Additional Praise for Rubén Martínez and *Crossing Over*

"*Crossing Over* is dark, brutal—and brilliant. Rubén Martínez gets under the skin. He takes us back and forth across many borders and reveals points of view that will startle both Mexicans and Americans. All the people who are making decisions about the border should read this sharp, gritty, true book. No other journalist could have written it; Martínez is truly our *coyote*."
—Sandra Cisneros, author of *The House on Mango Street*

"This is a deeply affecting celebration of the ordinary heroism of migrant families. It is also a brilliant reflection of the struggle to preserve fundamental solidarities amid the pandemonium of globalization. Martínez writes with moral clarity and razor-sharp wit—no wonder he is setting off sensors all along the border."
—Mike Davis, author of *Ecology of Fear*

"In the tradition of Oscar Lewis's *The Children of Sanchez* and James Agee's *Let Us Now Praise Famous Men*, Rubén Martínez takes us on the quintessential and often tragic journey from the promise of America to the reality it offers. By putting a human face on the experience, Martínez gives us a thorough and thrilling portrait of two countries, two cultures, and a family caught between them. Meticulously researched and passionately written, *Crossing Over* will become a seminal work on the Mexican migrant experience and on the border where the two Americas, north and south, are still discovering each other."
—Julia Alvarez, author of *In the Time of the Butterflies*

"This is a book that George Orwell might have written. What begins as a work of journalism about people at the borders of our lives, ends up, like a work of literature, forcing us to wonder about ourselves."
—Richard Rodriguez, author of *Brown*

"In blisteringly accurate prose, Rubén Martínez lances the wound that is the Mexican migrant experience. Uncompromising in its intensity, *Crossing Over* is a great testimony to life on this blessed, complex, and turbulent continent. We who live on *la frontera* look for books like this the way we wait for rain."

—Denise Chávez, author of *Loving Pedro Infante*

"*Crossing Over* is one of the few truly great border books ever written. Like his spiritual forebear, John Steinbeck, Martínez knows things about the migrant's heart that enrich us all. America needs to read this book now more than ever. Part travel epic, part act of moral witness, part cry in the night, *Crossing Over* is sure to become an instant and enduring classic."

—Luis Alberto Urrea, author of *Across the Wire*

"Rubén Martínez: he is our bravest."

—Helena María Viramontes, author of *Under the Feet of Jesus*

CROSSING OVER

Also by Rubén Martínez

East Side Stories: Gang Life in East L.A.
(with Joseph Rodriguez)

The Other Side: Notes from the New L.A.,
Mexico City, and Beyond

RUBEN MARTINEZ

CROSSING OVER

A MEXICAN FAMILY ON THE MIGRANT TRAIL

PICADOR USA

A METROPOLITAN BOOK

HENRY HOLT AND COMPANY

NEW YORK

www.picadorusa.com

Picador® is a U.S. registered trademark and is used by Henry Holt and Company under license from Pan Books Limited.

For information on Picador USA Reading Group Guides, as well as ordering, please contact the Trade Marketing department at St. Martin's Press.
Phone: 1-800-221-7945 extension 763
Fax: 212-677-7456
E-mail: trademarketing@stmartins.com

Library of Congress Cataloging-in-Publication Data

Martínez, Rubén.
    Crossing over : a Mexican family on the migrant trail / Rubén Martínez.—1st Picador USA ed.
        p. cm.
    ISBN 0-312-42123-0
    1. Mexican American families—Social conditions. 2. Mexican Americans—Biography. 3. Immigrants—United States—Social conditions. 4. Immigrants—United States—Biography. 5. Illegal aliens—United States—Social conditions. 6. Illegal aliens—United States—Biography. 7. Migrant labor—United States. 8. Chavez family. 9. Cherân (Mexico)—Biography. I. Title.

E184.M5 M388 2002
306.85'089'6872073—dc21   2002067330

First published in the United States by Henry Holt and Company, LLC

First Picador USA Edition: October 2002

10 9 8 7 6 5 4 3 2 1

For Benjamín, Jaime, and Salvador Chávez,
in memoriam

For María Elena Chávez, her daughter, Rosa, and her
granddaughters, Anayeli and Emily-Elizabeth: the future is yours

For my parents, whose journeys inspired mine

And for Joseph Rodriguez, whose eyes helped mine to see

Black markets flourish everywhere there are restrictions. Like connecting vessels, they equalize pressure between supply and demand without regard for laws, regulations, and ethical norms. Since in the real world there are no completely closed systems, illegal transactions can be impeded by controls but never quite prevented. Market forces seek and find the smallest gap, the tiniest crack, and eventually slip through every barrier. —Hans Magnus Enzensberger, *Civil Wars*

I looked into the lost and hungry faces of several hundred thousand Oakies, Arkies, Texies, Mexies, Chinees, Japees, Dixies, and even a lot of New Yorkies... and I got so interested in the art and science of migratin' that I majored in it—in a school so big you can't even get out of it. —Woody Guthrie

Han de ir por todos los fines de la tierra, a la mano derecha, y a la mano izquierda, y de todo en todo irán hasta la ribera del mar, y pasarán adelante.
(They shall go unto the ends of the earth, to the right and to the left, and in the end they will reach the seashore, and still they shall go onward.) —*Relación de Michoacán*, ca. 1540

contents

CROSSING OVER

PROLOGUE:
THE PASSION

I am close to the line.

The mostly invisible line that stretches two thousand miles along sand, yellow dirt dotted with scrub brush, and the muddy waters of the Rio Grande. Invisible, save for certain stretches near San Diego, Nogales, and El Paso, where the idea of the U.S.-Mexico border takes physical form through steel, chain links, barbed wire, concrete, and arc lamps that light the barren terrain at night. At these three crossing points—San Diego being the busiest port of entry in the world—the Border Patrol has cleared the land for miles around, so that the human figures who try to breach the line stand in stark relief and cast shadows. The Border Patrol swallows as many shadows as it can.

It is late summer in California and the hills that line I-15 in southern Riverside County are tinged rusty brown; the brilliant green wild grass of spring is a distant memory. This is one of my least favorite stretches of California highway, an interminable, mostly barren valley corridor.

I-15 is a necessary route for travelers and truckers shuttling between the Inland Empire and San Diego. It is also the preferred route of the "coyotes," the smugglers of human cargo who charge $1,000 a head or more to foil the designs of the Border Patrol and get their migrant clients on the road to their American future.

I am in the badlands of Southern California, en route to an appointment with the dead. I'm headed to Temecula, a growing city on the edge of Riverside County. It is arid country here, the westernmost point of the vast desert that spreads from the California beach all the way to the Gulf Coast of Texas.

For the American migrants who rode the wagon trains westward, California was once the "other side," just as it is today for the migrants heading north. Up from the fine yellow dust of these hills rise imported laurels, palms, sycamores, avocados, willows, oleander, eucalyptus. There are even apple and citrus orchards. But now and again, the old desert, a reminder of Mexican, or even Indian, California, appears in the form of an ancient, lonely stand of nopal cactus.

I take the exit at Rancho California Road. Temecula is picturesque, with its Western wagon-wheel décor. The elite live in the hills above town, in huge, recently built homes of the faux California Mission variety: red tile roofs, beige stucco, wrought iron. There are rose gardens and the occasional artificial pond gracing the spacious yards. One of the local realty agencies is called Sunshine Properties.

I head west along a winding two-lane that climbs into the Santa Rosa Mountains, a range that runs southward and eventually crosses the international line. The Santa Rosas are beautiful and bizarre: gently rolling hills of green give way suddenly to boulder-strewn peaks and chasms. On the Mexican side, the landscape is precipitous—and infamous. There, a stretch of Mexico Federal Highway 2 known as La Rumorosa (The Whispering One, for the haunted winds that blow through the canyons) has been the site of hundreds of fatal wrecks over the decades.

My destination is the intersection of Calle Capistrano and Avenida Del Oro. The names are, of course, Spanish—appropriated by the whites to romance their idyll with a dash of old California. The street signs are rendered in faux rustic, engraved wood. Most of the whites who live here now were once migrants themselves, belonging to subsequent waves of American wanderers—the Depression-era and postwar generations that pulled up stakes in the Midwest and on the East Coast to spend their lives in balmy paradise. This land was a final destination for them, the consummation of their California dream. You don't leave paradise once you've found it.

But for the Mexican migrants, Temecula is a stopover, not a final destination. Sure, there are Mexican gardeners tending to the rose bushes, cleaning the swimming pools, washing and folding the clothes, cooking the meals; brown women sing lullabies in Spanish to white babies. But the Mexicans are here for just as long as they have to be. They are mostly young and don't think of retiring, not only because they have no money to do so but also because they can't imagine themselves old yet. Most of the Mexicans in Temecula are literally just passing through, crammed into pickup trucks and vans driven by the coyotes. Temecula is just another of the hundred places they will blow through en route to St. Louis, Los Angeles, Houston, New York, Chicago, Decatur. But even these are not final destinations. The migrants will follow trails determined by America's labor economy: they will keep moving, from one coast to another, from picking the fields to working in hotels and restaurants, from cities to heartland towns.

Temecula was long a quiet town. But to the retirees' dismay, it is now a staging area for the battle of the border, in which two armies face off, usually under cover of darkness. It is a battle in which, occasionally, blood is spilled, though usually only on one side.

I turn right at Avenida Del Oro and pick up speed on a steep downhill grade. The road begins a long curve between hills dotted with rural mansions and avocado orchards. At the bottom of the gully, at the intersection with Calle Capistrano, I stop the car. The sun has fallen behind the hills to the west but still illuminates the higher terrain with a lush, classic California gold. Silvery plumes from the irrigation sprinklers arc over the fields.

This is where it happened. Where Benjamín, Jaime, and Salvador Chávez and five others, all of them undocumented Mexican migrants, "illegals," died crammed in a truck that sped along this rural road four and a half years ago.

I clamber down into the drainage ditch below the road. Yellow dirt and sickly weeds. I find a screen from the window of the truck's camper shell and a blue piece of plastic from the shell itself, about a foot long and six inches wide. And another piece of black plastic: a fragment of

4 • CROSSING OVER

the truck's running board. I pick up and examine a faded, crumpled tube of Colgate toothpaste, its ingredients listed in Spanish. There is an equally faded and torn McDonald's medium-size Coca-Cola cup.

Above the ditch, an anonymous artisan has built a small altar by taking the trunk of a California oak, slicing it in half, and carving out seven small crosses that he has filled in with light blue paint. (There should be eight crosses; the artisan was apparently unaware of the last victim's death in a nearby hospital several days after the accident.) It is a simple, beautiful monument.

I walk a ways up the hill, the bed of dead avocado leaves crunching underfoot. There is very little traffic and it is quiet, except for the leaves of the avocados rustling in the warm wind and, suddenly and eerily, the voices of men. Men speaking in Spanish. It sounds like they are nearby, but it takes me a while to spot them, high on a hill south of me. They are Mexican farmworkers, chatting casually as they pick avocados. They are a good half mile away, but the wind has brought their voices very close. These men traveled the same road that Benjamín and his brothers did. They are farmworkers now. Benjamín, Salvador, and Jaime Chávez are not. This is where their road ended.

It is five o'clock in the morning on Saturday, April 6, 1996. Two weeks before Easter, two more weeks of Lent before the Passion. The sun will soon break over the Temecula valley. The moon is a little less than half full, dipping low into the southwestern sky. The stars have dimmed with the approach of the sun. Only the planet Jupiter is visible, and it is just about to fall into the leaves of a stand of avocados on the south side of Avenida Del Oro. It is a clear and dry morning, and although it is early spring, the temperature is already seventy degrees; it will reach into the nineties at midday.

Avenida Del Oro is an east-west rural two-lane road of pitch-black asphalt and a bright solid yellow dividing line that runs for several hundred feet across the intersection with Calle Capistrano. Here, Avenida Del Oro falls into a steep gully along a long, sharp curve, the kind that creeps up on you and causes you to instinctively hit the brakes as you come to the bend. Calle Capistrano is a smaller road that runs north toward a few residences and orchards. The point at which the two streets join is precisely the bend in Avenida Del Oro's curve.

Deck lights glow amber from a ranch house high up on a hill to the east. There is no breeze. Occasionally there is the sound of an avocado falling, at first slithering through the branches, then hitting the thick bed of dry dead leaves below with a loud, brittle crash.

At five-fifteen the eastern sky is pale yellow. Shades of dusty pink rise into blue-greens and finally into deep blue at the zenith and in the west. A 1989 GMC truck, blue with silver trim, equipped with a camper shell of darkly tinted windows, speeds westward down Avenida Del Oro. Twenty-seven people are inside, twenty-five of them in the camper and two in the front seat. All are undocumented Mexican migrants.

The reason the coyote is on this isolated rural road is the inauguration of the U.S. Border Patrol interdiction effort known as Operation Gatekeeper. In 1994, a massive new steel wall was built along several miles of the border running east from the beach at Tijuana. After the Border Patrol claimed success with Operation Gatekeeper, it followed with similar measures in Nogales, Arizona (Operation Safeguard), El Paso, Texas (Operation Hold the Line), and McAllen, Texas (Operation Rio Grande). Consequently, the Mexican coyotes, not to be outdone by gringo technology, have chosen more circuitous routes through rugged terrain eastward. These new routes are extremely dangerous. Dozens of migrants have died of exposure in the torrid heat and bitter cold of the Colorado Desert since 1994. There are hundreds of such crossings between the beaches of Southern California and the Gulf Coast of Texas, and the cat-and-mouse game between the coyotes and the Border Patrol is never-ending.

A Border Patrol truck spots the GMC several miles south of the intersection of Avenida Del Oro and Calle Capistrano. What the BP agents see is a vehicle clearly overloaded, its fenders practically scraping the tires. From this point on, there are differing versions as to what occurred. The BP maintains that their personnel followed the vehicle at a discreet distance, with its emergency lights off. Lawyers representing the victims say that the BP wrecklessly and needlessly endangered the lives of the migrants by engaging in a high-speed pursuit.

For most of the hour-long ride up from the border, Benjamín, Jaime, and Salvador Chávez and their compatriots in the camper shell see nothing, not even one another's faces, because very little of the approaching dawn's light penetrates the camper's tinted windows.

When the coyote notices the BP truck in his side mirrors (he couldn't have seen much in the rearview mirror, given the dark glass and the twenty-five bodies piled like a cord of wood in the back), he speeds up, the tires screeching on the curves.

Inside the camper, panic rules. Those closest to the small window that looks in on the cab of the truck pound on it and scream at the coyote to stop. Several survivors recall that Benjamín Chávez shouted the loudest, a deep-throated yell. But it is to no avail. The coyote has been drinking. He has been snorting coke. He is hunched over the steering wheel, oblivious to everything but the BP truck behind him and the dark, winding road ahead.

Increasingly desperate, the migrants pop the camper's rear window open. They throw their small travel bags, their water bottles, and even a tire jack in the direction of the BP vehicle, but these fall harmlessly by the side of the road. They make dramatic hand gestures at the agents, imploring them to give up the pursuit, not because they want to avoid apprehension but because they want their driver to slow down. They are in fear for their lives.

The Chávez brothers, crunched against one another in the truck bed, see very little even when the rear window is opened. They are deep inside the camper, hemmed in by twenty-three other bodies. They only feel the lurching of the truck and hear the men's groans as they are slammed about on the curves.

The GMC hurtles down Avenida Del Oro at close to seventy miles an hour. About three hundred feet from Calle Capistrano, the coyote realizes he can't negotiate the curve and slams on the brakes. The realization comes too late.

There is a long skid, and the truck spins 180 degrees.

Then there is silence for a split second, as the truck flies off the road and turns over in the air.

And now a thousand sounds at once: the crumpling, the breaking, the crushing, and the snapping of glass, metal, plastic, and bone. The truck comes down roof-first in the ditch. Most of the bodies inside the camper shell spill out. Not all are completely ejected. Several are crushed underneath the mangled chassis of the truck. A cloud of dust rises from the impact.

The sun crests the horizon in the east now. It is possible that one of the last things some of the migrants saw, for just a fraction of a second, was the yellow glow on the horizon. Or maybe some of them saw the dust from the crash hanging in the air and heard the silence of the desert return as the groans of the dying faded.

Benjamín, Jaime, and Salvador were crushed under the truck. They had departed their home in Cherán, an Indian town in the highlands of Michoacán, a few days earlier and were on their way to Watsonville, California, to their usual stint of seasonal work picking strawberries in the fertile hills east of Santa Cruz. The accident made headlines in the United States for the enormity of the tragedy (eight people killed, nineteen injured, many critically) and because just a few days earlier another incident involving Mexican migrants had attracted attention. A videotape reminiscent of the Rodney King footage had aired on the evening news showing Riverside sheriff's deputies beating unarmed Mexican migrants, none of them visibly resisting, by the side of a Southern California freeway at rush hour.

Over the last decade, the numbers of casualties at the U.S.-Mexico line have begun to look like the tallies from a low-intensity conflict in a corner of the developing world. A University of Houston study counted some three thousand deaths in the last half of the 1990s, a conservative figure. Many bodies, the researchers concluded, will never be found. The bones of these migrants are hidden in the sludge at the bottom of the Rio Grande and scattered across the open desert.

And yet the migrants continue to cross, because ideals of paradise die hard, especially for Mexicans, who for several decades have regarded the Rio Grande as a river of life more than of death, notwithstanding accidents like the one at Temecula. They continue to cross despite the tragedies and despite Operation Gatekeeper because the odds remain in their favor. To truly "hold the line," as American politicians say, the United States would have to spend hundreds of billions of dollars—currently it is spending some four billion a year—to either build the Great Wall of America or amass all along the line, like at the border between North and South Korea or at the old divide between East and West Berlin, thousands of troops and all manner of physical obstacles, weaponry, and technology. Despite continuing anti-immigrant sentiment in the United States, there are no credible proposals to do so at this time. After all the rhetoric, the line is still more an idea than a reality. Most of the border between the United States and Mexico is represented not by Operation Gatekeeper's twelve-foot-tall steel barriers but by barbed-wire fences often little more than a few feet high. In hundreds of places, the wire has been cut. You can stand on the line through most of California, Arizona, New Mexico, and Texas and hop from one side to the other, screaming at the top of your lungs, and no one will see you, except perhaps a desert tortoise or a real coyote.

In publicity campaigns aimed at deterring prospective migrants, the BP has tried to use the dead as a cautionary symbol—even as an example. But the migrants' awareness of unscrupulous coyotes and the BP's determination to stop the migrant flow is not nearly enough of a deterrent. The reason is very simple. In 1994, Mexico was crippled by a profound—and prolonged—economic crisis that sent a flood of refugees north. The United States, on the other hand, enjoyed throughout the late 1990s a historic boom in practically every corner of its economy, and among the fastest-growing was the "service sector." Its jobs—typically in hotels and restaurants—along with hundreds of thousands of seasonal agricultural jobs, are largely filled by a vast pool of illegal, unskilled migrant labor. It is an arrangement that keeps U.S. employers, migrants, and the Mexican government generally content.

This state of mutual dependence has existed for the better part of a century, but the migrant business has not always been conducted this way. After the Mexican Revolution of 1910, some 700,000 migrants were received in the United States legally. And during the 1940s, a federally sponsored *bracero*, or guest worker, program imported hundreds of thousands of Mexicans—again, legally—to relieve wartime labor shortages. Then in 1965 the U.S. increased quotas from Latin America, and in 1986 the Immigration Reform and Control Act granted amnesty to millions of undocumented migrants, allowing them to legalize and bring family members north.

The one sensible binational policy that recognizes the presence of Mexican workers is the INS's border resident identification program, which grants a limited number of Mexican nationals living in border towns a safe-conduct pass to cross into U.S. territory for a certain distance (depending on the region, up to fifty miles) for business purposes. The program acknowledges that, without cross-border commerce, the towns on the American side would wither away. These days, hundreds of cities and towns in the American interior would probably suffer without the presence of the hardworking illegals. But the idea of U.S.-Mexico integration—as in the radical libertarian proposal to simply open the border and allow market forces to regulate the migratory flow—would cause too much conflict on both sides of the line.

Only a handful of faith communities and human rights organizations have questioned America's contemporary immigration policies, despite the growing number of deaths on the border during the 1990s. Yet the United States pulls, with its job-magnets, its porous border, and its selective enforcement of the immigration code: every migrant and practically every major employer of illegals in the country can tell you that the INS usually puts the heat on only after the crops are picked and on their way to market. For decades the message has been: We have a job for you. Today it is: We have a job for you but you'll have more trouble getting across the line.

From the migrant perspective, the Chávez brothers and the thousands of other migrants who have died over the past decade in car wrecks or by drowning or from exposure have become martyrs in a cause: to have the freedom to move, or at least to get the hell out of provincial towns like Cherán, whose timber-based economy is in tatters. Like Indian Joads, they have fled the Mexican dustbowl.

To move, to make some money, to buy some gold chains, or a 1984 Plymouth with 145,000 miles on it but a nice interior, or an Osterizer food processor so that your *madrecita* back home doesn't have to chop-chop the vegetables every night, or some snazzy snakeskin boots for yourself—or hell, to just come back home with a wad of greenbacks in your billfold, enough to peel off a few Jacksons and pin them on the statue of your patron saint and buy a dozen bottles of Bacardi rum, enough to get your entire block drunk for at least one night.

And then, after a winter's rest, to return to California . . . to Arkansas . . . to Wisconsin . . . to North Carolina . . .

This migrant trail is a loop not only in space but in time. The future lies in America, the past in Mexico. The past is tolerable only for so long, especially in the impoverished lands of the south. But the future can also be painful for a migrant in America; the distance from loved ones in the homeland can become unbearable.

It all works out perfectly for the migrant who shuttles between the two. It is best to stay on the road, to keep moving.

Lent in the Year of Our Lord 1996 was, for Mexicans, the darkest hour before the dawn. Certainly they hoped it was the darkest hour. The thought that there could actually be more suffering visited upon their country was too much to bear; Mexicans always prefer to invoke the resurrection.

This was the third consecutive Lent observed in a time of crisis. Since New Year's Day 1994, the stock market had plunged alongside the peso, the jobless rate had soared, and the black market had exploded. The rich tightened their belts, the middle class strained under massive debt. For the Mexican worker or peasant, it was yet another round of survival. The streets of Mexico City were choked as never before with street vendors, prostitutes, pickpockets, and incipient youth gangs aping their counterparts in Compton and East L.A. And then there were the poorest of the poor, the Indians living in the provinces, a good many of whom had become convinced that, in the face of such adversity, revolution was the only recourse. That or crossing the border.

In the border states, narco-wars raged. Mob-style hits were carried out on the streets in broad daylight. Much of Mexican airspace was ruled by a man nicknamed El Señor de los Cielos, the Lord of the Skies, aka Amado Carrillo Fuentes, a cartel godfather who shipped his cargo, by the tons, on chartered jet planes.

Despite forecasts of better times (the Clinton administration even chipped in $50 billion in credit to prop up its free-trade partner), the darkness lingered on. Assassinations, corruption, street crime. In everyday conversation, Mexicans referred to the phenomenon as, simply, "*la crisis.*" They uttered the phrase with almost sentimental familiarity, as if referring to a long-lost relative who unexpectedly shows up on one's doorstep. People said that *la crisis* was responsible for every malady that afflicted them, a deus ex machina that was cause, not effect. "Because of *la crisis*, I lost my job . . ." Because of *la crisis*, you borrowed a thousand dollars and risked your life sneaking across the U.S.-Mexico border.

I spent the better part of Lent adjusting to life in Mexico City, the biggest metropolis on earth, to which I had just moved. I wasted endless hours in bureaucratic queues (phone company, water and power, immigration) that looked more like soup lines. In the evenings, I sat in my apartment writing at a desk next to soot-streaked windows that looked down upon strangely empty streets—strange for the fact that there were some twenty million souls in the immediate vicinity.

And yet Mexico City, capital of a nation in tatters, approached Easter with rapturous anticipation; holy was the great highland city whose belly button the gods tickle to remind it that no matter how poor, crowded, contaminated, or violent, it was still just an inch below heaven. If you stared into the zinc-tinted pall hanging over the valley long enough, celestial forms came into view, writhing in the smog-ether.

But the actual heavens were something else again. There had been several smog alerts since Ash Wednesday. Pigeons fell from the skies, asphyxiated. Head pounding, I wandered the labyrinth, breathing in Volkswagen fumes and smoking Mexican Marlboros, at one with one of the world's last armies of True Smokers. Mexico City dwellers love to show off their tobacco prowess despite, or precisely because of, the fact that they live in the most polluted city on earth. I spat black balls into my handkerchief.

La crisis was, above all else, a public event. Yes, there was brooding and violence inside homes, within families—in the tabloids, we were treated to the typical tales of husbands chopping up their wives and sons killing their parents. In this family-values country, you could rest assured that if you were murdered the last face you'd see would be that of a friend or relative.

But the pressure of *la crisis* was too great to bear in private. Every two weeks, *la quincena* came, the bimonthly payday, and we spilled into the streets, into cantinas and dance halls and strip joints. God knows where the money came from. But I'd seen it before, this end-of-the-world excess, in the barrios of San Salvador during the darkest days of the civil war, in Managua at the height of the U.S. embargo against the Sandinista regime, in Havana back when Castro prohibited mention of the word *glasnost* and quarantined the island from contact with the outside world. When apocalypse is at hand there's nothing left to lose, and inhibitions fall. There might not have been enough money to pay the rent, buy clothes, or even eat decently, but, by God, there was enough for a round of drinks. Solidarity.

Thus, Mexicans escaped *la crisis* through the spectacle of public ritual. No one ever did anything alone. If you had a doctor's appointment, you called up your best friend; he'd take the day off from work to escort you, and stand by your side even during the embarrassing rubber-gloved examination. Same thing for trips to the bank, to get a haircut, to buy groceries. There was always great chatter as people lined up to do their business.

The ultimate Mexican public ritual, the fiesta, derives its tremendous energy from the tension between spirit and flesh, between Indian and Iberian, between Christianity and pagan pantheism—in a word, from Mexico's "mestizo," or mixed blood and culture. *La crisis* only poured fuel on the fire. In 1995, December 12 (the Virgin of Guadalupe's feast day), 24, and 31 were days of national paroxysm. On Valentine's Day, practically every hotel in the country, from the swank joints to the barrio hovels, hung a No Vacancy sign and ecstatic shrieks echoed along the halls: a national fuck. The provinces partied as hard as the capital; every town has a patron saint and the feast days were excuses for weeklong bacchanals on the order of decadent Rome. In the Indian territories, pagan agricultural rites only thinly disguised as Catholic were celebrated as never before. What all these fiestas had in common was that we celebrated the spirit *through* the flesh. We alternated between the extremes of mortified piety and Dionysian abandon.

And then there was Easter.

Throughout Lent, Mexicans performed the Catholic rote of abstinence and fasting, physically representing the economic collapse with their very bodies. Economic forces, after all, are invisible but for the effect they have on our physical form: where we live, what we eat, what we wear, how we dance. As Lent drew to a close, Mexico prepared to nail itself to the cross.

A gray wind blows in Iztapalapa. The rains of summer are months away and the dust of ancient, infertile earth rises in choking clouds. Lying on a fallow plain south of downtown Mexico City, the district of Iztapalapa, by the looks of things, was a rough-and-tumble barrio long before the Spaniards arrived. It has the color of old poverty: dark brown, almost chocolate-brown skin, the color of little or no cross-breeding. Iztapalapa's Indian population was poor around the time of the Conquest, and it's poor now.

I come up from the bowels of the metro into a plaza adorned with graffiti murals, of the officially sanctioned variety. There are eco-sensitive messages, tributes to the dead of the great quake of 1985. And a monument to *la crisis:* ESTAMOS EN LAS MANOS DE DIOS (We Are in the Hands of God), reads a banner flowing above the two hands of the Great One, which cradle a cityscape rendered postapocalyptically with sky-scrapers become tombstones and a blood glow tinting the twilight sky.

Iztapalapa is famous for two things: a soaring crime rate inspired by *la crisis* (which led authorities to temporarily deploy regular army troops on its streets) and the best *representación* of the Passion in all of Mexico. The pageantry of the event is on the order of Cecil B. DeMille—practically every barrio resident plays a part. In the United States right now, people are watching *The Ten Commandments* and *The Greatest Story Ever Told* on television, preparing for quiet Passover or Easter family gatherings and religious services. But in Mexico, half the population, from the capital to the Indian countryside, is starring in its own version of the Passion.

It is the 153rd annual *representación* in Iztapalapa (there is a region in the state of Guerrero where the ritual goes back four hundred years), and locals speak of *la tradición* with mystical reverence. The peso may have tumbled, we can't buy ham for Easter, my son was mugged last night, but we're keeping tradition alive! Just because there's a Price Club in every major city doesn't mean that Mexico has lost its essence. If Mexico didn't stop being an Indian nation five hundred years ago—mestizo identity, after all, is at least half pre-Columbian—why should it now? Still, Iztapalapa is a place contaminated by the germ of rest-lessness. Indians migrate from the countryside looking for the better life in the city; often, after a generation or two of urban poverty, they hit the road again, trying their luck in the States.

The barrio is decked out for the Passion: fully costumed Roman soldiers, Samaritan women, Pharisees walk the streets, snacking and smoking, shooting the breeze. But it's the *nazarenos,* the Nazarenes, who are omnipresent, roving packs of teenage boys who've built their own crosses and had their mothers stitch together simple white robes with purple sashes so they can play Jesus as penance. Five thousand or so *nazarenos* trudge along the streets of Iztapalapa this year, straining under crosses weighing up to ninety kilos. Many of the kids have been training for months.

There are dozens of simultaneous *representaciones*. A mega-spectacle plays out in the plaza on a stage about fifty yards long, floodlit by arc lamps and ringed by a bevy of Televisa remote trucks that transmit the performances live nationwide.

The *representación* of the Last Supper takes place. There are easily 100,000 people gathered in the plaza before the stage, but the concentration on the scene is absolute; the only sound that can be heard, aside from the dialogue, is the hum of the remote trucks. Judas rises from the table. He frets, wrings his hands. He paces back and forth interminably, throwing anguished looks at Jesus, at the disciples, at us. The roles are taken so seriously by the residents of Iztapalapa that the brave souls who play Judas are occasionally shunned by their neighbors, as if by representing Judas they're actually betraying Jesus himself.

The Last Supper table is carted away by stagehands; foam rocks and potted trees are rolled in for the Gethsemane scene. The Iztapalapa resident who has played Jesus for the last six years pleads, with old-school theatricality, to "let this cup pass from me" while the disciples lie sleeping a few feet away.

Then the chaos: Pharisees and scribes rush in, Judas offers his last kiss, a sword is drawn, an ear is lopped off, the disciples scatter, and finally Pilate: "Which of the two do you wish that I release to you?" And the entire plaza, every last man, woman, and child, as per *tradición*, shouts: "BARABBAS!"

Afterward, the crowd begins to disperse, but thousands of people remain in the plaza overnight, laying down blankets and passing around *champurrado* and *atole*, hot beverages that predate the Conquest. These fervent Indian Catholics will stay up with the Savior on the longest night of his life, the night before his death. They will also get the best seats for his crucifixion.

Good Friday begins as a startlingly clear day; somehow, we've been given a respite from the smog. Legions of visitors—an estimated two million—descend on Iztapalapa. The army of vendors fares well among the multitudes as the wait for the Crucifixion grows longer and hotter (the Red Cross tends to hundreds of sunstroke victims), selling crucifixes, sunglasses, cardboard visors, caps, mango, papaya, and bottles of Coke, Sprite, and Fanta chilled atop slabs of ice that drip puddles into the gray dust.

I join the *nazarenos* on their serpentine path through the barrios. Five thousand Christs accompanied by the sound of the wood of five thousand crosses dragging along the asphalt. The kids range in age from preteens with crosses only about four feet long to twenty-somethings with several years of *representación* experience, carrying the better part of a tree over their shoulders. Some of the crosses are painted black, others red. Some are carved with flowery designs, others varnished so well they look like they're encased in glass.

The pilgrimage begins at seven in the morning and winds through the better part of Iztapalapa before arriving at Golgotha in the late afternoon. The *nazarenos* start out in high spirits, perhaps guilty just a tad of the sin of pride. But by noon, the Red Cross is carting kids off on stretchers. It's the feet that suffer the most. A good many Christs go barefoot—on asphalt baking in the hot sun and sprinkled with broken glass. Some wear Ace bandages, which soon grow filthy and unravel. Others wear cheap huaraches; these, too, fall apart after a few kilometers. The kids jump onto pieces of cardboard—thrown down on the sizzling street by store owners along the route—and then, wincing, back onto the asphalt.

At times, the procession grows scraggly as, overpowered by the sun, kids fall out of the ranks, but the organizers rush in, shouting and whistling like Romans. I stand in the shade of a corner general store, drinking Pepsi and smoking Marlboros along with the crowd of onlookers, and suddenly there appears before us the most unlikely of *samiratanas*, dressed in a floor-length red velvet cloak but showing an inordinate amount of cleavage, her face made up like a transvestite's. Maybe she *is* a transvestite, who knows? The sight of this sexy Samaritan, eyeliner running down her cheeks, taking uncertain steps in five-inch stilettos is too much for the gaggle of mothers and grandmothers around me. "In *heels!*" cries one of them with glee. "Now that's really a love of art!"

Amazingly, the vast majority of the procession will make it to Golgotha, to Cerro de la Muerte. A fourteen-year-old carrying a cross he claims weighs seventy kilos says: "My father did it, my older brothers did it, now it is my turn to fulfill the tradition." And an eighteen-year-old wearing a real crown of thorns, drops of dried blood on his temples: "There's no pain that I couldn't bear with my faith in the Lord." Every kid is followed by a support crew of siblings, parents, and grandparents urging them on, carrying water bottles and cotton and alcohol to swab the aching, blistered feet.

Again and again the theme of *la crisis* comes up in snippets of casual conversation. Seems that there are more *nazarenos* since the peso fell. Seems like there are fewer vendors but more *tradición*, more *devoción*. A barrio grandmother sums it up: "It's the crisis that is making people come closer to God. More sinners, more penitents. The problem is, the really big sinners, *los políticos hijos de la chingada*—politico sons of bitches—never do their penance. We wind up doing it for them."

Finally, close to three in the afternoon, the *nazarenos* and *romanos* and *samaritanas* make their tattered, triumphal approach to Cerro de la Muerte. Kids sprint the final yards up the hill, throw down their crosses, collapse, strip off robes and T-shirts. Soon the hill is littered with five thousand crosses and the panting, half-naked bodies of five thousand brown Christs. Three great crosses crown Golgotha, with five thousand *nazareno* crosses scattered helter-skelter at their feet.

Surrounding the hill, held back from the *representación* area by a chain-link fence, are the two million onlookers. The sea of people in all directions is like a huge, unified organism, a great jellyfish, nudging its way ever closer to the *representación*, straining against the fence and the army of cops, Indian kids armed with ancient service revolvers.

Now trumpets blast. Romans on white stallions charge up the hill.

The proclaimer: "And having committed these and many other crimes . . . we condemn him and sentence him to be taken along the streets of the Holy City of Jerusalem, crowned with thorns and with a chain about his neck, carrying his own cross, and accompanied by two criminals, Dismas and Gestas, unto Golgotha, and that there he be crucified between the two criminals, where he will hang until dead."

He is nailed to the cross, the ninety-kilo cross that he himself built, the one that he has dragged in procession through Iztapalapa every day since Palm Sunday. The sound of the hammer resounds through the great banks of speakers. Stage blood spouts from hands and feet. A camera crane moves in close for the dizzying Scorsese shot.

Christ, Dismas, and Gestas writhe on their crosses, and all of Mexico's children see themselves. On Golgotha hangs every dream ever denied in this land: the three crucified might as well be named Benjamín, Jaime, and Salvador Chávez.

In the final moments of the Passion, the gray wind of Iztapalapa rises in great clouds above the massive crowd. It is the gray of the great dust of the city, not just the arid topsoil of the Cerro but particles of ash from the billion cigarettes of the chain-smoking city, refuse from the garbage dumps on every street corner in the barrios, sooty exhaust from the trucks and taxis and the passenger cars of the rich and poor, especially the poor with their jury-rigged eight-cylinder smoking Chevys—the dust of poverty, the dust of corruption, the dust of hell on earth.

As we bring handkerchiefs to our faces and rub our eyes, everything that was white turns gray: the robes of the *nazarenos*, the blocks of ice at the vending stalls, the pages of my notebook.

On this Good Friday the holy, fallen country has come to watch itself die.

And live.

It is accomplished.

Before Easter and after Easter, for many years before *la crisis* and every year since, a procession of Mexican *penitentes* has marched out of barrios like Iztapalapa and out of provincial towns throughout the republic. Migrants heading north, fleeing Egypt for the Canaan just across the Rio Grande, a million migrant souls searching for redemption and resurrection, a Mexican Manifest Destiny to be won on streets paved with gold, on American streets.

For over two years I was on the road, following Mexican migrant families. I did not live what the migrants lived, but I saw a bit of what they saw. I watched that ribbon of highway curl over and over the horizon. I saw a lot of hard work and a lot of love and a lot of drunken fights and a lot of long separations between lovers, between mothers and daughters and fathers and sons.

And I saw death. I logged some fifty thousand miles on my Chevy Blazer, most of it in cross-country travel. I suppose when you're on the road all the time, the chances of running into tragedy increase.

I saw diamonds of glass glittering on the asphalt and stiff cows with legs skyward.

I saw a Mexican man sitting in the mangled remains of an old Datsun, just sitting there, oh so relaxed, in the passenger seat, like he was dozing on the long ride up the eastern seaboard. But he was never going home.

I saw a young Chicano thrown from his truck on I-10. He and his ride were separated by four freeway lanes when the macabre ballet ended. He looked down at his leg, marveling that his kneecap was completely turned around, while I marveled that he was still alive.

I began my journey alongside the migrants in Cherán, Michoacán, the Indian town that Benjamín, Jaime, and Salvador hailed from. I followed their ghost steps across the border. And then, across the United States.

ONE

POINTS OF DEPARTURE

Joseph Rodriguez

I

HOME

The six-hour bus ride from Mexico City to Zamora, Michoacán, begins at midnight, at *la central del norte*, the sprawling depot in the industrial zone on the outskirts of the Monster. It's one scary place, a grim Mexican version of New York's Penn Station. It's always bustling, whether at three in the afternoon or at three in the morning, and vendor anarchy and traveler paranoia reign. As I make my way through the mass of exhausted, exasperated, wary bodies with wild hair, burning eyes, pasty mouths, and crumpled clothes, I'm accosted by an atypical beggar, a middle-aged woman, smartly dressed, looking like she belongs at a tea party in Coyoacán, the capital's old-money district. "Please help me," she says, showing me her purse, sliced open with a blade and emptied.

I will grow accustomed to the Mexico City–Zamora route over the next several months. The one luxury afforded working-class travelers these days is the sleek buses. No more tattered rattlers for the Mexicans. Gleaming Mercedes-built cruisers with VCR monitors hanging from the ceiling and enough legroom for Michael Jordan are the norm for both first and second class. Upon boarding, you are handed a cheese sandwich and a can of Coke by a bronze beauty in miniskirt and navy-blue company blazer, who, after all the passengers are seated, welcomes you and reassures you that the driver complies with all Mexican traffic laws. She points to a red light at the front of the bus. If it goes on, she tells you, the bus is traveling in excess of ninety kilometers per hour, the maximum speed on any federal highway in Mexico. We have the right to complain to the driver if this occurs.

The red light will be on all the way to Zamora.

No one will complain.

The chassis of my bus is fat enough to devour the whole narrow lane on the *periférico*, Mexico City's beltway, threatening passenger cars, the concrete center divider, and our lives. We barrel through the nocturnal haze, past apartment buildings crowned with tangled antennas, past a thousand roadside taco stands starkly lit by naked bulbs hanging from frayed wires that pirate juice from the utility poles.

I'm headed out of the city for the provinces, out of the center for the margins. Since moving to Mexico City and experiencing its bizarre mestizo identity—an ancient Indian city rendered in European baroque—I've come to believe that the future lies in the provinces, not in the capital, which is exactly the opposite of what the *chilangos* (as capital dwellers call themselves, adopting a derogatory pre-Columbian name coined by rivals of the Aztecs) think. The elites of Mexico City, their gaze ever fixed on New York and Paris—especially Paris, recalling Mexico's brief tenure under Maximilian and Carlotta—have always thought of it as a European island in an Indian sea, the future rising up from the sad muck of history and leaping ahead of the timeless, poor, pastoral provinces. But these days it is Mexico City that feels like the past. Its restaurants are presided over by bow-tied waiters. Its most famous neighborhood, Coyoacán, a quaint Marxist bohemia (erstwhile home to Diego Rivera and Frida Kahlo), has long since lost its vibrancy. Its "activists," mainly the bored children of stodgy aristocrats, glorify the Zapatista rebellion in Chiapas, ignoring the millions of Indians living right under their noses—in many cases serving them.

On the city's grand boulevards, its golden-era monuments ape the Arc de Triomphe and other Parisian feats. Dusty, old. Even its attempt to forestall the arrival of McDonald's on its downtown streets is a French affectation. The migrant towns of the provinces saw the future long ago and brilliantly negotiated the terms of their surrender. McDonald's did not conquer them; rather, the Indians made McDonald's their own.

So good-bye, then, to the past!

Good-bye to Popocatépetl volcano grumbling and spewing ash rain, threatening a new Pompeii!

¡Adios, adios!

The video monitors are flashing a ninja movie dubbed in Spanish, and the passengers are enthralled by the kicking and twirling. You look out at the moonlit Monster, at its tentacles glistening over the dusty hills twenty-five miles north of downtown. Onward we go, through the plains, past the fair colonial city of Querétaro, its church spires glowing eerily under the highland moon, and on through the dreary industry of Irapuato and into the slaughterhouse city of Pénjamo, where the air smells of pig shit and blood.

I stare out the window and I become my wide-eyed father in the early fifties, a pudgy teenager with slicked-back hair who devoured the nocturnal landscape from the cramped cab of a 1948 Ford double-axle truck. The canvas-covered truck bed was packed with American knick-knacks to sell to Mexicans—ladies' stockings, Lionel train sets, blue jeans, and assorted other merchandise that my grandfather bought in downtown L.A. between Second and Fifth Streets, where he'd haggle with the jobbers, Jewish guys with Old World accents as thick as his. The trips included all-night drives from L.A. to El Paso, Grandfather pulling out his wallet to pay tithe to the corrupt Mexican officials as soon as the truck crossed the Rio Grande.

On through the desert they'd go, saguaro cacti silhouetted against orange sunsets, and then the impenetrable darkness along the two-lane. The old man hunched over the steering wheel, the old lady nodding off, the night road endless. Grandfather, always irascible and impatient, insisted on the all-nighters, despite the risk of encountering bandits. The Mexican night was beautiful in its mystery, and full of terrifying memories. In the 1950s, the atrocities of the Revolution and the Cristero war were recent enough for my father to conjure the image of bodies hanging from telephone poles, the skin drying and curling up like old leather in the sun.

Chihuahua at dawn...Durango at nightfall...a forlorn motel where the grizzled proprietor warns my family of spirits haunting the rooms ... unsavory characters at truck stops ... a cow suddenly framed by the headlights, the great impact of fender and bovine belly and a tremendous blast of cow shit over hood and windshield. And one night, in the wee hours, suddenly the blackness broken by a great white flash in a cloudless sky. My father remembers bringing his hand up to cover his eyes. There was no other car on the highway. Was it a meteor, a nuclear test in the American desert, a freak bolt of dry lightning? Scared the wits out of him.

Mexico was a grand adventure for my father. Having grown up in L.A., he was more the American boy than the Mexican, and so the road must have been exhilarating. For my grandparents, the journey must have been much sadder, filled with dying dreams and ambivalent memories of the Old Country they left behind and to which they returned again and again, never letting go of it entirely and yet never staying.

Now the VCR monitors show snow and everyone's asleep as the bus heads south-southwest into the fertile valleys of Michoacán, the lights of Zamora breaking like a star-dawn as we crest the hills ringing town. The vision of my father fades and I'm left with the thought that I'm on the same road he traveled, a road he eventually left for family and mortgage, ninety-hour workweeks, alcoholism and recovery, and now retirement. I remember his telling me what his father had told him, the old Mexican proverb about the dangers of the road: "If you walk through fire, you're going to get burnt."

It is five-thirty in the morning, and I sit in the bus station in Zamora, where I must transfer to get to Cherán. Let me be clear about Zamora, and may the Zamoranos forgive me: it's ugly. True, the town is nestled in a fertile valley of strawberry fields surrounded by gently rising hills of green. But Zamora is one of those towns, like so many provincial Mexican towns today, that are growing too fast for their own good. Once it may have been sleepy pretty. But now it's congested with mufflerless traffic cruising the old narrow streets, and a pale cloud of baby smog hangs over the town, obscuring the stars at night.

Mexico's economic crisis has torn Zamora in half. The poor barrios of crumbling adobe are ruled by bands of forlorn cholos, American-style gang members who while away the endless rural hours searching for the perfect combination of mescal and glue. The rich neighborhoods feature garish two-story stuccos sporting satellite dishes and ringed by tall walls topped by electrified fences. There is no middle, just an ever-widening chasm between these two worlds.

Zamora is a typical Mexican provincial capital—population 100,000, agribusiness the mainstay of the economy. No one in Zamora believes that there's a future here, neither the big-time landowner nor the cholo. There's a *past*: this is where your folks were born, where the streets smell like childhood and the traditional fiestas are still celebrated more or less the way they were before the Conquest. But a future? The more Zamora is aware of the world beyond the little green valley—through the satellite dishes, through the music and clothes and tall tales that arrive with every migrant returning from the big cities of Mexico or the United States—the more Zamora wants to shed its skin.

And so practically everyone in Zamora, and everyone else in the entire state of Michoacán, for that matter, is getting the hell out—or coming back after having gotten the hell out. The movement is circular: you meet the future by moving out, render tribute to the past by coming back home to visit and spend your hard-earned American dollars.

If you want to leave Zamora, you come to the bus station, *la central*. If you want to arrive in Zamora, you come to *la central*. Even if you've got your own car or truck or eighteen-wheeler, the highway takes you right past it, for there is only one entrance to Zamora, and only one exit—Mexico Federal Highway 35, which heads north to Guadalajara and south to the highlands where Cherán is nestled and on through the Paracho Valley to Uruapan. Here gather all kinds of Zamoranos and outsiders. Indian vendors on their way to the city loaded down with overstuffed straw baskets of tamales or sweet breads or salted fish or hand-embroidered tablecloths. An army of young men headed north to the States or on their way back, wearing the uniform of the migrant soldier ready to battle the gringo *migra* and *patrones*: baseball cap, polyester shirt, faded jeans, sneakers. And, as at any bus station anywhere in the world, a curious collection of locos and down-and-outers, paupers and nouveau riche, narcos and cholos and *putas* and *putos*, innocents taking their first trip away from the family, and those long fallen from grace, perpetually running from fate and the law. Mostly, they're teen-agers. They walk with purpose, strutting as if through Times Square, arms swinging wide and high, chins up, got somewhere to go, man. And finally, the Wild One, a type no *central de autobuses* can do without. His biker jacket crinkles audibly, a pirate hoop dangles from his left ear, and his short, greased hair is spiked up. He smacks his gum loudly as he strides along, ignoring the peasants all around him.

It's a drab ochre mausoleum. There's a cafeteria presided over by an obese teenage chola with heavy mascara and a ton of attitude. A TV set hangs from the ceiling and all the patrons' eyes are glued to a dubbed rerun of *Adam-12*. There is a *farmacia* with a sign that says *"Abierto 24 horas,"* but it's closed. There's a colossal digitalized Coke machine painted with icy blue mountains and festooned with colorful little flags and a big banner announcing the 1994 Winter Olympics and proclaiming Coca-Cola the perfect Olympic companion: *¡Refresca tu espíritu Olímpico con Coca-Cola!* There's a magazine kiosk with outdated copies of *Vanidades* (the Mexican *Cosmopolitan*) and *Time en Español*, plenty of *fotonovelas* featuring grubby villains pawing at the big breasts of fake blondes and Clark Kent types who kill the ruffians before paw-ing the big breasts themselves.

And there's Dulcería la Zamorana, proffering snacks for the great journeys about to be undertaken: bags of Doritos and Ruffles, a pyramid of Santa María purified water, and behind the counter stacks of burritos and *tortas* (sandwiches) and tacos and *hamburguesas*, plastic cups of blue, yellow, or red Jell-O, and a soda fountain with Coca-Cola, Sprite, and Fanta Orange. And there is the attendant: a short, stocky, dark, Asian-eyed, jet-black-haired woman. A pure-blooded Purépecha Indian straight out of Michoacán history, serving you *tortas* stuffed with pre-Columbian ingredients: *aguacate, tomate, cebolla* . . .

It's five minutes to six. The station suddenly bursts with activity. There's a mad rush to the bathroom. With trembling hands, an *abuelita* is retying the frayed strings that hold together an overstuffed cardboard box. The Wild One is buying water, more gum, Doritos, and cigarettes. A *rockero* in black is picking up his guitar case with the B-movie grace of the title character in Robert Rodríguez's *El Mariachi*. Flush-faced, Buddha-bellied bus drivers rush into the main hall, whistling, shouting: "*¡Morelia! ¡Salida a Morelia!*" and "*¡México!*" and "*¡Guadalajara!*" and

"*¡Tijuana, vámonos!*" Everywhere, people are slinging bags over shoulders, heaving baskets up onto their heads, giving tearful good-bye hugs to sons and daughters and fathers and mothers.

And then I see her. She makes her way through the bustle like a Mafia don. A short, tough Indian woman with the trademark blue-black rebozo of the Purépecha Indians. Age has begun to crease her face, but her hair is dark black still and she's got the don't-fuck-with-me look of our adolescent Wild One. She is followed by about fifteen dirt-poor Indians, all of them carrying small vinyl bags. They look tired and scared, doing everything they can to not draw attention to themselves, but everyone notices them anyway. They are *pollos*, chickens—or *mojados*, wetbacks. In the States "wetback" is a racist epithet, but the migrants often use the Spanish word to describe themselves with pride—after all, they're braving the river and every other obstacle in their way to cross over to the other side. As for the Indian woman, she is their *coyote*, a nickname that refers to the wily ways of the smugglers.

She's all business. Another journey north. She barrels through a crowd of customers at one of the counters, makes a quick transaction. Her *pollos* sit nervously in a few rows of chairs, uttering not a word.

At precisely 6:00 A.M., the roar of buses gunning accelerators and grinding gears and pumping air brakes drowns out the monotone voice of the woman announcing the final call for a dozen buses over the PA system. It's as if a convoy is heading out of Zamora, a battalion or an expedition, a mass of fleeing pilgrims or exiles or evacuees.

The *pollos* get their own chartered bus. The coyote readjusts her rebozo before she walks up the steps, wrapping it over her head and across her shoulder. She is the last one to board.

Our third-class beast rises into the denuded hills, tapped by the Indians for timber and pine resin. Dirt roads to remote villages veer left and right off the potholed asphalt. We stop in nowhere towns where the Indian women crowd around clucking in their ancient tongues, aggressively hawking salted fish, soft drinks, gum, and mayonnaise sandwiches. We climb ever higher, our aviator-shaded teenage driver blasting narco-corrido anthems—odes to fallen drug lords—and navigating the hairpin curves at hair-raising speed.

Higher still, the cooling air is scented by the remaining trees (all bleeding resin into tin cans), and then I see the volcanoes, cute little pencil-gray baby volcanoes announcing that I'm just a few minutes away from Cherán, which is ringed by a half dozen dormant cones. The volcanic landscape brought the region its share of fame back in the 1940s. About forty miles south of Cherán is Parikutín, a smudge on the horizon from here, the most recent of the *volcancitos*. Parikutín erupted in 1943—just shot up from the ground on some poor tenant farmer's cornfield. It made the cover of *National Geographic* and served as the spectacular backdrop for *Captain from Castile*, starring César Romero and Tyrone Power as conquistadors.

After a series of tight S-curves, the bus negotiates a final bend and suddenly the town of Cherán opens up before me.

Cherán lies about two hundred miles almost directly west of Mexico City in the northeastern part of the state of Michoacán, on a highland plateau known as "La meseta Purépecha"—named for the Indian tribe that has inhabited the region since long before the Conquest—which itself is part the great central plateau that encompasses the middle third of Mexico. At an elevation of 2,430 meters, Cherán, whose population is around 30,000, is precariously situated. The town's name, which in the Purépecha language means "a place of fear," is a direct reference to the painful landscape of abrupt, irregular peaks and chasms. One step in the wrong direction and you plunge off a cliff. The only "flat" stretch is the steep grade of the highway, which doubles as Main Street and is known simply as *la carretera*, the highway. The region is generally tropical, but because of the altitude, the climate is cooler than in the lowlands of the coast and the jungles of the south. The harshness of the landscape and the relative tranquillity of the climate give Cherán a peculiar kind of geographical tension. It's no Eden, but there's a hint of paradise.

I hop off the bus and immediately leap and pirouette to avoid stepping into potholes filled with fetid water and floating fish heads from the market. Not knowing where to go—I don't know anyone here—I instinctively cross the highway toward the church, which, as in every other town in Mexico, is the center of the landscape. I take two steps across the scarred asphalt before I am almost run down by a semitrailer hauling timber. And there I stand, for the next few minutes, waiting for a break in the decidedly unfriendly-to-pedestrians traffic—more semis, and buses, and tractors, and Mexmobiles (clattering midseventies Datsuns and smoking

Chevys), and a fleet of late-model pickups with license plates from Wisconsin, Kansas, Connecticut, Mississippi, Nebraska, Arkansas, and, of course, California, a few of which are blasting gangsta rap or the latest West Coast house-music mix.

Every semi and bus that rolls by causes an earthquake of about 3.1 on the Richter scale for about half a block east and west of the highway. I stand by the side of the shuddering road and behold the parade.

It is market day in Cherán. Nonagenarian Indian women sit in crumbling adobe doorways and Indian teens cruise the streets in their Chicago Bulls windbreakers and authentic Air Jordans. The walls of the houses are covered with Chicano-style graffiti, in tortured Spanglish (FACK YOU, PUTO!). Along the street next to the church, where the vendors ply their wares, you see heads covered by cowboy hats and by backwards Oakland Raiders caps. There are burros carrying loads to market and there are video arcades where Indian kids become ninja warriors. Steven Seagal scowls from the window of the local *videocentro*, next to the swarthy Mexican-cowboy face of Vicente Fernández, the venerable ranchero troubadour of the provinces.

I sit on a bench in the plaza. Three buildings dominate the cobblestone square: the church, a modest, eighteenth-century model; the *presidencia municipal*, guarded by a few hungover blue-suited cops; and the establishment that no migrant town can do without—the *casa de cambio*. It's the first place you stop at when you return from the States. Here, you exchange your dollars like you'd cash in chips at the end of a Sin City binge.

I get up from my bench in the plaza and do a 360. Perched on the hills around me are a few hundred modest adobes and several dozen not-so-modest Michoacán dream homes built by those migrants who've braved the gringo frontier and come back home to play the millionaires. The American dollar, as of this writing, is worth nearly ten pesos, meaning that Mexicans returning with savings of a few thousand dollars are basically wealthy. (The average denizen of Cherán earns about three dollars a day.) The adobe dwellers are generally those who have yet to migrate or who have just begun to do so. Then there are the in-between homes: modest one-stories with iron reinforcing rods jutting up from the roofs—with another few years of picking cauliflower, washing dishes, or leaning over a lathe, there might be enough money for that second story. On many of these homes there are wooden crucifixes planted amid the iron rods. May God, Jesus, the Virgin, and the saints bless this endeavor, that the future may be ours, that the third and fourth bedrooms may soon appear, that our satellite dish may be christened and our home blessed with CNN and MTV.

This is not the kind of Indian village that Americans or, for that matter, middle-class non-Indian Mexicans are attracted to or can even easily imagine. There is no tourist trade in Cherán (the gringos and wealthy Mexicans head to Pátzcuaro, a stunning lake in central Michoacán, for the picturesque premodern Day of the Dead celebrations). After all, we like our Indians, well, Indian. Barefoot, in folkloric dress, burning incense in rites to the gods of rain and wind and fire, preserved as in a diorama at the Museo de Antropología e Historia in Mexico City. You want a town where you can take pictures of yourself towering over the beaming natives or of a ski-masked revolutionary brandishing a rifle in the jungles of Chiapas.

But I feel a sense of familiarity. Cherán is, somehow, a more radical version of what I grew up with back in Los Angeles, in between the Old World (Virgin of Guadalupe votives always aglow at my grandparents' house) and the New (the tube flashing with *The Brady Bunch* at my parents'). That cultural swirl is what I've always thought of as the living definition of "Chicano," although many who claim the moniker prefer a connection to the mystical Indian past, as in Carlos Castañeda's peyote visions, or urge righteous rebellion against the white man. Cherán, in all its rapid transformation, is taking a sledgehammer to the stereotype of the Indian, and Cherán is what most of provincial Mexico is coming to resemble, because it is the Indian who for several decades has done most of Mexico's migrating, and each migrant who goes north and returns adds another layer of Americana. Which is not to say that Cherán isn't an Indian town. All the things we associate with the Indian past (the Purépecha language, the ancient rituals like herbal medicine and sorcery) are here, coexisting with MTV. Cherán is an Indian town with one foot in pre-Columbian times and the other leaping toward the twenty-first century, spanning in its stride the five hundred years in between—five hundred years of *mestizaje*, a term that refers to the mixing of European and Indian blood resulting from the Conquest and to the negotiation of cultural identity that continues to this day.

Here, in the center of Cherán, I think about my own connection to Indian Mexico, if I even have one. My grandfather looked like an Indian—wide nose, bronze skin, short stature. But my grandfather also sang opera and drove a Cadillac in Los Angeles in the late 1950s. Was my grandfather still an Indian? And me—I've got a thin Castilian nose and the hair of a Moor. In Persian restaurants I am often addressed first in Farsi. But perhaps it's in the mix that the connection lies—and in the fact that I, too, am on the road. Throughout Mexico the Purépechas are renowned for their tenacity as wetbacks. Local authorities estimate that about one-third of Cherán's population travels north each spring and returns around the time of the fiesta for Saint Francis in October, bringing back not just dollars but the best and worst of U.S. pop culture.

Indeed, according to official figures, some three million Michoacanos are living and working in the United States today, although the number varies according to the season. There are towns in the highlands whose population decreases by 60 to 70 percent during the spring and summer months, when the majority of able-bodied men—and a good many women—between the ages of seventeen and forty-five go north. Many thousands return at the end of every year. Only a handful of seasonal farmworkers are hired legally for contract labor under the provisions of the U.S. government's H2-A visa program for temporary labor; most Mexicans picking America's crops are undocumented.

American farmers need the Mexicans and rural Mexico needs the jobs. Legal and illegal workers together bring back or wire home some $5 billion a year to Michoacán, whose total state budget in 1999 was only about one-third that amount. In addition, the state government reported in 1998 that there were nearly nine thousand workers (these would be among the legals) who had officially retired from their jobs in the States and returned to live out their years in Michoacán, receiving, collectively, some $2,765,000 a month from Uncle Sam in Social Security and pension benefits.

This state of interdependence is nothing new in the region, although Mexico's crisis has exacerbated the situation. Purépechas have been traveling the Wetback Trail since the early twentieth century. The very word *purépecha* means, loosely, "a people who travel," a pre-Columbian tribute to an indigenous nation that, long before the arrival of the

Europeans, exhibited what the Mexicans call *patas de perro* (literally, dog's feet). It was from the home of these peripatetic people that Benjamín, Jaime, and Salvador Chávez set out on their fateful journey.

It has been three weeks since the accident that took the Chávez brothers' lives. I am the only journalist in Cherán. It is my job—my ghoulish job—to interview the grieving Chávez family.

The Chávez house is at the end of Galeana Street, on the outskirts of town. More like a flood channel than a street—it becomes a mud flow when it rains, and it rains about nine months of the year in Cherán—Galeana is a deeply rutted dirt path that will cause a car axle to snap if a driver attempts to go faster than five miles an hour. Like practically every other dwelling in Cherán, the house is built against a hill. There is a rectangular concrete room at street level, with a wood-shack bedroom perched above it. Adjoining the shack are the kitchen, which is barely enclosed by scrap wood, and another shack that serves as the second bedroom. About thirty feet up the hill is the outhouse, equipped with newspaper for toilet paper.

There is little furniture in the rooms. Four double beds, two dresser drawers. No tables. In front of the shacks stand the only chairs, miniature wooden stools about the right size for a three-year-old, but adults and children alike sit on them. The only decorations are the Catholic beach towels that are a popular item throughout provincial Mexico and the Mexican barrios in the States, neon-bright renditions of the Last Supper, the Sacred Heart of Jesus, the Virgin of Guadalupe, and the rest of the constellation of saints.

It is a Sunday, and the members of the Chávez family are dressed in their best, having just returned from church to pray for their dead. The mother, doña María Elena Chávez, is a woman in her early fifties, but right now she appears to be approaching seventy. She is extremely thin, wrists and ankles like twigs, with the deeply lined dark brown face of an Indian matriarch. Her eyes glow an unusual grayish green. These days, they are almost always moist, filling with tears that I never see drop. Doña María Elena stands about five feet tall. Like most of the other Purépecha women of Michoacán, she wears the traditional rebozo, the embroidered shawl of blue and black bars divided by thin white lines, over a plain checkered country-style dress of thin cotton, and knee-high dark blue stockings that have lost their elasticity and bunch up halfway down her calves. Her shoes are low-heeled, of cheap black felt, with gold buckles of plastic.

Rosa Chávez, María Elena's daughter, is twenty-one years old. She has small black eyes set in a baby face, a round figure, and medium-brown skin. Although she isn't smiling today, over the next two years I'll get to know her smile—the slightest curling of her lips, a dimple on her right cheek—and pleasant laugh quite well. Sunday best for Rosa is what she wears most every other day of the week—a succession of T-shirts (ranging from Bruce Springsteen to CHOOSE LIFE) and jeans (today, white; she also has blue and black) and a rebozo draped across her shoulders. Hers is the look of women who've lived in the United States. Up until very recently, wearing anything but a dress and rebozo in Cherán was a scandal. Some women now even walk the streets of Cherán without the rebozo—to the consternation of many a macho elder.

Fernando, at thirty-one the oldest surviving son of the family, is wearing a white dress shirt of the polyester variety and equally modest dark slacks. He is darker than his mother or his sister, nearly chocolate brown. A handsome Indian face with a thin mustache, a somehow plaintive face. His voice sounds just like he looks—soft-spoken, tentative, and occasionally, suddenly earnest. He walks and talks slowly. If Rosa tends toward the tomboy in the Purépecha highlands, Fernando breaks type the other way—he's anything but the macho. If he wears a mask at all, it is one of quiet stoicism.

There are kids running around, bare feet and sneakers pattering along the hard-packed tan earth of the spacious yard, where chickens and roosters scratch and cluck and chicks chirp and the women wash clothes in big tin basins. Seven in all, the children of Fernando, Rosa, and Florentino (the other surviving son, currently in the States) and of the dead, Jaime and Benjamín. They range from José Iván, a loud eighteen-month-old who's always falling down and crying for a few seconds before getting up and playing again, to César, a dark, handsome, sensitive twelve-year-old, now a de facto father or uncle figure to the younger ones since three fathers and uncles have left home never to return.

I sit on one of the small chairs. Dreading the interview, I make small talk as long as I can. Fernando speaks softly now and again, as does Rosa. María Elena is silent, doesn't even make eye contact, instead turning her head away, staring in the direction of the highway that winds westward down into the valley. Mostly, there is quiet. I hear myself making conversation and shut up. A cool wind rustles the leaves of a plum tree that shades the entrance of the second bedroom and of a tall cherry tree farther up the hill. Even the kids play quietly.

When María Elena finally speaks, it is not to demand an indemnity from the U.S. government. Instead, she wants to warn about the danger other sons and daughters face on the road. Keep your children at home, she counsels. "I don't want another mother to suffer what I've suffered."

Fernando, in a voice that begins soft and slow and gradually gathers emotion—and the stronger his voice the more he looks you in the eye— says something he feels everyone should know about his brothers: they didn't die because they were reckless and flouting death, no. "You never think about what can happen on the road," he says. "When you make that journey you're thinking about your dreams, that things are going to get better, that you're going to be able to support your family, give your kids an education." The Chávez brothers were thinking of the future, not the past.

Fernando says that he will return to Watsonville, where all five brothers lived and worked for a few seasons of strawberry picking before the crash. Florentino is there now, apparently in a bad way, living in the same trailer where they all ate and slept together, facing the ghosts with only the camaraderie of his friends and a few beers after work.

I am surprised that Fernando speaks of returning north in spite of the tragedy. I'd assumed that all the brothers were illegals—as the vast majority of Cheranes who roam the northern roads are—but Fernando and Florentino can travel without the risks: both have temporary work permits to pick the fields of California. The three who were killed didn't.

Rosa and her husband, Wense (short for Wenseslao, a Slovenian name whose appearance in Cherán no one, not even Wense himself, is able to explain), are both illegal. Wense has been crossing the line back and forth since he was thirteen years old and knows the better part of the American Midwest, having grown quite fond of St. Louis. Rosa's first and only trip north had been with Wense to Missouri shortly before the accident. On the one hand, she would like to return to the "other side," as migrants often refer to the States, with her husband, who can't imagine staying in Cherán, tragedy or no tragedy. Besides,

Rosa, invoking the migrant creed, says that it's the only way that she can be sure that her daughter, Yeni, will have a future. On the other hand, she is well aware of the anguish she'd cause her mother if she attempted to cross illegally once more. What the matriarch wants is clear to all: that everyone remain in Cherán rather than face the risks of the road again.

But the Chávez family, despite the deaths, is possessed of the migrant spirit. In some ways, the brothers have become martyrs who make the journey all the more necessary. Their sacrifice would be meaningless if the family stayed in Cherán, stuck in time, frozen in a futureless poverty.

Over the next several months, whether to stay or to go will be the main topic of conversation between mother and children. I can already tell, by the very fact that Rosa is ambivalent about the future, even during this season of loss, that she will take to the road again. It is only a question of when and where and how she will cross the line.

The Chávez brothers' funeral was a majestic affair, perhaps the biggest Cherán had ever seen. Every resident who could walk attended, from the toothless lady who claims to be 103 years old and flirts with passersby on the highway, to the young gang members who furiously tag the town with spray cans, to the nouveau riche migrants who return from the States with thick gold chains dangling from their necks, looking more like Dominican baseball players than wetbacks who've worked fifteen years picking fruit from California to Florida.

The cemetery is at the western edge of town, a few hundred feet below the level of the plaza, bordered on three sides by the highway. The deathscape is as divided along the lines of class as the town. The rich get elaborate tombs of polished stone; the poor, simple wood crosses rarely more than a foot tall, which disappear after only a few years owing to the wet climate of the highlands.

The Chávez family can by no means be considered rich. Although the sons had been migrating for several years before the accident, they had yet to graduate from fieldwork to the better-paying jobs of the city, which allow Cheranes to save substantial amounts of money and transform their lives on both sides of the border.

The tragedy will give the Chávez brothers a middle-class existence, albeit in death. The three are buried in a spot usually reserved for the illustrious, under a tall cherry tree at the very center of the crowded cemetery, affording them shade every day of the year, especially welcome at midday, when the tropical sun is punishing summer and winter alike. A stonecutter in the state capital of Morelia heard of the tragedy and offered to build, free of charge, three large monuments in the shape of church steeples, the preferred style—for those who can afford it.

When I get there, a cemetery worker, Ramiro Payeda, a graying man who works a shovel like someone far younger, is laying the foundation for the tombstones, which have not yet arrived. At the entrance to the cemetery, he mixes the concrete by forming a volcano cone and pouring water into the crater. The scraping sound of the shovel can be heard all over the cemetery. Then he takes the mixture down to the graves in a wheelbarrow.

Don Ramiro is upset with the news—actually, a rumor that I pass along—that the local loan shark who lent the Chávez brothers money for their fateful trip is still demanding payment from the family. Such loans are common among the migrants; they need cash to pay the coyotes to get them across the line, repaying the loan with money from their work in the States. There is no bank in Cherán, and this allows the loan sharks to charge exorbitant interest rates—often 20 percent.

"It's an insult to the dead," Ramiro says. "And it's just adding insult to injury for that poor family. They don't have much. They're living off what their neighbors have given them in the last few weeks. It hurts me, I don't like it. That's it, my friend."

Ramiro pours the concrete over the graves.

He predicts that the family will not have to repay the debt. How can you make a dead man pay? He remembers an incident from a few years ago. A wealthy landowner wanted to evict a poor farmer from his land to expand his own holdings; the small farmer's lot had gone into default because of a few seasons of bad crops. But that farmer—he'd been on that lot since everyone could remember. Word spread through the town, and on the day the police showed up to evict him, there was a crowd of about a hundred standing by the farmer. The only ones evicted were the cops. To this day, the farmer remains on his plot. That's how it is, my friend.

Ramiro expertly smooths the concrete with a trowel.

And that is how it will be for the dead, should that loan shark persist, Ramiro tells me.

"You should have been here for the funeral," Ramiro says. "A lot of reporters, like you. There'll never be a funeral like that again. It was as if they were burying Purépecha princes from the old days. There was Father Melesio in his brilliant white smock, and the *presidente* in his new blue jeans and smart boots, and the widows wailing as only widows can wail, and the mother, can you imagine the pain of a mother who loses three sons at once? There were great bouquets of flowers and beautiful wreaths, a thousand votives flickering in the breeze, and all the rebozos making a blue-black sea as the mothers rocked back and forth moaning, and the men with their hats in their hands crying just as hard as the women, because those boys who died were just like all of us—*they were us.* Because we've all taken that road.

"You should have seen the bodies," Ramiro says. "The Americans didn't even bother to wipe the blood off their faces. And the stitches from the autopsies! The Americans must have thought our boys were dogs."

The sun is setting now in the Purépecha highlands, shadows lengthening over the hills of Cherán. A sudden gust of wind shakes the branches of the tree, and a shower of cherries falls onto the nameless gray slabs. Don Ramiro kneels down and picks them off the concrete, one by one. Then we both just sit there quietly, looking away in opposite directions, he toward the north, I toward the south. I hear the sound of a bus grinding into first gear, straining against the steep grade of the highway. It is heading north.

María Huaroco is the Chávez family's next-door neighbor. A short, tough-bodied Indian woman, she has jet-black hair despite her fifty-something years. A gold tooth flashes in her occasional smile. Her son, Pedro, grew up with the Chávez brothers and accompanied them on the journey northward. He survived the crash in Temecula but saw his closest friends crushed under the truck. Miraculously, he walked away from the wreck with a sprained ankle.

María Huaroco sits in the cool, dark living room of her house, another shack perched on the hillside. As in almost every other household in Cherán, there is an altar against the far wall, where a large old-fashioned doll of a blond, light-skinned Jesus stands amid votive candles, glasses of water, and flowers in vases. Smoke wafts over from the wood fire in the kitchen a few paces away. From the small window that looks down the hill, I can see several large tin basins filled with sudsy water on the front patio.

María speaks broken, Purépecha-accented Spanish. It is a rapid speech of clipped vowels and clucked consonants, the sounds of the indigenous language transposed onto Spanish. The emphasis is on verbs and nouns, often with articles missing and scrambled genders and tenses. The pitch rises and falls dramatically, from aspirated whispers to near shrieks, punctuated with a laugh that sometimes sounds cruelly sarcastic and at other times seems softer, like a bittersweet acknowledgment of the absurd.

I do not have to prompt her much to speak about the accident. It has been the main topic of conversation in town since it happened.

She told me: I was at the wake, sad, crying, what else could one do but cry? Nothing but crying. Those boys are friends of my son. I, too, have three sons. Those three dead are my son's best friends. Everyone suffered the death.

God is great, God gives strength when things happen, yes? Because God made the world and God will give us strength and God alone has all things, that's what I say, but who knows, who knows if it was an accident, if it was the coyote or the driver or the *migra*, nobody knows; we will know nothing—it just happens, ha! When they came to tell us of the accident, they said, "Señora, do you know the Chávez sons?" Oh, *los chinitos* [the Asian-eyed], I said, because that's what we call them, *los chinitos.* "Well they're hurt bad." Eh? I said. How? "Because they had an accident in Los Angeles or somewhere around there." Ay! I said. And so we ran out of the house, and ran, ran like mad. It felt to me like the ground was giving way beneath my feet, it felt like a mountain was rising up before me, but she wasn't there, doña María Elena wasn't there, she was asleep at her daughter-in-law's house. And there we were, running again. And then I found out that my son wasn't dead, but her sons are dead, and she cried and cried and she has reason to cry because the three died together . . .

I have a son on the other side. I don't even know the name of the place. He doesn't call. He doesn't send money. Six months, he doesn't call. Eighteen years old. My youngest. When my children leave, I pray: "My God, accompany my sons, my God, I want you to take care of my sons." I don't know if that's why my son was saved. I don't know . . .

And I say to my children: "Behave yourselves, and write me, don't forget me, and try to send me money so that I can save it for you, don't spend it foolishly."

You see this little house here? I built it myself. How? Washing other people's clothes. Never anything but washing and washing and washing for others. And the clothes I have—all given to me by generous souls. Look at the way I'm dressed. Me, I'll never go to the other side. Think of it! I can't read, can't write. If I go, what will I say to them, the gringos? How will I order a plate of food? Or even say "Good morning"? Ha! All the sons and daughters of our families are spread out over the earth. Separated like that, what good is it? It's no good.

I don't know what people are thinking. Some say they'll still go, others say no. Some say that lightning doesn't strike twice and that's why they go. I heard a group left last night. I know the mother of one, and she said to me, "Will he arrive or will he die?" And I said, "Who will know?"

Joseph Rodriguez

2

PAISANOS

The church bells clang madly for morning Mass, rung by a local teenager who performs the task 365 days a year, at seven in the morning and at seven at night and several times a day during fiesta. The shroud of mist that blanketed Cherán during the night slowly lifts, allowing shafts of pale light to dot the hills, but the cold remains. The houses of Cherán lack insulation; at night they might as well be refrigerators. The highland cold chills you deep inside, tensing the muscles until they ache. The only consolation is that this is pure mountain air, clean and spicy, smelling of earth and dry leaves.

Cherán awakens slowly. The plaza is empty but for the cops who are ever shooting the breeze before the *presidencia municipal* and a few enterprising vendors setting up their pyramids of fruit and vegetables for early customers. Cherán is not a lazy town—it is impossible for a town so poor to be lazy; the poorer a town, the harder it must work—but it struggles to banish the highland night. How deeply one sleeps in Cherán! The cold forces the soul to dive deep into the body, far from the world, from the twenty-four-hour dissonant symphony of the highway, from the imposing, fog-shrouded hills and volcanoes that everyone here knows are haunted by a thousand suffering, trickster, or downright malevolent spirits.

At the taxi stand a block from the plaza, the drivers, almost all of them heavy drinkers, blow on their hands and rub puffy eyes. Like ants, the peasants carry loads that appear to be twice their weight in large baskets held on their backs with a strap wrapped around their foreheads. Oxen pull carts of lumber slowly down the highway, exasperating the twentieth-century vehicles.

The interior walls of the Saint Francis of Assisi church have yet to be plastered, the gray concrete dimming an already dark cavern. But right now one great tube of light pours through the east-facing windows, spotlighting a row of Purépecha women kneeling in the pews, all of them wearing rebozos and clicking the rosary. It is a scene straight out of colonial or even missionary-period Mexico. It is the image of Mexico I grew up with in Hollywood Westerns, an image even more deeply ingrained in me by my father's recollections of my grandmother's provincial hometown of Jerez, Zacatecas, which he visited occasionally as a child.

Sparrows chirp loudly, vying with the voices of the women. There are a dozen nests around the altar, where Saint Francis, Cherán's patron, stands in his friar's cloak, a green neon halo glowing over his head and the rest of his body gaudily ringed by yellow, blue, and orange tubes.

The pews begin to fill with the faithful, peasants all of them, the poorest of Cherán's poor, men in sweat-stained straw hats and grimy wool jackets, their muddied sandals and boots shuffling across the floor, and women with hair sooty from the cooking fires, their rebozos fraying.

Father Melesio strides to the altar, a striking man with wide jowls, a heavyweight boxer's body, and bright green eyes—a color that contrasts eerily with his bronze skin and is one of the most obvious physical signs of *mestizaje* in the Mexican provinces: for centuries, the Spanish conquistador has been represented in Indian fiestas by a mask of blond hair and green eyes. Three weeks after the accident, Father Melesio's sermon allegorizes the tragedy.

"The shepherd finds the lost sheep trapped, badly hurt," he says, his voice booming in the cavernous cathedral. "The good shepherd always goes looking for those that need him the most, just as we cannot remain content to be among only those who are healthy and strong. What of those who find themselves lost and hurt, far away from us? We must go searching for the lost sheep."

During the celebration of the Eucharist, Father Melesio very nearly performs a pagan rite.

"For life," he intones, "for the sun, the earth, the rain, and the wind, we sing to you our thanks." He raises the Host heavenward, and the Indians kneel: in that moment, it feels like a doorway into time opens before me, and I sense Cherán's history receding into the immemorial and also surging forward: the continuity of the Indian past, albeit in Catholic garb. Thousands of prayers have been offered up in Cherán on behalf of the Chávez brothers. While the three of them will never stand next to Saint Francis or Saint Anthony or the brown Madonnas, their memory permeates the church, the entire town.

"It was an incredible shock to this community," Father Melesio tells me after Mass. "After the burial, everyone went back to their daily lives, but there's no doubt that the deaths have left a deep scar and helped people become more conscious of their situation."

Father Melesio, clearly of the liberation-theology tradition that melded Marxism and Catholicism among the poor throughout Latin America in the 1970s and 1980s, analyzes Cherán's story with materialist precision. People know why those boys died, he tells me. Not because of a coyote's irresponsibility, though that certainly contributed to the accident, and not just because the *migra* was chasing them. They died because their lives were governed by a global economy. By an economy that ties Cherán's well-being to the United States.

"All sides share in the responsibility for these deaths," Father Melesio says. "It's like a chain. The coyotes make money off the people who cross, and the farmers in America make money off them too, and of course the families and the government in Mexico are remunerated as well. It's a chain looped over many gears. We can't say that it begins in Cherán or in the United States. It's everywhere at once."

The chain has always produced tragedy. After Mass I visit with Cherán's *presidente*, or mayor, Salvador Sánchez Campanur. His office overlooks the plaza. There are a fax machine and a few manual typewriters but no computers. On the wall there is a blown-up black-and-white aerial photograph of Cherán and its immediate surroundings. The town is dwarfed by the imposing landscape, the craters of the volcanoes winking at the heavens. It looks as if Cherán was the target of a cruise missile attack and was miraculously spared.

"It's not the first time we've received the dead from the other side," says Sánchez, a bespectacled, gold-toothed populist type, wearing blue jeans and a denim jacket with a fluffy lambswool collar. Each year, Sánchez says, the bodies come back from the north. Some die in accidents on the job, others from illnesses. Some are victims of the border, dying from dehydration or hypothermia, from car wrecks or falls into steep ravines, from banditry on the line.

Sánchez points at the few flat, open spaces on the aerial photograph. It is not the best land for agriculture; there is virtually no exportation. The staples, corn and beans, are for subsistence. Neither is there any industry to speak of in Cherán, except for the production of a modest amount of furniture, most of which is sold in the region. But even this livelihood will soon be a thing of the past if the timber supply continues to dwindle at its current rapid clip.

So these are the options for Cheranes today: ply some food or wares at market, tap the pines for resin, build wood tables or chairs. You can try opening up a small general store (but brace yourself for the competition: there are stores on every block in Cherán, sometimes two or three). Or you can drive a taxi (there's a fleet of twelve, and most of the day they sit idle at the plaza).

Or go north.

But while Cherán is poor, it is by no means the poorest town in the Purépecha highlands, nor is it among the poorest in the Mexican provinces. Compared with Indian villages in the deep south of Mexico— say, the jungles of Chiapas—Cherán is relatively well-off. While malnutrition is not unheard-of here, you don't see naked kids running around with distended bellies.

The *presidencia municipal* conducted a survey in 1996. Among

Cherán's population of approximately 30,000, health authorities reported only six cases of malnutrition, although they did find a high incidence—943 cases—of serious respiratory infection and a relatively high rate of intestinal maladies, mostly owing to poor hygiene. Electricity is pretty much universal, but running water is rare (perhaps half the population avail themselves of the communal spigots in every neighborhood) and hot water even rarer. Telephones are for the migrant aristocrats: there are only 130 private lines. Most people use the half dozen long-distance public *casetas* to communicate with relatives in the States, and the calls are usually paid for by the relatives. Perhaps the clearest sign of overall poverty, and a clear and present danger to Cherán's health, is the lack of sewage lines in most of the town (only recently has construction of a city system begun). Most families still have outhouses. Untreated commercial and domestic "gray" waters run openly along the streets.

Poverty, then, but no famine. People will not die if they stay in Cherán. Still, Cherán survives as a quasi-modern town only because its people migrate and return the richer for it; the local economy is based almost entirely on work performed in the north. The U.S. dollars brought back to Cherán each year represent the entire municipal budget multiplied dozens of times over.

And beyond the money, the Cheranes are drawn north by ideas. Education, for example. There is no way rural parents can provide more than an elementary school education for their children; children are expected to work as soon as they're able-bodied—and women are expected to marry and have children in their early teens.

In the "liberal" north, women don't have to wear rebozos, no one cares much if you shack up with your lover without getting married first, and any night of the week teenagers stay out past midnight without facing a severe beating with a belt from Papá. In the north, Mexican women can drive cars, and their husbands might even help wash the dishes and tend to the children. In the north, workers take retirement, a concept that does not exist in Mexico.

Ironically, there are not a few migrant veterans who ultimately opt to return to Cherán for good, complaining that the liberal north is not so liberal after all. They complain that there are "too many laws," that you can't just crank up the *cumbia* on your boom box at any hour of the day or night, that you can't drink a Bud on the sidewalk in front of your house, that you can't discipline your kid for fear of being arrested on charges of child abuse.

But the biggest draw is the world, and what is going on beyond the Purépecha highlands. From the perspective of Cherán, the entire world is on the move: commerce, culture, and people. The Cheranes want to be a part of the movement. Were it not for the migrants, Cherán would be forever trapped in the past. To move is to live. To move is to head toward the future. Working in the States not only elevates Cherán's economic status but also connects it, culturally, to the whirlwind of globalization.

When I ask Sánchez if he's made his way north, he smiles and answers, like any good lefty Mexican pol, with the collective pronoun. "Yes, we've gone to United States," he says, "when we were young. And we found it to be"—he pauses, searching for the word—"quite exciting."

Delfino is a taxi driver whose real passion is playing guitar with a local ballad trio, serenading lovers young and old. By day, he sits by his late-seventies Plymouth, waiting for a passenger alongside a dozen other drivers. Sometimes the cabbies have to wait hours for a fare, which rarely amounts to more than a few pesos. Cherán's fleet of taxis are identifiable not just by the town's name, in Old English lettering, painted red on the white doors of the cars. They are also all marked with Cherán's unofficial emblem: the silhouette of a *bruja*, a witch in pointy hat astride a broom. "Here, we're all *brujos*," Delfino says with a smile.

I notice a light-skinned girl, in her early teens and clearly pregnant, selling fruit on the sidewalk alongside the church. Delfino tells me she's American. Barely speaks Spanish. The story is that she is the daughter of a Cherán migrant who married an Anglo woman in the States. The mother died and the father returned with his American-born daughter to Cherán. And here, she gets knocked up by a local Indian boy, bringing things full circle. That baby will be mestizo several times over.

The cabbies in Cherán, as everywhere else on the globe, always have the local gossip. Today, the talk is of the latest group of wetbacks to head north. Forty-five men left on a bus the previous night. All of Cherán will carefully follow the news (gleaned from Spanish-language CNN by the satellite dish owners, then by word of mouth to the rest of the town), waiting for reports from the border.

José Luis Macías Murillón, a local schoolteacher, notices me walking aimlessly about town with my tape recorder slung over my shoulder. Macías has been waiting for his moment to say just what he thinks of the world.

First off, he wants to say that he thinks that the beating of his *paisanos* in Riverside, California (the infamous videotaped incident that occurred just a few days before the accident at Temecula), is an affront to all citizens of the world who respect human rights. And he thinks that there might be a connection between the Riverside beating and the accident in Temecula—who knows?—perhaps a secret policy of intimidation. The Border Patrol agents are renowned for their brutality, Macías notes, like the time they shot that kid in Texas (a disputed incident in which a U.S. Marine with an M-16 killed a teenage goatherd armed with a .22).

But what he most wants to tell the world is that the situation really hits home because many a local has fought with the Americans in their wars. In World War II, there was Alvaro García Alamos, one of the 201st Airborne boys (a modest Mexican contingent that fought with the Allies in Europe), and he actually came home alive, although a bit, you know, psychologically affected. Macías's own brother, Sebastián Macías, fought in Vietnam with the American army, and he also made it home alive. The Americans called him up several times, Macías guesses to give him his pension or some such, but Sebastián never returned their calls; he's never talked to a soul about what he saw in the jungles. Another local boy, Vicente Sánchez Muñoz, served in the Persian Gulf war, as a drill instructor in the army.

All these men from Cherán lent their support to the Americans and, well, Macías thinks that the Cheranes have done their part for their northern neighbor, in the picking fields and on the killing fields.

Now the people of Cherán will keep going to the States, Macías says. There's nothing that can be done to stop them.

And he just wants to say that he's very concerned about this situation.

And another thing. Many Americans have come to Cherán. Years back, a lot of Americans came, with their religion. There was one by the name of Max Lenthrop, who bought a piece of land and built this great house and he stayed many, many years, and he studied the Purépecha language, and everyone treated him very well. When he left, Cherán bade him farewell with much tenderness.

So the Cheranes have graciously hosted the Americans on this side of the line, and yet they are received quite ungraciously on the other side. This makes no sense to Macías. Maybe someone has spoken badly of the Cheranes in the States?

Macías tells me that his wife and children are in Wisconsin. Now that school will be letting out for the summer, he's going to see about getting a passport and a visa to go be with them. And if he doesn't get his visa, well, he's just going to have to go illegally. And he thinks that the people of the United States should understand this, that there should be some kind of diplomatic negotiation. Maybe a bracero program, like in the old days. You know, people moving back and forth according to their needs—and of course the needs of the bosses in the United States. Simple and just.

Finally, he wants to say that the other day he was talking with the *presidente* about maybe setting up a register down at the *presidencia* where the migrants would leave their names, their destinations in the States, and the names and addresses of their relatives here, so that Cherán can keep track of its own. Because there are a lot of people who haven't come back, you see. They leave and no one ever hears from them again. They just get lost up there.

He thinks that maybe the Cheranes die and the Americans toss them, nameless, into a mass grave. You know, like they do in a war.

¡Pinche perro!

Goddamn dog!

Pedro Fabián Huaroco shoos the rambunctious black puppy away. He sits on a tiny stool on the patio in front of his house, eyes puffy at eight in the morning. He seems wary of me, and I think I know why.

Pedro was with the Chávez brothers when they died, but he survived the accident and was assailed by the media in its wake. Now the talk in town is that Pedro has changed his story. According to some locals, he was seen on TV just after the crash, telling a national Mexican audience that he heard a couple of loud explosions just before the truck flipped over into the ditch. The reporter asked Pedro if he thought these were gunshots (presumably fired by the BP at the fleeing vehicle, perhaps blowing out a tire and causing the accident). Pedro said he didn't know. His comments, however, raised the possibility, at least in the Mexican media, of something much worse than just a tragic accident. It suggested a murderous BP that hunts wetbacks like game.

Upon returning to Cherán, Pedro seemed to backpedal. He now says that he can't remember anything clearly or whether there were any explosions at all. This has caused a rift in Cherán. The Chávezes think Pedro is lying and the families have not exchanged a word since the funeral. The rumor—no one knows who started it—is that Pedro was paid off by the BP. And so, no matter how many questions I ask, Pedro only lightly sketches out the events at the border for me.

He does, however, tell me, in a shaky voice, of his journey home after the accident. He was checked at the hospital in Temecula for a sprained ankle and then interviewed by BP agents (during which either he did not mention hearing the explosions—they do not appear in the transcript of the interview—or, if we subscribe to the conspiracy theory, the BP paid him off to never mention them again). The BP drove him back to the line, where they gave him five dollars for taxi fare to La Casa del Migrante, a charitable way station in Tijuana, where he had a hot meal and got a ride to the bus station.

From that point on, from nine o'clock on Monday morning until he arrived in Cherán at two in the morning on Wednesday, Pedro was alone, sitting near the back of the bus as it charged along the perilous route of La Rumorosa. During those interminable hours on the bus, the scenes played over and over in Pedro's mind: the darkness inside the camper shell, the smell of the sweaty bodies jostling against one another, the violent swerve as the truck left the road, and that split second when they were airborne, causing a sensation in his stomach that reminded him of the rare occasions when his father, a mean drunk now dead, would playfully toss him into the air and catch him in his arms. Then the impact of the truck hitting the hard, rocky earth of the wash, like an anvil smashing an aluminum can, and the sudden light of day, the dust hanging in the air, the screams of the injured.

He saw Salvador Chávez's feet—he recognized the shoes—sticking out from underneath the remains of the camper. They twitched a couple of times and then were still.

This is what I remember, Pedro says. Please don't ask me anything else. Please, don't ask me anything else.

Dr. Adalberto Muñoz's office is a block down from the church. Everyone knows him as Dr. Tito, the dimunitive of his Christian name. He is a former *presidente* of Cherán and continues to be an important political powerbroker, a local stalwart of Cuahutémoc Cárdenas's Partido de la Revolución Democrática (PRD), which for several years has ruled the town by almost unanimous consensus. When your child has diarrhea, when you can't get rid of that bronchitis, when you're hungover as hell, when you just want to shoot the breeze, you sit in Dr. Tito's handsome waiting room, with its colonial-style windows and wooden shutters carved with floral designs and its finely worked benches and tables, which are almost always occupied by a bevy of Indian women and their suckling children.

While there are thirteen doctor's offices and fourteen doctors (not counting several dozen Indian healers, the *brujas*) for Cherán's thirty thousand residents, Dr. Tito lays claim to the title of town doc hands down. This is because he is a Purépecha through and through. Yes, his lighter shade of brown speaks of strong *mestizaje* in his bloodline and he's got a dozen cousins in the States, but, unlike most of the other doctors, who are descendants of mestizo families that have lost touch with the town's Indian roots, Dr. Tito speaks the Purépecha language fluently. This bonds him to the Indians in a way that his closest competitor, the Jehovah's Witness doctor who hands out copies of *The Watchtower* along with the penicillin, can only pray for.

A generous soul with the best of bedside manners, Dr. Tito has a winning smile, a reassuring belly on his short frame, and a beautiful

Purépecha wife who's several inches taller than he is. When he speaks Spanish, it is still with that clipped, clucked sound of the mother tongue. He also happens to be one of the town's amateur historians, a keeper of pre-Columbian artifacts and legends.

And he's got stories to tell. He receives me in his *consultorio* with the glass cases filled with antibiotics and syringes and the obstetrical chair in the corner. He sits at his big, old wooden desk. Under the glass tabletop there are snapshots of himself with friends and patients, and postcards he's received from some twenty-five states in America. He offers a glass of lemonade and talks, at a leisurely pace (despite the many women and children in the waiting room), with great enthusiasm, of the past, the present, the future.

In the last few days, the doc says, he's seen about a dozen men, ranging in age from fifteen to forty-five, all asking for routine checkups and a certificate of good health—necessary paperwork for an American H2-A visa, which will allow them to cross legally for contract farming jobs. He has also heard that yet another busload of illegals left Cherán last night. (Migrants lacking visas often visit him before a journey, as well; they'll ask for antidiarrheals and the like, in case they fall ill while working in the States.)

Ever since he was a child, Dr. Tito has seen the legions of men, and, these days, increasingly women, make their way north and return with tales of their adventures. He himself is among the select few in town who have never made the journey. "This is my home," he says simply. "I just never felt like I had to leave."

It is the past that Dr. Tito really adores. Up by the *ojo de agua*, a natural waterfall and pool a couple of miles northeast of the highway, above the barrio of Parikutín (affectionately nicknamed Paris by the locals), he's found archeological remains amid the basalt rock. They seem to be evidence of mining operations, of the time when the Purépechas worked the silver, copper, and gold that once abounded in the mountains, riches that wound up in Spain or in the Vatican.

He brings out a huge cloth-covered tome and opens it delicately, as if about to peruse the original Dead Sea scrolls. It is the *Relación de las ceremonias y ritos y población y gobierno de los indios de la provincia de michoacán*, which is popularly known, thankfully, simply as the *Relación de*

Michoacán, the most complete historical narrative of the region, a classic early Mission-era text. Although the book is unattributed, its author emerges from the prose quite clearly. He is obviously fascinated by the history of the region; he is also guilt-ridden over the barbarous treatment of the Purépechas by the conquistadors—making it likely he was a Franciscan missionary.

Dr. Tito leafs through the yellowed pages, which tell of ancient Michoacán, a rich and mighty empire. This is not mere boasting of an illustrious mythical past, as all Mexicans, even the descendants of the poorest, most decadent, and most violent tribes, are wont to do. The *Relación*, while a subjective history (like all the other *relaciones*, it is based on the author's firsthand interviews with elders, so that it is often difficult to separate fact and myth), appears to be precise in detailing the pre-Columbian culture of Michoacán.

The Mexicas (popularly known as the Aztecs), who for centuries had dominated—through the most barbarous of imperial means—the better part of central Mexico up until the arrival of the Spanish, were never able to conquer the fearsome Purépechas, the descendants of nomadic Chichimeca tribes. These early peoples established themselves in and around the Lake Pátzcuaro region in central Michoacán—possibly fleeing drought in the north—and with their knack for hunting, fishing, agriculture, and war eventually came to dominate an ever-expanding region in southwestern Mexico.

The Mexica and Purépecha cultures developed independently of each other. The closest similarities to the Purépecha tongue are found thousands of miles away among the Quechua of the Peruvian Andes and, strangely, among the Zuñi of the American Southwest, raising the possibility of complex ancient migratory links between the Northern and Southern Hemispheres.

Whoever wrote the *Relación* was the James Agee of his day. It describes, in remarkably minute detail, the meals, clothes, fiestas, weddings, and funeral ceremonies of the Purépechas, along with a political and military history of several hundred years, up to and including the Conquest. The voice of the narrator sounds like a Purépecha speaking Spanish. Often, instead of affirmations, the dialogue is anchored by interrogatives. (For example, a Purépecha prince, instead of declaring, "We aren't afraid of anyone," says, rhetorically, "Whom are we afraid of?") The author detected this linguistic tic and thought it important enough to maintain throughout. "I advise my readers to accept the questions in this text . . . and to adapt to the [Michoacanos'] way of speaking . . . because most of them speak through questions."

It is the way the Purépechas speak today, whether in the mother tongue, in Spanish, or in English, a style of speech that, as the *Relación* narrator points out, affirms an idea—often ironically and rhetorically, sometimes with bitter sarcasm—through negation. ("The *migra* didn't have to chase the boys like that, did they?") It is the way a people who are at once proud and humiliated speak. It is a subversive tongue.

For several hundred years, the Mexicas and Purépechas went about their respective business, eyeing each other warily. In the end, it was the Mexicas who were humbled, groveling before the Purépechas after Moctezuma's embarrassing defeat by Cortés's ragged Spanish forces in Tenochtitlan, pre-Conquest Mexico City. The Mexicas begged the Purépechas to join them in a last-ditch effort to beat back the Spaniards and the tribes that had joined the conquistadors against the hated Mexicas.

The *Relación* tells a tale of conquest as sadly ironic as any on the continent. First came the signs. A few years before the arrival of the Spaniards, the high priests were perturbed by the sudden appearance of cracks in the walls of the great temples ("They closed the fissures but they would open back up") and two comets that glittered across the night sky. The priests thought that these sure signs of impending destruction were messages from the gods urging the Purépechas to conquer a neighboring tribe. But then priests and commoners alike began to dream of strange men riding atop terrible beasts who entered the sacred cities and took up residence in the temples. Fear seized the empire.

A final, apocalyptic vision came to a concubine of a Purépecha lord. One night Cueravaperi, the mother of all the gods, came to the young woman and led her to the road outside of town. The goddess told her to walk until she met the one who would give her a prophecy to take back to her people. And suddenly before her, in the form of an eagle, was none other than Curicaveri, son of Cueravaperi, the god of fire and supreme deity of the Purépechas. The girl climbed up on his wings. Together they flew across the mountains to a great mansion perched on a towering peak. There, all the gods were waiting, wearing wreaths of flowers and colored ribbons in their hair, and before them a feast of wine and honey and plums and other delicacies. Curicaveri told her to sit and listen.

"New men have appeared and they will come to our lands," the gods told her. They said that the gods of Michoacán would no longer come to the mansion with their wines, that no new temples would be built, and that the old ones would be left in ruins. There would be no more sacrifices or offerings, no more ceremonial fires or incense rising up to please the heavens.

"All will be deserted," they said. "For there come now other men to our lands . . . and the song will be one, there will not be many songs as there were before."

In fact, the conquest of Michoacán actually began in the early 1500s before a single Spaniard had set foot in the kingdom, with the arrival of measles and smallpox, imported from Mexica lands where expeditionary forces had already arrived. Neither the priests nor the healers nor the gods of the Purépechas could cure the diseases. "An infinity of people died, and many priests," the narrator tells us. The political conquest didn't take much longer.

The Spanish forces, led by Cristóbal Olid, arrived in Michoacán in 1522, a year after the Mexica surrender in Tenochtitlan. The Purépecha *cazonci*, or king, the inept and easily swayed Tzintzicha, son of the great Zuanga, who had perished in the plague, made the same mistake as Moctezuma, the Mexica ruler, by mistaking the conquistadors for gods. Counseled on the one hand by zealous priests and on the other by those who coveted his throne, he initially amassed a strong army against the enemy. And then he committed a series of blunders. He told the army to stand down, fearful of the wrath of the white-skinned deities, whose imminent arrival, he became convinced, was a fulfillment of the apocalyptic prophecies; he threatened to commit suicide, along with his entire high command, and then changed his mind; when the Spaniards showed up, he abandoned his capital;

and finally, forced to return, a virtual prisoner, he willingly led the conquerors to all the hidden palaces of the empire, ultimately giving away the riches of his crown and his people.

And thus, without having had to fire a shot, without having lost a single man, the meager and ragged forces of the Spanish crown burned the Purépecha temples to the ground with the very fire that the Purépechas had believed to be the property of their own god, Curicaveri.

Franciscan missionaries arrived in 1533, founding a church and naming, of course, Saint Francis as patron. It's been nearly five hundred years since Michoacán was defeated. "Defeated," Dr. Tito says, not "conquered."

Had it been an outright conquest, the doctor reasons, would there be a population of some 200,000 Purépechas today, a quarter of whom speak only the ancestral tongue and a great many more who are bilingual (and a growing number who are nearly trilingual, having added a basic migrant's English to their lexicon)? Ask Dr. Tito, ask anyone in Cherán how they identify themselves, and they will say Purépecha before they say Mexican.

Their identity is not a matter of language, not even, strictly speaking, one of bloodlines—*mestizaje* abounds here. In the end, it is a matter of who the people of Cherán think they are. And so Cherán, according to Cherán, is a Purépecha town. Albeit a Purépecha town cruised by late-model pickup trucks blasting hip hop, an Indian town whose homes are crowned by satellite dishes, an Indian town that follows NBA box scores as closely as it does the weather's impact on the cornfields.

Go to Father Melesio's church and see the rebozo women pray. They pronounce the rosary in the adopted Iberian language. Then they carry baskets of fresh tropical fruit to the altar, muttering prayers in Purépecha, as if the church of the conquistadors were merely a facade, as if the church were still the old temple presided over by Curicaveri.

Nonetheless, Dr. Tito is worried. Many of today's generation, the sons and daughters of the Great Migration, have lost the mother tongue almost entirely.

"You walk down the street and you see kids with their ponytails and baggy jeans," he laments. And the women who've cast off their rebozos. And the graffiti. Even Dr. Tito's mother's house has been tagged by kids who scrawled their crew name—BUNKER 15—atop a fresh, pretty coat of burnt-orange paint.

What's different today, Dr. Tito says, is how swiftly the culture is changing, in direct proportion to the number of people who leave and how long they stay on the other side. Each migrant who goes north brings a bit of America back home. No one in Cherán is untouched by this cultural revolution. Take Dr. Tito's own family. His mother, while born in Cherán, migrated during the turbulent years following the Revolution of 1910. His Uncle Abraham and his Aunt María were born in the north. Dr. Tito has two sisters living in Los Angeles and one in Yuma, who is married to an American evangelical.

Dr. Tito remembers his grandfather saying that back in the 1920s the border was a port of entry, not the wall that it is today. Many an old-timer in Cherán recalls arriving at the border and being asked merely to show his hands instead of undergoing the careful and often insulting interrogations that anyone who "looks Mexican" is subjected to today. If the prospective migrant had all ten fingers and no obvious disfiguration, he was allowed in.

Before leaving Dr. Tito's, I ask one last question.

"What of the Indian healers?" I tell him that I've heard that Cherán is a town of witches.

"They're my competition," the doctor says with a chuckle. Actually, time was when not a little enmity existed between the *brujas* and the doctor, both counseling their clients to forsake the other and his "bad medicine." But these days, they're getting along just fine.

"There's enough illness here for all of us," Doc Tito says.

When I have time to kill in Cherán I walk the entire length of the highway through town, about three quarters of a mile. I begin at the northern end, near the mansion owned by the local coyote millionaires, which is crowned by a huge green Sprite billboard. Then I pass the bus stop and teeming market stalls, on to the long-distance phone booth where a pretty, lonely single mother named Nena, who's never gone north, asks me to describe the places she takes calls from (Memphis, New Orleans, Chicago, Madison, Portland) and hints that I should take her back with me to one of those gleaming cities. Across the street I'll chat with the taxi drivers, who are always telling me I should talk to so-and-so, like the guy who just came back from North Platte, Nebraska, with a gleaming new Chevy S10.

Half a block down, at El Tizol, Cherán's only full-fledged restaurant, I'll greet Salvador Romero, who sweats over his chicken grill; farther down the street, his brother, the veterinarian, tells me that the ox he treated this morning might not make it and wonders how its owner will manage without a beast to haul timber from the mountains. Then there's a stretch of handsome houses with tinted windows and pretty tile and wrought iron; many of them are empty for most of the year. Their owners are *norteños*, northerners (as the people of Cherán call those who live in the States), and they use them like vacation chalets. And the car repair shop, where a group of cholos hang out every afternoon and evening because the owner, himself a young, hip migrant, sells NFL caps and NBA windbreakers. And the fruit stand in front of taxi driver Marcos's house, although often these days the stand isn't up, because his wife is at the hospital, fifty miles away in Uruapan, the nearest city with decent emergency medical facilities, with their baby daughter, who was born severely underweight.

And on every block, at least one store, and sometimes two or three, all selling the exact same goods—Marlboro cigarettes, Modelo beer, yam candies in plastic tubs swarming with flies, eggs, and Pan Bimbo, the Mexican version of Wonder Bread.

At the southern edge of town is the Pemex station. Here the highway bends and there is a panoramic view of the valley below. Directly west stands Juanconi, the baby volcano, a perfectly shaped cone but for its strangely flat top, still young enough to not allow any real vegetation to grace its gray sides. Beyond Juanconi is a long, fertile plain that blooms with a beautiful carpet of white wildflowers in the spring.

The city of Paracho, the only tourist destination in the highlands, renowned for its expert guitar artisans, lies in the distance. At the bend, the highway intersects with three streets, which lead south to the high school, a couple of poor barrios, and the bullring. On the horizon looms massive San Marcos Mountain, a brooding sentinel overlooking the cornfields below its massive, thickly forested folds, one of the last virgin areas in the Purépecha region, protected from poachers by armed guards.

At the Pemex station I visit with Sergio Velázquez, the attendant, who greets me jovially and shoots the breeze as he tends to an endless stream of motorists. He sees all of Cherán from here. Everyone arriving or leaving town stops at the Pemex.

Sergio is twenty-three years old and has survived the migrant road. He's got homemade Chicano-style tattoos to show for it, including "I Luv Irma" across his eight knuckles. He's not going north this year. After several years of work in Texas, Mississippi, and Louisiana, he was able to build a house for his family (he's married with a baby son). He confesses to missing life up north, though. Right about now, he figures, they're picking tomatoes in Arkansas. In the Carolinas, the tobacco leaves are thick and oily, almost as tall as a man, and in Kentucky, the watermelons will soon be ready. Half of Cherán is up there, Sergio says, but they'll all be back soon. Midway through the summer, the migrants are already dreaming of October, when Cherán holds its annual fiesta for Saint Francis, which, luckily for the migrants, coincides with the end of the picking season in the States.

Sergio tells me that the reason he spent all those years in the States comes down to a bicycle. When he was a kid, he wanted one more than anything else in the world, a shiny aluminum motocross model with hand brakes, the same kind a neighbor kid had. Though his father did his share of work in the picking fields on the other side, he never brought home enough money for luxuries like that. Sergio was nineteen years old, in his third year of working in the States, when he was able to buy his first bike.

"It might sound kind of funny," he tells me, nearly shouting above the din of half a dozen idling motors and the trucks and buses hauling ass around the bend. "But I risked my life for a bicycle."

They used to rent bikes in Cherán when he was a kid. But that wouldn't have satisfied him. And he wouldn't have been happy just renting a house.

"You've got only one chance in this life, and if you make it, then you've got something to look back on," he says.

Which is another way of saying that you create a future so that you can have a past, a past that reflects your own will rather than a past imposed by history, one that crushes the very idea of independence. It is an American ideal, of course, and Sergio isn't the only one who believes in it these days. It is flourishing all over the highlands of Michoacán.

Joseph Rodriguez

3

FAMILY

Now it is June, and the rains have come to the highlands, great mountain thunderstorms. I return to Cherán, on the second leg of what will become a year-and-a-half-long pilgrimage. The town's only hotel is now my second home, a dilapidated two-story structure that sits by the side of the highway. The rooms are spartan provincial, with moldy straw-filled mattresses and water-stained walls. Acrid truck exhaust wafts in through the broken windowpanes day and night. The accommodations, which are used only by sleepy truckers and itinerant salesmen of the snake-oil variety, are presided over by a surly matron and her even surlier adult son. They grudgingly serve me hard tortillas and cold beans every morning for breakfast.

The days begin misty-cold in Cherán during the summer. I go out in the morning with a jacket over a shirt and T-shirt but have to peel off two layers by midday, when the sun is searing. The clouds begin to gather in the early afternoon, billowing up fast before you like time-lapse photograghy. They tower over the hills and volcanoes, as if they're issuing from the craters themselves. By midafternoon, the white sun and deep blue sky of the highlands disappear and you begin to hear the thunderclaps, slapping the hillsides and echoing from a half dozen directions. You shiver in the sudden rising wind.

The church bells toll four o'clock, and the vendors down at the plaza scurry to cover their wares, while a group of schoolchildren play in front of the kiosk. Now the wind comes with all its fury, sweeping up the dust of the dirt paths (there are only a few paved streets in Cherán, and these are cobblestone; the only asphalt stretch is the highway). People bow their heads and cover their eyes. Fat drops begin to slap the plaza stones. Lightning strikes close now, close enough for flash and clap to be nearly simultaneous. This delights the children, who shriek with feigned fear. The vendors head for shelter under the eaves of the buildings facing the plaza or run for the church. But the children stand their ground, looking up into the roiling gray expectantly. And then it comes, another summer downpour in Cherán. You can see it rushing up the street from the direction of San Marcos Mountain, which looks like a great eagle protecting or menacing the town, depending on the time of day and the quality of light. Right now, the eagle is descending on Cherán.

When the rain hits the plaza with its full force, the children twirl about and stamp their sneakers in the puddles. The vendors watch them from behind the sheets of runoff pouring from the roofs. They stand with arms crossed, weary and brooding—more business lost—except for one, the toothless lady who claims to be 103 years old, who never moves from her doorway, kneeling night and day by a basket of nuts no one seems to buy, calling out lewdly to passersby and muttering about the Revolution and all of Cherán in flames. She is smiling her mad, toothless smile. She starts to clap her hands, though the sound is drowned out by the rain, and without moving from her post she is there in the plaza dancing gaily as she did a century ago. She is laughing now, loud enough for the vendors to hear, and on a few of those beaten faces the slightest of smiles begin to show.

Rosa Chávez's husband, Wense Cortéz, is the most unpredictable member of the grieving clan. While Rosa's surviving brothers, doña Maria Elena, the in-laws, and the widows all display a painful confusion born of the shock of the three brothers' deaths, Wense, who has just celebrated his nineteenth birthday, is the most volatile and variable. He might get drunk tonight or he might start a dry spell of several days or weeks. His demeanor is often sullen, sometimes testy, but then suddenly he'll throw his head back and laugh. And there are times when he'll act mature beyond his years, thinking not of himself but of his wife and daughter and their future in the States.

Rosa has decided to stay in Cherán for an indefinite period while her mother recovers from the loss. But Wense is restless. He is trying to decide whether to return to St. Louis without Rosa. He knows the Wetback Trail well, both its light and dark sides. There is the mature, responsible route, and then there's the *desmadre* (literally, "dis-mother," a versatile Mexican colloquialism that describes an anarchic state—as in a great party, or a barroom brawl, or a fucked-up relationship). The *desmadre* trail means going it alone on the road, hooking up with other unsupervised kids and living outlaw fantasies.

As I get closer to the family, Wense begins to look to me as something of an older brother and adviser. He assumes that since I'm from the north I must have intimate knowledge of the border and the latest *migra* tactics. I do the best I can, feeling inadequate not just because I'm no expert on migrant routes but also because, at thirty-six, I am neither married nor a father. At nineteen, Wense is dealing with far more responsibility than I ever have had. We are both nomads, but there is a vast gulf between us. My road is essentially middle-class; I travel because I can. Wense and his migrant brothers and sisters travel because they must.

One day, Wense asks if we can talk alone, the first time he's ever done so. We head down to El Tizol, which serves just one meal, a plate of grilled chicken that many migrants compare favorably to that at Pollo Loco in the States. There aren't many options for eating out in Cherán besides El Tizol; there are a couple of taco stands on the highway near the bus stop and a handful of cantinas that serve appetizers.

Ambling along the dirt path toward the plaza, we pass oxen pulling timber and crews of kids wearing hip-hop regalia. Wense himself wears his trademark white baggies, an equally oversize black T-shirt, and a baseball cap emblazoned with Jesus' upturned face in that "My God, why hast thou forsaken me?" look. Beneath that countenance is Wense's own face, striking for its black-brown color and intense dark eyes.

When he takes his cap off, Wense reveals hair that is buzzed in the latest American urban fashion. Coupled with his hip-hop uniform, inspired by the African American youth of St. Louis, his home in the north, it underscores his urban hardness. This is the look he needs in order to fend for himself not just up north but here in Cherán as well.

Wense is the darkest of the clan, except for his daughter, Yeni, who, at barely two years old, is already aware of color lines. In St. Louis, Wense tells me, she is comfortable among her African American playmates. But on the rare occasions when she sees white skin, she shrieks with terror. The hierarchy of color is omnipresent in Mexico, almost as powerful a dynamic as in the States. The types are clear: the bluest eyes and the fairest skin are money in the bank, whether you're rich or poor. Even in Cherán, where practically everybody's poor, the light-skinned are always considered the most handsome. It's the same all over Latin America. In my mother's El Salvador, on the birth of a light-skinned cousin, my entire family marveled at the beauty of his porcelain skin. God had favored the family with a kid whose skin was the same color as Jesus' and whose eyes sparkled like a young Paul Newman's.

The light-skinned are, of course, overrepresented among Mexico's elite—these are the descendants of the *criollos*, Spanish nobility that never much mixed with the natives. They make up only a tiny percentage of the population. The largest segment is mestizo (in class terms, mestizos range from a smattering in the upper class to the working-class majority). The pure Indian is at the bottom of the ladder, the poorest of the poor. Some thirty percent of Mexicans today fall into this category.

The Spaniards distinguished some fifty-two separate castes during the colonial era, combinations of European, Indian, and black-African blood. But the bottom line was that the whites were *gente de razón*, people of reason, whereas those with dark skin were perceived as primitive, the darker the more primitive. To this day, "*pinche indio*," damned Indian, remains an insult in Mexico. A small number of black Mexicans live on the coasts of Veracruz and Guerrero; they endure de facto segregation and racist jokes, which have yet to be considered politically incorrect in Mexico.

And yet, since independence—and especially since the Revolution—*criollo* ideologues have attempted to foster a sentiment of national unity by claiming that *mestizaje* is the national culture, the common link between Indian, European, and African. This myth is invoked much like the American "melting pot" (into which only white ingredients have been poured, leaving blacks, Latinos, and Asians out). Today, after several years of *la crisis*, the divide of color and class is ever more apparent.

A very dark-skinned Indian, Wense is doubly scorned. Here in Cherán and on the migrant trail he never really fits in. Even among his siblings he is the darkest, the most Indian of Indians, and it seems as if he's fulfilled the low expectations of him by playing rough on the road and paying the price. He walks with a limp, his left leg chronically stiff from a whacking he took in a bar fight in Missouri with a crew of rival wetbacks from Zacatecas. He's been in more than one car wreck resulting from binge drinking. He plays Cain to the Abels, represented by his fairer-skinned siblings and in-laws and the other, more law-abiding Cheranes who make the trek north and faithfully send back their *remesas*, monthly money orders to their families in Michoacán. Wense barely hides his envy of the well-to-do migrants. Confronted with condescending attitudes—even outright hostility—wherever he goes, he's done his best to confirm people's fears.

But it is not the outlaw Wense before me right now as we sit down at El Tizol and get our hands and lips greasy on Salvador Romero's tasty, if skinny, chickens. This is the dilemma Wense lays before me: he wants to go back to St. Louis, but Rosa isn't ready to leave her grieving mother yet, and he's conscious of the painful anxiety he'd cause the family by embarking on the illegal journey alone. Each time a crew of wetbacks heads out on the local bus for the first leg of the journey down to Zamora, Cherán collectively holds its breath and waits for word of a successful crossing—or tragedy. The odds are on the side of the migrants, of course; even with the beefed-up Border Patrol, thousands still cross the border every day and make it to their destinations. But the fate of the Chávez brothers, even two and a half months after the accident, still echoes loudly.

"Yeah, I'm scared," Wense says softly, a rare admission for any Mexican man, much less Wense, who's done his best to cultivate a fearless persona. "I'll be scared the whole way up to the border, I'll be scared at the line. I'll be scared all the way to St. Louis."

Wense asks me, rhetorically, because I can tell that he's already made up his mind, whether I think that the pain he'll put his family through is an acceptable price to pay for a better future. The future is an American education for his daughter, Yeni, a nice apartment in St. Louis or perhaps Chicago, a new car for himself, and some land here in Cherán. Practically everyone in Cherán dreams this dream—a piece of land here on which to build a two-story house with hot and cold running water, a gas stove, and a huge satellite dish on the roof.

For most of the conversation, I have been staring into Jesus' pained face on Wense's cap, since he's been talking down into his plate of food, but now he looks up at me and waits for my answer.

Principally, I think about María Elena, the grieving mother. Rosa is strong enough to handle anything. But if Wense leaves, so will Rosa, maybe even at his side. So I tell him to think more about doña María Elena before making his decision, hinting, not so subtly, that he should wait. He nods, grows quiet.

We order another round of beers to stretch out a lazy afternoon. Through a haze of barbecue smoke, we watch the traffic pass El Tizol. Peasants trudge by with stacks of corn stalks on their backs. A local brass band carries trumpets and tubas and drums, on their way to a wedding. A burro slowly shuffles past, the poor beast's hide branded not by an iron but by local wannabe cholos, who have spray painted an illegible moniker. Now a trio of *norteños*, whom Wense eyes warily, strides toward us.

The crew steps into El Tizol, and Salvador Romero, the savvy host, greets them as warmly as he does everybody else; his customers range from newly rich migrants to families who scrape together a week's earnings for one meal out on the town. The *norteños* are the former, veterans of the other side, young men in their twenties who, by the look of their clothes, most likely have legal work permits and jobs not in the picking fields but in the city. They wear Gap shirts and jeans, clearly new, and project an attitude that nonmigrant Cheranes have come to loathe, a kind of yuppielike arrogance and largesse. Wense loses his train of thought. Our bond is broken.

The *norteños* order two beers apiece, and Salvador hops to it, asking them how the weather is in California. Then one of them turns toward our table and, without acknowledging me, addresses Wense:

"Look how famous you've gotten, that reporters come to interview you."

Wense does not reply, but I can tell that he is seething. Salvador is at the bar, watching the scene carefully, probably wondering whether he's going to have to intervene. The eternal peacemaker, I attempt to make small talk with these assholes so that they'll get off Wense's back, but Wense beats me to the punch.

"Who do you think you are, showing up here with your *norteño* airs?" he says, barely raising his voice, his hands off the table now and at his sides.

There is the requisite silence for several beats, as everyone considers their options for saving or splitting face. The standoff highlights the chasm that class has become in Cherán. On the one side are three well-to-do migrants who, through ingenuity, or a couple of extra years of schooling, or sheer luck, struck the mother lode in the States and have come back to Cherán to strut their stuff. On the other side is one poor migrant who, perhaps because he is darker, or spent less time in school, or just had some bad breaks, can barely feed his family. Three kids in preppy Gap wear and one in hip-hop warrior regalia. All Indians.

One of the *norteños* speaks up next and, to my surprise, chooses to back down. "Hey, we were just having fun, you go on and eat with your friend," he says, and turns to his buddies. Perhaps the *norteños* deferred to me, a stranger who no one in this town wants to leave with a bad impression. Wense, sensing victory, mutters a few parting shots and even starts to get up from his chair in menacing fashion. But Salvador immediately comes over and jovially sets a fresh beer before him. I tell him it's not worth it. The tension dissipates.

Wense will not get drunk tonight—a good thing, considering that sometimes when he starts drinking he won't stop. Without uttering a word, we walk back to the Chávezes', where he sleeps with Rosa in the wood shack by the plum tree. He's considering my advice, I know. But by the time we arrive at the house, it's all set. It's a matter not of whether but of when Wense will leave.

There is no altar in the Chávez house, an anomaly in Cherán. In the wake of the accident the family followed Catholic custom, reciting the rosaries and novenas, but they haven't been in church more than the bare minimum required by tradition.

"Oh, my dear Lord, I don't believe in you anymore," says María

Elena Chávez. She is standing, with her surviving children and grand-children, behind the counter of the family's new general store. The stock came gratis, a charitable gesture from government officials in Morelia, the state capital. The impact of the accident on the Purépechas did not go unnoticed by the Partido Revolucionario Institucional (PRI), which governed Michoacán. This is the party's classic brand of patron-izing benevolence: long on symbolism and short on practicality. What the family needs is cash or, even better, visas for legal travel to the States, not cans of tuna and cartons of cigarettes.

Nevertheless, the family is pinning its hopes on the store; the only other income at the moment comes from Florentino, who is working the picking fields of California, supporting an extended family of fifteen by sending three hundred dollars a month home in money orders. They've set the store up in the street-level room where Salvador, the youngest of the dead sons, once slept. So far, the store has generated what amounts to spare change. One of the reasons is that the stock sent from Morelia is good for a store in Morelia—a major city—but not for a town in the highlands. There are several jars of Nescafé, although virtually no one in Cherán drinks instant coffee—people prefer to grind beans bought at market and boil them, with cinnamon and a ton of sugar, in a big ceramic pot for *café de olla*. Nor is anyone in Cherán accustomed to bars of fancy facial soap. The thought of using canned *mole* is an insult to any self-respecting mother in Cherán. And the cig-arettes, unfortunately, are Mexican brands like Farolitos and Delicados, the kind that the drunks buy late at night when money is running out; most Cheranes are Marlboro men—a migrant affectation. (The one item that's caught on is a Mexican version of Gummi Bears.) Another problem is the location of the Chávez house—it is the last one on Galeana, a street that leads toward the bullring at the edge of town. Directly across from the house is a large empty lot. Customers closer to town shop at the stores on their own block. The Chávezes are lucky to have five customers a day.

In truth, the family never had much reason to believe in God. The accident was the family's second great tragedy, the first being the father's alcoholism and abuse. Like Pedro Páramo in the eponymous Juan Rulfo novel, Efraín Chávez nearly laid waste to everything and everyone around him. It is a story all too common in the highlands.

María Huaroco, the neighbor, also had an alcoholic husband; both men are now dead.

Efraín Chávez himself had no use for God. "He'd say, 'Why do you go and pray to those wooden monkeys?' " doña María remembers. He'd also say that the real reason people went to church was to see if their Sunday best measured up to everyone else's. Rosa recalls him saying, "It's better to go confess to a tree than to a priest."

Doña María, on the other hand, once believed enough to attend Mass regularly. After all, Jesus was one of the only men she knew of who didn't drink himself into a stupor and beat women. Even though the thought made her feel terribly guilty, she often found herself kneeling before Saint Francis and praying that her husband would die.

María met Efraín when she was eighteen—by Cherán standards, she was practically an old maid and her mother was anxious for her to marry quickly. He was already a drunkard, a *desmadroso*. One night María was walking home when Efraín and a friend of his appeared, both stumbling drunk. Upon her rejection of Efraín's advances, they dragged her by arms and legs and hair along the street until Samaritans intervened. But in those days, doña María says, a woman didn't have much recourse against unwanted advances.

"I never loved him," María Elena says. She tried to convince her mother that he was a bad man, but her mother would hear none of it and they were married against María's will.

He drank every day and they had constant fights that ended with his slaps and, on occasion, punches. One time he even tried to strangle Benjamín, the oldest; the boy's face turned purple and it took the combined energies of María Elena and her other sons to break Efraín's death hold.

Efraín Chávez was, simply, a demented dictator. In a rage, he'd take the kids' clothes off the line and throw them on the cooking fire. He'd wake the boys up at two in the morning and send them into the woods to tap the pines, while he'd stay home and drink, sleep it off, and drink again, supporting his habit with money from the resin the boys gathered and sold. During these binges, he'd disappear for days at a time.

When doña María couldn't stand it anymore, she and the children would seek refuge at her mother's house. But he'd show up eventually, throwing rocks at the windows, bellowing like a madman, crying pitiful tears, and pleading with her to return. More than once, mother and children hid in the brush of the deep gorges surrounding Cherán while he prowled the town looking for them.

She pleaded with him to stop drinking, if not for the children—who already hated him and probably always would—then at least for his children's children. But it was too late. The blood in his veins was mad with the poison.

"This is all true," doña María tells me. "It's good enough for a movie."

One of her only pleasures during the marriage was cooking. She stocked her kitchen with pots and pans, plates, tableware. But over the years Efraín smashed just about everything. Today the family eats out of plastic bowls and uses tortillas instead of spoons and forks, like the poorest Cheranes. María's children begged her to leave him, to buy her own lot and build her own house. This is why, initially, the oldest Chávez boys, Benjamín and Fernando, started migrating to the States: they dreamed of saving up money to buy the land and build a house for her.

And María Elena is proud of her boys, the dead as well as the living, for not having turned out like their father. It's as if the children went out of their way to avoid causing anyone to suffer the way they did. Nevertheless, the boys were marked by their father's reputation. It wasn't easy for them to find girlfriends, much less wives. The available women of Cherán were warned by their parents about the Chávez brothers: watch out, they're liable to end up like their father.

He died in 1989, at forty, a not uncommon age for men in Cherán to die at, especially if they're alcoholics. She had managed to move out of the house and stay with her mother for the last two years of his life. Now and again she'd see him stumbling along the street, his face always flushed and shiny with sweat, as if the alcohol were burning him inside. He collapsed with a bottle in hand at one of the local bars at five in the morning. María Elena never shed a tear.

Gradually, the family's fortunes changed for the better. Benjamín, Fernando, and Jaime had been working in California since 1985, and now that the old man wasn't drinking their money away, they saved conscientiously and bought property in Cherán on which they were each able to build a modest home. Later, Florentino joined his elders on the yearly treks to the picking fields, and finally, in 1994, Salvador came on board. The five brothers traveled north together that spring and the next. Rosa married Wense in 1995, and the couple lived and worked in St. Louis up until the accident.

The brothers were set to take a third trip in 1996, to continue to rebuild the future that Efraín Chávez had destroyed. All five would work together for $7 an hour, six days a week, from April through September, and return to Cherán with about $25,000 between them, in addition to what Wense and Rosa saved in St. Louis. They would build doña María Elena a new house. They would buy new shoes for all the grandchildren.

And then the accident. Which is why doña María Elena doubts God. "What have I done to deserve this?" She asks. Why the punishment? Why three of her sons? She could understand one. But what mother could stand the pain of losing three at once?

Now her voice trails off at the end of each sentence. When she spoke of her husband, at least she had the energy of her rage.

Since there is no reason to stay inside the customerless store and since the sun is setting, the family comes out onto the street as most of Cherán does at this hour, the elders sitting on steps or tree stumps, the kids running wild in the street, everyone facing west. Florentino's eighteen-month-old son, José Iván, has taken a liking to me and keeps tugging at my jeans. He wants me to pick him up so he can see the dramatic view of the valley where the Juanconi volcano stands in stark silhouette, a bright gold corona dancing above it in a cloudless sky. I lift José Iván and he stares, wide-eyed and wordless, into the distance. After a few moments, he mutters something unintelligible, pointing with his finger to a spot on the horizon.

María Elena Chávez has filed suit against the federal government of the United States of America, as well as against the Santa Rosa Community Services District (which maintains the road her sons died on), for what her lawyer calls the "negligence" of the Border Patrol in its high-speed pursuit of the truck her sons rode that April morning. Tort culture has come to Mexico. Persuaded to file by Austin Johnson, an American attorney then living in Mexico City, María Elena is moved by concern for her children and grandchildren. The first thing she thinks of doing if she receives a settlement is keeping the family together. She's just not sure where. She could use the money to get herself a visa (the most important requirement for which is a healthy bank account), cross the border legally, and head up to St. Louis to live with Rosa and Wense, if they go back. Or she could journey to California and join her surviving sons in Watsonville. Or she could bring all her children home and build new houses for them and for the widowed daughters-in-law.

The Chávezes desperately need a future to believe in. Since the accident, depression has taken its toll. Fernando suffers from stomach problems, apparently psychosomatic, preventing him from traveling north. María's back bothers her more and more. Yolanda, Benjamín's widow, is the most visibly affected. Along with Josephina, Jaime's widow, she has discovered that some alcohol brings a bit of comfort. In the evenings, they'll walk to a cantina downtown, buy some beers, and return to drink them quietly in the house Benjamín built with his own hands.

Ironically, the family's present economic situation is all the more precarious because the rumor in town is that they've profited from the accident. When the women go to market, they sometimes get hard looks from total strangers. This is a classic case of *envidia*, envy. It is an oft-used word in Mexico, where the vast majority has reason to feel envious of the well-off few. One story has it that the Chávezes have received tens of thousands of dollars from the government in Morelia, when the only help they've had is the useless stock for the store. But this rumor may be the reason for the loan shark's insistence that the family pay off the debt of the dead, the money fronted for the fateful trip.

Immediately after the accident, the Chávezes did receive genuine charity, in the form of food and drink, mostly from neighbors. The only money they were ever given was a few hundred dollars collected among Cheranes in Los Angeles by Salvador Romero's cousins, who own an upholstery shop and have done quite well for themselves. Beyond that, most promises of help have gone unfulfilled. Nearly five months after the tragedy, the stonecutter in Morelia has yet to deliver the monuments he promised for the brothers' graves. Beneath the cherry tree in the cemetery lie the unadorned concrete slabs that don Ramiro put down at the end of April. Not even the dead can rest yet.

And then there's been the succession of *estafadores*, con artists, who've called upon the family in recent weeks. The first to arrive were the *húngaras* (literally, "Hungarians," as gypsies are known in much of Latin America), with their beads and tarot cards and feigned sympathy for the bereaved. They told María Elena to lie down and passed an egg slowly over her entire body. Then they cracked it into a glass. The egg white was speckled with foul matter, clear evidence that some "bad magic" had been visited upon the family by *envidiosos*, and thus they were in bad need of a *limpia*, a spiritual cleansing.

The *húngaras* then asked about the family's financial situation. Pretty bad, María Elena told them. The gypsies said they could change that right then and there. All they needed was the Chávezes' money, however much they had, and they'd "make it work" for them. The gypsy way of making money work was a simple sleight of hand in which they pocketed the cash—a few hundred pesos, just about all the Chávezes had at the time—while they pretended to mix it with dirt and a special potion, grinding it down into a thick paste that they then placed in a pouch and buried in the yard. The Chávezes were told to unearth the pouch in two weeks and behold the miracle of alchemy.

Fernando wasn't home when the gypsies visited. He saw through the scam immediately. He unearthed the pouch and showed his mother that there was nothing but mud inside, but by then the gypsies were richer and well on their way to the next victim in another Indian town.

But even Fernando, a veteran migrant and more worldly than the rest of the family, fell for the next scam. One afternoon a good-looking mestizo kid came calling to offer his condolences. He said he was Eric Morales, the well-known prizefighter who has been compared to Golden Boy Oscar De La Hoya of East L.A. He was young, charismatic, well-dressed, with the impressive, lithe body of a lightweight contender. The Chávez women were delighted with his flirtatiousness and Fernando and Wense were impressed by his macho gallantry. He even produced a glossy 8 × 10 and signed it "With love and affection from Eric Morales."

Eric said he had come because he'd read about the tragedy in the papers. He was so moved, he said, he just *had* to do something. After all, he too had grown up poor in the provinces, in a town not unlike Cherán, and had made the long journey from poverty to stardom, a journey the Chávez brothers themselves might have made had the *migra* not cut their precious lives short. Well, he felt it was his duty to help people like the Chávezes, because he knew that was why God had showered such good fortune on him, so that he could share it with others in need. Of course, he knew that money would never really compensate for their loss, but it would give them some comfort in their grief. He told them that soon he'd hold a press conference to announce that he would donate $10,000 from the purse of his next fight to the family. He said he'd already talked to the governor in Morelia about it. He wanted to hold the fight right here in Michoacán, he said, in honor of the fallen brothers. He also said he'd contacted Oscar De La Hoya's people, who offered to contribute another several thousand as well.

Eric Morales played with the children, ate some cans of tuna (becoming the first customer at the store to do so), and generally won everyone over. But just now, he had a favor to ask. He said that his car had broken down in a neighboring town and that he didn't have the cash to pay the mechanic (he pulled out his billfold at this point, showing an impressive collection of credit cards), and, though it embarrassed him to ask, would they mind letting him borrow some money, just for a few hours, so that he could pay the mechanic, after which he'd drive his car to the nearest bank and then return to pay them back?

The Chávezes never for a moment doubted his sincerity and asked him how much he needed. "As much as you have," he said. After all, his car was an expensive late-model Ford, and there'd been a problem with the head gasket and it would surely be a costly repair. The family scraped together 1,000 pesos (at the time about $125 American).

"Eric Morales" never returned. He didn't even pay for the cans of tuna. He did leave an address and a cell phone number in Tijuana, where he said his manager's office was located. I dialed the number one day; it was disconnected. To be absolutely sure, I also called a sportswriter friend in Los Angeles and, ultimately, Eric Morales's real manager. "Eric Morales has never even *been* in Michoacán," he told me.

Not only does María Elena not believe in God anymore, she doesn't believe that there is kindness in the hearts of strangers. Not even among her townsfolk, who are busy spreading rumors about the family's supposed windfall.

I mention these incidents to Father Melesio and ask him which he thinks is worse: an enduring naïveté, which is equal parts ignorance and an innocent faith in the world, or a pervasive cynicism that forbids any belief in even the possibility of goodness from strangers. Father Melesio mulls it over and then quotes Scripture: "Jesus said that we have to be harmless as doves and wise as serpents."

Wense decides to consult a witch to see whether crossing the border is a good idea or not. Yolanda, a great believer in Purépecha mystical traditions—her dead husband often appears to her in dreams, to counsel or simply to soothe her—recommends a woman named Ana who lives at the base of a large hill called Kucumpakua on the eastern edge of town. Ana is a distant relative of Yolanda's—more proof, it seems, that in Cherán, as the saying goes, everyone's a witch, or at least has a relative who is. In any case, family relations go some way toward reassuring Wense that he won't be a mark for charlatans like the gypsies or "Eric Morales."

Ana and her family live even more poorly than the Chávezes do, in a flimsy series of shacks with no panes in the windows and newspaper serving as insulation against the bitter chill of the Cherán night. Among her only luxuries is a boom box blasting Selena's "Amor prohibido" so loud when we arrive that the speakers distort the sound. (A Chicana who could barely speak Spanish, Selena made it to Mexico only after her murder.)

Ana is a diminutive woman in her midthirties, with a gold-toothed smile and a mane of light brown hair pulled back tightly in a ponytail, revealing a round, freckled face. Everything about her speaks poverty except for a handsome pair of gold hoop earrings. Ana cannot read or write Spanish, but she can read the tarot. A recent convert to the esoteric, she tells us that life had always been an uphill struggle for her, filled with financial and romantic failures and chronic illness, until she realized that a spell of *envidia* had been cast on her some thirty years ago. She was apprised of this fact by a *brujo* she consulted once in Mexico City after suffering a strokelike attack that left her partially paralyzed and with severely diminished eyesight. The local medical doctors had found nothing wrong, hence her journey to visit the renowned *brujo*, who spotted the malevolent spell. The old sage also told her that she herself had the secret powers to become a witch, a gift that if ignored could cause her even more grief. After following the master's spiritual instructions to the letter (several *limpias*, or cleansings, and special prayers to the dark powers, services for which she paid several hundred pesos), she recovered her health and started her own practice in Cherán.

Wense enters Ana's *consultorio*, a small square addition to the main house. Candles burn everywhere—you can feel their heat in the room. Incense rises in great clouds from a couple of conch shells. On the floor and on shelves sit dozens of saints, a wildly eclectic collection including a black ceramic rendition of a beaming Buddha, Saint Francis, baby Jesus, and the *Santísima Muerte* (Most Holy Death, one of several dark powers that Latin American esoteric healers work with). There is also a large pyramid, about a foot high, made of transparent resin, inside of which float miniature horseshoes, garlic cloves, pesos, crucifixes, and several postage stamp images of a constellation of saints of both the official Catholic and the underground variety.

She peels the cards from the deck and places them before Wense, tapping on each with her right index finger. "Let's Talk about Sex, Baby" has now replaced Selena on the boom box, deejayed by her teenage daughters next door.

You need work, she tells Wense. You and your family have very little, but you can make things better. You want to go north, but you're unsure, you're scared. You must have a *limpia* before you go. You need to clean out your house as well. There is a pile of rocks that someone has placed near you that holds a spell over you and your family; I see it in some room where no one sleeps. Take some Clorox, pour it on the rocks, and toss them away. Ah! And your mail is late because of those rocks, too! And over by the cherry tree, some kind of animal likes to stand around there at night, isn't that so? There's bad energy there, too. And also where your mother-in-law cooks. Clean all these places out. If there are any open bottles, cover them or discard them; the bad spirits like to gather there, you know. Now, you have to understand that Rosa, she gets anxious sometimes. You must always remember that it's her nerves that make her snap at you, not that you're doing anything bad. And your mother, I can see her dreaming of your brother, who is somewhere far away, because there's something that he hasn't figured out in his life yet. You and yours are going to make it, don't get desperate. You'll see how different you'll feel after the *limpia*.

Wense, not exactly a great believer in the esoteric, comes away amazed. "I never told anyone except you how I felt about leaving," he says. He's also happy that Ana has given him a green light for his journey north—provided that he performs the *limpia*. There is indeed a pile of rocks in a room of the abandoned house next door to the Chávezes', and an owl often perches at night in the cherry tree. These, of course, are all things Ana herself could have seen on any one of her visits to her relatives' house. And Wense, while not accustomed to confessing his insecurities to Rosa or his in-laws, can be read, emotionally speaking, about as easily as a billboard.

But that is not what matters here. The witches of Cherán tell their supplicants what they want, or need, to hear by confirming the existence of the obstacles in their lives, and give them a ritualized way to clear them away. Ana has given Wense a prescription whose physically therapeutic value might be questionable, but she has also reassured him that this season of suffering will be rewarded with a brighter future. What Wense needs right now is confidence to face the road again, and Ana has given it to him.

I, too, find myself needing reassurance on the road these days because, frankly, I have no idea where I'm headed on my journey alongside the journeys of the migrants. It's time for me to visit the witches.

The war between Dr. Tito and the witches of Cherán ended in a treaty largely brokered by doña Elisa Herrera, the treasurer of the local chapter of the National Association of Traditional Indigenous Doctors. Time was when the witches would warn their clients against visiting that fraud Dr. Tito and he'd return the favor by advising his patients that the witches were charlatans. So great was the enmity that all sides recognized something had to be done. Doña Elisa and Dr. Tito met face-to-face, and after some initial mutual recriminations, they found common ground. They shared case studies and treatments, each coming to realize that their respective traditions were complementary.

The reconciliation was made possible by the witches' belief that there are two categories of illness, "good" and "bad," the good being a purely physiological phenomenon and the bad a result of black magic. A deal was struck: if the witches encountered "good" diseases that they couldn't treat with simple herb remedies, they would recommend the patient see the doctor, and the doctor, in turn, would hand over cases where he could find no evidence of physical pathology. The agreement has worked out quite well for both sides, and it is Dr. Tito himself who facilitates my meeting doña Elisa. We sit in his spacious living room, which, like his *consultorio*, is furnished with big rustic sofas and chairs. When I see doña Elisa for the first time, I feel like my grandmother has returned from heaven. Everything about doña Elisa is round—her eyes, her face, her body. She wears a light blue knit sweater that stretches over her huge chest, a red checkered skirt, and blue stockings. Her hair is done up in the traditional braids of Indian women. She is relaxed and friendly, showing no sign of the typical Indian distrust of strangers. She speaks a broken Spanish, often saying a word first in Purépecha and then searching for the translation.

"*Shurikis* is what we call ourselves," she says, using the Purépecha word for healer, "and we use *hitzakecha*, herbs, to heal."

For thirty years she's been working "this thing," she says in Spanish. For the first fifteen, she often fretted over whether her knowledge was enough to meet the challenges of her profession. The men clearly on the verge of beating or killing their wives. The teenagers about to kill themselves over their first love. The criminals who'd confess to her. The elderly gentlemen whose bodies had finally given out and whose pride had disappeared along with their strength. The families who had lost a season of crops to sudden plague, wondering what the future held in store for them.

"I'm not scared anymore," she says, grinning. "I feel like I can go up against anything. I feel my power."

Doña Elisa invites me back to her *consultorio*, just a block and a half down the street from Dr. Tito's. It is market day in Cherán, the street choked with makeshift stalls and pickup trucks hauling in loads of fruit and vegetables, but it's as if people can sense her coming—she parts the crowd as Moses does the Red Sea. She tells me that she stocks up on her herbs and saints at the world-famous *brujo* market, the Mercado de Sonora in Mexico City. Familiar with a few Mexican practitioners of the Afro-Caribbean animist religion of Santería who work in the

Mercado, I ask for her opinion of their healing powers. "Oh, there's one or two good ones," she says, with the air of *bruja* royalty.

Her office is adjacent to her spacious hacienda-style house, where chickens and roosters strut over a wide dirt patio. She opens the door onto a fairly large room dominated by an altar with a nearly life-size statue of Saint Joseph, whose beard flows white over his yellow raiment, dwarfing a smaller Saint Martin. On the wall there is a large Last Supper clock whose battery has obviously wound down, and, on a series of shelves, dozens of jars and bunches of herbs: verbena, rockrose, chamomile, basil, maguey, yucca, mint, rosemary. There are little plastic containers filled with pine resin pomades and soaps, which she cooks up in a huge vat on the patio. Each has a handwritten label for the malady it treats: asthma, kidney stones, bronchitis, gastritis, nerves.

As with Dr. Tito and the *brujas*, there has been an accommodation between Indian and Catholic tradition. The futility of the Church's effort to completely Christianize the Indians was apparent only a few years after the Conquest. The first goddess of mestizo America, the Virgin of Guadalupe—equal parts Mary and ancient Indian fertility icon—was born barely a decade after the fall of Tenochtitlan, and there wasn't much the Spanish ecclesiastical authorities could do about it; she was ultimately allowed into the pantheon of the official church and has performed the lion's share of miracles in the Americas ever since.

Five hundred years after the first painful meeting between Old and New Worlds, the rites of the Church and those of the Indians coexist naturally. When I ask Father Melesio about the *brujas*, he tells me he regards them with "*mucho respeto.*" Besides, he reasons, theirs is in essence a Christian gesture: "They're looking out for their neighbors." It's only the "black magic," which invokes the dark powers—including Satan himself—that he thinks deliberately and cynically preys on people's ignorance. It would be too much for Father Melesio to condone lighting a candle to Most Holy Death.

These are tough times for healers and clients alike, doña Elisa tells me as she invites me to sit down at a small wooden table where she's read the tarot thousands of times. The number of people seeking her advice has increased dramatically, but their ability to pay has diminished just as much. She long ago stopped charging a standard rate; people pay what they can.

The work is also exhausting, because these days it's not just a simple matter of tending to the locals. The *norteños* consult with her as well—via letters sent by special couriers and AT&T's long-distance lines. She's summoned to the phone booth down by the bus station a couple of times a week. A concerned mother from Cherán who's lived in Chicago for the last ten years explains that her baby daughter's cough just won't go away; the gringo doctors have prescribed their antibiotics and nothing's happened. Doña Elisa will ask the mother to send her a picture of the child; often a relative in Cherán will have one. Then this venerable *bruja* will light a candle before the photograph, holding in her mind everything she knows about the family—where and how they lived in Cherán, whether the husband is an alcoholic, any enemies the clan might have, the things she's heard from other migrants about Chicago and how the weather is up there this time of year. Then she deals the cards. From their alignment she'll know whether it's a medical problem or whether it "belongs to us, the *shurikis*."

If it's a "bad" illness, she'll recommend chamomile tea with honey and lemon for the cough, but she'll also work her white magic against the black that's gotten hold of the child. This is performed at night, when doña Elisa is asleep, that is, when doña Elisa's body is asleep, the time when her spirit can leave her body. She'll seek out a friendly eagle or owl to take hold of and fly—a kind of transubstantiation in which her energy is passed along from creature to creature on the winds—all the way to Chicago, directly to the child's bedroom, where she will reappear in her grandmotherly form, placing the palm of her hand on the child's forehead to cast out the blackness.

The doña's tale reminds me of a story I heard earlier, from a couple of teenage boys with whom I talked about the preponderance of satellite dishes in Cherán. They told me that one morning, walking through the blue mist of a Cherán dawn en route to their cornfield, they saw something stirring in one of the *parabólicas* on top of a house that belongs to a renowned *brujo* who was also well known for his alcoholic binges. And damned if it wasn't don So-and-so curled up in the great antenna, butt-naked, shivering, hugging himself in the cold breeze. The boys called up to him and he awoke with a start. "What are you doing up there?" they called out to him, barely able to contain their giggles. The *brujo* looked about him and then at his own naked form. "Don't worry, boys," he said, climbing out of the antenna and standing upright. He yawned, stretched, scratched. "I'm all right. I guess I didn't quite make it to bed after that house call in Detroit." He climbed down from the roof and crawled into the house through the bedroom window.

Doña Elisa has never actually been to the United States. She is, however, completely aware of the world to which Cherán is connected through the incredibly complex web of migration, the lines of communication that transmit not just dollars and reruns of *Baywatch* but also new legends (hip-hop gangstas) new diseases ("EH-stress" is a full-fledged concept in Mexico these days), and a new sense of pain. Doña Elisa suffers when her son walks on the wild side with the outlaw migrants, drinking and getting into trouble. She's done everything she can for him. "There are some things that the *shurikis* cannot cure," she says. "If the person does not want to be cured, there is nothing I can do." There is little that doña Elisa does not know, despite the fact that most people would consider her, at best, a colorful character out of a Carlos Castañeda novel and, at worst, just another poor Indian, trapped in the past.

Envidia is rampant in Cherán these days, doña Elisa says. "It's the crisis. Because so many have lost what they have, they turn to evil to get what they want. But they hurt others and themselves. You, too," she says as she fixes me suddenly with an intense stare, "are in crisis."

She asks me to shuffle her well-worn tarot deck and then deals, laying the cards before me in four rows, ten cards across. She considers the images that appear: The Tower, the Lovers, the Queen of Pentacles, an inverted Two of Cups, the Fool, the Queen of Swords, an inverted Ace of Wands. I am now among the sick, the lovelorn, the mourners, the luckless migrants, the alcoholics and outlaws, the poor—all those who come to doña Elisa for succor. Perhaps there'd already been some subconscious suggestion that laid bare my wounds for doña Elisa. She just happens to carry the name of a woman I fell in love with in Mexico City during the summer of 1994, the year when all hell broke loose in the capital and throughout Mexico. The year the Indian rebels of Chiapas made the front page of the *New York Times* and caused jitters on Wall Street, the year *la crisis* entered the popular lexicon to describe a devalued peso, a million business failures, skyrocketing unemployment, hunger in the provinces, and a mass of refugees gathering at the border.

That was the year Popocatépetl, the volcano on the outskirts of Mexico City, started spewing ash—I toasted it with a shot of tequila from the roof of a hotel in the Zócalo, watching its rhythmic exhalations of billowing gray. Narco-lords battled bloodily in the northern states and bought off INS inspectors so their shipments could cross the border along with the illegals. The first Chicano-style gangs formed in the forlorn barrios of the capital, and the Virgin of Guadalupe appeared here, there, and everywhere, because she always comes when Mexicans need her most.

In the summer of 1994, a summer of apocalyptic thunderstorms, of sinkholes big as Cadillacs and sometimes big as houses opening in the asphalt, the natives of Mexico City understood that the pain of the provinces had arrived at the gates of the capital. That summer I met Elisa, and though I will not tell the whole sad tale, I will write what doña Elisa said to me that afternoon in her *consultorio* three hundred miles from Mexico City and several months after my separation from my lover.

She flicks a cracked fingernail at the cards, and with her broken Spanish she speaks, in a gentle but serious tone: Here is woman whom you love more than anything. But she is far away. And she is married. She is married to an American, far away. And this one whom you love most, this one married far away, will forever be far away. You follow her across the land, and she runs, she always ran. And when she comes to you, you run away! But she will never love you well, never love you the way you love. Find another one. (She confuses gender in Spanish— she actually tells me to find another man.) And here—doña Elisa has counted forward seven cards, coming to the image of a princess holding a chalice above which a butterfly floats—here is another one. She loves you well, and still you run away! It is a sad thing, this. She counts forward another seven cards. And now here is the man that first woman married, the American who is far away. This card—flick, flick, and she pauses, sighs a theatrical sigh—is a warning to you. It is the man, the American, and he may have the sickness we call AIDS. This disease is *de la chingada*! We *shurikis* have tried many herbs, many, many herbs we've tried. And prayers to all the saints, and dreaming of cures, but nothing stops this disease, which is very, very powerful. More powerful than I am, and I am powerful. It is a warning: he may have AIDS. And if he may have AIDS, then the woman you love most may have AIDS, and if you are with that woman, and then with the other woman who loves you most, then all have AIDS! But you are in time. So go far away from them. Leave them both far away. This is a hard thing, the hardest of all things. But look. She counts forward another seven cards. Here is your work, here are the words that you write. The words that you will write about me. She flicks, laughs. There will be money, and you will be alone, which is good. You work well alone, isn't that so?

In broken Spanish sprinkled with the words of a dying tongue, without my prompting, without any mention of triangles or long-distance relationships, a seventy-year-old *bruja* in the hills of Michoacán warns me about unsafe sex and unsafe love.

Now this woman with her deeply lined face and obsidian eyes stands me in the center of her altar room and, with two little blue plastic spray guns, one filled with water of rosemary, the other with water of basil, sprays me with aromatic mists—my groin, my legs, my back, the back of my neck, the back of my knees, my feet—whispering prayers in her tongue the whole time.

There is a storm gathering outside, clouds rolling together, lightning bounding about the hills and gorges of Cherán, rain starting to slap the asphalt of a highway that has no visible beginning or end— trucks and buses and charging, revving, backfiring, slamming brakes on slick black road. And I can hear the town's stray dogs out there, too, barking and biting at and dodging those tires that never stop spinning.

Joseph Rodriguez

4

WAITING

Ladies and gentlemen, finally the moment you've all been waiting for!" The voice, tremendously loud, echoing with cavernous reverberation, punches through the great banks of speakers. "Here for you, these gallant young men, these warm, simpatico, romantic young men, who will serenade you with their lovely, their profound, their passionate, their inspired compositions, the wonders of the ballad world . . . LOS SOLDADOS DEL AMOR!"

Rosa, Wense, and I are seated at a table in the empty lot a block down from the marketplace that serves as Cherán's concert hall. It has been raining off and on all day, and the concert had been delayed about an hour for fear of electrocution, but finally the Soldados appear in cadet outfits, their blow-dried pompadours struggling to stand high in the humid air. Fireworks explode and lasers shoot out from behind the drum riser as the deejay spins a *Star Wars*–like anthem for the band's entrance.

It is one of the bigger concert events of the year in Cherán, which, because of its status as a county seat, receives its fair share of name acts. The town's high migrant society—the middle-class minority that can afford the exorbitant thirty-peso admission price—is out in force. Rosa and Wense insist on treating me, even though it's clear that the price of tickets and table (which is paid for separately) and beer is beyond their budget. When Wense walks up to the makeshift box office, a battered pickup truck whose passenger-side window is cracked only about an inch to make transactions, he haggles with the vendor endlessly but to no avail.

Tonight, the Cheranes are dressed in their finest. Young men sport fresh buzz cuts and gleaming, puffy nylon jackets emblazoned with the names of several NBA and a few NFL teams—Charlotte Hornets, Portland Trailblazers, St. Louis Rams—but it is the logo in black and red, the colors of revolution as well as of the Chicago Bulls, that predominates. The team jackets, which can cost upwards of a hundred dollars, are worn with great pride by the Cheranes.

Historically, basketball has always lagged behind soccer and baseball in Mexico and throughout much of the rest of Latin America, but of late it has seized the Purépecha imagination. Basketball is now the town sport, hands down. Around the corner from the concert grounds is a concrete court where kids gather every afternoon and evening. That the Bulls are the most popular team with the teens and twenty-somethings of Cherán is no coincidence. There are several hundred Purépechas living and working in Chicago and a dozen other cities in Illinois these days—and in the 1990s the Bulls ruled the Windy City, Michael Jordan was king, and Scotty Pippen and Dennis Rodman princes. Their personas exemplify urban Americana— fast, flashy, hard—for the Purépechas. After all, the Cheranes who work in the big cities of the States invariably live in poor, predominantly black neighborhoods. And, being provincials, they are naturally attracted to the "hardest" style because it helps them blend in on the mean streets of America—at least this is what they believe. Even the migrants who work on farms prefer the urban style because no one wants to return to Cherán with stories of picking fruit and vegetables. They want to tell of conquering the cities—and a nylon Bulls windbreaker helps authenticate the tale. What's more, basketball, like hip hop, is a perfect metaphor for migrant life. The fast break is much closer to its rhythm than the much slower and more lyrical beats of soccer or baseball.

Wense is dressed tonight in a pair of baggy pants that glow an incredibly loud orange. He wears his dark blue, XXXL shirt untucked; it falls nearly to his knees. He's also got his white high-top Nikes. But the pants are smudged with what looks like paint, the material of his shirt is visibly thin, and the sneakers are badly scuffed. He can't compete with the rich migrant boys and their brand-new sneakers and cooler-than-cool beanies (also bearing the names of American sports teams) pulled down low over their eyes. Or with the *banda* music aficionados, who look like American cowboys in spotless beige Stetsons with snakeskin bands and colorful feathers, pearl-buttoned cowboy shirts, and shiny, pointy boots. *Banda* is a classic migrant pop phenomenon. At first glance, its popularity would seem to be a kind of nationalist reaction against Americanization, since *banda*'s roots lie in the nineteenth-century brass band music of the state of Sinaloa. But today's version, bearing the stamp of migrant culture, is every bit as urban as hip hop or rock—synthesizers and electric guitars, along with a much faster beat, have transformed the folk form.

Rosa has her hair up in a ponytail. She wears a simple white blouse, a gray sweater for the chill of the night, loose black cotton pants, and brown felt shoes that remind me of old-fashioned Hush Puppies. She doesn't wear makeup—she doesn't own any. She's dressed well enough not to be entirely dismissed by the chic migrant women, but she's no match for the girls dressed like Selena in thin blouses knotted at the waist and white pumps with tall, fat heels. Or for the more elegant of the tradition-minded women who show off with the finest of rebozos. The poor woman's rebozo is made of thickly woven wool that is rough on the skin. But these women wear soft, finely knit rebozos of light gray or beige (and look, ironically, like the actresses who play poor women on the Mexican soap operas). Still, Rosa has made a point by casting off her rebozo and wearing pants. She and Wense are dressed in their migrant ambition.

I sit next to Rosa for most of the evening, engaging in conversation every time Wense gets up to buy a drink, which is often. Rosa says that although she is certain she will return north some day, she is equally certain that she should stay at her grieving mother's side for the time being. But Wense does not appear to be in a waiting mood, and this has caused increasing tension between them.

"I don't think he's going to wait," Rosa says, shouting over the din of the Soldados' overblown love ballads. "He's getting bored."

It's not so much that Wense can't get a job in Cherán. He could work on a big farm or maybe at one of the few sawmills. But Wense considers those jobs beneath him now, at least in Cherán. In the States, he does precisely that kind of work; he has yet to move up from field-work to a city job, the ultimate migrant goal. Nevertheless, Wense gets paid twenty times more for farm jobs in the States. To take such jobs here would be a step backward and a blow to his pride.

Rosa, facing the possibility of months or even years in Michoacán, is thinking of how she can earn her own livelihood, with or without Wense. It is a measure of how much the devastated Mexican economy and a taste of life in the less patriarchal north have influenced women's roles here that Rosa is pondering what amounts to single motherhood. After all, Wense may not make it safely across the border or find steady work up north, and he might drink the money away. Rosa has to be ready to fend for herself. There are dozens of stories of Cheranes who promise their wives a better life but then are not heard from. Her latest plan is to embroider tablecloths and take them to market in Guadala-jara. It's a long shot, but if she is going to stay on here, something of this sort is her only chance for a semblance of an income.

Rosa has a junior high school education, which is more than most women or men in Cherán have, but that doesn't make much difference in the local job market. She could wash laundry for well-off families, like the Chávezes' neighbor doña María Huaroco, but that would be akin to Wense's accepting farmwork in Cherán. Both Wense and Rosa have been profoundly marked by their journeys north. In the months before the accident, they'd earned real American dollars and lived in a genuine American apartment with hot and cold running water and an electric stove. They've had their first taste of social mobility and now they want more. They are still by all accounts dirt-poor, but they're also starting to think like the middle class. They have started moving and they don't want to stop.

"I don't know whether I'll succeed or not," Rosa says. "All I know is that my brothers died trying to make something better of themselves, and I'm going to keep trying, down here or up there, whether Wense's around or not."

Synthesizer blasting and guitars twanging, the Soldados play ballad after ballad of love lost and love betrayed and rich-girl-breaks-poor-boy's-heart. For the first several songs no one gets up to dance, but slowly the couples make their way to the muddy space between the tables and the stage. The couple that stands out the most is the man everyone knows as El Músico and his latest girlfriend. El Músico (The Musician, for his long hair) and his mother, La Licuadora (The Blender, because, it is said, she will dice you up like fruit in a blender if you cross her), are the most successful coyote team in Cherán. El Músico is also one of the tallest men in Cherán, maybe six foot one, a powerful, barrel-chested type with a blunt and bronzed Indian face. His thick, light brown mane trails well past his shoulders. His snakeskin boots are the fanciest on the dance floor, his tight jeans gleam a bleached white. His mauve rayon shirt is opened several buttons down his chest, showing off a large gold crucifix between his muscled, hairless pecs. His date is a pretty local woman who wears a white dress and a fancy rebozo draped over her shoulders.

El Músico and La Licuadora are the most talked-about personalities in Cherán. They are among the richest families in town, and their private life is endlessly scrutinized by the local folk. The rumor mill has it that El Músico is no longer living with his wife and that his date tonight is also married and separated from her mate—a veritable scandal, if true. And, to top off the soap opera, El Músico's wife is supposedly dating his new girlfriend's husband. The elders point to this as clear evidence of gringo immorality invading Cherán.

The Cheranes at the concert glance not so furtively at the illicit couple with looks of awe and envy, as if El Músico and his new girlfriend were Charles and Diana in their better days.

Wense returns with another beer in hand and sits down next to Rosa without a word. They stare straight ahead, together but separate, watching the Soldados and the twirling couples. Wense will not ask Rosa to dance. He's not exactly the romantic type. Maybe he feels he just doesn't fit in with the royalty of Cherán on the dance floor.

I lean back a bit to watch Rosa and Wense silhouetted by the stage lights. They still love each other, no doubt. It is a quiet, tense love, and compared with the many truly abusive relationships in this town, theirs is a relatively healthy marriage. Although Wense's gotten into his share of macho trouble, he has never physically hurt Rosa. He knows that Rosa has sworn to herself that she would never endure or allow her children to endure what her family suffered while her father was alive. Rosa would leave and not look back if Wense ever crossed that line.

But Wense has a mean streak in him, and Rosa, despite her increasingly assertive demeanor, is still in shock from the accident. Their lives will be changed—are changing already—as a result of what happened in Temecula. They will either stay close or be torn apart. Either they will dream bigger dreams or their pain and fear will destroy their hope. They'll have good luck at the border (lightning can't strike twice, can it?) or they'll find more trouble on the road. In the end, their love, their future as a family, is, after all, only partly an act of personal will. The rest is up to history.

Rosa and Wense have strong commitments that pull at them in opposite directions. Their family pulls them back to Cherán, Cherán's economy pushes them away; the economy of the United States beckons, the Border Patrol agents stand with their shields at the line. Rosa and Wense live smack on the line between the old world and the new, between Cherán and St. Louis, Missouri.

After half a dozen midtempo ballads, the Soldados suddenly burst into what sounds like a punkish, honky-tonk Mexican version of *Appalachian Spring*. The dance floor explodes with energy as the Cheranes try out the two-step. I ask Rosa what the hell it is that the Soldados are playing.

"Cohn-tree?" she says, tentatively.

As the night wears on, a cold mist rushes down from San Marcos Mountain, the stage lights glowing blue and red through the gathering fog. I see a horse standing stock-still on a hill above town, looking in our direction. He seems unreal, like a stuffed animal. And on the rooftops surrounding the concert grounds the poorest of Cherán's poor huddle, looking down into the swirling rainbow fog of the pit. Their faces flash in the strobe light.

Because I want to watch the news," responds Moisés Acuapa Carrillo, when I ask him why he's parted with $106.66, the first installment on principal of $3,200 with a thirty-month term, for a spanking-new *par-abólica*, which two young men from Uruapan are currently securing to the roof of his modest one-story adobe. It is an old-style dish, about six feet in diameter, with a heavy counterweight and pedestal, the kind that, in the States, is rapidly going the way of the eight-track cassette. Even in Cherán there are already a few families in town with DirecTV setups not much bigger than the ceramic plates they eat from.

The Carrillo family makes ends meet with a small corn parcel worked by the men and textiles knitted by the women. The payments will probably strain their finances to the limit—they are not migrants, and they don't plan on ever leaving the Purépecha highlands—but they want to watch the news anyway.

"I like to know what is going on in the world," Carrillo says.

On the basic subscription plan, he will receive Spanish-language CNN, which will connect him to Atlanta, and MTV Latino, which will connect him to Miami, in addition to the colossus of Mexican media, Televisa, which will connect him to Mexico City. And, of course, he will be connected to Hollywood. Every Sunday night, at roughly the same time that millions of households across the United States tune in to *The X-Files*, so will Moisés Carrillo, although he'll be hearing Scully and Mulder debating the existence of aliens and ghosts in a dubbed Spanish that doesn't match the movement of their lips.

We stand on the roof, watching the workers train the dish on the heavens, as the youngest of the Carrillo brood shriek and dash about. Someone brings out a disposable camera and asks me to capture the historic event. The family gathers in front of the dish for the portrait, all striking a giddy, prideful pose. Geraniums bloom prettily in old jalapeño tins at their feet. Volcanoes tower in the distance. And the dish, a huge monochrome peacock fanning its feathers, crowns their heads with a postindustrial halo.

How the Cheranes love to tell their tales of conquering the northern frontier! I get word that José Jiménez, a local representative of a contractor in Morelia, who in turn represents a contractor in Texas, who in turn supplies labor to farms in the States and across the Caribbean, has placed an open call for migrant workers. This is the *legal* side of

Cherán's migrant story. These workers will all get special temporary visas to work for a season, in full compliance with the laws of the country at hand—in this case, the Bahamas.

"Our brothers shouldn't have to risk their lives to earn a respectable wage," Jiménez says, generously cracking open Modelo beers for all who stop by his house to inquire about the gig. He explains the details of the job and the paperwork involved. They'll be working in citrus fields. They all have to go to Dr. Tito's for certificates of good health and to the *presidencia* if they don't have their birth certificates.

Once that piece of business is out of the way, it's time for some more beers. And some wetback stories.

José's son Mario holds court. In his late teens, he's tall, thin, and gregarious. He sits on a tree stump before the prospective workers, who range from nervous first-time teenagers to wizened veterans. Mario wears a Charlotte Hornets cap, holds a cheap Farolito cigarette in one hand, a can of Modelo in the other. He tells of the time he worked in North Carolina—tobacco country, and a favorite Purépecha hunting ground, especially for young migrants with a taste for adventure. Everyone and their mother goes to places like California, Texas, and Illinois. But North Carolina! The very name—in Spanish, it comes out quite poetic: *Carolina del Norte*—sounds like it could well be another country, a savanna of tall grass flowing in the breeze like the hair of some ravishing blonde in a gringo shampoo commercial.

Last September, through his father, Mario got a legal contract job on a cucumber field near a dust speck of a town called Pikeville (southeast of Raleigh) owned by a German American farmer with a name something like Schmidt. The conditions were typical, the kind that quickly erase whatever romance the migrants might feel about the land of Jesse Helms.

"Just about everything you earn, you wind up spending," Mario says, to nods and mutterings of agreement from the men. The kid earned seven hundred dollars a month, but a month's worth of bus fares from Pikeville to Schmidt's alone was a hundred dollars. "And the German would take advantage of us by selling us cans of Coke for two dollars," he says, and pauses, letting this unthinkable injustice sink in. "And so one day we're in the field and I tell him, 'Hey, *patrón*, I think I'm paying you more than you're paying me.' "

This last line is delivered with great bravado. The eyes of the younger men bulge at the thought of such outright rebellion. The elders cackle knowingly. They know that kind of asshole *patrón*; they've worked for him. The name might be different than Schmidt, and the field might've been in Georgia, or Nebraska, or the San Joaquin Valley of California, but they remember, they certainly remember. They also know that the kid is about to start spinning a tall tale, but this actually makes the story all the more enjoyable. It's a movie now, a new Cherán myth being born, everyone's fantasy of playing the hero against a villainous *patrón*.

Mario continues. "And so the *patrón* says to me, he says, he says something so crude I won't repeat it here, and then he yells at me to get back in the field."

The *patrón* stands tall over the workers and our teenage hero from Cherán. Work has ceased in the field, even the cicadas have grown quiet. All eyes are focused on the combatants. The sun is hot and still and everyone's sweating, drops rolling down their foreheads and stinging their eyes.

And our hero says: *¡Ni madres!* Which is difficult to translate, because literally it means "Not even the mothers," but closer would be: Fuck no!

Mario strides over to the *patrón*'s van, which is used to ferry the workers to and from the bus stop a few miles up the road.

"Take me to the bus station!" the kid demands.

The farmer is stunned. No Mexican has ever talked back to him! It takes him a few beats to recover. "Sure, I'll take you," he says, and a sick smile forms on his lips. "For two hundred dollars."

"Fine," Mario says, "I'll walk."

But Mario doesn't walk away. No, he walks up to Schmidt and throws his basket of cucumbers down at the German's feet—you have to pick about two hundred buckets of that damn vegetable every day just to break even—and he tells him that every Mexican in this field has the right to a fair wage, to decent working conditions, to not be robbed by the company store, and, furthermore, every Mexican in this field has the right, if these basic conditions aren't met, to protest, because this is America, and there are laws here, not like in Mexico, not like in Germany! This is a democracy, and Schmidt will treat the men dem-o-crat-i-cally (he enunciates each syllable), or else. Mario shouts that he has his rights, even if this is not his country. (The origin of this last epigram is actually a popular song by Los Tigres del Norte, a *norteño* band that has made a career of setting wetback tales to a polka beat.)

"You have no rights," the *patrón* says, but his voice has lost some of its edge. He is aware, for the first time, that he is surrounded by fifty workers boring a hole through him with their rage, staring straight in his eye, not down at the dirt, where peasants usually cast their eyes in the presence of the boss.

Mario decides to show Schmidt his rights. After a long, theatrical pause, the kid makes a fist with his left hand. He tells the *patrón* that this hand, this hand that picks those stinking cucumbers, is now going straight up that German ass! Mario's hook lands squarely on Schmidt's jaw. The *patrón*'s hat flies off, and Mario starts running, because he's sure the cops will be there any minute, and he looks back over his shoulder to see what's going on. Oh, and what he sees in that hot, dusty little field! All the paisanos are cheering and laughing, the *patrón* is picking himself up from the dirt. Finally he's been humiliated like he's humiliated the Mexicans all these months.

Although Wense is trying hard to walk the straight and narrow, there's still a part of him that wants to be just like José Izquierdo.

Depending on whom you talk to, Izquierdo is either a wetback hero or a guy who scares the locals with his cholo style. Izquierdo stands out. Even if he's half a mile down the highway, you notice the long, slicked-back jet-black hair, the mirrored shades, the fat gold crucifix bouncing on his chest, his denim short-sleeved shirt buttoned all the way up, the black baggies and white high-tops. But it's the walk that really sets him apart. That so-slow-and-cool saunter, which he achieves by leaning back against his stride, making it look like only his feet are moving forward while the rest of his body threatens to fall back. It is the classic cholo swing, the gait originated by the zoot-suited Chicano youth of the 1940s, the highest of high Mexican American styles, maintained to this very day, with some modifications, on the streets of East Los Angeles. And in cities and towns across the Americas where barrio kids born to immigrant parents search desperately for an identity through a style that negates both Mexican *and* American culture so ferociously that it winds up exaggerating both, creating a surreal hybrid in the process: in essence, Chicano culture.

But at this moment, José Izquierdo is no cool cholo. He is staggering along the dark streets of Cherán, Wense and I trailing him. His hair is disheveled, drool spills from the corners of his mouth. He mutters unintelligibly, except for the occasional whimper of a name: Laura. The macho gait is gone. With each laborious, off-kilter step, he threatens to collapse.

This is not the José Izquierdo I met a few hours ago. Wense and I had been walking through town when we ran into him, and the two had greeted each other warmly. They'd grown up together in Cherán and had also shared stints on the migrant trail, in St. Louis and Chicago. I noticed immediately that Wense regarded him not with the seething envy he displays in the company of the middle-class migrants who cruise ostentatiously through town in their gleaming Chevy trucks. He looked at José with the innocent admiration of a kid in the presence of his hero.

José had been in rare form. He was only beginning the day's drunk and was in a generous mood. We headed for the *casa de cambio*, getting looks of awe or reproach all along the way. He had three gringo C notes—bona fide counterfeit, he assured me—burning a hole in his pocket. He told me he'd just gotten in from Chicago a few days before. Came back, he said, to visit his aging *madrecita*, to see his *prometida*, the sweetheart he'll marry the day he finally decides to settle down, and, of course, to do some serious partying. At the *casa*, José performed a masterful act of *norteño* flirtatiousness with the teenage clerk. She didn't inspect the bills at all.

Next, we made for Ven a México (Come to Mexico), the only upscale bar in Cherán, where you get good appetizers with your beer, rum, and tequila. The owner and host is a flaming *loca*, an incredibly effeminate gay man named Salvador who made good money as a maitre d' up north. He ran into some kind of trouble (a dark secret that no one's ever gotten out of him) and made it back to Cherán with just enough cash to start up the bar—a bar, mind you, not a cantina.

It was clear that Salvador doted on José. Some locals in the bar stopped their domino game to give him hard looks, others were obviously impressed with his outlaw persona. Holding court, José told us what America is really all about.

Speaking in a highly urbanized Spanish, he said that he'd been all across the States, from California to the Carolinas, but he liked the middle of America the best, the lake and river cities: Chicago, St. Louis, Memphis, Little Rock. Like every other migrant from Cherán, he started out working in the fields. But he itched for city life: the traffic, the polished glass and steel of the skyscrapers and malls, the white girls in miniskirts, the sun sinking into a ruddy smog horizon. But there's only one way to make good money when you're an unskilled worker in a big city.

He began small-time, moving dime bags of weed for a Puerto Rican dealer in Chicago. Gringo businessmen in suits would come down to the barrio in their Blazers and 4Runners for drive-through service. The wisdom José had grown up with—the harder you work, the less money you earn—was suddenly turned upside down. Now he worked less for more money. He graduated to coke, crack, and crystal. Quarter and half bags became gram and eighth-of-an-ounce bags. Soon he was off the street. Having proven his trustworthiness, his boss singled him out for the most important job of all—transporting large quantities across state and, eventually, international lines.

The pace of our drinking accelerated in direct proportion to the ambitions José described in his story. He got a nice car—a ninety-something Camaro. He bought the 14K crucifix he was wearing today. He had white girls clinging to both arms as he strolled along Milwaukee Avenue. He drove trucks and vans across the Texas desert and up and down the Mississippi River Valley on all-night deliveries, partying along the way.

Gradually, as he told his tale, José's demeanor changed. He'd begun with the sweeping gestures of a braggart. But by the time he was talking about moving pounds and pounds of the stuff, his speech was slurred, ever more rapid. He began to sweat.

And then he was in jail. He rolled up his left sleeve to show us his tattoo—the popular cholo rendition of the tragicomic masks with the slogan "La vida loca" in Old English lettering. It was a short stint, he said; his boss's lawyer got him out after only a few weeks. But I wasn't so sure. I wasn't sure if José Izquierdo was telling the truth about anything. He might indeed have lived *la vida loca* or he might merely have seen the classic Chicano gangbanger films *Bound by Honor* and *American Me*, both of which are available at Cherán's *videocentro*.

He started knocking back tequila with beer chasers with reckless frequency. This was no longer a party but a desperate attempt to outrun the phantoms gaining on him. There is that moment in every outlaw movie when karma kicks in and the free ride has to be paid for. José was moving quickly to that moment.

He got out of the joint with a fresh tattoo and, apparently, some unspeakable trauma. "It was hell in there," is all he said, head nodding drunkenly at his beer. And then, finally, he exploded.

"He can't run my life!" he shouted, causing the bar to fall silent for a few seconds before the dominoes started slapping the tables again. He was talking about his boss—the guy he owed for getting him out of jail. José proclaimed that he was on the run twice over: he had a court appearance pending in Chicago and his boss had work for him. The kind of work you can't refuse.

And with that, he burst out of the bar. For the next two hours, Wense and I follow José on a hellish tour of the darkening streets of Cherán. We visit several piss-poor cantinas where aging alcoholics cry, puke, and pick their pointless fights. Later, he wants to hail a taxi down at the plaza for a ride to Paracho and the nearest brothel. (Cherán once had one, Wense tells me, but the local wives and girlfriends ran the whores out.) The cabbies will have none of it, no matter how many dollars he waves in their faces. José is now at that stage where only one of two things can happen—he'll either pass out peacefully or be arrested for violating one law or another.

José's dilemma is similar to Wense's, just more extreme. Should he stay or should he go? He doesn't want to get any deeper into the business. Lose your life, for what? So some gringo can powder his nose, so some poor black kid can drag on a crack pipe? So some skinny whore will cling to you for your drugs and money? But he can't stay in Cherán either, growing old watching the cornstalks rise and fall with the seasons and the forest thin out and die, listening to thunderclaps echo off the balding hills. Cherán, who gives a fuck about Cherán? Stay *here*? When you've seen the lights of Memphis swirl on the waters of the Mississippi at four in the morning?

José heads to Cherán's only travel agency, where you can book flights to anywhere in the States. He bangs on the shuttered windows. No one answers. Then it's on to the *caseta de larga distancia*, where calls come in from dozens of cities and towns across America. He'll call his boss, after all. There'll be a package waiting for him in Brownsville, or in Harlingen, or Laredo. There'll be a meeting in some decrepit house in the worst part of town. He'll be looking over his shoulder the whole way to Chicago.

But it's too late. The blinking lights of the sign above the *caseta* door are off. So it's on to the plaza, where we sit and listen to José ramble and to the bells of the church tolling each quarter hour. It's only about nine o'clock, but there is no nightlife in Cherán. A couple of dogs bark and we hear the strains of a few boom boxes playing ballads. We sit on the cold concrete benches whose ancient whitewash is fading and chipping away. We sit and we listen to José howl.

"Laura!" José calls with a raspy bellow. Laura, his nickname for the one he planned to marry when it was finally time to settle down. But he won't be marrying Laura. Not because he doesn't want to settle down but because when he returned from Chicago a couple of days ago, he went to her house and her mother broke it to him that she'd married a man from Uruapan. Laura had waited all those years he'd been wandering around up north, her mother told him, but now she was nineteen years old and she couldn't wait any longer. "I'm so sorry, José," Laura's mother said. "You know how much I wanted you to marry my daughter."

By midnight, José has made his mind up four times. Twice to go back to work for his boss, twice to stay in Cherán, kill the fuck who stole his Laura away, and win her back, to grow old with his love and watch the cornstalks rise and fall. He refuses any attempt to get him home. Finally, Wense and I leave him staggering along the highway, bickering with his ghosts, shouting for his Laura, and cursing America.

It is almost impossible to hear El Músico over the din of traffic rushing along the highway. We are standing just outside the front door to his house, separated from the northbound lane by only a few feet of dirt.

He is not inviting me in. Wense is at my side, tense and quiet as usual. I am here to see if I, too, can become a wetback.

There is no keeping Wense in Cherán. He wants to leave as soon as he can raise the money. I've convinced myself that to accompany him is the writerly thing to do. Nevertheless, nightmarish scenarios keep flashing through my head. An accident at the border: Wense's killed, I survive. I bring the body back, explain how it happened, but the Chávezes hold me responsible. *He only went because he thought you could help him . . .*

I also find myself thinking that Wense should feel responsible for *my* well-being. I have no smuggling expertise; I'm not even a good swimmer. But to Wense I'm the older brother, the older gringo brother, the one who should know about the border and its risks and how to cross it without losing your life, because, after all, the fortifications on the line are my country's idea, not his.

This is my second attempt to convince Cherán's premier coyotes to let me tag along. The first was an utter failure. On that occasion, La Licuadora answered the door. I asked for El Músico—you always ask for the man of the house to do business in Mexico—but she told me he wasn't in and fixed me with a fearsome stare, as if to say, Who the hell are you and what do you want with my son? An impressive woman, La Licuadora. Purépecha women are sometimes used in Mexican tourist publicity as an example of exotic beauty—quiet, docile beauty. But in Cherán, women often think of themselves as macho, tough as nails. Though women have yet to hold elected office in Cherán, many are politically active, often voting as a bloc.

La Licuadora is Asian-eyed, with a dry, cracked, dark brown face. She is short though anything but frail, with broad shoulders and sturdy legs. Most locals agree she's in her fifties, but there is not a single gray hair in her long black mane. I was nothing more than fruit for the blender. She shot a few words at Wense in Purépecha. They went back and forth for a while, Wense in an overly friendly tone that must have made her suspect me and my proposal all the more. Wense dutifully translated for me. "This guy's not a reporter," La Licuadora said, "he's *migra*." Wense could go for the usual price, but no "reporter."

In the end, she relented somewhat. She actually admitted, after her initial denials, that she was indeed in the smuggling business. But she played a minor role in the operation, just jotting down the names of the migrants who wanted to head north, until there were enough to make a new trip across the border worthwhile. This, too, was a lie—she was involved in all aspects of the family business—but I was in no position to argue.

So today I'm trying to convince the son of the toughest Purépecha woman in Cherán that I'm on the up and up. El Músico converses pleasantly, not letting on that he's suspicious. Sure, he's in the coyote business, he says. And a good business it is. He motions to the car parked alongside the house, a late-model Dodge sedan, gold, with Illinois plates. The money for the car and the home improvements (the entire facade is covered with new tile, the kind generally used for bathrooms and kitchens, but in Cherán a popular *norteño* style) comes from the smuggling fees. These days, the going rate for a door-to-door trip is $1,000—preferably in U.S. currency. He often takes more than thirty, sometimes as many as eighty locals at a time. There is high overhead in this business—bribes to federal police at several checkpoints along the route to the border, fees for the managers of the "safe houses" on both sides of the line, the purchase of vehicles for travel within the States, gas, food, and so on. And yet, even though El Músico says he might spend as much as 75 percent of his take to get the job done, I figure his profit could be over $10,000 a trip.

Just when he's got me thinking that all I have to do is negotiate a fee for my first illegal journey across the border, he starts in about the gringo cops. Surely I know that the American police are the real problem for the coyotes. The *migra*? Ha! They mean nothing to El Músico. The cops are another story. Because, you see, the cops and the *migra* work hand in glove. He could get a traffic ticket in Lincoln, Nebraska, and then every *migra* checkpoint in the country will have his name on the computer. It becomes obvious that El Músico is sending me a thinly veiled message. Whether he thinks I'm actually a cop is not the point. He doesn't want his name in the papers. He probably doesn't even want his nickname in the papers. He doesn't want to do time—hard time. On this count, he is not exaggerating. Currently, federal sentencing guidelines call for an automatic ten years for smuggling human beings into the country. My guess is that so far, he's avoided being nabbed the way most coyotes do, by posing as just another wetback when they're pulled over. The *migra* typically interrogate everyone, trying to ascertain the identity of the ringleader. But all the illegals are told beforehand to answer that they're a wildcat crew, traveling without a coyote. It is extremely difficult, without extensive undercover work, to catch a coyote.

In the end, El Músico says that he's on vacation, no smuggling in the foreseeable future. I walk away, defeated. A few days later, I'll hear that El Músico and La Licuadora are readying to cross the line once again.

Salvador Estrada is one of those Cheranes who fiercely defend Purépecha tradition, an Indian who won't abandon the homeland or its history. He is also the owner of one of the two long-distance *casetas* in town, which is set up in what would be his living room.

A tall, portly man who sweats profusely when he pontificates on a subject he cares about—and he cares about every subject under the sun—he opens his doors for business early in the morning and keeps them open well into the night, when the *caseta*, lit by intensely bright fluorescents, is a beacon just off the highway a couple of blocks down from the plaza.

Estrada, his wife, and his children take turns working the switchboard. There are five phone lines, each with its handsome old-fashioned wood-and-glass private booth. There are always a few people hanging out at the *caseta*, some placing calls but most receiving them. American dollars go much further paying for long-distance tolls, and, in any case, calls are actually cheaper when made from the States. Since almost all migrant Cheranes work six days a week, Sunday is the busiest day at the *caseta*. It can get pretty hectic. The procedure is always the same. Let's say that Florentino Chávez in Watsonville rings and asks to speak to his mother, doña María Elena. He is promptly told to call back in half an hour. One of Estrada's sons is dispatched to the Chávez house (about ten minutes round-trip) and delivers the message that Florentino has called. María Elena has just a few minutes to fix her hair and put on something nice to wear—going to *la caseta* is like taking a stroll to the plaza, a very public stroll to a very private matter. People are always dressed in their best for a Sunday *caseta* appointment.

Doña María Elena will invariably arrive a few minutes late, but that's okay, because Florentino knows she's getting on in years and isn't as quick as she used to be. If it's Sunday morning, María Elena will find about twenty other Cheranes waiting for calls from their loved ones. Florentino will call back about forty minutes after he placed the first call, and he most likely will be told to call back in another fifteen minutes. He might actually have to call once or twice more before a booth is free. I've seen many Cheranes spend well over half an hour talking to their relatives, connecting in the only way they can, save for postcards and letters, which aren't all that common; while many young migrants are literate, their parents and grandparents are probably not.

Salvador Estrada remembers the call from the Mexican consulate in Los Angeles with the news that the Chávez brothers were dead. It was a Saturday, late in the evening. The consul asked him to inform the town judge, whom he called at home. Then he sent for the family members. It was at the *caseta* that the judge informed María Elena that her sons were dead and María Huaroco that her son had survived. And so every time one of Estrada's kids shows up at the Chávez house, it reminds everyone of the night they will never forget.

It was not the first time Estrada delivered such news. "Every month or two, we get a call about another death up there," he says.

Estrada gives me a grand tour. Up until a year ago, he had just three separate phones, the old heavy black ones with fraying cloth cords. Originally, he couldn't dial or receive calls directly and had to be patched through an operator in Uruapan. Now, of course, he just dials the long-distance access code and receives incoming calls directly. His telephone number is written on dozens, perhaps hundreds, of scraps of paper tucked away in the wallets and purses and jeans of migrants across the United States. Soon, he plans to install five more lines—so long as the border is crossed, business will boom. The calls pour in from Illinois, California, Pennsylvania, Missouri, Arkansas, North Carolina, Texas, Oregon, and the latest locale, New York City. Yes, the Cheranes have arrived in Manhattan, Estrada notes with pride.

After I exhaust my questions, Estrada asks me one. He's heard that I've interviewed doña Elisa, the venerable *bruja*, and he just wants to know if it's true. Then he leads me back through the interior patio of the house to his office. There are dozens of glass bottles lining the shelves, each filled with the essences of native plants and animals.

"I don't have an altar or anything like that," Estrada says, taking down a bottle of aloe. "But I preserve the traditions, too." I realize that I'm talking to yet another *brujo*, albeit a rather secular one. He belongs to the same *brujo* association as doña Elisa; as a matter of fact, he is a founding member of the local chapter. The man who owns the most profitable long-distance *caseta* in town (he takes a commission on every incoming call), a man who makes a decent profit because his *paisanos* are scattered along the migrant trail, picking up the best and worst of Americana—this man is a Purépecha *curandero*, a traditional healer.

"We've allowed ourselves to be influenced by other cultures, at the expense of our own," he says. "As Mexicans, we should follow the traditions of our ancestors."

Estrada explains that his style of healing avoids the "white" and "black" magic distinctions favored by many of his Purépecha colleagues. His potions, variously concocted with scorpion tails, dove feathers, deer antlers, and his favorite, the juice of the aloe, can, he insists, treat practically every known disease. Except, of course, AIDS, which, he emphasizes, "is not the wrath of God, like some say. It's just another disease, one that we bring upon ourselves and one for which we ourselves will find a cure eventually."

Estrada has obviously read some American self-help books, which have become increasingly popular in Mexico over the last decade. Together with herb extracts, then, he treats his clients "psychologically," so they can "do something for themselves and achieve a healthy emotional life."

I mention the acute retinitis I've suffered for years, and before I can finish detailing the symptoms, Estrada launches into a diagnosis that seems to have been gleaned from Chinese medicine. He tells me my eyes are too "hot" (which, in essence, is true; my American doctors have told me that the tiny vessels in my retinas are pumping too much blood, causing leaks that cloud my vision). The prescription: each morning, I am to awaken just before dawn and walk outside. I am to relax my body by breathing deeply. I am to lie facedown, my head pointing toward the rising sun, preferably on barren ground, but if that is impossible a concrete surface will suffice. I am to lay my forehead on the cool earth, with my arms stretched wide, palms down. I am to remain in this position for ten minutes. I will thus begin the day with my retinas cooled. Whenever I suffer an acute attack, I am to find a cool surface and perform this ritual.

The early morning hours are Estrada's favorite time. Did I know that the dew on the leaves of the plants is the sweetest water on earth? It is cool, he tells me, and soft as air, and flavored with the essence of God, for God is all things and resides even in the leaves of the plants.

"I don't want all this to be lost," Salvador Estrada tells me as we part outside his *caseta*, where parents and grandparents wait their turn to hear the voices of loved ones from afar. Maybe instead of writing a book, he tells me, I should make a movie about the traditions of Cherán.

The summer wanes. The cornstalks begin to dry and wilt. From the hilltops, the town appears surrounded by an unbroken sea of rustling yellow-green. Billowing clouds still gather every afternoon, but it doesn't always rain now. The sunlight slants toward us from south of the meridian. The nights are clear and starry—the Milky Way an intense brush stroke of light splitting the sky in two—and they are colder, because the fog doesn't rush down San Marcos Mountain now.

At the Chávezes' house, the big news is that Wense has left to try his luck at the border. He set out with a younger brother on the morning of September 17, the day after Mexican Independence Day. Now a week has gone by without word from him, and the wait is all the more anxious because reports from the line are nothing short of terrifying. August, September, and early October are dog days in the American Southwest. The greatest risk now is no longer from the tricky currents and sudden undertow of the Rio Grande but from dehydration. As Cherán begins to cool down, Texas and Arizona reach the peak of late summer's heat. The temperature can hit 120 degrees in the shade.

Not much has changed at the Chávez household. The general store downstairs is still fully stocked with useless goods, and there are still no customers. Often when I arrive, there is no one minding the store, either. Doña María Elena, the widows, and the kids are upstairs doing the chores. But there are a couple of new additions to the family, mascots for the kids: a frisky puppy and a baby lamb, a stray that doña María Elena couldn't resist taking in. She gives it milk from a baby bottle. The one luxury doña María Elena has allowed herself is a pair of new shoes, black felt, low-heeled, with gold buckles, similar to her other pair.

Waiting. Waiting for word from Wense and waiting, six months after burying Benjamín, Jaime, and Salvador, for the stonecutter from Morelia to make good on his promise of tombstones for the dead. Mayor Salvador Sánchez Campanur has made calls on behalf of the family. The answer is always the same: "They're on their way."

During one of my afternoon visits, Florentino Chávez's wife, Eudelia, a short, round woman who often hides her smile behind her rebozo, brings out a photo album. It is filled mostly with shots of her husband, pictures he's sent her from the other side, where he remains. Here he is, jeans tucked into knee-high black work boots, nearly lost in the immensity of a Carolina tobacco field. The plants are almost as tall as he is, their thick drab-green leaves split by huge yellow veins. And then the dead appear. Benjamín and Salvador, in a poorly focused shot taken in a California supermarket, in violation of those strange but strict rules chain stores have against taking photos on their property. It is Salvador's second trip north. He beams amid the rows of packaged products, while Benjamín, playing the older brother, stands formally, a stiff arm around Salvador's shoulder.

Eudelia, María—Fernando's almost gaunt but prettily freckled wife—and the pleasantly plump and round-faced Yolanda, Benjamín's widow, shiver in their rebozos as the afternoon turns to twilight and a cold breeze comes up from the Paracho Valley. Fernando is up at his house and so it's just the women sitting in the darkening store, looking out at the blue-gray horizon. The women's mood is lugubrious, in sharp contrast to the hyperactivity of their kids running and screeching out on the road. As they talk quietly, I realize that it's no longer just the pain of the loss that depresses them. Leafing through the photo album has also reminded them that they have always stayed behind when their husbands went north.

María is the one who says it first. "I'd go up there if it weren't for the fact that the men won't let us."

Ironically, it was Rosa, the wife of Wense, the most outwardly macho man of the clan, who was first allowed to accompany her husband. Rather, she forced her husband to take her along. Fernando and

Florentino, by most accounts more sensitive to their wives, have yet to relent.

María isn't the only one who's tiring of sitting home in Cherán waiting. Eudelia breaks her usual silence to second the motion. "If you ask me, we'd all be better off up there."

Yolanda has nothing left to lose but is terrified of crossing the line. "I can't say what it's like up there, because I've never been, but just think of all the people who've died up there. And those are the ones we know about. There's probably thousands more, but their bodies will never be found in the desert." Then she contradicts herself. "But I guess most people make it just fine, or else why would they keep going?"

Doña María Elena sits grim-faced in the corner of the store. I am expecting her to beg her daughters and in-laws to remain focused on the risks—the border has already taken three Chávezes, God forbid the *migra* or the river or the desert leave her grandchildren orphaned. But when the young women turn to her, she surprises us all. A sudden smile breaks through her tense wrinkles.

"God willing, we'll all be there someday," she says. "But I'm not as young as my daughters-in-law, I might not escape the *migra*." We all laugh. It is one of the few occasions I've heard her make a joke.

Cherán's taxi fleet is made up entirely of aging Plymouths but the cabbies take pride in keeping the interior vinyl in good condition. Taxis here are usually only used by well-to-do matrons returning home after shopping at market or, late at night, by drunken *norteños* with American dollars burning their pockets. The poor either use the town's cheap public transportation (tattered VW vans) or walk. Because Cherán consists of only a few square miles, the rides are rarely more than a few blocks.

Mostly, Cherán's cabbies wait.

There's Delfino, who whiles away the idle hours by strumming his guitar in the backseat of his car. And El Chaparro (The Short One), a stocky guy well under five feet who is nevertheless renowned as one of the best barroom fighters in the highlands. El Indio, of the dark, almost chocolate-colored skin, on the other hand, is one of the taller men in

Cherán, but he would never raise a fist against anyone; he loves telling tales of the old days, especially *bruja* stories. El Poeta derives his nickname from his ability to insult your mother with an infinite number of adjectives.

And then there's Marcos, the only cabbie who's a veteran of the migrant trail, with whom I've established a bond beyond the jocular banter I share with the others. He is of average height, his striking good looks accented by longish curly black hair and a hip mustache and goatee. He usually wears white sweatshirts and jeans, which fit well on his masculine frame. He can look tough, but he's one of the most sensitive men I've met in Cherán.

Often, we'll sit in his cab parked at the curb, waiting for a fare. We'll swap stories or just listen to the radio, tuned to the town's only station, XEPUR, "The Voice of the Purépechas," which plays the melancholy highland ballads known as *pirekuas*, laments sung in Purépecha over simple guitar arrangements in heartbreaking duet harmonies.

It is early evening, and the fares are few and far between because everyone's either already home or huddled at the cantinas. We chain smoke Marlboros despite the fact that the windows are open only the slightest crack to protect against the cold autumn air. There are four cabs in line ahead of us, the drivers cocooned in their second homes. Whenever the lead taxi picks up a fare, everyone moves up a few feet. Marcos doesn't bother to start the motor to move ahead. He just releases the brake and gravity takes us down the slight incline of the street.

It's been one hell of a year for Marcos, for Cherán, for Mexico. His wife and infant daughter have been gravely ill since the baby's premature birth a few months ago. The doctors in Uruapan told him that chances were fifty-fifty for the baby and not much better for his wife. The child was born at six and a half months, her tiny lungs filled with fluid, and his wife suffered an embolism after giving birth. Marcos stayed at the hospital for several sleepless days and nights. Finally, a miracle: both his loved ones survived, although his daughter continues to suffer setbacks that send the family scurrying to the hospital several times a month.

Marcos feels the pressure building. The illnesses. The tremendous debt he's accrued at the hospital. The meager earnings and stress of his job. He tells me he feels trapped—he feels it in his very body, in the form of chest pains and back pains and stomachaches. He admits that sometimes he crosses the line with alcohol. So far, he's been able to pull back whenever he's about to pitch into the abyss, but these days the abyss beckons constantly. He wants a drink right now. But he's never been drunk on the job.

In Cherán, he has no alternative to driving a cab. The fourteen-, fifteen-, sometimes eighteen-hour shifts are his only hope. With luck, he can make the better part of a week's pay with one fare, say a mid-night run to Zamora or the jackpot, the two-hundred-mile trip to Gua-dalajara, for which he can charge several hundred pesos. But that happens, at the most, a few times a year, usually during fiesta or at Easter, when the *norteños* are vacationing in Cherán and have money to burn. And these runs are extremely dangerous. At night, Mexico State Route 31, the two-lane road that connects Cherán to Zamora, is a bandit's dream. There isn't a single street lamp along the thirty-five-mile stretch. There are no regular patrols in the area, and if there were, corruption being what it is, the authorities would probably aid the bandits rather than their victims. And carjackings are not the only danger. The road is hair-raising even in broad daylight, with several terrifying curves, and the buses and semis blast by at harrowing speeds. In the darkness, the dense foliage along the road seems to reach out for your car. It feels like the night will swallow you whole. But there is no choice, that's the road, the only road, connecting Cherán to the rest of the world, to Zamora, to Guadalajara, and on up the Pacific route to the border at Tijuana and the cities and towns of the States.

Marcos is thinking of taking to that road himself. He admits that it would be tantamount to abandoning his family and his duty as a father. It wouldn't be the first time he's made the journey. He's got his border war stories. The best time was when he crossed at Tijuana with a cheap *mica chueca*, a fake green card he bought at Plaza de Santa Cecilia, the old smugglers' headquarters a mile from the line. They took a Polaroid photo of him right there on the street, some-one holding up a kerchief behind his head for the requisite pale back-ground. He crossed without a hitch. And there were other, more difficult times, battling the *migra* on their turf, in the hills and gullies of southeastern San Diego County.

But for every high-tech weapon the *migra* employ, Marcos says, there's a guerrilla-like response from the wetbacks and coyotes. Take the laser traps, for example, grids of beams that, when breached, immediately alert the *migra* to movement. One wetback crew Marcos crossed with was equipped with spray cans. You sprayed ahead of you in an area already known to be a problem from previous busts. The beams glittered in the mist, and you made your way around the grid. The coyotes claim that the Border Patrol constantly relocates its tracking equipment. But each group of migrants that gets caught actually helps new migrants cross. Each bust is valuable intelligence gathered.

In the States, Marcos seems to have been a typical migrant, working hard, partying hard. One night in L.A., weaving around drunk on his bicycle—he has never owned a car; even the taxi belongs to a local entrepreneur—he was stopped by the infamous LAPD. Marcos says the alcohol inspired him to raise holy hell about his rights as a citizen of the world and curse them in his migrant's English. Ultimately, he says, they let him go on his way. Another migrant tall tale? If I'd believe anyone, it'd be Marcos.

But the moments of levity in the conversation evaporate and Marcos returns to his dilemma: he wants to get the hell out of Cherán, and he knows that he should stay with his family. His jaw is set tight. He bounces his knee up and down, taps the dashboard with his fingers. He wants to escape. It's an astonishing admission for a Mexican man. Mexican men are always escaping, of course, but they usually justify their wanderings: I'm leaving so I can send money back home to my family; I'll work there for a few years and then bring my family up. What Marcos is saying is that he wants to quit his life in Cherán.

He's thirty-three, Christ's age when he died. In fact, Marcos has already been crucified—he's played the role of savior in Cherán's Easter Passion play three times. You have to have a marathon runner's endurance for the role, and Marcos is among the few in town who does.

He'd rather have this cup pass from him, though. He's actually gone as far as packing his bags. His mother pleaded with him: Think about what you're doing. Don't abandon us, don't run away from your responsibilities as a man, from your loved ones, your town, your state, your country, from your *life*. Think about it, my son. And so he unpacked and he's still here. But he is not at peace.

The engine of the taxi in front of us growls awake. We roll forward a few feet. We are now the first in line, but there's no one to be seen along the highway. It is one of the quietest moments I've ever experienced in Cherán. A quarter moon dangles from the southern sky; the dim outline of the Juanconi volcano rises up from the darkness of the Paracho Valley.

Marcos has never been at peace. His father was killed when he was just fourteen, in a dispute involving pride, alcohol, and a gun. Still in junior high, Marcos, the eldest son of the family, went looking for vengeance. In a story that sounds like something out of the L.A. nightly news, he arrived at school one morning packing a pistol. Walking home after class, he spotted the man who killed his father—the bastard had avoided justice by bribing the authorities. He opened fire from a distance of half a block, in broad daylight, right here along the highway. Amazingly, neither the murderer nor innocent bystanders were killed, but one bullet did find its mark. Marcos was hauled away by the local cops, who kicked the shit out of him in jail, but was ultimately bailed out by his family, and that's the last he ever heard from the authorities. Seems like everyone in town agreed that the boy's crime was more than justifiable—it was justice itself, rural justice. Thus a legend was born in Cherán, and rural legends are powerful things. A year later, his father's murderer asked for peace. "But I don't want peace with him," he says. "Not in this lifetime." Which is not to say he's going to gun him down. He's older than that now.

He learned early on to be a fighter. He's a scrappy boxer and if he never raises his fists again, the legend will still follow him to the grave. No one fucks with Marcos. But no matter how well he defends himself—with a gun, with his fists, with his legs outrunning the *migra*— the world comes back with its unpredictable blows, against which not even legends can prevail. The world gives him a premature baby that can't breathe. It causes his wife to suffer an embolism hours after giving birth. It topples his country's economy. It deprives him of dignity even if he has a dignified job, because that job won't pay him what he deserves and what he needs. It causes him to start out on a journey of thousands of miles. It changes his life without a second's notice.

Marcos is still waiting for a fare. He offers me a ride, but I tell him I'll walk. I watch the Plymouth roll down the highway, its flickering red parking lights dimming into the blackness, Marcos tied to the road.

One of the most prevalent sounds in Cherán on a typical autumn day is that of hammers clubbing nails into wood. The hammers are wielded by *norteños* who have returned from the States after a season's work and are transforming American dollars into the material symbol of their migrant success: the addition of a second story to their homes. Some families are even going for a third story. Along the dirt streets where packs of barefoot kids play alongside emaciated stray dogs, there is the bustle of construction. Trucks pull up in front of migrant residences and deposit loads of lumber, iron reinforcing rods, bricks, sand. Everyone's in on the action. Teenagers wield shovels, women and children carry buckets of water, grandparents hoist small piles of wood. There is great gaiety in the work, because it really isn't work at all. There is no gringo *patrón* overseeing the job. And the finished product will be enjoyed not by some white middle-class family that will never invite the migrant laborers to dinner. These rooms will be inhabited by the migrants themselves. Soon the shouts of children will echo along freshly painted hallways. In the evenings there'll be whispers and grunts and groans in the bedrooms. The whole family will sit before a Samsung TV with the volume turned up full-blast so that the voices of Scully and Mulder can be heard clear out to the middle of the street. And if you happen to be walking by you'll see the ghostly light of the tube flashing through homemade curtains.

Look down on Cherán from the hills ringing the town and you can practically watch the houses grow, the rusty reinforcing rods jutting up, the men placing brick atop brick, the new roof crowning the achievement.

The Enríquezes are a *norteño* family, the most talked-about family in town next to La Licuadora and El Músico, and, like the coyote ring leaders, they are adored and loathed, envied and maligned. I first caught sight of the Enríquez clan one afternoon while I was sitting down to my usual lunch of charred chicken at Salvador Romero's place. Suddenly I heard the unmistakable *thud . . . thud-thud . . . thud . . . thud-thud* of a hip-hop bass line pumping from an unseen source on the highway. The rumbling grew louder, like the approach of a Cherán thunderstorm, entirely drowning out the *pirekua* music crackling through Salvador's vintage transistor radio.

Then they appeared: a fleet of four gleaming Chevy Silverado trucks cruising slowly, very slowly down the highway. The tinted windows were open only slightly, so I couldn't see the drivers. But I did catch the tailgate of the last truck, bearing a beautiful airbrushed rendition of Jesus crowned with thorns, soulful eyes looking up toward the Father. Below him was a Wisconsin license plate.

It was an awe-inspiring sight, even for a place as turbulently transcultural as Cherán.

"You haven't met the Enríquezes yet?" Salvador asked me incredulously as the trucks made a left up a cobblestone street and disappeared. "Everyone knows them. They just drove down from . . . where is it they work? Wisconsin, I think."

A while later, I am in the Enríquez house, sitting on a tiny stool, the household whirling with activity around me. Kids push wheelbarrows to and fro. Bags of cement crowd the blue-tiled floor of the living room. Out on the patio not one but two washing machines slosh away, next to a grinding cement mixer. The family is putting the finishing touches on the second story of the second house on the same property. They added a second floor to their original house a few years back. Both structures are painted a handsome, rather American Southwest pastel that, I am told with great pride, is called "coral." The windows of the new house, currently being installed by local workers hired by the Enríquezes, are modern, with brass frames and blue-tinted glass. There is a large carport between the two structures, the whole enclosed by a twelve-foot wall topped with shards of glass. This last touch—the aesthetics of security—makes the property look much like a typical upper-class household in any Latin American capital.

The design of the second floor of the back house is more Mission-lyrical than the conventional rectangle of the one out front. Three large arches loop before a long, open-air corridor. A narrow iron exterior staircase spirals between the two floors. About halfway up the wall that shields the property from the street and neighbors, there is an altar, a small, half-oval enclosure where votive candles burn before a statuette of Jesus, casting wavering shadows over the patio at night. A bougain-villea spills over a planter in the middle of the carport. Draped over the staircase railing and hanging from several lines strung between the arches, the family's drying clothes, including about a dozen pairs of jeans, seem a rainbow quilt against the understated stucco. Two washers but no dryer. Not yet, anyway.

"We feel great now that we're home," says the patriarch, Santiago Enríquez, who wears a sleeveless T-shirt, a pair of bright green jeans, and rubber sandals. Despite the commotion, he looks as relaxed as can be. There is a thick gold bracelet on his right wrist, a gold watch on his left. He's got a great paunch but also the bulging arms of a butcher. He, his wife, María, their five children, and their four daughters-in-law all work at a meatpacking plant in Norwalk, Wisconsin. I have never heard of Norwalk, Wisconsin, but it appears to have done right by the Enríquez family.

The eldest son, Santiago Jr., takes a break from plastering and sits down next to his father. He fixes me with a hard look, apparently try-ing to discern just what threat this outsider represents to his father and clan. He is taller than his father, less paunchy and even burlier. In typical *norteño* fashion, he's adopted American inner-city style. Thick gold chains hang from his neck over a black T-shirt. He wears a leather cap backwards, the way the pride of Compton, Ice Cube, does, black jeans, and brown leather motorcycle boots; and he's grown a wispy goatee on his chin (not easy for an Indian). By local standards, he does not look very Purépecha; his build, in fact, makes him look more like a Samoan gangsta rapper from Long Beach. San-tiago Jr.'s three brothers are all cut from the same cloth. Woe to locals who challenge these men to an arm-wrestling match or, for that matter, a car stereo duel. They cruise up and down the mile-long stretch of highway in their Silverados a few times a week, just to make sure that everyone knows they're in town. When they walk around the plaza, they do so side by side, like gunslingers. Their act is incredibly persuasive. I am told that the brothers never get into a fight. Everyone's too scared of them.

As Santiago Jr. and his brothers realize that I just want to hear about their path toward migrant success, the hard looks give way. Santiago Sr. leans back and with pride tells of the routes, the jobs, the years. Arkansas in '78, cutting down pine trees. Then Nacogdoches, Texas, near the Louisiana border, also pines. There were stints in Florida, Illinois, Kentucky, Michigan, California: oranges, chiles, tomatoes, cucumbers, tobacco. By the time of the Immigration Reform and Control Act of 1986, which allowed over two million undocumented immigrants, mostly Mexican, to legalize their status, he'd done enough time in the States to qualify for amnesty and gain legal residency and green cards for most of the family. Still, the youngest children lacked papers; they'd lived in Mexico while their parents and older siblings worked in the States and hadn't qualified yet. In 1987, the torch of Mexican migrant optimism guiding them, Santiago Sr. led the remaining Enríquezes, including his daughter, Marta, who was seven at the time, across the Rio Grande illegally and wandered through the desert for seven days and seven nights. They followed the harvests, riding the highways in a van loaded down with pots and pans and blankets. There were times, Santiago admits, when they were *bien tristes*; he even had to beg for money at one point.

"But now," he says, "I don't have to ask for anything."

Santiago Sr. first heard of Norwalk, Wisconsin, through the migrant grapevine, the rumors of work that constantly ripple through the community in the United States. Word was that a meatpacking plant was hiring. All the able-bodied of the clan, except wife, María, and daughter, Marta, signed on at the Valley Pride Meat Plant, seven in all, each averaging $10 an hour apiece. Simple math reveals that the family collectively made $70 an hour, ten hours a day, six days a week, some forty-five weeks a year. That's about $189,000 a year, an upper-middle-class wage for a working-class family. They bought a house in Norwalk. They have their property in Cherán. They have their cars. Today, the entire family is legal, and they travel back and forth across the border with ease. And yet, it would be inaccurate to call the Enríquezes middle-class in the true American sense. First of all, the American middle class would never consider them their social peers. And then the family's relative success is the result of a collective economy. What white suburban middle-class family—parents and adult children—works together in a meatpacking plant, lives together in the same house, pools its money, and allows only the father to make important financial decisions? The Enríquezes have molded their American dream according to Purépecha principles. Then again, one of the defining characteristics of the American middle class is the ideal and practice of mobility in pursuit of the bigger house, the nicer neighborhood, the family vacation, and a golden retirement. In this sense, the Enríquezes are profoundly American.

Ever since their first family trip north, the Enríquezes have continued to make all their crossings together as a unit. They like to keep their caravan of five Silverados together—the road back to Cherán can be as dangerous as the road to the States.

"The *federales* try to take advantage of us when we return home," says Santiago Jr.

The *federales*, Mexico's infamous federal police, charge exorbitantly for permits to enter the country with American cars, not counting the bribes exacted at several checkpoints along the route home. There's also the risk of falling prey to the bandits that scour the main north-south highways in the fall, at the end of the American harvest, when tens of thousands of migrants return. The bandits know that the migrants are bringing home new cars, appliances, and cash. And so the Enríquezes blaze along the highways together in their wagon train, stopping only to eat and go to the bathroom.

All the Chevys are '89 models in mint condition. Roberto's is the one with the Jesus mural. From close up, the savior's visage hovers surreally over a blacktop highway bisected by broken white lines. On that road is another truck, a replica of Roberto's own, only it has the word MICHOACAN airbrushed on the tailgate instead of Jesus' image.

Like his brothers, Roberto bought his truck unmodified and started adding on accessories paycheck by paycheck. That was the one luxury their father allowed; the rest of their pay was conscientiously saved. First came the black rubber running boards, American Racing rims, wide-track radial tires, and a spoiler over the cab. Then the paint job, metallic magenta with blue-green highlights. And, of course, the powerful CD player and the tinted windows.

Santiago Sr., not to be outdone by his son, has a red-and-white truck that features the Last Supper on its tailgate. And then there's Jacinto's metallic-silver truck, and Enríque's ocean-blue, and Santiago Jr.'s pearl-white paint job with an airbrushed depiction of Cherán. There they all stand in a row for all the townsfolk to admire, parked not in the freshly cemented carport but out front, atop the potholed street, before the coral mansion with tinted blue windows.

When the Enríquezes finish work on their property—probably next year—the two houses will have a total of nine bedrooms, bathrooms with hot and cold running water, dining rooms and living rooms in each. "Little by little, each year a little more," Santiago Sr. says. "But it's been hard to finish it." This year, he's spent 80,000 pesos—over $10,000. All in all, it's taken fifteen years to develop the Enríquez property.

"I don't think I'll spend too many more years up north," he says. "Maybe ten more. And then I'll come back here to enjoy what I've made, if God grants me the years."

Jacinto, half a life younger than his father, shares the vision. "I'll make some more cash," he says, "and return."

This notion runs contrary to the classic American migrant narrative. Many European and Asian first generationers dreamed of returning home but wound up dying on American soil; the American future swallowed their Old World past with the incentives of pensions and Social Security and the amenities of life in the First World. But for increasing numbers of Mexicans, the idea of retiring to the Old Country is more attractive, and not just because of the social status of Mexican migrants in the United States. Here, Santiago Sr. says, there is more freedom. He can play his Mexican music as loud as he wants, whenever he wants. He can drink a beer on the sidewalk in front of his house or—why not?—carouse about the plaza at three in the morning. The cops won't stop you. They'll probably join you.

"It's a more delicate issue up there. I've learned how the Americans are," he says, pointing at his head with his index finger. American-style democracy, it seems, doesn't quite translate, at least culturally, to Cheranes like Santiago. Thus, the members of the Enríquez clan come back to enjoy their freedom a few weeks a year. They come back to finish their dream home. And they come to replenish their spirits' reservoir of memory for the long months in Norwalk, Wisconsin. The irony is that "home" is beginning to look more and more like Wisconsin, something that the Enríquezes prefer not to dwell on.

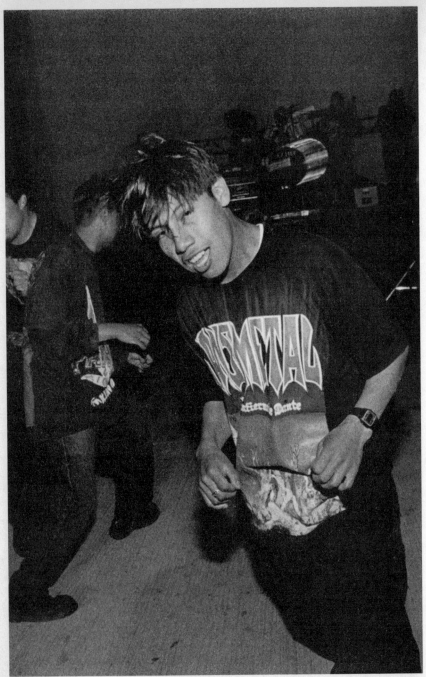

Joseph Rodriguez

5

HIGHLAND
HIP HOP

Güiro is standing guard over his posse, looking up and down the highway. When a car cruises past the auto body shop that is his *cholo* crew's official hangout, he juts out his chin, on which he's grown a King Tut–like tuft of hair, and stares. He wears a beanie low over his eyes and a Fila T-shirt under his Bulls jacket. I'm trying to talk to him about how life is different on the two sides of the border, but it's hard to compete with the whine of oldies tunes (at the moment, Ritchie Valens's "Donna") pumping into his headphones from a Sony Discman.

He tells me he's not supposed to be hanging out on the street after nine o'clock. The local police imposed a curfew on him in response to the clamor of elders demanding that the authorities do something about the *cholos* tagging up the town, picking fights with nonmigrant teenagers, and wooing Cherán's virginal fourteen-year-olds with their cool northern style.

"I'm wanted on both sides of the border," Güiro says with an outlaw's pride. I suppose that he's exaggerating when he says he's got a court date in L.A. next week. He mentions a stint of one month and four days in the Correctional Training Facility in Soledad, California—

a claim that certainly sounds far-fetched. No one does only a month in state prison unless there's been some bureaucratic mistake. I don't know if Güiro is a legal or illegal migrant, and I don't ask. (Either way, he would have broken the law by leaving the United States with a pending legal proceeding.)

A local drunk, a nonmigrant, judging by his disheveled highland look, stumbles toward us. Güiro stiffens. *"Y tú, ¿quién te crees, puto?"* Who do you think you are, faggot? The drunk manages a slurred challenge. *"¡Ni sabes con quien hablas, güey!"* hisses Güiro. You have no idea who you're talking to, you dumb fuck. The drunk stands there, rocking back and forth on his heels for a few seconds, taking this in. He mutters something under his breath and starts off down the highway, past Güiro and his crew of *mocosos*, kids who emulate him in dress and speech and petty crime.

"Soy tu sombra, güey," calls out the drunk over his shoulder. I'm your shadow, you dumb fuck. It's a great line, but it doesn't amount to much of a threat. Güiro owns the highway tonight.

These are the kids Cherán's elders fear and loathe, the *cholos* transforming the Michoacán outback into inner-city America. This particular clique calls itself "La Raza" (The Race, a term Mexicans often use to refer to themselves, even though mestizos aren't technically a race at all), and they claim membership in "Sur XIII" (South 13), the umbrella gang that every Mexican migrant from Michoacán to Wisconsin belongs to. (Thus, Mexican gang members are generally referred to as *sureños*, southerners, while Mexican Americans are called *norteños*, notherners—not to be confused with term that denotes migrant status in provincial Mexico—and there is more than a little enmity between them.) These kids are not the AK-47-toting, drug-dealing kind. They talk the talk, walk the walk, wear the clothes, sport the "tats," but in the States they rarely get into trouble beyond the occasional barroom brawl or DUI. Here in Cherán, they look mean and hard sauntering down the dusty streets and they scare a number of the locals, but they're usually home before the church bells toll nine o'clock, sitting with their *abuelas*, bantering in Purépecha, model Michoacán kids. The ranks of La Raza thin out during work season up north. But now with October's fiesta approaching, they are big enough to make a show of force.

There's no glue sniffing or rock cocaine among La Raza, and this is due to Cherán's overall innocence of drugs. Even pot is hard to find in the Purépecha highlands. Whatever is cultivated here is consumed by the gringos or Mexico City hipsters and only rarely by the Indians themselves. As for the all-important gang tattoos, only a couple of the kids have them, and these are hidden under shirts and pants—hidden, that is, from the kids' parents. The crew talks about fights in the north, in Pico Rivera, the Los Angeles working-class suburb in which two of the gang's elder members live for the better part of the year. But the violence sounds like it's out of another era. Fists, sometimes a knife. One kid boasts of kicking someone in the gut with a steel-toed boot. But no guns.

The auto shop where the kids hang out is owned by a guy named Chaco who is no cholo and who, in fact, often makes fun of the kids and their Chicano ways. Chaco happens, though, to own a beautiful 1986 deep blue Camaro with a personalized California license plate emblazoned with AARON1—Aaron is his Christian name—and so the kids adore him. Chaco himself claims no gang affiliation and dresses down compared with the kids. He tolerates them because he's making money off them, selling, along with auto lubricants and spare parts, sneakers and baseball caps, items he buys from a vendor in Zamora. "There's a demand," he says. "Even the kids who've never made it past Zamora want a pair of shoes, a baseball cap that says 'Raiders.' It would be bad business to ignore them."

Despite his standing among the *norteño* kids, Chaco is something of a Purépecha nationalist. He doesn't speak Purepécha, the language of Indian Michoacán, doesn't even understand it. Light-complected, he's clearly mestizo. And he listens to a combination of house and *banda* music, loves Chevys. But, says Chaco: "I'm 100 percent Purépecha." So someone who defines himself as 100 percent Purépecha simultaneously helps the kids of Cherán maintain their aesthetic connection to East L.A.

And it doesn't stop at aesthetics. True, Cherán is not Zamora, which like other midsized provincial cities has a fairly hard-core gangsta scene. The local chapter of Sur XIII in Zamora is a truly fearsome set of glue-sniffing kids who've committed their share of violent felonies. I hung with them one night, a privilege I had to buy in the form of several bottles of rot-gut mescal. The Zamora kids were clearly on the edge of self-destruction, a menace to themselves and to others. They lamented their station in life, trying as they were to be true cholos in the provinces. "If only we had guns!" the crew leader told me. "If only we had guns!"

In Cherán, though, the signs are there. One cop told me that he doesn't feel good about tossing local teens in jail—he knows each kid's parents by name—but that the situation demanded action. If the local authorities have already pinned a curfew on Güiro, such a tactic against the entire La Raza clique might not be far behind—yet another way in which Cherán is coming to resemble the cities of the north.

Before he left, Wense recommended that I look up his friend Alfredo Román, who had just returned from the States after several years in Missouri and Illinois. "He's a *norteño*, but a good man," Wense said. "I learned a lot from him."

So one afternoon I stop by Alfredo's, which is easy to find because Wense told me to simply look for a smoke-gray 1983 Buick Regal parked in front of a house a block off the highway. When I arrive, Alfredo, who is thirty years old, is leaning on his ride, knocking back a few beers with a group of younger Cheranes admiring the car. Gray trim, Krager rims, darkly tinted windows. It strikes me that Alfredo is a lot like José Izquierdo; he fancies himself a migrant outlaw. But unlike José, Alfredo has struck a bargain with the life. He dresses like a gangsta, he drives a tricked-out gangsta's car, he's down with the home-boys of the Sur XIII clique he helped start up in St. Louis ten years ago, when he was still a youngster on the migrant trail, but he's also a married father of two and a foreman at the greenhouse nursery where he works. A responsible cholo. In the borderlands, that is no oxymoron.

Alfredo's parents went north with a couple of older siblings while he was still a toddler, leaving him with his maternal grandmother. Years went by. Alfredo came to call his grandmother "*mamá*"; she raised him until the day she died. When his real mother arrived for the funeral, she asked him, "Why don't you call me *mamá*?" He answered: "Because you don't even know your own son."

The reunited family followed the harvests to Murphysboro, Illinois, where they lived in a trailer and picked apples. The young Alfredo was a loner. "There was nothing but *bolillos* in that town," he says, using a slang term for gringos—"white bread." There's no love lost between Alfredo and gringos. "I've never had a white friend," he says. "Bunch of racists."

He quit high school, met and fell in love with a migrant girl who was also from Cherán. The young couple moved to St. Louis and worked like the devil. In the U.S. legally, this is the first time he's been home in several years.

"I just wanted to see what things were like," Alfredo says. "I figured if I didn't come this year, I might never come back. So here I am."

Among the cholos fawning over Alfredo is a kid nicknamed "Coco," the tag he uses on the walls of both St. Louis and Cherán. Ten years younger than Alfredo, he's enthusiastic about life on the other side. "You can have a good time up there," he says. He bought an '82 Oldsmobile this year on his fruit picker's salary. "Everyone down here dreams of having a car like that, but you just can't do it in Cherán. Down here, they've only seen cars like mine in the movies." As if on cue, two Silverados cruise by us slowly. The Enríquez brothers.

"They're acting like they're all that," says Coco. "But they work in a stinking meatpacking plant. At least I don't smell like a cow when I come home from work."

But the harsh words don't amount to much—here in Cherán, anyway. As more teenagers gather around us, the talk turns to the gangsta scene in St. Louis, the tensions between the cliques from Michoacán and Zacatecas, natural rivals. Coco mentions the black gangs in East St. Louis. The guns, the drugs, the deadly encounters on the streets.

"It's not like that down here," Coco says. "Here, it's all show. Imagine if it was for real, with guys from the Parikutín barrio challenging the guys from Amaru. No way! Down here, they don't even know how to tag up a wall right."

An old Indian woman in a rebozo trudges past us, carrying a small wooden table over her shoulder. "Buy table?" she whispers, in heavily Purépecha-accented Spanish. The boys are quiet for several moments, watching as she takes step after painful step up the cobblestone street.

Alfredo asks if we want to go for a ride. Seven of us pile into the pristine white vinyl interior of the Buick. Alfredo drives the entire block and a half to Ven a México, the bar presided over by Salvador. In honor of the upcoming fiesta, Salvador has decorated the place with checkered tablecloths and plastic roses in plastic vases.

The afternoon turns to a long, languid evening of drinking, the beer bottles collecting on our table like bowling pins, as if we're vacationing at Lake Pátzcuaro or at the beach. And it is a vacation, the only vacation Cherán's migrants ever have—coming home for fiesta. The talk at the drinking well never varies. Not just for my benefit or through any prompting on my part, the main conversation is about migration, about the good and bad points of life down here or up there—a conversation almost always decided in favor of there.

But now, Salvador plays devil's advocate. "Come back home, my sons," he lisps melodramatically. "They're just exploiting you. That thing you call a future is an illusion." He talks bitterly of his own experience with the gringos, "their discrimination, their bad influences, their silly freedom and drugs."

The migrant kids scoff at him.

"Just because it went bad for you doesn't mean it's bad for us," Alfredo retorts.

Later, we float out into the cool air and back into the Buick.

"Time for cruising," Alfredo says, switching on the CD player and blasting a rap tune by Crucial Conflict:

It's just an everyday thing in my neighborhood . . .

Alfredo's is the only car cruising the highway tonight. The Enríquez brothers are nowhere to be seen; they're probably wooing some pretty local girls down at the plaza. We stop by a store and buy a bottle of *charanda*, a powerful regional cane liquor, and a jug of horrid-tasting artificial orange drink as a mixer. Under the dim amber of the two street lamps that illuminate Cherán's one-mile length of highway, Alfredo cruises the Buick at five, maybe ten miles an hour, as far north as the church, as far south as the gas station. On this Saturday night in Los Angeles, Oakland, Chicago, Miami, even St. Louis, there are Latino and African American kids on similar rides, also pumping the hip-hop bass, honking their horns at pretty girls, throwing hard looks at rival gangstas.

Alfredo slips in a Tupac Shakur CD, and suddenly the kids are debating, in minute detail, the various possible scenarios behind the late hip-hop legend's assassination.

"It was payback between Bloods and Crips."

"Nah, Suge Knight sent someone to get him."

"I heard that it had to do with some Mafia guys in Las Vegas."

"Maybe it was the Mexican Mafia? Didn't he rap on the last album about blacks and Mexicans getting together?"

The what-ifs. Tupac had a bullet-proof vest with him that night—why didn't he use it? The could-have-beens. Hadn't Tupac said that he wanted to leave the life behind? Hadn't he had a conversion in prison when he did time on that bum sexual-assault rap? The implacability of it all: Tupac had survived a previous attack in which he'd taken a bullet to the head and had lived on for nearly a week after the shooting in Vegas. It had seemed like he was going to pull through again.

The kids turn the story over and over again, mesmerized by the urban epic. But Alfredo, leaning back in the front seat and steering with only the index finger of his right hand, remains quiet, in his own world. Finally, he speaks.

"You punks don't know anything," he says cuttingly. "You just don't know."

And it is obvious that Alfredo does. He turns the volume on the stereo up so loud that we feel the bass pumping as if it were our own hearts, and we cruise like that for a long while along the highway, above the plain that stretches to the horizon, the black night of the Paracho Valley broken only by the tiniest clusters of city-stars in the distance, most of them small towns, smaller than Cherán, but like Cherán in every other way.

I'm standing in the midday sun at the junction of the highway and the access road to Jocotepec, a small town some seventy-five miles north of Cherán whose only claim to fame is its proximity to Ajijic, a popular resort on the shores of picturesque Lake Chapala. Jocotepec is in the state of Jalisco, which neighbors Michoacán to the north. These are lowlands, and the climate is gentler here, warmer and more humid than in Cherán. But the social climate resembles that of Michoacán in many ways. Jalisco, like Michoacán, is among the top four migrant "sender" states in Mexico.

I am waiting, in vain, for a ride into town, which is a long mile off the highway. I spy on a young couple on the other side of the road, a rather ragged boy hanging all over a pretty provincial girl. He's dusty-haired, she's got an Aqua Net do. His shirt is hanging out, her dress is ankle-length. I can hear the bus coming from a long way off, and the guy gets more and more agitated as it approaches. The brakes squeal. The bus blocks my view. The motor groans into first gear again and slowly moves on.

Now he is there alone, standing like a stricken Bogart, looking after the bus until it is out of sight and the blast of the motor fades away. Only then does he cross the highway, passing within five feet of me, making brief eye contact, heading straight for the roadside store.

I wait another ten minutes and then head over to the store myself, thinking of getting a bottle of water for the now-inevitable walk into town. He is there, drinking a Modelo beer from a plastic cup. He's a handsome young man, despite the weathered, grimy look of someone who's been on the road a long time. Silky blond hair, a faint scar over his left eye, a sparse mustache that looks even lighter than his long, bright mane. Suddenly, unexpectedly, he's got his arm around my neck and he's telling me that we'll walk into town together. He just got his hair cut, he tells me. "I had it past my ass before. The town didn't like that too much. But I didn't cut it for the old fucks. I cut it because I felt like cutting it, you know?"

He introduces himself as Ambrosio. Fast friends, we walk past abandoned houses and fallow fields and cicada-singing trees, until Ambrosio pulls me into an empty, weedy lot. Across the way is a long, low building with a corrugated tin roof. The walls are unpainted concrete. It is the town whorehouse. But at four in the afternoon on a Sunday, not a prostitute in the world is awake. We sit on the floor with our backs to the cantina wall, waiting for the bartender to show up and slake Ambrosio's thirst.

He's in a bad way. Twenty-eight years old, apparently alcoholic, 3,000 pesos in the bank—borrowed money that he suggests he, in turn, is loan-sharking out. But things weren't always like this. At fifteen, Ambrosio made his first trip north, crossing successfully under the cover of night in Tijuana. *Quería hacer algo*—he wanted to make something of himself—as the Mexican migrants say. His brothers already had. Both had studied at the University of Guadalajara, one becoming a schoolteacher, the other an engineer. As the youngest, he'd had the weight of their success bearing down on him. Fifteen years old and nowhere to go but north; he just wasn't cut out for school. His father, a worn-down man who'd worked the land all his life, gave the young Ambrosio his uninspired blessing. "Who knows if you'll have good luck or not?" he told his son at the bus stop.

Then came the days without food or shelter or money, sleeping outdoors. He made his way to Santa Barbara, where a distant relative put him up. But work wasn't easy to come by, and the blonde beach bunnies weren't giving him the time of day, so he headed farther north, hanging out at 7-Elevens along the way, panhandling like he'd seen the gringos do.

He arrived in San Jose, California, looking for an uncle. He had no phone or address, but his one artistic talent served him well. He sketched a profile of his relative, took it around the Mexican barrios for a few days, and lo, he found him. The uncle showed him the ropes of hard migrant work and hard migrant partying, taking him to cantinas and table-dance bars; at one, Ambrosio lost his virginity to an African American woman. That's how he learned that all the women of the world are beautiful— Chinese, Arab, African, white—though after all these years on the road he now swears he will marry and have children only with a Mexican girl. "I have to do something for my *raza*," he says.

Once the cantina opens, I buy him a beer. He buys me three more, all of which I must accept and drink because the code of the cantina is sacred and refusing a drink is an invitation to bad feelings or worse. We are the only ones here, served by an effeminate teenage boy who bats his eyelashes at me. Ambrosio asks the boy if he "works," and the boy testily says no, "I only serve drinks."

Now Ambrosio tells me of an attempted-murder rap. "Yeah, I stuck the nigger," he says, in between sips of beer. "Stuck the blade into his stomach and clean up into his lungs."

Two and a half years in Folsom, followed by deportation, which included a free flight to Guadalajara. He arrived with $500 in his pocket—every cent to his name after five years in the States.

Suddenly an old campesino appears, literally out of nowhere—I didn't see him enter the doorway, he's just there, hovering over our table, hat in hands, quiet, sad. Ambrosio sighs and says that it's his grandfather.

"You didn't come to eat," the old man says softly.

"I'll be there, I'll be there," Ambrosio dismisses him, without looking up.

The old man repeats himself. And so does Ambrosio. Now the old man is trembling. With age, with sadness, with shame. Or maybe he's an old alcoholic too? He is looking down at the floor and does not acknowledge my presence. The gay kid watches from behind the bar. The old man waits a while longer and finally turns away and slowly, achingly makes his way back outside.

The sun is setting. A pure gold light shines through the small windows that ring the cantina, and its beauty turns the place momentarily into a church with panes aglow.

What does my life have to do with that old man, Ambrosio snorts. My adventures, my madness, my bloody hands, my asshole gringo *patrones*, my black girls in San Jose, what does anything in my life have to do with that old, ignorant man? Him and his farm animals and his cornstalks?

A couple of beers later, Ambrosio relents. I am a romantic because he was a romantic before me. I must travel the road he quit. I returned to this dusty town because, in the end, his animals and his cornstalks are mine too, and they are a beautiful thing, no? Are they not beautiful, my friend?

"I am independent of his generation, and yet I depend on his generation," Ambrosio says, with the wisdom of a mature man.

Where to now?

Canada, says Ambrosio. Canada.

So Ambrosio will go north again, but this time he won't fuck up, he's not fifteen years old anymore. He'll go north and then he'll come back. Funny how it goes: you leave home precisely because you have to return. Or you return because you have to leave. Something like that. May they bury me here, in my land, *México, ¡ay, ay, ay!*

With all the talk of the amorality unleashed on Cherán by wayward youth returning from the United States, now is probably not the best moment for the *rockeros* to stage the first-ever rock concert in the town's history. There's plenty of rock music in Michoacán—on the airwaves, in the record stores, on the Walkmans belonging to the kids strolling the streets and even to the young peasants wielding machetes in the fields. There are also a fair number of concerts in the region, especially in Zamora, which name acts include on their tours, and even occasionally in Paracho, the town southwest of Cherán. It's curious that Paracho is a *rockero* site, given its international fame as the home of the best crafters of acoustic guitars in all of Mexico. With these guitars, Mexicans young and old alike strum bolero and ballad rhythms for Old World serenades.

In a sense, *banda* music has laid the foundation for rock 'n' roll in Cherán. Both *bandas de vientos*, European-style brass bands, and modern *banda* groups, playing a ¾ polka beat with electric bass, guitars, and synthesizers, are hybrids of Old and New World style and instrumentation. The brass bands play instrumental versions of regional hits, some dating back a century or more. They tour the streets and accompany Saint Francis's daily processions, as well as play at the numerous wedding parties that are traditionally held at fiesta time. The contemporary *banda* groups are even more mestizo than the original groups that appropriated nineteenth-century European instrumentation and married it to regional tonalities. Today, *banda* is just one step away from rock 'n' roll. There is a resurgent national *banda* craze, partly because of the intensely physical—and intensely sexual—form of dance called *quebradita* (loosely, break dancing). Significantly, the craze initially took off not in Mexico but in the migrant barrios of Los Angeles. The aficionados of *banda* might be flush with Mexican pride when they don their cowboy hats, but in the end, this music is all about the whirlwind of migration and its influence on culture.

Rock 'n' roll, though, is another story. Despite mainstream acceptance of bubble-gum pop, the real thing can still cause horror among Mexico's elders, like Elvis scandalizing Eisenhower's America—especially in the conservative provinces. The young people producing Cherán's rock concert say that there is nothing to worry about. One of the organizers, Dante Cerano, is a deejay at XEPUR and, as far as he knows, the sole Indian jock in all of Mexico who is allowed to program—albeit only one hour a week—rock music on a state-subsidized indigenous radio station. (Urban commercial stations regularly feature rock on their playlists, but in most of the Indian provinces, there is only state-sponsored—and, therefore, state-censored—radio.)

Cerano has titled the event "Etnovidiun," a neologism combining the Spanish words for "ethnic," "life," and "unity." Cerano offers the definition: "Let the ethnics live." In other words, a rock concert proclaiming the autonomy of indigenous peoples.

The concert is held at the abandoned movie house (the local *videocentro* knocked out the old picture shows years ago). When I enter the cavernous theater, the promoters and band members are busy sweeping up huge piles of trash from the last gig, a wedding party several months ago. There are no stage lights, just a few dim fluorescents that barely light the space. A chaotic sound check ensues, with drum slaps and the whine of badly tuned guitars echoing painfully off the bare concrete walls.

All of Cherán's *rockeros* turn out for the bash—about three dozen kids in sneakers, jeans, and black concert T-shirts featuring the names and mascots of Mexico's best-known "hard" bands: Transmetal, Psicodencia, Atóxxxico, and an anarchist group from Los Angeles called Brujería (Witchcraft). Brujería's emblem includes the visage of Mexico's most famous non-Indian Indian revolutionary, Subcommander Marcos, spokesperson for the indigenous rebels of Chiapas, in his world-famous ski-masked, pipe-smoking pose. Brujería hit it big in the underground scene a few years back with barbaric songs that included lyrics about raping and dismembering the pope.

Today's featured acts, a crew of light-skinned kids from Uruapan who call themselves Mentes Vacías (Empty Minds), all backwards baseball caps and growling voices, provides the thrashing noise for the slam dancing. The kids bounce off one another with glee in the immensity of the empty, dim, dusty space. One of them takes time out to proclaim the birth of Cherán's new rock scene, even though the town doesn't have its own band yet.

"The older people criticize you for liking this music," says David Rojas, who is eighteen. "They think that it automatically makes you a drug addict. It's time they let go of those bullshit attitudes."

José Velázquez, the most Indian-looking of the bunch, lithe, dark-skinned, and Asian-eyed, says that he's fifteen and "has been a *rockero* for six years." He loves the music because "the lyrics speak about the corrupt government that treats the people badly."

Although a couple of the kids speak derisively of the *pirekua* acoustic ballads the Purépechas are famous for, most say they respect the music of their elders. "It's a way of expressing yourself without losing your roots," says Gonzalo Juárez, at twenty-one a veteran of the scene. "We like the *pirekuas* as much as the hard stuff. Maybe one day some kids from Cherán can come up with a *pirekua*-rock sound."

The concert goes off without a hitch, though it's obviously a financial disaster for the promoters, what with the dismal turnout. But for Dante Cerano and other like-minded *rockeros* in Cherán, this is just the beginning.

After the show, I share a couple of beers with Cerano at Salvador Romero's place. Cerano tells me that rock is not just some passing fad. It is at the center of Mexico's cultural and political wars. Cerano, with his gig at XEPUR, is on the frontlines of the battle. The state-sponsored indigenous radio stations are bastions of Mexican nationalism—a peculiar, depoliticized brand of it that leftist critics have long condemned as the government's attempt to keep the Indian population docile. Part of the government's long-standing effort to create an official "national culture," the project focuses on folkloric, premodern traditions. The practitioners of traditional culture—healers, dancers, artisans, fiesta organizers—who follow the government's line are rewarded handsomely with grants, and those who don't are marginalized. It's a policy that the PRI employed effectively over its seven decades in power and whose purpose has only recently been called into question by the Zapatistas and other sectors of the burgeoning civil society movement that includes independent unions, student groups, and even middle-class citizens who've been crushed by the economic crisis.

Rock 'n' roll, a cultural sensation crafted largely by poor kids with a cynical attitude toward government—and with plenty of rebellious energy—is regarded with great suspicion in official circles. And Dante Cerano, a striking-looking young man whose skin tone lies somewhere between the chocolate brown of his pure Indian brethren and the tan of the mestizos, is thus a pioneer in the Purépecha highlands. A rebel to be co-opted or snuffed out. So far, the local authorities have been able to do neither, because it is clear that he has the support of Purépecha youth. The authorities are still trying to figure out what to do with him. Meanwhile, he keeps spinning the devil's music.

Cerano himself is the embodiment of the clashing and melding that define Purépecha identity in the twenty-first century. Completely bilingual, speaking a flawless Purépecha and a Spanish peppered not just with the usual regionalisms but with urbanspeak from Mexico City.

Cerano has much to say about the transformation of ancient Purépecha culture under the influence of *mestizaje* and migration. What's survived is something more than rebozos, dances, and recipes—these, in the end, are just metaphors for—he searches for the word—a *philosophy*, a way of seeing the world, the mores, and the values that Purépechas share as a people. Such as collectivism and solidarity, clearly visible in certain rituals, like the *cosecha*, the autumn harvest, in which the entire town of Cherán participates, old and young, male and female, rich and poor. "It's more than work—it's tradition, it's celebration, a community event." Solidarity of this sort can be a people's saving grace but also a vulnerability that stifles individual pursuit, as in the indigenous elders' disapproval of their rebellious young.

There is always a tension between culture and class, Cerano continues. Class dictates the material conditions of life and, under the harshest circumstances, can give rise to cynicism, fatalism, apathy—or rebellion. The Purépechas chose the latter, and their rebellion is migration itself. Through migration, they can improve the material conditions of their lives and also transform their culture. Through culture, people create their identity, their sense of place in the world; they tell their own stories with the aesthetic of their choosing. According to Cerano, a conquered people can regain their self-image by sorting through what remains of pre-Conquest history—for not all was lost, not all is irredeemable—and by taking stock of what the conqueror offers. What occurs in the cultural sphere is also inherently a political act, a public expression of desire and will.

The migrant culture of the Purépechas is emblematic of what is happening all across Mexico and in many parts of the developing world today. Cerano seems to be saying that the Purépechas can have their cake and eat it, too: they can partake in—indeed, be protagonists of— transnational or "global" culture even as they nurture the vestiges of their roots. In this context, the regional is global and vice-versa.

There has been more than one conquest in Mexico's history, Cerano says. By the Spaniards, the French, and generations of their *criollo* offspring (who to this day rule the nation, politically and economically), and of course by the Americans. For a century and a half, by the Americans, and today more than ever. But to paraphrase a couple of old Latin American proverbs, no ill here lasts a millennium and there's no soul that can't be saved.

"Rock 'n' roll among the Purépecha," Cerano says, "can be a measure of our being conquered. But it can also become a measure of our independence." After all, didn't rock 'n' roll serve as a kind of cultural liberation—and part of a political one, exploding as it did at the very birth of the civil rights movement in America?

As Cerano continues his riff, I find myself thinking of Otis Redding's subversive version of "White Christmas."

"We are indigenous people who know our culture," Cerano says. "Rock is an international form that lends itself to different cultural settings. Here in the highlands, it is a music that speaks to the passions and anxieties of young people who are seeing the rapid changes in the world around them, even if they haven't left Michoacán."

In Michoacán, Elvis has not yet left the building.

Another funeral in Cherán.

This time, it's for a venerable matriarch. Death always brings the better part of Cherán down to the cemetery. The thousands of wooden crosses and stones leaning this way and that make for a cluttered, claustrophobic tableau. There is practically no space left for the newly dead. I pay a visit to the Chávez brothers' graves. The Chávezes might not have their tombstones, but they do have the shade of the majestic cherry tree and the sibilance of the wind through its leaves. Their graves, covered with concrete slabs, will endure the elements better than will those of the poor, with their foot-high crosses of unfinished pine, which rarely last more than a few rainy seasons.

As the funeral party breaks up after the first clods of dark earth are shoveled into the new grave, I notice a kid I once saw hanging at one of the local cantinas with José Izquierdo. He's wearing impossibly baggy jeans, an oversize T-shirt, and a fresh buzz cut. He also has tinted prescription glasses. He's obviously *norteño*. I try to strike up a conversation in Spanish, but he responds in English.

"My Spanish ain't so good," says the kid, who introduces himself as

ndrés) Tapia, a distant relative of the dead matriarch. We
English, getting quizzical looks from the bereaved peasants
Andy doesn't speak your garden-variety immigrant's American English. He speaks it like a native—with the unmistakable laid-
back, softly melodic drawl of an Arkansan.

"Well, I was born in Michoacán," he says, "but I really grew up in
Arkansas, y'know."

A little while later, I am in the Tapia home, just a couple of blocks
up the hill from the cemetery. The family sits in the dim, blue-walled
kitchen around the large table—kitchen tables are always big in Mexico;
this is no American 2.5-kids-per-household country. They eat the typical Purépecha meal of *churipo*, to which I am graciously invited. I'm
soon sweating from the nuclear-grade red-chile broth in which the soft
chunks of beef and cabbage have been stewing for hours.

Around the table are the patriarch, Raúl, a stocky, dark Indian man
in his fifties with an acne-scarred face and small, plaintive eyes. His
wife, Yolanda, pleasantly plump, carries herself with the self-confidence
of Cherán women who've long lived on the other side. There are five
children. The youngest is Maribel, sixteen, a pretty girl with a quick
smile and big eyes as black as her shiny hair. Adán is nineteen, the
tallest of the kids, with a hip haircut long on top and buzzed on the
sides. Raúl Jr. is chubby like Andrés and sports a cut like Adán's. Jordán
is the oldest at twenty-five, and he plays the part, smart and somewhat
aloof. Andrés is the quietest of the bunch except when I speak with him
one on one, a sensitive kid who's feeling out of place in Cherán and, I
sense, out of place just about anywhere in the world.

A few days ago the Tapias were sitting down to dinner together at
their home in Warren, Arkansas (population 6,455), a town surrounded
by timberlands and tomato fields about eighty miles south-southeast of
Little Rock. They packed up the van and drove east through Texarkana
and south to Laredo, where they crossed the border, paid the usual
bribes along the central route, veered west at Mexico City toward Guadalajara, and south again to Zamora for the final stretch up into the
highlands.

The Tapias don't make this journey every year. The last time they
came was in '94, before that in '92. Over time, the trips have become
less frequent. The special occasion this time is Jordán's marriage to a

local girl he's been courting long distance for several years. The ceremony will take place with all the traditional pomp and circumstance here in Cherán, and then the newlyweds will head north to Arkansas. The only member of the family who remains in Cherán is Raúl Sr.'s mother, a woman in her eighties who spends most of her days alone in this house. It is a *norteño*-style abode. Like the Enríquezes, Raúl Sr. began adding extra rooms several years ago, fantasizing about a luxurious retirement. But Raúl is no longer so certain that he'll return to Cherán in his later years. America has slowly but surely been swallowing up the Tapia family's future.

You can see it most clearly with the kids. Maribel, Adán, Raúl Jr., and Andrés stand out painfully in Cherán with their brand-name clothes, fresh faces, and halting Spanish. Only the eldest, Jordán, speaks the language well. For the younger siblings, visiting Cherán is like a vacation in some exotic locale, albeit one with an *abuela* whom they have trouble understanding.

Andrés and Jordán are the only children actually born in Michoacán. Jordán spent his first five years here, Andrés his first two. Their Michoacán past is nothing more than the memory of a distant childhood, idealized by time and their parents' tales. The Cherán of today cannot possibly match those visions. When I ask for the bathroom, Andrés sheepishly says that there is no toilet, only an outhouse.

Even Raúl Sr. finds himself complaining about the conditions in Cherán. "We miss the comforts of our other home," he says. "It's not very clean here. I even get stomach problems now. And the gasoline! It's terrible for our cars."

The family's migration began in the mid-1960s when an ambitious Raúl Sr., then a kid, headed north to try his luck. He had uncles already working in the north; there'd been migrants in his family dating back to his maternal grandfather. As a boy, Raúl had heard tall tales from the elders when they'd gather in the evenings to drink beer and smoke cigarettes.

"There was this one old guy who told me about the *migra* back in the old days," Raúl recalls. "There was a time when crossing the border was like going through the gate into a ranch. There'd be two gringos who'd ask you where you were headed and charge you nothing but a dime to get across."

The road beckoned and Raúl took to it, arriving first in the San Joaquin Valley and then in Los Angeles, before making his way eastward across the country, eventually ending up in the Deep South. Raúl Sr. is clearly infected with migrant optimism. "Within a decade," he declares, "Hispanics will be the largest minority in the United States." This statistic, which is now cited with regularity in American media, has been a Bible truth among migrants for several years; it's not the first time I've heard it quoted in the highlands. The idea is simple: power in numbers. For the better part of the twentieth century, Mexican American political power was marginal and stagnant, partially because of massive deportations that prevented migrant workers from developing social, economic, and political roots in the United States. (Gerrymandering—and ballot stuffing—worked against those who did.) But the Immigration Reform and Control Act of 1986 was a watershed event. Overnight, millions of Mexican migrants became eligible for citizenship (the Tapias early on took advantage of this amnesty), and a measure of political power came within reach.

After several years of carrying a green card, Rául Sr. will soon become a naturalized citizen and vote for everything from president all the way down to Warren's city council.

It has taken Raúl Sr. twenty years to achieve all this—twenty years on the road. He first heard of work in Arkansas on the migrant grapevine. Tomato picking, lumber mills. Warren was far away from the gangs and drugs of the big cities, dangers that worried Raúl as his children approached adolescence. He'd seen the *cholos* getting into trouble on the streets of Los Angeles; he swore to himself that his children wouldn't go that route.

When the Tapias arrived in Warren, there were only four other Mexican families living permanently in town. That was a decade ago. Now there are about sixty families, many from Cherán.

"We feel at home there," Raúl says, as strange as it might seem to hear a Mexican Indian claiming as home a good ole boy town like Warren. Indeed, Raúl Sr. sees Warren as something like the Cherán of the north. A rural town much smaller than Cherán, a verdant, peaceful place, with the pastoral rhythms that are slowly being eroded away in Cherán and the kind of intimacy big American cities never had.

After the meal, Raúl Sr. and his sons tool around in the backyard while the women clean up—at least in this sense, they are a traditional family still.

"The roots always lead me back," says Jordán. "But when I come back, I feel comfortable just for the first few days, and then I start to miss the life that I'm used to. I guess I've got roots in both places now."

Raúl Sr. has grown quiet. He is wearing his gleaming white straw cowboy hat, the one that he puts on only in Cherán. He snips at a few weeds growing at the base of a retaining wall whose tangle of iron reinforcing rods jutting skyward speaks of an unfinished task. As I look at those rods, they suddenly start to clang together. It takes me a couple of seconds to realize what is happening. The air fills with the hollow sound of groaning earth. The temblor lasts only a few seconds, but I imagine the chaos that will strike Mexico City, two hundred miles away, within the minute. (Earthquakes off the coast of Michoacán and Guerrero are often minor events locally but, through a seismic quirk, are magnified by the liquid foundation of the ancient lake lying underneath Mexico City.) There is no damage in Cherán. In tomorrow's papers, I'll read about the panic on the streets of Mexico City when the 6.5 quake struck.

Raúl Sr. shrugs it off. "It happens all the time around here," he says.

Raúl's mother calls out to her son from the kitchen. He tells her that he'll be right there.

Then he turns back to me, and when he speaks, his voice cracks.

"This might be the last time we're together here as a family," he says. "It might even be the last time I see my mother alive. It's hard to be far away from her, you know? When I'm on the other side, I think about her a lot. I think about her all the time."

The earthquake of migration has brought changes to practically every family in Cherán, for better and for worse—changes that follow fault lines extending from this highland town all the way to Arkansas and hundreds of other points north. It tears families apart and reunites them. It destroys an ancient language and creates a new one. It makes what is far away near, and what is near, far away.

Joseph Rodriguez

6

FIESTA

LAX. At the check-in counters for Mexicana, Aeroméxico, Lacsa, TACA, and the half dozen other airlines that serve Latin America, the serpentine lines are bulging—you can feel the breath of the person behind you on your neck. The line swells, not just with passengers but also with dozens of cardboard boxes of varying heights and widths, many nearly as tall as the travelers, most secured with fraying rope or sealed with duct tape. The effect is of a miniature city of cardboard buildings, replete with billboards: the logos of Samsung and General Electric and RCA and AIWA and other migrant sponsors.

But this city is on the move, being swallowed up at the ticket counter, the boxes disappearing as they are heaved onto the conveyor belts—only after considerable haggling between passengers and airline officials over excess baggage charges.

On the migrant trail, you create your world and carry it with you. Home is no longer located in a single geographical point. The towns from which the migrants hail are joined with the towns of the north to create a city space of the mind—a migrant lives and works in the States and he visits home at Christmas, New Year's, Easter, and the fiesta.

Migration has forged a line of communication between and among these spaces.

Come fiesta time and the end of the picking season in the United States, the migrants pack up the material landscape of their cities— boxes filled with VCRs and ghetto blasters, the ever-popular *licuadoras* and other handy kitchen appliances, and clothes, and computer games— and take them home to towns in Jalisco or Zacatecas, to San Salvador or Managua. But that is only half the transaction. After fiesta or New Year's, the migrants carry back other kinds of goods, ones that reside in the head and the heart, comprised of language and myths and rituals.

The migrant universe encompasses all the cultural and material space of and between two points—the picking fields, the church where you were baptized, the church where your children will be baptized, the desert, the subtropics and the tropics, the land where it rains during the summer and the land where the winter is dry, the *maquiladoras*, or factories, on the border where legions of Mexican women assemble the electronic components that the migrants buy as finished appliances on the other side, only to bring them back to the homeland. It occurs to me that we cannot use the term *homeland* the way we used to. The homeland no longer exists.

At LAX, this red-eye, or "*vuelo tecolote*" (owl's flight), as Latin Americans call it, is full. These flights always are at this time of year. That's why the airlines charge more during the holidays.

Most everyone is dressed sharply for the trip home. They want to arrive back in the *pueblo* looking good, to prove they've done well in the States. There's the unmistakable smell in the air of new leather jackets, plenty of audible crinkling.

The flight to Guadalajara is, thankfully, a cruise through calm skies. Everyone in the cabin has covered themselves with those prison-issue blankets or are crushing pillows into the cracks between seats and windows. But Humberto, the paisano next to me, wants to talk. It's been a long day for him and his two comrades, who are seated in the row ahead of us. They set out from Portland, Oregon, after a season at a food-packaging plant, where their asshole gringo *patrón* pays just a cut above minimum wage. The flight from Portland was inexplicably pushed up an hour, so when they arrived at seven for what they thought was a seven-thirty flight, the plane had already left. Living in a trailer with no phone, they weren't apprised of the scheduling caught another flight a few hours later and winged it t then the fifty minutes to L.A., but their original fligh had already left. So here they are now, with another two thousa to go. Once they touch ground in Guadalajara they'll splurge on a taxi to the bus station and then it's another few hours up to Los Altos de Jalisco, about 120 miles north of Chéran. They'll get there by noon tomorrow.

Humberto doesn't have time to take English classes, what with his twelve-hour shifts, but he's doing the best he can to educate himself by watching CNN in English (when he could just as easily watch CNN *en español*) and picking up the *Oregonian* to scan the headlines. He looks at the magazine in the seat back in front of him. "*Reader's Digest?*" he says, tentatively. I nod; he's pronounced it pretty well. "This is a magazine about digestion?" he asks. I explain. He nods.

We look out at the expanse of lights of Guadalajara in the predawn. On final approach, we trade travel histories. He's been everywhere I've been in the States and knows bus stations and backcountry routes that I don't and never will know. He will travel back and forth until a plane crashes or he can't get out of bed, he says. He can't stop moving now. To stop moving would be like turning off the irrigation on your farmland. The cornstalks would dry up and wither long before the crop matured, the ears would be stunted, worthless.

Humberto is the modern man. He is poor. He is on a journey. He is in awe of the glittering expanse of city lights below us. He is not afraid of the sudden prelanding turbulence. He is thinking only of seeing his family.

Cherán may be undergoing its most radical transformation since the Conquest (or at least the Revolution), but it still follows a calendar rooted in pre-Columbian life-and-death rhythms. The holy Indian days correspond to the Catholic liturgical year—Indian rites in Catholic drag. And so, Easter falls around the time of the ancient Purépecha fertility rites, and Saint Francis's feast coincides with the autumn harvest, when Indians give thanks to the gods of rain and sun and corn.

These days the fiesta in Cherán takes on even more significance as the migrants return home from the north—from the tobacco fields of the

Carolinas and the citrus groves of California, from picking mushrooms in Pennsylvania and tending to greenhouse nurseries in Missouri, from the tomatoes of Arkansas and Washington's apples. Husbands and wives, parents and children are reunited; best buddies who were separated at the border seven months ago and gave each other up for dead now give each other tearful, drunken embraces. Kids return to find a grandparent or an uncle in the grave; a father sees his newborn child for the first time.

Fiesta marks the end of nearly a year's worth of fear and anger, sexual frustration or infidelity, stinky clothes and deportations, jaywalking tickets and sleeping on the floor of an apartment in a crumbling part of some big American city. Nearly a year's worth of hope often denied.

They come with new clothes or still in the dirty jeans in which they picked the last of the crops or washed the last pile of restaurant dishes. They come back with billfolds thick with dollars or as poor as they left, perhaps even deeper in debt to the local loan sharks. Often they come in a car they just bought with cash, because most migrants don't have checking accounts or credit cards and hardly ever apply for bank loans. They have gassed up the car at fluorescent-lit pit stops on all-nighters down I-5, I-19, I-25, or I-35, the interstates that lead to San Diego, Nogales, El Paso, and Laredo. They'll be packed ten-deep among the luggage, in some ways recalling the discomforts of their original journey north, except that the long drive home is relatively stress-free. This time no Border Patrol jeep will chase them. The BP does not patrol the highways' southbound lanes, because they know the migrants are heading home and thus deportation is unnecessary. This is the only BP policy that indirectly results—unintentionally—in a humanitarian gesture from the American government: the Mexicans can take home the cash and belongings they've accumulated. Ironically, it is the Mexican customs officials who pose the biggest threat to the returning migrants. Free trade or no, customs officials exact exorbitant bribes and sometimes confiscate goods they have an appetite for.

The talk in town revolves around the fiesta—which bands have been hired to play, which bullfighters will dazzle in the ring, who will get the honor of cleaning Saint Francis's statue, which families in town can't come up with the cash to pay the fiesta tithe, whether the girl who promised her hand to the boy who's been in Iowa all year will have her heart broken.

Even the Chávezes have been getting into the mood. Like all my other acquaintances in Cherán, they take pride in their town's customs, which they see as unique, even though they are practically identical to those of every other small town in Mexico. One day, the family invites me to the neighboring town of Nahuatzen, whose fiesta falls a few weeks before Cherán's and serves, for the Cheranes, as a kind of warm-up. It is in all ways like Cherán's, although not as big, which the Cheranes point out with pride. It is one of the Chávezes' first family outings since the accident, and all, from doña María Elena down to the tiniest tot, dressed for the occasion.

We pile into Fernando's white Ford pickup, a dented late-seventies workhorse, tired but enduring. We head out of Cherán on the two-lane, an unseasonable drizzle falling on me and the kids sitting in the truck bed, a drizzle that turns into a downpour as we pull into town. The rain causes havoc. A much poorer town than Cherán, Nahuatzen has only a couple of cobblestone streets; the rest are dirt paths that become flood channels in the rain. The vendors all have the usual blue plastic tarps over their stalls, but this is a measure against the sun. The tarps grow huge bellies of water, some of which burst onto those seeking shelter from the storm. We are all drenched by the time we make it to church.

I recall the family's cynical attitude toward religion, but as we enter, their eyes fill with wonder. Wreaths of pine needles hang along the walls, strings of white paper flowers arch above our heads. Women carry lilies and red, white, and orange orchids as they slowly approach the suffering Christ, gently and sensually brushing his writhing form with the petals. They retreat from the altar by stepping backward, keeping their eyes on the deity, just as they would have adored a god from the Purépecha pantheon long before the Spaniards arrived with their white God-man nailed to a wooden cross. Hundreds of votives burn at the shrines before the saints, so many that there is an official fireman appointed to keep the flames from burning the church to the ground. Months later, Rosa will tell me that the only reason her family goes to church is to pray for her brothers—they, too, are martyrs.

The kiddy rides are stalled and dripping in the storm, but the children eat pastries with delight. María Elena carries José Iván, her youngest grandchild, slung across her breast inside her rebozo. She struggles in her new black felt shoes with gold buckles as we walk the mile from the fiesta back to the truck over slippery cobblestones and loose rocks and broken concrete, taking long, strained steps over torrents of muddy water. No one gives her a hand and she doesn't ask for one; she never stumbles, and I realize that those twig legs I once thought so fragile aren't fragile after all, that she's willing them to be strong enough to carry her child through the storm.

We are following 330 years of tradition," says señor Seferino Flores. "At least, that's what tradition says." The grizzled old-timer was elected *comisionado* of the Parikutín barrio this year and is now overseeing the preparation of an *estandarte*, or standard, for the fiesta, which will be propped up alongside Saint Francis in the church. Every year, Cherán's thirteen barrios are assigned responsibilities that must be fulfilled to the letter. There are four main tasks: music, fireworks, bullfights, processions and other church preparations. Each year, these rotate among the neighborhoods. The first official year of this celebration may have been 1656, but there is ample evidence of the pre-Conquest roots of Cherán's fiesta. For the standard, a dozen kids husk a great pile of blue corn. The cobs are lashed to the horseshoe-shaped frame amid bunches of pine needles, daisies, carnations, and a string of colored lights that will be plugged in at the altar and blink night and day. Thus the pre-Columbian symbol of the harvest god who decides whether to make the earth fertile takes its place on the altar alongside the man from Assisi.

"The corn is what this *pueblo* mainly produces," says señor Seferino. "Our *patrón* watches over the corn, and so for fiesta we represent him that way." The fiesta rites also give thanks for successful migration. Seferino himself is a veteran of the northern campaigns, with stints in Alabama (watermelon, potatoes, yams) and Alberta, Canada (timber). "All of us who go to the other side ask for our Saint Francis's blessing. And when we return, we thank him with masses, processions, and standards."

There is nothing quite like Cherán's fiesta in the United States, although successive generations of southern European immigrants have brought a taste of it to ethnic enclaves in cities and towns across America. Fiesta—seven days and seven nights of absolute, excessive, anarchic, sublime, and at times scandalous partying—is an elemental part of small-town economies, for better or worse. Every household pays the required fiesta tithe and also spends a substantial amount on food, booze, and trinkets. The concession stands in town line the pockets of both local and itinerant entrepreneurs. In this scenario, the rich get richer and the poor get the shaft, although the latter are, at least during fiesta days, usually quite happy with the arrangement. Fiesta can also be quite a political issue. After all, if it's poorly organized and, say, the beer runs out, the local *presidente muncipal* will have hell to pay. Conversely, a good party means good political fortunes for the *caciques*, the town bosses.

Ask Father Melesio about fiesta and he waxes romantic about the *colectivismo* of the event, of *solidaridad*. After a year's worth of trials and tribulations on the migrant trail, why the hell not?

"Considering the blows they take," he tells me, "they, too, have a right to happiness. You can't look at the fiesta as wasted money. It's not an escape. It's the spirit of life itself."

Sure, there might be a little too much drinking, and a couple of fights might turn nasty. But Father Melesio's parish will receive most of its donations at this time of year, *norteño* dollars for the church's coffers, money that will help run social programs that do indeed perform good works. There are those on the left who decry the tradition as part of the machinery of control that ultimately forestalls rebellion against the forces of capital. In the Zapatista-controlled territories of Chiapas, for example, fiestas are now celebrated without alcohol, because indigenous leaders identified alcohol as a form of political and economic repression.

But Cherán is nowhere near a revolution, and not because of alcohol. In Cherán, pent-up frustration is diffused largely through migration. The day the Cheranes can no longer imagine a life beyond Cherán is the day the town will explode. Border Patrol or no, that day is a long way off—it's not even visible on the horizon. What we're left with is the bacchanal of the fiesta.

I'm lost in a sea of cholos and drunken *norteños*, brass bands and buzzing market stalls smelling of new clothes and greasy food, church bells ringing and flashy cars cruising. Amid the chaos, a Jehovah's Witness medical doctor who apparently considers Dr. Tito a godless charlatan begs me to interview him. He says that the fiesta is utter profanity, an idolatrous perversion of Christianity, that he and his family will cloister themselves inside their home—they have no satellite dish but plenty of

Bibles—for the rest of the week. They will hold marathon prayer sessions for all these lost souls. And no, he's never even thought of moving to the States, thank you!

As for the rest of Cherán, every day from six in the morning through the wee hours, the skyrockets whiz upward and burst, the detonations echoing off the town's craggy hills. The streets downtown are choked with stalls. They ring the plaza and line both sides of a side street for about a mile, all the way to the open space next to the high school, where there are kiddy rides and the Ferris wheel that no fiesta can do without. The vendors stack their pyramids of fruit and piles of T-shirts and rows of shoes; slabs of stewed pork glow under amber heat lamps. At the *lotería* games (like bingo, except instead of numbers, there's an assortment of archetypal Latin characters and symbols), announcers drone the command to place your beans on *el soldado* (the soldier), *la rana* (the frog), *el catrín* (the dandy), *la muerte* (death). Barkers implore you to pop the balloons with darts and shoot the ducks with pellet guns. There are Taiwanese toys for sale, including a special-agent set complete with a .38, handcuffs, and a walkie-talkie. And rows of kitschy portraits—a cute little white fluffy dog, blue ribbons in its hair—inscribed with words to live by ("Our friendship is forever"). And towering Virgins of Guadalupe, coronas blinking with rainbow lights. Cowboy boots alongside imitation Nikes. Caps and windbreakers: Charlotte Hornets, Phoenix Suns, Pittsburgh Steelers, Oakland Raiders, Chicago Bulls, Los Angeles Dodgers. Popcorn, cotton candy. Beautiful rebozos, from the roughest blue wools to the softest of pastels, proffered by both venerable matriarchs who actually wear them and younger women in tight Guess jeans.

The *norteños* strut about, their silver belt buckles gleaming and gold chains glittering. In the church, the older women make their way on bloody knees to the altar, where Saint Francis, fresh from his annual makeover, stands handsome and holy under his green neon halo. His frock is festooned with twenty-dollar bills (a couple of hundred dollars of which were donated to the church by the Enríquez family), a symbol of migrant gratitude.

Rosa Chávez's husband, Wense Cortéz, does not have any bills to pin on Saint Francis's frock. He managed to make it only a few dozen miles inside United States territory this time. Probably the timing was bad—he was among the few trying to enter the States at the beginning of fall, when most were headed the other way. When the migrant stream heading north diminishes, the chances of getting caught at the border are all the higher.

I find Wense at home with Rosa, looking rather sheepish. Nevertheless, as he begins to spin the tale of the crossing, he warms to it, like any other migrant telling of conquering the northern territories.

"The river was low," he says, tugging on the bill of his dusty crucified-Christ cap. "It was only up to my belly button. It was no problem to cross. We laughed at how easy it was." The coyote, too, was overjoyed at the ease with which they breached the Grande near Matamoros; with this blessing, he told his clients, surely the rest of the trip would be just as easy. The fact that the coyote had taken along his two teenage daughters was also taken as a good sign by the migrants.

But it was not to be. A *migra* helicopter spotted them soon after they crossed. Suddenly, Wense says, the coyote and his daughters disappeared. Typical. Coyotes have a way of disappearing when you need them the most. The BP truck showed up a few minutes later and hauled them back to the line.

They waited for the coyote to reappear at the appointed place on the Mexican side, but after a day and a half Wense and his younger brother Melchor, who was making his first trip north, decided to strike out on their own with a wildcat group of down-on-their-luck migrants, all of whom had already been deported several times or robbed by border bandits. Since the brothers' money had just about run out, they figured they had nothing to lose.

This time the river was over their heads; they had to pay two men whose sole source of livelihood was ferrying migrants across the treacherous waters on a makeshift raft of tractor tire inner tubes. It was a Friday night and in the darkness the river looked more like oil than water, but they made it across just fine.

For the next four days, they wandered in the desert. "Have you ever been so thirsty you thought of drinking your own piss?" Wense asks. It was well over a hundred degrees, a typical south Texas late-summer day. They stumbled through the sand and scrub, searching in vain for shade. They ditched their empty water bottles and drank from stagnant pools of water in gullies or potholes on farm roads. On the third day, they ran into a Mexican rancher who offered them food and a chance to shower at his house. Wense had come across many such angels of the road in the eight years he'd been crossing. The newspapers never talk about them. The stories are always about the *migra* or their vigilante cousins, the gun-toting gringo ranchers. Wense swears that for every person trying to block the migrants' path, there is someone else out there in the borderlands willing to help the midnight train reach its destination.

Unfortunately, the Samaritan could not cover the tracks the migrant crew had left through the desert, which the BP assiduously followed. On the fourth day, the migrants were back in the wild, out where there wasn't even a ranch house in sight. They heard the familiar sound of helicopter blades slicing through the dead, hot air. There was nowhere to hide except among isolated clumps of scrub and the occasional wash. Still, Wense and Melchor gave it their best. When the BP jeep arrived, they were the last ones to get picked up. They might very well have escaped, had it not been for the German shepherd that sniffed them out.

Only now does Wense admit that he'd considered giving himself up to the *migra* even before the bust, more for his brother's sake than his own. The boy was severely dehydrated, on the verge of delirium. His lips were a cracked white, like the smile on a Day of the Dead sugar skull. Real tragedy might have occurred had the BP not picked them up.

Throughout the story, Rosa has been sitting at an old manual Singer, stitching together a pair of red denim shorts for her daughter. She has been quiet the whole time as Wense waves his arms and raises his voice, casting himself as the hero. Rosa glances up at me and gives me a strange look—half annoyed, half bemused. She's crossed the border only once, but because of her family's loss, she can't think of the border as just another migrant tale.

For Wense, on the other hand, this is an adventure to add to Cherán's migrant lore. He laughs at the horrors of the road as he recounts the experience—as if somehow he feels he's cheated the *migra*, the road, or death itself by having returned alive. But Wense's will to move is far from broken. He says he'll perform odd jobs in town, maybe a bit of construction work on some *norteño*'s second-story addition. He might as well stay around for a while. After all, it's fiesta time.

"After fiesta, I'll go up again," Wense says. "For sure I'll make it then."

The next day, I return to the Chávezes to find Rosa seated once again at the Singer and Wense nowhere in sight. "The fiesta," says Rosa bitingly, "swallows up the men. They're all a bunch of drunkards this time of year."

Rosa's been doing a lot of thinking about the future. Fiesta is a natural time to look back on the past year as well as toward the next. I am shocked to hear Rosa say that she is considering going north soon herself. Seven months have passed since the accident, and she has fulfilled what she saw as her role: to stay with her grieving mother. In recent weeks, the old woman appears to have pushed aside much of her pain, mostly by concentrating on her grandchildren. Rosa knows now that her mother will hold on for them, if for nothing else. They are the only hope the family has.

So Rosa compares visions of her life here and there. Here: Stay at home, mend clothes, stitch doilies that won't sell at market. Fill the tins in the yard each day with sudsy water. Mind a store that has no customers. Wait for calls and money orders from Wense, wait for rumors of his drunken carousing or infidelities up in St. Louis. Watch her daughter, Yeni, grow up, attend a few years of elementary school, and get knocked up by a local boy who will surely run away to the north himself. Perhaps one day Yeni will sit at the Singer like Rosa does now, thinking about making a break for the north.

There: Rosa drove a tractor once when she and Wense worked on a farm outside St. Louis. Up there, they have an apartment of their own, with hot and cold running water, an indoor bathroom, a sofa, an electric stove. Wense acts differently up there; he even helps with the dishes. She can probably convince him to teach her to drive the white Buick he recently bought and left behind in the care of a friend. It is impossible to imagine mobility in Cherán. But when Rosa thinks of St. Louis, all kinds of visions come to her: cosmetology school, college for Yeni, and someday a house of their own. Where her mother will live. Where the widows and Rosa's nieces and nephews will live.

Even María Elena has come to consider the possibility of moving north one day; she is now resigned to giving Rosa her blessing for the trip. María Elena asks me if I think that the U.S. government will eventually ask her to testify in court. She is hoping the Americans will put her on a plane so she can land on U.S. soil without having to cross the line that killed her sons. Then, no matter what happens in court, she thinks she will stay on the other side with her surviving children, papers or no papers.

I tell her I don't know, although I suspect that free plane fare to the States is unlikely—the INS will probably settle out of court to avoid political and economic liability. I could advise María Elena to wait for the settlement, which will take years. But it would be hard to convince the Chávezes to abandon the path they seem intent on following even in the wake of the tragedy. I think about the U.S. immigration service's "Stay Out, Stay Alive" publicity campaign, initiated in the wake of dozens of deaths on the line this year. The approach of the videos and posters was as simple as it was cruel: use the bodies of the dead as a warning to prospective border crossers. If they don't deter the Chávez family from crossing, they won't deter anyone.

After the fiesta. Everything will happen after the fiesta.

I stay at don Francisco Payeda's house for most of the fiesta, on the recommendation of Father Melesio, who took pity on me after I told him that I'd been staying at Cherán's only "hotel" during my frequent visits. I was glad to leave those dingy rooms, which shuddered whenever a bus or truck passed on the highway.

Francisco's is also a shaky structure on the highway, but it is a generally happy home. Four generations of Payedas share space here, from the octagenarian great-grandfather, who was among the early migrant pioneers (he picked fruit in Oregon in the forties) to the son of Francisco's daughter Nena, the sad-looking but friendly girl who works at the *caseta* next to the market. The family mascot is Lobo, an amazingly wild but ultimately lovable dog, some sort of mix of German shepherd and short-haired hound. He always leaves my jeans streaked with muddy paw prints.

Francisco is nicknamed Pancho Villa because he's a legend in the local teachers union, a fiery activist who always walked at the head of the march and faced down the soldiers and their rifles. But that was in the old days. He's now retired and has taken heavily to the bottle. He is not a mean drunk; on the contrary, the alcohol just accentuates the sweetness of his character. But his body is showing the effects of the poison. One morning after, he extends a trembling hand. "D.T.'s," he says. He's been trying to quit, but how can you not drink during fiesta?

Returning to the Payeda house one day, I lie on my sagging bed for a nap but suddenly hear a tremendous din. There is a knock on my door. It is Francisco, waving a bottle and apprising me that the bull-fighters have arrived in Cherán and that it is his great honor to host them in his home.

A short while later, I meet the three bullfighters who've been invited for the fiesta, an old tradition. They're from Jalisco, the source of all of Mexico's great macho men, the best soccer players, the hardest drinkers—and the finest-looking ones, I might add. Owing to a mix of French and Indian blood, the mestizos there (men and women alike) are tall, light-skinned, and green-eyed, with finely sculpted asses—and you need a finely sculpted ass to be a bullfighter, of course.

Juan Carlos López and Sigifredo Loza, aka El Cerillo (Toothpick, for his thin body), are in their midtwenties, dressed casually like a CK ad in pullovers and jeans held up by thick leather belts with big silver buckles, their hair longish and slicked back. Their group leader, Ricardo del Toro, is thirty-nine and his graying hair is receding. Shorter than the other two, he is less striking-looking, but he makes up for it with a gregarious demeanor.

They are accompanied by Enríque Carranza, an affable, somewhat plaintive guy, perfect for the role of rodeo clown, and his brother, Santiago, who's just along for the ride. And then there's Nora, a large Indian girl from a nearby Purépecha town, playing the part of groupie; she rarely says anything and when she does say something it's sarcastic or snide. Clearly she's a rebel, the bad girl who's proud to be hanging with bullfighters. Nora's always got Walkman head-phones on, and you can make out the faint whine of tearjerker Mexican ballads.

The men proceed to prepare for the bullfight, scheduled for five in the afternoon, only a couple of hours away. They get ready by searching for that ever-elusive perfect combination of alcohol, coke, and weed.

Though few townspeople know it, Cherán has welcomed a trio of bull-fighters about as decadent and wasted as they can be and still manage not to get killed in the ring.

In between tokes and snorts and shots, the bullfighters are recount-ing the long and winding path that led them to Cherán. They grew up in Los Altos de Jalisco, the highlands above Guadalajara. They've been traveling since they were child prodigies in the ring. All bullfighters know life on the road; this group knows it in spades. They fight twenty bulls every couple of days for what amounts to spare change; they are the *toreros* of the poor, traveling from village to village, usually for fiestas honoring patron saints. They are away from their families (they're all married with kids) and hometowns upwards of 250 days a year. They've fought bulls with their worn and torn capes and wooden sticks-cum-muletas (they rarely fight to the "moment of truth"; most of the places they visit can't actually afford a kill) in every pueblo and cow town from the desert outposts of the borderlands to villages in the steaming tropics.

"This is the only way to get through it," Ricardo says, dragging hard on a fat joint of pungent weed and then holding it up high as if it were a sacred pipe. "How else could I get into the ring 150 times a year with those *cabrones*? We never kill them, but they could kill us anytime."

These are true rock 'n' rollers, I think to myself. As close to the dark side as Jim Morrison or Kurt Cobain, as reckless as Sid Vicious, as hyper as Little Richard, as devilishly sexy as Elvis. For they make a living facing death on stage and off—wooing it, dancing with it, and, every once in a while, coming quite close to consummating the rela-tionship.

It's time to get the costumes on. They peel off their clothes at a slow, stoned pace, without the least bit of modesty, for bullfighting is a sport and all sports are about the body, but this sport in particular tells the body's story in an extreme way, with scars that only a bull's horn or hoof can make. Our *toreros* seem to take pleasure in showing skin, practically posing, as if for *El otro lado*, Mexico City's slick gay zine. Ricardo, the veteran, has the most scars. A three-incher above the right breast with an exit wound through his shoulder blade. A nasty tear along his left hip. There are also several small streaks across his balding dome. And he tells us of the one that almost killed him: gored clean up the ass and into his bowels once in some forgotten Indian village. It's a wonder he can still shit, he laughs.

The younger fighters' bodies are still more or less intact. Mostly because, I come to realize, they are conservative in the ring. Ricardo, on the other hand, is a verifiable madman. "I do handstands in front of the animal," he says, "something no bullfighter before me has ever done, and I don't think anyone else ever will." He promises to perform the feat in honor of his new friend from the States. "You take picture," he says in English, his finger pressing down on the imaginary camera. "Yes?"

Cerillo, Juan Carlos, and Ricardo lounge about in various stages of undress, smoking a bit more, drinking a bit more, as if putting off their date with the bulls as long as possible.

Ricardo goes on with his story. A bullfighter doesn't just twirl a cape before a snorting bull, he explains, "it's a way of life." To be a bullfighter, you don't joke with death, you joke with life. You are expected to be a *character*, flouting all the rules, living life to the fullest because tomorrow that raging bull might gore you again and this time the peritonitis might actually kill you.

There was that time that Ricardo stepped off the bus in Guadalajara after yet another grueling tour, and it was pouring rain. There he stood dripping, waiting for a bus to get up to Los Altos, when he noticed a fine black '82 Mustang with gleaming rims idling at the curb. He reached into his pocket and felt the wad of bills from the dozen performances he'd just given. "How much do you want for it?" he called out to the guy at the wheel. The driver quoted an exorbitant price. With the flair of an Italian don, Ricardo peeled off the exact amount, and the stunned driver walked away richer but wet. "A bullfighter should not suffer the indignity of being soaked by a Guadalajara thunderstorm," Ricardo says, "when he can ride home in a black '82 Mustang."

And there was the time he was walking down the street in he can't remember which town and came upon a house with its doors and windows wide open; he heard the crying and laughter of a Mexican wake. Without knowing anyone, he walked in and went straight to the widow to offer his condolences—and his considerable manly charm. The wailing widow was laughing within minutes, begging him to stay. "A bullfighter always looks out for those who are in pain, because he knows so much of it himself," he says with a wink.

And then there was the Long Walk for which Ricardo will go down in the annals of bullfighting history. You see, despite his handstanding heroics, Ricardo never made it to the "the show" in Mexico City, the country's premier bullfighting venue. Time and again he was passed over while colleagues he considered to have less *cojones* got the nod to stand at center ring under the rain of red roses. He was convinced that official corruption was to blame for the boycott against him—bullfighters with wealthy patrons greasing the wheels, no doubt. So he decided to let the world know his plight. He dressed in his *traje de luces*, the gleaming sequined uniform of the bullfighter, and set out from Guadalajara to Mexico City on foot (a three-hundred-mile trek), handing out flyers decrying the dirty politics of the sport. The pilgrimage made headlines in papers all along the way. Now and again a friendly driver gave him a ride, and total strangers would take him in at night, feed him, urge him on the next morning. A month after his departure, he arrived in Mexico City, his feet blistered and bleeding, his knees shot through with excruciating pain, his *traje* in tatters. And no, the bullfighting powers that be never gave him a shot at the ring in Mexico City.

But that's not the point, Ricardo says. The point is that he fought. The most famous bullfighters, after all, are the ones who lost their greatest battles, the martyrs of the ring like Manolito and Juan Belmonde. At thirty-nine, Ricardo will never get that chance at Mexico City. He will tour the towns of broken-down rings and fiesta-drunk Indians until the day comes that he meets the bull that'll take him to bullfighter's heaven. He loves these towns, he really does, the towns where most Mexicans live—towns full of people just like him, who never got that shot at the big time, who are forever condemned to pack up their bags and move on to the next town, the next state, the next country, looking for something better.

We can hear the ragged brass band that will accompany the bullfighters on their procession through town to the bullring. The bullfighters grow quiet. As slowly as they took their clothes off, they now start pulling on their *trajes de luces*. First the stockings, the hip-hugging pantyhose rolled up over hairy legs. Then the white shirt— white; the collars are hopelessly ringed with soot and the ⟨ wearing so thin on Ricardo's that you can clearly see his tanneo Next the thin black ties. Juan Carlos has a neat little silver crucifix serves as a tie pin. Now the spangled pants and the suspenders up an, over the shoulders. And the gleaming vests, perhaps not as gleaming as they once were; several dozen sequins have fallen off and the silk is fraying.

And, finally, the pièce de résistance—the sunglasses. Ray Ban Way-farers for Juan Carlos and Cerillo, aviator shades for Ricardo.

Thus they strut out into the gray afternoon, stoned and floating, their eyes glowing behind their shades. The band starts up a raucous tune. Mayor Salvador Campanur effusively shakes hands with the hon-ored guests. As the procession picks up momentum, more and more of Cherán joins in. The teenage girls half hiding their coquettish smiles with their hands. The local gang kids with their crew cuts and baggy jeans. The town drunks. The just-back-from-the-States wetbacks dressed in their Guess best.

It's a magnificent bullring for such a small town—clearly, migrant dollars contributed to the two-thousand-capacity all-concrete stands. A full *banda sinaloense*, an electrified version of the brass band with a mas-sive sound system befitting a heavy metal band, starts playing Michoa-cán's anthem, "Caminos de Michoacán," a song whose lyrics tell a classic tale about a guy who lost his love and is now chained to the road, searching for her from town to town:

Caminos de Michoacán
y pueblos que voy pasando
si saben en donde está,
porqué me la están negando
díganle que ando en Sahuayo
y voy pa' Ciudad Hidalgo.

(Roads of Michoacán / and towns I'm passing by / since you know where she is / why do you deny me? / Tell her that I'm in Sahuayo / and headed for Ciudad Hidalgo.)

The road (and those dead-end towns rising up on the horizon and receding in the rearview mirror) is denying the forlorn boy his love. The road is often a character in Mexican ballads—always denying or fulfilling dreams, leading toward a fiery end or a successful crossing of the border.

It's five o'clock. From the bandstand, Cherán's prettiest young women, in Indian dress with rainbows of ribbons dangling from their hair, wave white scarves to the frenetic *banda* beat. The band will play nonstop throughout the performance; the girls will never stop waving their scarves.

It is beginning to drizzle now, but there are no rain outs in bullfighting. The ring becomes a squishy swamp of deep brown, almost black Michoacán earth. Juan Carlos and Cerillo complain that this makes avoiding a horn up your ass all the more difficult.

Chaos in the ring. Since this is the town's own event, bought and paid for with Cherán pesos (actually dollars converted into pesos at the *casa de cambio*), the locals feel they have as much right to the bulls as the bullfighters themselves. So the warm-up festivities include an amateur "running of the bulls" for the locals. As the animals are released into the ring, one by one, teenage kids run about gleefully, leaping behind the barricades when the snorting beasts come too close, pulling at their tails after the horsemen lasso them. One kid in particular catches my eye—he wears a stars-and-stripes bandanna around his head and has a gold loop dangling from his left ear, quite the binational pirate.

Finally, the kids run back into the stands for the main event. The *banda* strikes up the Iberian bullfighter's anthem, and Juan Carlos, Cerillo, and Ricardo enter the ring, doffing their black felt hats to the crowd. Then the bulls come, each one meaner than the last. Juan Carlos and Cerillo maintain a discreet distance from them, letting Ricardo do most of the work. He doesn't have that much grace out there—rather than the balletlike movements I remember from watching bullfights on TV with my grandfather, Ricardo's are stiff, a bit awkward. But he more than gets the job done, twirling the cape this way and that, eventually dizzying the bull to a standstill and earning an ovation from the crowd, which is egged on by an announcer who shouts encouragement above the *banda*'s incessant blare. The drizzle turns to a steady rain. But everyone stays put; they open umbrellas or buy sheets of plastic from the vendors, those entrepreneurial geniuses who always think of everything.

Now a tremendous blond beast charges into the ring, the meanest of the afternoon. Juan Carlos and Cerillo look really nervous; Ricardo runs behind one of the barricades and takes a tremendous shot of Don Presidente brandy straight from the bottle, for which he receives another ovation. The crowd senses a momentous encounter is about to take place and understands Ricardo's need for a drink to steady his nerves. Ricardo throws me a look. This is the one! He will perform the feat that no other bullfighter has ever attempted: the handstand.

He makes a grand show of taming the animal, a dazzling display of cape twirling, standing arrogantly with hand on hip, then down on one knee, over and over until the bull stops in its tracks, disoriented. He turns to me, makes a snap-the-picture motion with his hand, then turns back to the bull. Down he goes, his hands sinking into the wet brown earth, and his feet come up and together in a perfect gymnastic execution of a handstand. A crazy act—and a terrible insult to the bull: an insult hurled at death itself. Ricardo gets back up, mud dripping from his hands, which he now places on his hips as he cocks his head, thrusting his chin out, the bullfighter's arrogant parting shot at the defeated bull. Another ovation.

Ricardo comes back to the barricade, to handshakes and slaps on the ass and an offer of more booze, which he readily accepts. Out in the ring the horsemen are tossing their lariats and the kids run about, now modestly imitating Ricardo, attempting their own handstands before the roped animal.

A few minutes later, a black bull rushes out of the pen and Ricardo, visibly drunk now, goes at it again, and again he dizzies the bull to a stop. To my horror, he goes down for another handstand, this time only about a yard away from the beast. "Behold the valor of the Mexicano—!" the announcer shouts, holding the final vowel with a tremendous, near operatic bellow. Ricardo remains upside down, rain falling on the soles of his muddied black slippers. Juan Carlos's face is tightened into a nervous scowl. The Indian girls' scarves reach the top of their leftward arc.

"—oooooooo!" Ricardo comes up, turns his back to the beast, raises his arms in a Y to his fans—and in the next instant is airborne as a collective, aspirated "*¡Ay!*" comes up from the crowd. When a two-thousand-pound animal hits a man of five foot five weighing maybe 150 pounds, the impact is like a human kicking at a twig. Ricardo twirls in the air, ultimately completing a full somersault. Cerillo and Juan Carlos are stunned motionless for a second or two; in that interval, the bull stampedes straight for Ricardo's crumpled form, first flipping him over with the slightest tap from its huge nose, then running completely over him, hooves coming down here on earth and there on skin and bone.

It takes all the combined energies of Ricardo's apprentices and the clown and the horsemen to finally distract the bull. All eyes are on Ricardo's still body. Slowly, he moves a hand and pushes the rest of his body back up from the muck. He comes upright like a trembling fawn standing for the first time. He slowly waves to the crowd and forces a strange, feeble smile. But nobody else is smiling. We are all looking at Ricardo's face, which seems to have been torn in half. And now we notice a funny white spot, about the size of a fifty-cent piece, high on his forehead. It is his skull. He takes one step toward the barricades and collapses.

When they carry him away, there is no skull showing, just a persistent gush of blood from the wound. The ambulance wails. The performance is over; the stands empty quietly and quickly. Juan Carlos and Cerillo gather the capes and muletas, and since no one can tell us where they've taken Ricardo, we head back to Pancho Villa's to wait for word on the fallen master. "This is the worst time, maybe this is the last time," Juan Carlos says. They light joints. They drink. They wait, swapping stories about Ricardo's exploits with bulls and with women, about the law's respect for him despite his excesses—that Ricardo, he's got friends in high places. But our laughter is forced and the solemnity starts to feel like the beginning of a wake.

Night falls and the rain is relentless.

The goring is certain to be the talk of Cherán for months to come. Every fiesta has at least one memorable moment—often involving serious injury or even death. We saw Cherán's Passion in the ring today. Some urged the *toreros* on, others the bulls. Summoning life, secretly praying for death, a symbolic chance to settle subconscious and sometimes very conscious scores—the opportunity offered by every great sport. And there are many scores to settle in this town. Cherán, a town of wetbacks, who the hell gives a shit about Cherán, who even knows it exists except the fifty thousand or so people who live in the highlands of Michoacán? Once a year the Cheranes gather at the ring, drinking, laughing, crying at the multiple ironies of it all (a bullring bequeathed by Spanish conquerors, Purépecha kids wearing the hip-hop uniform of black American kids who a few generations ago were slaves, Indians become cowboys in their rough-and-tumble enthusiasm for *gringolandia*). Laughing and crying because their dreams are so great and their pasts so painful and this limbo of a present is one hell of a tense place to live.

Why does Cherán love the ring, aside from its being a fiesta tradition that goes back centuries? Because Cherán is running with the bulls 365 days a year.

A couple of hours later, there is a knock on the door. Ricardo enters, his head completely swathed in white. He walks feebly, supported by Nora, the Indian rebel girl, and a local aficionado. He utters not a word; neither does anyone else—no one is sure whether he's survived or is in need of last rites. Nora undresses him, hanging the torn, bloodied, and muddied *traje* on a chair. He lies there cradled by her, naked but for a small towel across his loins—a poor Mexican study by Michelangelo.

It's then that Ricardo looks around the room, a smile beginning to curl his lips. And he shouts: "So where's the party?"

Sunday morning begins with the mad clanging of bells. An old man stands alone in the center of the plaza lighting skyrockets with his cigarette, letting the bamboo shoots slip through his fingers. If the bells and rockets don't wake you, the dozen brass bands playing "Las mañanitas," the traditional Latin American birthday anthem for Saint Francis, will.

Despite its collective hangover, Cherán opens its eyes at the crack of dawn for the last day of fiesta. The faithful stream down from the hills with bouquets of flowers, the twenty-dollar bill they'd debated giving Saint Francis or saving for the postfiesta depression, and baskets of bananas, cherries, and greenish oranges. The church is now one massive altar, pungent with incense, a thousand votive candles, pine needles, roses, gladiolas, and rotting fruit. The rebozo women pray fervently. The men stand on wobbly drunk legs, hats in their hands, crossing themselves again and again.

They are giving thanks for returning home safely. They are giving thanks for finding their families in good health when they arrived. They are praying for a bountiful corn harvest now that the stalks are yellow-dry and withered, waiting only for hands to pick the cobs. They are praying that next year's journey north will go well, that all the Cheranes will arrive at their destinations.

Although it's just the beginning of Cherán's winter, the end of fiesta carries the premonition of spring and a new wave of departures. The great wheel of migration never stops spinning.

At the Chávez house, the family is dressing up for one last tour of the plaza, the fiesta stalls, and the kiddy rides. The granddaughters wear matching angelic-white dresses, the grandsons white shirts and black pants. Doña María Elena has made a curious fashion choice: over her typical flower-print dress, she wears a large white T-shirt that reads simply—in English—LIFE.

But the giddiness of fiesta is finally giving way to renewed grief among the clan. All the sons and daughters of Cherán have returned except Jaime, Benjamín, and Salvador. The family spends the morning remembering. Rosa says that in the days before the brothers' departure there had been several *malavisos*, bad omens. Yolanda, Benjamín's widow, saw an owl perched strangely in a tree behind her house, and a hungry coyote entered the kitchen. Benjamín trapped and caged it in the yard, but when they returned after running some errands, the animal had disappeared. There'd also been an extraordinary whitewashed sky the morning the brothers left, long cirrus clouds streaking across the blue.

But when Benjamín, Jaime, and Salvador bid their loved ones farewell at the bus stop later that day, there was no sign of anything amiss. Salvador was nervous with excitement; this was only his second trip north. Benjamín talked of returning to Cherán for Easter. There were hugs and kisses and tears on the women's faces but no untoward worries. No one in Cherán could have imagined the possibility of such a loss.

I accompany the Chávezes downtown. The kids are all smiles and shrieks, but the adults, including Rosa, are taciturn. They receive salutations from many of their neighbors, but these are the kind of pitiful greetings reserved for the bereaved. It is difficult to imagine that the family will ever truly enjoy fiesta without the undertow of pain.

All of Cherán is downtown, swirling among the stalls, eyeing the goods more than buying. Stacks of Silver Tab Levi's, little bags of rainbow-colored plastic farm animals, black Barbie dolls, pastries smothered in honey, hand-painted dishes, a thousand rebozos. The Chávezes do buy something, a set of tiny ceramic cups and a kitschy piggy bank—a farewell gift for me. The gesture brings me close to tears because it reminds me that I, too, am on the verge of leaving.

On Sunday night, Wense and I head to the plaza. He buys a bottle of Bacardi, two liters of Coke, and a stack of blue plastic cups. He drinks straight from the bottles and invites everyone he runs into—long-lost relative, total stranger—to a toast on the street. This, too, is a fiesta tradition. Hundreds of men are stumbling about the plaza like Wense (there are women here, too, but most are sober; macho tradition dictates that a drunk woman might as well be a whore).

There are two stages set up, *banda* outfits playing alternate sets with the requisite swirling lights and stage fog. On the dance floor between the stages, a sea of cowboy hats bobs up and down. Wense drags me into the middle of it, but not to dance; apparently, he just wants to be in the crush of the crowd, at fiesta's ground zero. He is drunk, urging me to toast as often as he does. Compared with the dancers, Wense is dressed down tonight. Usually, he makes his best attempt at matching *norteño* fashion with his faded shirts and stained pants. But now he wears a grimy gray sweatshirt moist not only from the night's drizzle but also with snot and spit.

Suddenly, Wense's got to take a piss. He barrels through the crowd toward a feed store on the south side of the plaza and relieves himself behind a stack of fertilizer bags. I am glad no one notices. Back to the plaza. Wense is now getting to that inevitable stage of a drunk where anything can happen: he could pass out, get in a fight, get busted by the cops, slapped by a girl.

Now he rushes into the dancing area again, straight up to a well-dressed *norteño*, a huge, bug-eyed bull of a man with a long mane of hair like El Músico's. Wense insists on introducing me to the *norteño*, apparently to impress upon him that he, too, has connections in the north. But the *norteño* is just as drunkenly aggressive as Wense and starts talking tough—to me.

"You're no *norteño*," the dude says, sizing me up. "You're from Jalisco, I know who you are, and let me tell you, I work for the FBI, so don't go around impersonating a gringo or I'll have to arrest you." I am laughing at the bizzare claim, but the *norteño* is not. He thinks I'm laughing at him. Now Wense starts talking back. I look down at the man's pointy snakeskin boots and wince at the thought of Wense crumpled on the plaza, taking kicks to the stomach. Sensing that blows are imminent, I pull at him hard just as the *norteño* lunges forward, falls through the empty air, and hits the pavement face first. I drag Wense through the crowd, breaking up *quebradita* couples and shoving aside cholos who shoot back scowls. I look back into the pit and see a swirl of flying fists; the *quebradita* has turned into a slam dance.

"You don't understand, Rubén, you just don't understand," Wense keeps slurring as I pull him into a side street along the church, but we encounter violence here as well, crews of cholitos going at it with fists and kicks and fuck yous and *chinga tu madre*s.

All of Cherán is spinning around me as I try to stand still. I'm as drunk as the fiesta itself. But Wense insists on pulling me back deeper into it all and now I can apprehend only fragments of images. Salvador Romero, the one sober man on the plaza, handing out greasy chicken from a cart . . . Nena, Pancho Villa's daughter, standing alone in a crumbling doorway, rebozo up to tearful eyes . . . The taxi stand abandoned because on this night even the *taxistas* party until dawn . . . A *quebradita* dancer taking off his leather belt with the huge silver buckle and twirling it over his head, the buckle suddenly flying off into the crowd . . . *¡QUE VIVA MEXICO, CABRONES!* . . . A couple of kids whom I take for cholos because of their freshly shaved heads, until I realize they're just poor Cherán teens with lice . . . Father Melesio laughing hoarsely at the gates of his church, beholding the spectacle . . . Cars swerving around a drunk lying on the highway in a pool of vomit . . . Potato slices frying in a vat of golden grease over a menacing coal fire . . . The *lotería* barker calling out: "*¡LA MUERTE! ¡LA MUERTE!*" . . . And at the center of the plaza, *el castillo*, the castle of fireworks that soon will fill

the night with pinwheeling sparks and mortar whistles, an
end of fiesta.

Suddenly it is quiet. Somehow, Wense and I have
blocks up the highway, far from the devil revelers. We sit on the sidewalk next to a lonely taco stand presided over by a Purépecha matron
who is clearly not in a fiesta mood. Wense has his head between his
knees, hands over his head, like a prisoner of war. The bottle of Bacardi
is long gone. I'm thinking it's about time for him to puke, but instead
he raises his head and starts sobbing and talking at once.

"Rubén, you don't understand, you just don't understand. I wanted
you to meet my family, see? Haven't you noticed that over the seven
months you've been coming here, I've never taken you to meet my
family? I mean, you come to visit my wife's family, and that is good,
they're good people, but I have never taken you to meet my family and
do you know why, Rubén, do you know why?"

He is not looking at me. He is staring and gesturing toward the
highway, as if there were a third person in on the conversation.

"Do you want to know why, Rubén? Because I am ashamed . . ."

And now the tears really start to flow, rolling down Wense's
chubby face.

"Because I'm ashamed, because . . . my family is poorer than you can
imagine, I'm poor, my family is poor. You think my wife's family is
poor, ha! I saw my brother today, his shoes were taped together to keep
them from falling apart. He's fourteen years old, just fourteen, and look
at him! At his age, I was already across the border. And today I saw
him and I gave him the last of my money. I was going to buy myself
some jeans, but I gave it all to him so he could get some shoes. That's
how my family is, Rubén. Do you understand, do you understand me
now? Do you understand why I'm so angry at the *norteños*, at the *migra*,
at the cholos—well, not the cholos, I respect them, they are to be
respected, the cholos. But I get so angry and when I drink I get angrier
and I might be small but I can fight, Rubén, I can defend myself when
those assholes look down on me. They think they're better than me
because they know that my family lives west of the highway, below the
cemetery, where the poorest of our poor live, and now we're all here,
the rich, the poor, the *norteños*, for fiesta, but my brothers-in-law are
dead, and I don't tell you this so you'll pity me or give me money, but

if you do give me money, I'll pay you back, you'll see how responsible I am." (Nearly a year later, he asks me for five hundred dollars to help get his brothers across. He pays me back within the month.)

"I'm telling you this because it's the truth, my truth, and I'm going back up there, fuck the *migra*. That's my truth. I'm going to cross that line no matter what anyone says about it, and I'll probably drink too much sometimes but I'll work harder when I do, I can work on a hangover, no hangover ever kept me from an honest day's work, and I'll bring Rosa and my little daughter up north, too. We'll be together once again, in St. Louis, and my mother-in-law, and the widows, and all my brothers, and my father, even the old old man, we'll all be there together . . . You have to come visit us, Rubén, in my house that is your house, and you'll see how my life is there, you'll see it all, you'll see us working and living in an apartment with all these black people around us, and a lot of Mexicans, many, many Mexicans. One day there'll be more Mexicans in Missouri than blacks, I swear to you."

And now he looks me in the eye. "You'll have to come visit us, Rubén, you'll have to come visit one day, in St. Louis, Missouri."

Wense is gone. I don't know where he is. He wiped his tears on his sweatshirt, got up, started walking back toward the plaza, and then he just disappeared. I'm looking for him, wanting to tell him that I understand, that I'll visit him in St. Louis. I'm at the edge of the plaza crowd that is waiting for the *castillo* to explode, and whom should I run into but Pedro Huaroco. Pedro, the survivor of the deadly crash, who the Chávezes suspect was bought off by the *migra*.

He's wearing his humble migrant outfit, a Pepsi T-shirt and a cap commemorating the "Peanut Festival Road Race, Sylvester, Georgia, 1989." Soon he has his arm around me—during fiesta, fast friends are as common as fast enemies—and offers me his bottle, which is nearly empty. Time for another one. We walk to a cantina a few blocks off the plaza, momentarily leaving the fiesta din behind. There are mostly old-timers, mescal drinkers, at the counter. I'm recognized as an outsider, and everyone shakes my hand and slaps my back, congratulating me on being on hand for the grand fiesta of Cherán.

Then don Raúl, the proprietor, says to Pedro, "You're the one who was in the accident, aren't you?" Pedro will always be known as "the one who was in the accident" and, given the rumors that circulate about his role in the tragedy, regarded with suspicion. Small towns have long memories.

Pedro demurs and orders a round of mescal. But the old-timers will not let it go.

"So how was it up there?" one of them asks.

"It was a thing of destiny," Pedro says. "And if you want to know how it *really* was, well, I'm the one to talk to because, yes, I was there."

To my surprise, he begins telling the story, with much more detail than when I interviewed him. He begins as if it were just another border tall tale, in a loud voice filled with bravado. But his tone changes rapidly. He grows short of breath. He licks his lips.

The migrant crew that he and the Chávez brothers hooked up with slept together in the brush just north of the line, east of San Diego, waiting for the coyote's truck to pick them up. The land there was brutal, very little earth, mostly rock, and you know how cold the rocks get at night. He slept next to Benjamín, the oldest Chávez brother, the one Pedro felt closest too. They awoke with a start when someone shouted, "*¡La migra!*" But it was only a rattlesnake slithering about in the bushes. A few of the migrants tried to catch it for a quick meal, but it eluded their grasp. Someone remarked that the snake's appearance was a bad sign. Had it been a good spirit, they reasoned, it would have allowed itself to be caught, offered itself as food. Pedro himself never saw the snake. Only the Chávez brothers and a couple of others who also died in the crash.

It was one of those things of destiny, Pedro says again.

Inside the GMC, Pedro was squeezed in between Benjamín and another paisano. He knew something was wrong when the coyote accelerated suddenly. He could dimly see the headlights of the Border Patrol truck through the tinted rear window. Pedro started praying to the Virgin of Guadalupe. Benjamín Chávez cursed the driver at the top of his lungs, swearing that he'd kick his ass when they were deported back to Mexico. Pedro heard the screeching of the tires on the curves. Someone kicked the rear window of the camper shell open. The migrants closest to the window were shouting, flailing their arms in the direction of the BP truck. They knew that the coyote would not stop—destiny. Their only chance was to convince the *migra* to stop. In desperation, someone tossed the carjack out the window. It fell harmlessly by the side of the road. The driver took the curves at ever-higher speeds. The bodies crushed into one another inside the camper. Pedro knocked heads with someone—he thinks it was Salvador Chávez—hard, like in a soccer match when two players both go for the ball and crack skulls.

With a trembling finger, Pedro traces a map of the curving road, Avenida Del Oro, on the wood counter, the old, rutted, cracked counter of uneven planks stained by years of Coke and cigarettes and food and sweaty elbows. Now he traces the intersecting road, Calle Capistrano. He goes back to Avenida Del Oro, his finger representing the GMC approaching the intersection. The finger bends, and the knuckles of the rest of his hand knock the wood. The old men nod quietly.

He crawled out from underneath the camper—he was saved by a two-foot-high space under the chassis. He stood up and fell back when his ankle gave way beneath him. He remembers the cloud of dust and that it was dawning in the east. The truck was lying upside down, its front wheels still spinning, the camper shell crushed. There were legs and arms protruding from beneath the chassis: Benjamín . . . Jaime . . . Salvador. He pulled on Salvador's leg. He pulled with all his might. The shoe came off in his hand and he fell backward. The leg twitched, twitched, and went still.

The men around the bar are looking anywhere but at Pedro. Don Raúl wipes the counter. On the TV screen above us, Cantinflas is fast-talking a cop out of taking him to jail. One by one, the men leave, rather unceremoniously after the effusive greeting. They got more than they asked for.

A thing of destiny. How else could Pedro, or anyone else, possibly explain it?

For Pedro, this sliver of faith is small consolation. He will live his entire life with the memory of the accident, with the guilt of having survived, a guilt exacerbated by the Chávezes' pain. He hesitates when I ask him if he'll ever go north again. He must think of his son, he says, a cute five-year-old with a tightly braided ponytail trailing down his back, just like his father's. What of the day that will surely come when the child, as a teenager, takes to the road himself? Will Pedro try to stop him? What will the boy find on the road?

We walk out into the darkened streets of adobes with off-kilter, shuttered doorways and blackened windows like the eyeless sockets of skulls, and I remember my father's descriptions of Old Mexico, the small towns of the northern provinces that after nightfall seemed haunted by the bitterest spirits.

Now, for the second time tonight, I have beside me a Mexican man in tears. Pedro cries not for the Chávez brothers, that is, he doesn't give their names to his sorrow. Yesterday, his ox died. At first I, the gringo, think this is some kind of joke, but it's not. Eight years that *animalito* had trudged up into the hills and helped Pedro bring back pine and oak from the last free stands of trees in the region. He loved that animal. Because it represented his livelihood in Cherán and because it gave every ounce of its energy so his family might be provided for.

How he worked for us, that ox! How he thought only of us! Surely a bright, benevolent spirit resided in him; whenever he strayed in the mountains he'd make his way down all by himself, he knew the path home. When work was good, Pedro and his ox would make forty pesos a day, seven days a week, and they had to work those seven days because his family needed about three hundred pesos a week just for the bare necessities. But now the ox was dead. A new one will cost six hundred pesos, and if Pedro can't work with his ox, how will he get that money?

There is a sudden flash of light, followed by a bang that echoes along the hills. The *castillo* has been lit. Pedro runs for the plaza, and I after him. We arrive to see the plaza of Cherán erupt in a silver-blue light, with all the beautiful fury of its 331st fiesta. A bevy of skyrockets go up, some shooting straight into the sky and banging like antiaircraft fire, others streaking red like tracers, still others splitting off into several little missiles. Dozens of pinwheels shower the plaza with rainbow sparks and a great cloud of glowing smoke rises into the night. The *torito*—the brave man who straps a wooden carriage of firecrackers and pinwheels onto his back—meanders crazily before the *castillo*, scattering the crowd with its thousand faces: awed kids with mouths agape, elders tight-lipped, perhaps recalling the fiestas and the Cherán of long ago, drunken *norteños* dazed or sneering or hooting—but there are very few smiles. It is a violent beauty, after all, this fiesta climax, the release of a great and terrible energy that is the sum of another year's journeys.

Joseph Rodriguez

7

HARVEST

Wense made it. True to his word, he left a couple of weeks after the fiesta, and this time the river was low, the temperature mild, and the *migra* apparently on vacation. He had to walk only three hours through the desert before the van picked up his crew, and the drive east and north to Missouri was uneventful. He'll work all winter long at a greenhouse nursery in St. Louis, impervious to the brutal Midwest winter. It can get down to below zero outside, but in that nursery the temperature's always eighty degrees, the air heavy with humidity and the scent of thousands of flowers blooming.

In the highlands of Michoacán now it is cold and dry; the land has taken on the yellow and brown hues of winter. December in Michoacán is the time of the *cosecha*, the reaping of the town's only crop, maize. Now everyone is obsessed with the rustling sea of withered stalks hiding the ears of corn that will provide Cherán its tortillas and other corn-based meals and drinks in the new year.

At the Chávez house, there is more than harvest in the air. Florentino has finally returned from California. He'd remained in Watsonville after the accident, after identifying the bodies in Temecula. Because Rosa had returned from St. Louis for the funeral and Fernando had been at home sick, Florentino had felt that it was his responsibility to stay on the job and provide for the family.

The task proved far more difficult than he imagined. He'd go to sleep terribly alone in the trailer where all the brothers had once slept together. Everything around him triggered memory. The tiny black-and-white TV with the bent aerial that they all watched together in the evenings. The empty bunk beds. He'd get up, walk outside into the cold, misty air of Watsonville mornings—so similar to Cherán's—and there waiting for him in the carport would be just one pair of mud-caked work boots instead of five.

But now that he's back home, Florentino is sober and doing everything he can to lift his mother's spirits. He plays the radio loud, like his brothers used to. There had been no music in the house since the accident, a sign of mourning, like the black ribbon nailed into the wall above the entrance to the store downstairs. But Florentino said that the dead didn't want any more mourning, that they wanted the family to enjoy life.

Meanwhile, Rosa is finalizing plans for her own journey. Whatever reservations her mother or brothers might have about her decision to leave have gone unspoken. Rosa goes about her daily routine without any hint of apprehension. She is awaiting word from "Mr. Charlie," a local coyote who provides "door-to-door" service for a fee of $1,000. She will leave on a moment's notice, as soon as the coyote fills up the two dozen slots on his passenger list; word is that the group will depart by the end of the month. The only sign of the impending journey is that Rosa has packed an overnight bag.

The other news is that the tombstones for the dead brothers have finally arrived from Morelia. Part of them, anyway. The monuments, miniatures of gleaming white cathedrals with twin steeples, consist of a base and crown. Only the bases came, but the stonecutter sent his assurances that the graves would be done by New Year's, along with his profuse apologies for the delay in finishing the work. A year and a half from now an exasperated María Elena and her sons will pool their money together to pay a local mason to complete the task.

. . .

I get up early at Pancho Villa's. It is impossible not to get up early, what with the cuckoo clock that strikes twelve at five-thirty in the morning, the baby crying, and Pancho and his wife rustling and whispering in bed, sounds I hear as if they were in my own room because the doorway connecting the rooms has no door, just a blanket. Pancho's wife starts up the wood fire in the kitchen, filling the patio with the sweet smoke that will warm the sweetest coffee on earth, *café de olla*, the grinds boiled with a ton of sugar and cinnamon in a big earthenware pot. Nena gets ready to head to work at the *caseta*, another day of receiving calls from the towns and cities she dreams of living, and falling in love, in one day.

Pancho pours some cane liquor into his coffee and raises the cup to his lips with trembling hands. The younger kids run through the backyard scattering the baby chicks. No bath today; there's not enough water. The kids are given a meager meal of fried strips of tortilla. I am not offered any. There is not enough for the adults to eat today.

Finally, Pancho's father, Francisco Sr., opens the door to his own house, an old-style Purépecha *troje*, "house" in Purépecha, pine-plank walls and a roof of thatched cornstalks. Even when Pancho built the modern house that the rest of the family lives in, the old man refused to budge; he prefers the old ways. He wears his white hat, a Marlboro man wool jacket, and leather gloves against the cold. Almost ninety years old, he likes to talk to me of his *bracero* trips north, back in the 1940s.

There is great laughter when I announce that I will be joining the harvest today. The thought of a gringo in the corn rows is just too much.

But soon this gringo is sitting in the bed of a battered Ford pickup belonging to a Chéran family named Olivares. We hold on for dear life as we bounce along a dirt path out of town, entering the endless sea of corn. Seated next to me are none other than Güiro and his cholo crew. In fact, it was Güiro who invited me to this particular *cosecha*. He is friends with one of the Olivares boys, a former cholo who's gone straight and now commutes between the mushroom farms of Pennsylvania and Chéran.

I have been told that an invitation to a family's harvest is considered an honor, a sign of respect and friendship. Today, Güiro has dropped the cholo scowl. He's still got his Walkman on, but he's all smiles, leaning back against a stack of baskets.

Harvest for the Purépechas, as Father Melesio, Dr. Tito, and Dante Cerano have all told me, is much more than just a commercial venture. The lands surrounding Cherán are communal, owned not by the state but by the Purépechas themselves; most families in town have their own parcel. At harvest time, the communal life is truly manifest. Taking turns, each family reaps its crop with the aid of other families. In this way, most Cheranes are in the fields throughout harvest season, moving from parcel to parcel.

The pickup pulls off the road in the midst of the fields east of town that stretch across a long, gentle valley, where every inch of earth has been sown. The wind rustles through the stalks, the sound of a stream gently rushing over stones. Now I understand why the Purépechas, hundreds of years ago, chose the high, precarious land to build their village: it is surrounded on all sides by land perfect for agriculture, irrigated naturally by streams running down from the hills.

Everyone gets a large straw basket, about a yard in diameter and four feet deep, with a leather strap that you stretch across your forehead. The only other equipment is the picking tool, a small hooked blade with a wooden handle. We dive into the corn rows. Grab an ear, snap at the stem, husk it with the blade, toss the cob over your head into the basket, go on to the next ear, and on to the next stalk . . . and on and on, down the endless rows.

My companions are picking alongside me, though they're going much faster than me because I'm a novice, and soon I can't see my friends anymore, I catch only fleeting glimpses of them floating among stalks that are taller than any Purépecha. I hear them up ahead, joking like they're kicking back at home or at the cantina, Güiro and his homeboys rapping slowly of Chevrolets and Tupac, of *migra* busts and famous narco-traffickers, of the heat of the midday sun, of how condoms impede erections, of furtive trysts right here in the corn rows, of fiesta fights, of how good that cold one's going to taste at lunch. Hours through rows that have no beginning or end, under a slightly milky misty sky, our shoes taking on the hue of the thin tan earth that's seen these stalks rise green and wither yellow since long before the Conquest, since forever.

Grandmothers and toddlers make up the rear guard, scouring the stalks for stray cobs. The task is performed with great joy, as if it weren't work at all, because it really isn't. The migrants who've picked crops and run errands for America all year are now doing it for themselves: they will eat what they reap in the form of tortillas, and *atole*, a thick corn soup served piping hot, and steamed corn and grilled corn smothered in mayonnaise, grated cheese, lime, and chile. No part of the corn will go to waste; they will use the long, tough, fibrous leaves to weave baskets, thatch roofs, and even make raincoats for themselves as the Purépechas did before the Conquest.

We work from about nine in the morning to one o'clock and break for lunch. The Olivares women bring out the big earthenware pot of stew, huge chunks of soft beef swimming in a blood-red chile soup, which makes us sweat all the more but eventually cools us down. Across the valley, I can see other families partaking of the same traditional Purépecha meal.

Then it's back for another four hours of picking. My neck, shoulders, and back are sore beyond belief, my soft writer's hands painfully scratched. Every time I think my basket is full of corn, I return to the truck, which is now piled high with cobs, only to find that I've filled it halfway or even less, which causes knee-slapping laughter among the Indians.

With the gold light of the afternoon sun slanting across the fields, we load the last of the day's picking onto the old Ford, and everyone, all fifteen of us, gets into the cab and on top of the ton of corn in the back. The truck is so overloaded that the tires scrape the fenders. But the truck doesn't protest, it rumbles along slow but content, backing up along the dusty road out to the gravel road, cruising at ten miles an hour the mile or so to the highway that takes us to town.

Mr. Charlie isn't the trusting kind. In the coyote business, you've got to be careful whom you shake hands with, and he's not shaking mine, despite Rosa, Wense, and Florentino's best efforts at an effusive introduction. Short, dark, pot-bellied, oily-faced, unruly-haired, Mr. Charlie has had a long hard day of something. He lives three blocks down Galeana from the Chávezes. When he is informed that the reporter is willing to pay the same fee as every other migrant for the trip north, the conversation turns more cordial.

We reach a tentative agreement. No still cameras, no video cameras, no tape recorders. Full adult fare, half up front, half on delivery. Cash only, please. In Zamora, he'll charter a bus and hire a chauffeur—both of the highest quality, he assures me—for the trip to the border.

He reminds me that not all coyotes work like this; there are some in his trade who'll put you on third-class buses with layovers in forlorn northern Mexican towns. At the line in Nogales, coyote No. 2 will take over for the "short" trip across the line to Phoenix, Arizona, after a "short" stay in a safe house on the Mexican side. Mr. Charlie will then personally deliver you to a second safe house, in Cobden, Illinois. At that point, relatives in St. Louis have to pick us up.

Mr. Charlie says the passenger list is growing by the day, but we probably won't leave until after Christmas. I mull it over. Wait another ten days in Cherán or head to L.A. to spend Christmas with my family? I've missed only one Christmas with my family my entire life; it is not an easy decision. Family wins out.

"I'll be back a couple of days after Christmas," I tell him.

"No problem," he says. He shakes my hand.

And so I leave Cherán, despite the Chávezes' protests. You'll be missing all the Christmas traditions, they tell me. The *posadas*, the egg breads, Midnight Mass and the beautiful colors and smells in church, the dance parties held right out on the street in front of people's houses, the huge Nativity scene down at the plaza.

I take an early evening bus down to Zamora, the dim headlights barely illuminating the highway. But through the tinted windows I can see the magnificent light of a thousand stars hanging from the ink-black southern sky.

As we crest the hill just north of town, I look back. There is more light than I've ever seen emanating from the town. One more Purépecha tradition: the *norteño* families with their big two- and three-story houses dress their satellite dishes with blinking rainbows of Christmas lights. That is how I remember Cherán now: the dozens of great dishes of light flashing in the midst of the vast darkness of the highlands, lights blinking at the heavens, thanking all the gods of the Purépecha pantheon for a baby's birth, for the gift of life in the new year.

In the dimming twilight, my plane crosses the Sea of Cortéz, an amber lake amid the twilight gray-blues of the Sonoran desert. After the turbulence over mainland Mexico, the flight turns amazingly gentle. I am leaving *la crisis* far behind and, at this altitude, the drama of the border is invisible. There is no line, just this moment of peace far above it all.

Joseph Rodriguez

8

ROSA'S JOURNEY

Mr. Charlie showed up at Rosa's house at about ten in the morning on December 27. Today is the day, he announced, get ready. True to his warning that his migrant crew would depart Cherán on a moment's notice, Rosa had only a couple of hours to say her good-byes. When I phoned the Chávezes from Los Angeles on December 28 announcing my return, María Elena informed me that Rosa had already departed.

Everyone was to meet at the bus station in Zamora at seven that evening. Sensing Rosa's apprehension, Mr. Charlie tried to put her at ease. They were certain to make it, he told her, because they were going to cross on New Year's Eve.

A few years ago the Zapatistas had their revolution on New Year's Eve. The rebels had known that the Mexican army would be *pisteando*, drinking, carousing with whores, and not at their posts. That's how the Zapatistas took over nearly a third of Chiapas—for a few days, anyway. The coyotes figured they could mount the same surprise attack against the *migra*. The gringos might be stuck-up, repressed assholes, the coyotes reasoned, but surely they partied on the thirty-first of December.

Rosa took the bus, a beat-up VW van with worn-out shocks, down to the plaza. Inside the church, she lit a candle for Saint Francis and prayed to him, to the Virgin, and to her brothers. Like that of the rest of the family, her faith had been terribly shaken by the accident, but this was no time for doubting. If there was a God or angels who looked out for those facing the dangers of the road, she needed their help. "My brothers who are in heaven," she remembers whispering, looking up at Saint Francis with his face aglow beneath his green neon halo. "Help Yeni and me cross safely. Don't abandon us."

María Elena and Florentino accompanied Rosa and Yeni to the station in Zamora, just as they had done with Benjamín, Jaime, and Salvador. They left Cherán on a bus driven by a teenager with aviator shades. There was very little conversation among the family. Mostly, they looked out the windows as twilight waned and darkness engulfed the highlands.

The Zamora bus station was in its typical chaotic state. Arriving passengers collided with those departing at the gates, and the voice on the PA intoned the destinations monotonously: Mexico City and Morelia, Tijuana and Nogales, Tuxtla Gutiérrez and Oaxaca and Guadalajara. The Chávezes sat waiting in the plastic chairs before the colossal Coca-Cola machine at the center of the building. María Elena cried softly throughout the wait. Rosa didn't let go of her hand until Mr. Charlie called everyone together to board the Nogales-bound bus. Rosa told her mother not to worry and immediately felt silly, but what else could she say? She boarded the bus and felt the tears streaming down her own cheeks. A year ago, she'd seen her brothers off at this very station.

It was a cool, clear night and the air was filled with the scent of freshly tilled earth. The bus headed north on Highway 35 and then up the Pacific Route toward Arizona, passing the beacons of the Mexican night, the dozens of twenty-four-hour tire-repair shops lining the road, each advertising its services with a huge old balding truck tire and a dim, naked lightbulb hanging in the center of the wheel.

Rosa looked out the window and saw the homeless huddled in doorways, the greasy smoke rising from all-night taco stands, and the dusty open stretches of wintery farmland only faintly illuminated by the dim swath of headlights. Slowly, ever so slowly, the subtropical greens of the south gave way to the arid yellow immensity of the north. On the other side of the line, the desert would yield, again, to mountains and valleys and rivers. What one had to do was survive the desert.

The trip to Nogales took thirty-eight hours. Mr. Charlie told the migrants that it would take another three days to arrive at their destinations on the other side. For Rosa and the rest of the Cheranes, it was the beginning of a two-week voyage that would test their physical and emotional limits, but of course they didn't know that yet. All Rosa knew was that her husband was waiting in St. Louis, that her mother was sad and anxious back home, that the road to the border was interminable. Her brothers saw these very things with their own eyes, she thought to herself. They had felt each bump in the road that she felt now. She conjured up images of Jaime, Salvador, and Benjamín, placed them in the empty seats toward the back of the bus.

Yeni was fast asleep in her arms, but Rosa couldn't close her eyes for more than a few seconds at a time. She wasn't aware that she was crying again until the woman sitting next to her asked Rosa if she was all right. Aren't you scared? the woman asked. She'd heard about the accident. Everyone knew about the accident.

There were eighteen women, two men, and five children from Cherán on the bus. They whiled away the thirty-eight hours to the line watching video after video on the monitors hanging from the ceiling—mostly ninja knock-'em-ups, the preferred genre of Mexican bus drivers. They arrived in Nogales in the wee hours of the twenty-ninth. They slept a little in a cheap but clean hotel and the following day were taken by van to a squalid safe house that smelled of unwashed bodies. There was no furniture. They sat on the floor and ate a tasteless meal of meat, potatoes, and tortillas.

The coyotes came and went in their vans, receiving and making phone calls on their chirping cellular phones. At five in the afternoon on December 30, the group was hustled into a van whose middle and back seats had been removed. They were told to lie down flat, and since there were twenty-five of them, most everyone had to lie on top of or below somebody else, squirming about to find a way to not crush or get crushed.

They were driven for about forty-five minutes, probably eastward, to a part of the border where the massive steel wall separating downtown Nogales, Mexico, from downtown Nogales, Arizona, becomes a laughable barbed-wire fence about four feet high. They crossed the line without a hitch. It was so easy, Rosa thought. One step and you're in America. The migrants marched out into the dusk, climbing hills and descending ravines. When night fell, there was only the sliver of a moon and starlight to walk by, and the temperature dropped rapidly.

They moved at a steady, fast pace for about four and half hours. Rosa carried Yeni slung in her rebozo the entire time, her neck and back increasingly strained. They came to a deserted two-lane road, where they were told to wait in the bushes for the next coyote van. It wasn't long before headlights appeared in the distance. The van pulled over, the side door opened, and everyone ran for it, slipping underneath a barbed-wire fence by the side of the road and throwing themselves into the van one on top of the other.

They'd driven only about fifteen minutes when a police squad car pulled them over. They sat by the edge of the road until several Border Patrol units took them back to BP headquarters. Rosa was scared; this was the first time she'd been detained by the *migra* and she didn't know what to expect. The interrogation lasted all of a minute. Name, date of birth, home address in Mexico. They took her fingerprints on a digital pad. Every time the American agent spoke, all she heard was the strange accent with which he pronounced the words in Spanish. Soon she was laughing in the middle of her responses, relaxed, a bit giddy even. The high-tech surroundings were a surreal jump cut from the mountain terrain she'd just hiked through—and it was warm inside the BP head-quarters.

The agents didn't search Rosa's backpack, where they would have found her Mexican ID papers and discovered that she'd given them false information. Today she was María. Later, she'd become Julia, Rita, Iris, and Alejandra. Names she remembered from magazines: movie stars, rock singers. Names of people she'd fantasized being. Names of people that, in some way, she was becoming.

The group did not attempt to cross again on the thirtieth, exhausted as they were from their ordeal. And as for Mr. Charlie's grand New Year's Eve surprise attack, it came to naught. The coyotes, along with the other men in their group from Cherán, started drinking early in the afternoon and by midevening they were stumbling about town. The women were left behind in the safe house, of course, prompting a long discussion about macho irresponsibility. Machismo itself was one of the primary reasons that so many women were heading north these days. The old migrant tradition in small towns like Cherán permitted only the men to become adventurer-providers, journeying north alone to tame the frontier. After a few years, many were able to bring their families up to the States to join them. But the separations were hard on the women—there was the sheer loneliness, of course, but there were also the constant rumors that their men built *casas chicas*, love nests, with other Mexican women (or, worse yet, with gringas) up north. Then there were the truly sad cases where the man went away, never be heard from again, not even in the form of a fifty-dollar money order to help clothe the kids in the winter.

There were only three solutions to this problem, and one wasn't a solution: accept the man's philandering away from home and wait patiently for money and the occasional visit. The radical response would have been for the women to create their own *casas chicas*, but Cherán was, after all, a provincial town and to do so would risk one's being labeled a whore by the elders, men and women alike. The strategy many women came up with was to join their husbands in the north—whether their partners liked it or not. These days there were new tales being told among the Cheranes, stories from women who said they'd traveled north to surprise their husbands with their mistresses and how the whores were sent packing and the men suffered the wrath of betrayed Purépechas.

And so on this New Year's Eve the women talked about the men and their drinking and their *putas* in America, whom the women would shortly be able to confront. And yes, they found some compassion in their hearts for the men too, for they were just boys, really, and not all their stories about how hard they worked or about abusive *patrones* and gringo cops were fantasies.

The children became increasingly boisterous as the sound of fire-crackers—and live ammunition—crescendoed outside the safe house in Nogales. It was January 1, 1997.

The next attempt to cross, in the early evening of New Year's Day, was a cruel farce. The Cheranes had walked only a soccer field's length

ica before they were detained. The fucking gringo *migra*
party on New Year's, Mr. Charlie complained bitterly. They
at the safe house within a couple of hours.

That night they slept as well as they could, huddled on the floor.
The next day they sat around eating potato chips, sipping Coke, and
swapping dreams of saving up enough money to buy a house back in
Michoacán or, more humbly, to get a new TV set or pay off mother's
medical bills. Rosa said she dreamed of bringing her mother to the
United States, as well as her sisters-in-law, the widows, and their children. They'd live together in St. Louis, in one of those big old blood-
red brick houses with tall white wood window frames and a view of the
Gateway Arch and the Mississippi.

On January 2, at roughly the same time as the previous attempt,
they walked across the line again. The *migra* appeared to be waiting
for them. As they ran across a two-lane highway, they heard a man's
voice shout in thickly accented Spanish *"¡Párense, cabrones!"* (Stop, you
idiots!) This time the group broke up and scattered in half a dozen
different directions. Rosa stuck close to two of the local coyotes Mr.
Charlie had hired as guides for the crossing. They hid in the bushes
for about three hours, waiting for the *migra* to leave. Flashlights came
close to discovering their hideaway several times. When they thought
the coast was clear, they began looking for a way around the roadblock,
but even the coyotes seemed to have lost their sense of direction. It was
early in the morning and the cold began numbing their hands and feet.
A crescent moon was still high in the sky and the landscape glowed in
the spectral light. A woman in the group complained of cactus thorns
in her legs. After another hour or so, they again found themselves on
the deserted highway; apparently, they'd walked in a circle. Then they
saw several Border Patrol trucks with their headlights off, waiting.

One of the coyotes said they should try another route, one on which
they wouldn't have to walk very far, a prospect that delighted everyone.
This time they crossed underneath the twelve-foot-high steel wall that
separates the Mexican and American parts of Nogales. On the American
side, huge amber lamps attracted great clouds of moths. The spot the
Cheranes chose for the crossing was close enough to the town for them
to see the glow of city lights.

The new route did not change their luck. The migrants walked for about fifteen minutes after crossing the line and boarded a van. The *migra* caught up with them a few minutes later. They went through the same ritual at headquarters—interrogation, fingerprinting. At every turn, they tried to disrupt the *migra*'s procedures. The fingerprinting computer was their favorite. Only if the finger was pressed flat and firm on the digital pad did a clean image appear. Rosa would put her fingers down sideways or too lightly for the image to register, causing the agent to curse and mash her hand onto the pad with his own. Whether the trick worked or the *migra*'s technology wasn't all that it was cracked up to be, the computer, apparently, did not find a match.

Back at the safe house, they kept one another's spirits up by joking and coming up with nicknames for everyone, like the coyotes did. El Cantinflas went to a short, reedy guy who was quick with words and double entendres. El Washington was for the man who couldn't talk about anything but the most minute details of the varieties of apples he was going to pick all spring and summer long in Washington State. El Apagaluz (Turn Off the Light) was given to one of the men who returned to the safe house rip-roaring drunk in the wee hours on New Year's and turned off the light in the room the women slept, saying they should be asleep. La Novia del Pueblo (The Town's Girlfriend) was the pathetic moniker for the woman whose man had abandoned her years ago. And Lucero, the name of the ravishing, leggy blonde pop star who dominates Televisa, Mexico's mega-entertainment network, was chosen for Rosa's daughter, Yeni, whose skin is nearly chocolate brown and whose features are completely Indian.

Now the men in the group began complaining that the babies were crying too much and tipping the *migra* off to their location. The coyotes agreed and decided to split the men off from the main group. They tried the fence route once again, the men traveling slightly ahead of the women. The *migra* were waiting for them just as before, but the men were able to elude their grasp and they arrived safely in Phoenix that same night. The women and their children were detained again and deported back to Nogales.

The coyotes asked the women if they wanted to try once more, since it was still early in the evening. They did, crossing for the third time at the same spot. Within minutes they were detained once more. They arrived at the safe house at four in the morning. Exhaustion and depression were beginning to set in.

The next night there were a couple of new arrivals at the house, including a fully decked-out transvestite from Mexico City. Heavy makeup, skirt, high heels. She bonded, of course, with the women, who were delighted with her company. And instantly gave her the nickname of La Loca.

The women were driven east of town again, for about an hour. They hiked in rugged terrain, in an area that appeared similar to that of the first attempt—soft sand, occasional rocks, desert scrub. But this was by far the most difficult hike. Crawling underneath a barbed-wire fence, Rosa got her rebozo caught in the rusty metal and Yeni scratched her leg badly. Still, the two-year-old didn't cry.

This time they walked for six hours, the moon helping them with its silvery blue light. It was a clear and brutally cold night. They passed through ranch land where cows and horses slept, standing stock-still. Now and again, a real coyote howled in the distance. They crossed a deserted two-lane and two deer, elegant and shy, appeared before them, disappearing back into the brush without a sound a few seconds later.

The apparition caused elation among the group—it was the sign they'd been waiting for. For most of the indigenous peoples in the Americas, deer are a good omen. "We'll be sure to cross now," Rosa told herself, digging deep for the last of her hope and energy.

But the terrain only grew more rugged. Rosa lost her footing when she stepped on a rock that gave way in the sand, and her knee came down on another rock, tearing open both her jeans and her skin. Miraculously, she was able to cradle Yeni in such a way that the child wasn't hurt. Rosa felt blood trickling down her calf, strangely cold. She willed herself to take one step after another, her body feeling terribly heavy and slow now. She stumbled once more. The rest of the way she held on to the coyote's coat, using it as a walking stick.

Soon her thirst was unbearable and she asked a woman she'd seen carrying a water bottle for a sip. But the woman had discarded it hours ago. Indeed, the women had left everything behind by now, including backpacks and bags of food, in a desperate attempt to lighten their loads and move more quickly. Rosa's mouth was cold and dry, her face burning and wet with sweat.

The van picked them up at the appointed spot. The *migra* were nowhere in sight. Soon they were on the freeway headed toward Phoenix, where they would rejoin the men at another safe house.

So the apparition of the deer had indeed been a good omen—they were in America. What they didn't know was that the worst blizzard of that winter was beginning to blow across the Plains.

The safe house in Phoenix, where the women joined several other migrants who had crossed before, was presided over by a moody matron who charged five dollars for each meal of only slightly reheated leftovers. The woman watched TV in the living room, the only place in the house with furniture. The migrants were locked inside empty bedrooms.

Meanwhile, Mr. Charlie set about buying the van that would transport the migrants to safe houses in Illinois, Kentucky, and North Carolina, where relatives would pick them up.

Rosa spent money for only one meal; it was all she could afford, and she gave the food to Yeni. On their second day in the house, the matron locked the bathrooms, alleging that the *pollos* were making too much of a mess. When Mr. Charlie stopped by later that day, the group turned mutinous and demanded that he take them to another house or to a hotel; he grudgingly obliged. The woman in charge of the second house was as generous and hospitable as the first had been mean. Her warm meals tasted of home and she didn't charge anything. Mr. Charlie bought a powder-blue Astro van and worked on it in the garage, retrofitting the vehicle for the trip. He removed the middle and back seats, adjusted the shock absorbers so that the van wouldn't appear to be skimming the road from the weight of twenty-five bodies inside.

The work was completed at four in the morning on Thursday, January 9. Thirteen days after leaving Cherán, Rosa hadn't called either her mother back home or her husband in St. Louis. She assumed that they were worried sick, but there wasn't much she could do about it—she'd now run completely out of money, and, in any case, there was no phone available to the migrants at the safe house.

Another thousand miles to go. Rosa didn't see much of the landscape, since most of the time she sat cross-legged on the floor of the van. After a few hours, her legs began cramping. She asked the woman sitting next to her if she could stretch her legs out over hers, and soon everyone's legs were entwined.

At one point, probably in Colorado, the group was caught in a *remolino*, a tornado of snow and hail. A tremendous gust of wind nearly knocked the van off the highway and one of the side windows blew out. Frigid air poured into the van.

At first the cold hurt the migrants down to their bones, but after a while they were just numb. Rosa had only a thin sweater for the cold, her gray sweater, the one with a hole in the left elbow. Same thing for Yeni, nothing for the cold. But once again, Yeni didn't complain, didn't cry or even whimper. When she spoke to her mother it was in a barely audible whisper. It was as if she knew what they were doing, where they were headed.

According to the car radio, it's five degrees below zero, thirty below with the windchill factor. I am in St. Louis, where I headed after I learned that I'd missed Rosa's departure from Cherán. My mustache crinkles when I open my mouth; my hands and feet ache, despite my boots and gloves and one of those black hats with the furry ear flaps.

We're heading east out of town, across the bridge that spans the Mississippi, which tonight is equal parts water and ice, a million chunks of it streaming south below us on the rapid current.

We pass the famous Gateway Arch, monument to America's expansion west of the Mississippi. But tonight we're heading east and I'm with a crew of Mexican, not American, pioneers. For Mexicans today, the Promised Land lies toward the Atlantic. Driven out by anti-immigrant fever and a saturated job market in the West and drawn by labor shortages in the agricultural and service sectors throughout the Midwest and South, the Mexicans have arrived in the heartland.

At the wheel is Baltazar Cortéz, in the backseat his brother Wense; I, the visitor, get the honor of riding shotgun. Our mission tonight, other than trying to avoid sliding off the icy roads and dying from hypothermia, is to pick Rosa up at the safe house in Cobden, Illinois.

Our covered wagon is a gold 1989 Pontiac Grand Am with 150,000 miles on the odometer but a mint body, new tires and shocks.

I'd been with Wense as he waited anxiously to hear from Mr. Charlie. Finally, Mr. Charlie called from Phoenix to announce that they'd made it across the border at Nogales and were ready to head up to the Midwest. But before they could leave, he said, he needed another five hundred dollars in advance, on top of the five hundred dollars already paid, saying that two-year-old Yeni had to pay half the adult fare. Wense protested—the deal had been that Rosa and Yeni would travel together for one fare. "We've had some unexpected expenses, Wense," Mr. Charlie told him, explaining that they'd only crossed after seven attempts, a record for the coyote.

In his usual cordial tone, Mr. Charlie explained that if Wense didn't come up with the fee, Rosa and the baby would be left behind in Phoenix, without food or money. Through friends and family, Wense got the money together within a day and wired it to Phoenix.

Wense waited another forty-eight hours for the next call. The cordless phone in Baltazar's apartment in Berkeley, a West St. Louis suburb, finally chirped this afternoon at about 4:30, Mr. Charlie announcing their arrival in Illinois—and asking for yet more money, money that Wense, of course, does not have. "How does he think I can get it?" Wense sputtered. "We're just going to have to explain to him that I don't have it."

I wasn't too hopeful about counting on a coyote's sympathy—there are countless horror stories of migrants held hostage in safe houses for weeks, even months, until the debt is paid—but Wense is adamant that Mr. Charlie will allow him to bring his wife and daughter home to St. Louis tonight. "I know him," Wense tells me, smacking his hands together and blowing on them in the backseat. "There won't be a problem."

Rosa's imminent arrival is yet another block in the pyramid the Cortéz and Chávez families have been building in Missouri over the last several years. The pioneer was Baltazar, who arrived in St. Louis in 1991, recommended to a local rancher by his friend Alfredo Román, who had emigrated from Michoacán years earlier. Here, Baltazar met and married Victoria, a woman from Uruapan whose family had migrated to St. Louis in 1992; the couple had their first child, Stefani, the only American citizen in the family, two years later. Wense started making seasonal visits to St. Louis not long after his brother arrived, working for the same rancher. Wense then married Rosa, and in late 1995 brought her up for the first time; she, too, worked for the rancher.

The Cortézes are by no means the only Mexican family in the area. The Románs—a clan with three generations of family in St. Louis— trace the pioneers back to a distant cousin who followed the crops eastward from California in 1952, winding up first in the cornfields of Illinois and later on a tomato farm in Missouri.

We continue east on Interstate 64 toward the farmlands of southern Illinois, our headlights cutting into the slanting snow, the cars ahead of us puffing dragon steam, their tires kicking up grimy, salty ice; in the rearview mirror I can see the spectral cloud our own car produces.

There are few towns along the route to Cobden. Mostly it's frozen cornfields, grain elevators, water towers, the occasional gas station and accompanying Hardee's, Dairy Queen, or McDonald's, icicles like translucent daggers hanging from the eaves. Mini-tornadoes of snow dance strangely before us on the two-lane.

There is only one source of warmth in this car—and it's not from the heater, whose pitiful bursts are overwhelmed by the cold seeping in through the ice-covered windshield and side windows. The warmth comes from the one and only and omnipresent Virgin of Guadalupe, who looks down upon us from heaven, the roof of the Grand Am. Baltazar pinned up the beach-towel rendition a couple of weeks ago. "Now, she travels with me wherever I go," he says with an elfin smile, snuffing out a Marlboro in the ashtray and flicking on his high beams to peer through the blizzard.

We are the only ones out on Route 127 at eight o'clock tonight. Passing the time, Baltazar tells of his voyage across Mexico and across the United States, a trip that began nine years ago when he was seventeen and worked for a few months as a day laborer in El Rancho, California, not far from Temecula, the site of the Chávez tragedy. He used to sleep in the citrus groves, taking a shower when the irrigation sprinklers came on at sunrise. He and his fellow Mexican travelers cooked and ate from the same pan, heating up tortillas over an open fire.

It was like that for quite a while, Balta says, and he remembers thinking that when you're down on your luck people kick you down even farther, and the moment you make good, people envy you and talk bad about you. At the time, he couldn't possibly have imagined coming to St. Louis, having a microwave, driving a gold Grand Am with a Virgin of Guadalupe towel tacked to the roof.

Wense chimes in with his own hard-luck tales, recalling the cop who pulled him over for expired license tags and then suddenly threatened to deport him, yelling about "these fucking Mexicans." And he rhapsodizes about the time his hero, Alfredo Román, the smart and stylish veteran cholo, greenhouse nursery foreman, and family man, was approached by a tipsy *güera*, an American blonde, at a club, only to have the boyfriend, a Nordic mastodon, show up on the dance floor to challenge him. Alfredo managed to bust a beer bottle on the gringo's head before security hauled him away.

We've arrived. We know we are in Cobden (population 1,090) because there are three flags flying in the center of town: Old Glory, the flag of the Prairie State, and the one depicting an eagle swooping up a snake in its beak on a red, green, and white field—the Mexican national flag.

"Hardly any white people living here anymore," says Balta.

There is only one problem. We don't know which house is Mr. Charlie's safe haven. We stop by the home of some relatives of Wense's buddy Alfredo. In the ten seconds it takes to get to the door, the frigid wind seeps deep into my bones. The door opens with a blast of mist. We are told to go up the road and look for a trailer home with a van bearing Arizona license plates parked out front. We fall back into the car and cruise the streets of Cobden, the only car in town that's moving, looking for the pine-green plates. Baltazar points to a basketball court, now blanketed three feet deep in snow, where Michoacán and Zacatecas boys duel to the death. And there's the house of a venerable *bruja* from Cherán who realized she could make more money plying her trade here in the States than back home.

Finally, we see a trailer home with warm yellow light pouring out of its icy windows. The Astro van is parked alongside it, up to its fender in snow. The trailer is the brightest thing I've seen all night in this gray-white world. Even before we get to the door, it opens from inside and Mr. Charlie himself comes out, his round face beaming under a

Caterpillar cap. Handshakes for Baltazar and Wense—and then his eyes settle on me. He gives me a quizzical look, as if trying to place the face, and then it dawns on him. He shoots a concerned glance back at the brothers.

"Don't worry," Wense says, "he's with us." Mr. Charlie is now apparently convinced that I'm *migra*, but what the hell, if I am, what can he do now? We crunch through the snow and up the stairs to the trailer.

I had been thinking about this moment all night. About what must have been a harrowing trip, two weeks of battling the *migra* and the icy roads from Arizona to Illinois. Two weeks eating not much more than potato chips and sipping a little Coca-Cola but not a lot because you won't be able to go to the bathroom for another twelve hours. Two weeks marching double time up craggy hillsides in the desert, crawling under barbed-wire fences, sitting knees to chest in vans, breathing in the aroma of unwashed flesh and hair, nerves constantly on edge, feeling every bump on the endless road.

I guess I was expecting to see two dozen haggard, forlorn faces. I guess I was expecting grimaces of pain, kids with tear-stained cheeks and babies wailing.

But once my eyes can focus, I see none of that. I see beaming faces. Babies cooing in their mother's arms and teenagers huddled around the TV, enraptured at the sight of cowboys on horses thundering over the red dirt of Monument Valley. There's even a Mexican *cumbia* playing from an old cassette box. More women are chatting away in the kitchen around a grandmother stirring a steaming stew on the stove—the matriarch who owns this trailer turned safe house. She and her family emigrated from Michoacán decades ago, but the place is decorated with calendars from general stores back in Michoacán, posters of Purépecha Indians in typical dress.

And there is Rosa Chávez, sitting cross-legged on the floor in the back of the room, cradling Yeni. Rosa rises with a groan; her scabbed knee pokes through the tear in her pants. Wense doesn't move from the doorway as Rosa approaches. Rosa stops. The couple stand about a yard apart. They smile shyly at each other.

And then Wense says . . . *Hola*.

And Rosa responds . . . *Hola.*

That is it. But they are the happiest people I'd ever seen in my life. Because Rosa has made it. She is home. She is finally home.

The day before I leave St. Louis, Balta offers to show me the sights. The temperature is still near zero, there are two feet of snow on the ground, and the roads are icy. It's a Sunday and most of St. Louis is huddled behind frosted windowpanes, but we all put on our layers of shirts and sweaters and jackets and pile into the Grand Am with the Virgin of Guadalupe beaming down at us from the ceiling.

Mexican pride being what it is, our first stop is a Mexican store that offers the usual assortment of Old World spices and meat cuts, tortillas and salsas, Mexican B movies on video, and votive candles emblazoned with the saints to whom many a migrant prayer is whispered. We are received with great gusto by the owners, clerks, and customers, all intent on showing off the Mexico they've brought with them to this icy outpost of the American Midwest—*la tradición* that has foiled assimilation and the melting pot—and on demonstrating how the joke is on the gringos . . . even as the sons and daughters of these first-generation migrants are beginning to enunciate the consonants and vowels of an English-language future, even as the kids are listening to hip hop and oldies and wearing uniforms of American urban warriors, culturally communing with the *morenitos* ("the little black ones," as Mexicans often refer to African Americans) who are so misunderstood and despised by the elders. In the end, the joke will be on both the gringo and the Mexican guardians of reified notions of culture. The kids will be neither Mexican nor gringo but both, and more than both, they will be the New Americans, imbibing cultures from all over the globe.

No trip to St. Louis would be complete without a proper visit to the Gateway Arch, and after navigating the deserted streets of downtown we're standing near the riverside, gazing up at the mammoth gleaming thing, a marvel of engineering, a twentieth-century monument to nineteenth-century idealism. When the pioneers arrived in St. Louis and gazed westward across the river, there was nothing but prairie on the other side, cut by rutted wagon roads promising another coast, another world. There were still more than a thousand miles to go, through hostile Indian territories, through the severity of the desert, but it was God's plan that Americans cross that river, make that great expanse theirs however they could, and of course they did.

For most of the year, there is a vast meadow of prairie grass beneath the arch, but in the dead of this brutal winter, an endless carpet of fresh powdery snow is unmarked by even a single footprint. We are the only tourists to brave the storm. The stark, minimal tableau inspires a photographer friend who has come along for the ride to compose a picture. The family—Baltazar, Wense, Rosa, and Yeni in her mother's arms— are to walk out into the field of snow toward the arch. They are all stamping their feet and puffing misty breath, and Balta especially doesn't look thrilled by the bizarre idea. I am a guest and Mexican hospitality is as famous as the American South's, so soon they are trudging through the knee-deep drifts. Twenty-five feet out, they turn around to pose. We wave them on. Fifty feet. One hundred. Each time, we ask them to go farther, farther out. A football field away. They are dark specks now, lost in the white immensity, their futures a gamble, an enormous risk for ideals and realities shaped by hundreds of years of exploitation and opportunity, of migrant suffering and triumph. Theirs is the great rite of passage, theirs the symbol of America. And yet for most of America, they are invisible, pinpoints of brown on a field of white.

TWO

ANOTHER COUNTRY

Joseph Rodriguez

9

THE LINE

Years ago, I wrote several dispatches from the border at Tijuana, easily the most famous crossing point along the two-thousand-mile-long line. On many occasions, I hung out at the *cancha*, a soccer field that runs along the border just a mile from downtown. All there was back then was a scraggly fence, perforated in too many places to count. On a bluff a hundred yards north, Border Patrol jeeps were perched day and night.

Through the dusty heat of day, the *cancha* was empty. But as soon as the sun set, it turned into a veritable migrant fiesta. A great crowd gathered at the fence and began organizing the evening's expeditions. The migrants came from all over Mexico and Central America and from as far away as China, Iran, Pakistan. Packs of lone men, unshaven, dusty-haired, carrying only the clothes on their backs or small, cheap vinyl bags filled with just a handful of belongings. And families, entire families, from grandmothers with crinkled faces and braided white hair to wide-eyed tots in arms.

The crowd gave rise to a mini-economy of vendors exploiting the migrants' last-minute shopping needs. Hawkers pushed everything from booze and running shoes to girlie magazines and sheets of plastic for that unforeseen thunderstorm. Matronly women stood over coal-fired stoves stirring great steaming pots of *pozole*, hominy stew, or sizzling *carne asada*, grilled beef. Prostitutes offered farewell trysts.

Music blared from boom boxes connected through a few dozen extension cords to a socket in someone's living room a couple of hundred yards away or hooked up directly to the fraying, sparking wires hanging above our heads. And there were the soccer matches, intense battles between rival regions throughout the republic: Zacatecas versus San Luis Potosí, Michoacán versus Saltillo, Durango versus Tamaulipas.

Gooooaaaallll!

It was a fiesta back then, like a Fourth of July barbecue; everyone was celebrating in anticipation of crossing. Back then, chances were better than fifty-fifty that you would get across on your first attempt. And even if you were nabbed by the *migra*, you'd surely make it on your second try, probably that same night.

Later, after people had eaten, scored a few goals or a blow job in the nearby bushes, the coyotes would gather crews of twenty-five or more migrants, sometimes many more. The coyotes would huddle among themselves, drawing straws to see which route each team would take. There are hundreds of ancient footpaths in the hills above Tijuana, deep ruts carved over the decades by a million migrant footsteps.

All at once, the crews would move out, hundreds of men, women, and children streaming across the chaparral-dotted hills. The Border Patrol would spring into action, but the gringos would quickly be overwhelmed by the massive tide.

Gooooaaaallll!

Sure, it was dangerous sometimes, especially along the line in Texas, where migrants had to ford the trickster currents of the muddy Bravo. But back then migrants were more likely to get robbed or beaten by border bandits than to die of exposure in the middle of the desert.

The border wasn't a border. The line was broken. It was an idea, not a thing.

And then the idea became a reality. In the early nineties, California was in a deep recession. A lot of union jobs had been lost. The Firestone and Goodyear tire plants shut down, as did the last of the old iron and steel works, and aerospace companies laid off tens of thousands of workers. People were angry, and then-governor Pete Wilson looked back in time for inspiration. To the Great Depression and the "repatriation" of hundreds of thousands of Mexican workers. To the postwar recession and Operation Wetback, which deported hundreds of thousands more. And then *la crisis* sent a fresh flood of refugees north. Suddenly Wilson, a Republican who'd always sold himself as friendly to Mexico and Mexicans, a man who in fact once had an undocumented woman clean his house, pointed his finger southward.

"They keep coming!" he declared.

He hated the migrants now. Narco-satanic hordes were at the gates. He swore that he would draw a line in the sand that no wetback would ever cross.

American politicos have paid lip service to "holding the line" at the southern border for the better part of the twentieth century, beginning in the days of the massive migration spawned by the Mexican Revolution of 1910–17. But in 1994, the rhetoric took the form of concrete, steel, arc lamps, infrared cameras and goggles, seismic and laser sensors, and even U.S. soldiers with M-16s offering "tactical support" to a greatly expanded Border Patrol. Operation Gatekeeper sought to block the decades-old illegal crossing at San Diego–Tijuana with a twelve-foot-high steel wall that runs inland twelve miles from the coast. At night, it is lit a harsh amber. The glow that falls from the gigantic light towers straddles the line for several hundred yards in each direction, meaning that the gringo light actually falls on Mexican territory— illegal light, as it were, but the Mexican government has never complained about it or about the constant noise pollution from the helicopters on patrol.

The migrants have complained, though. They called the governor "Pito" Wilson, *pito* for "whistle," but also, in Mexico, for "penis." During the 1994 World Cup, Wilson was on hand to inaugurate a match at the Rose Bowl in Los Angeles. Among the 100,000 people in the stands, there were at least 60,000 Mexicans, Salvadorans, Guatemalans, Nicaraguans, Hondurans, Colombians, Chileans, Uruguayans, Brazilians—migrants each and every one. Wilson stepped up to the microphone. But no one heard a single word he said over the boos, whistles, and chorus of "Pito! Pito!" in great rhythmic waves.

Gooooaaaallll!

Pete Wilson has gone, but one thing remains of his nativist legacy.

After years of being lobbied to help the Golden State beat back the illegals, the federal government obliged with a new fence at Tijuana. To cross into California today, you have to go east of the fence. You have to hike in total darkness, through mountains that block out the beacon of city light from San Diego. You take a long walk in the dark.

East of Nogales, Arizona, my Blazer clatters down the rutted dirt of Duquense Road. At this point, the line consists of little more than a few strands of barbed wire about four feet high. Somewhere close by, Rosa Chávez crossed over with Mr. Charlie.

The sky is a deep Arizona blue, dotted with brilliant white cumuli. In California, the pale light tends to minimize contrasts; here, shadows stand out in stark relief. I am in the Coronado National Monument, named for Francisco Vásquez de Coronado, a sixteenth-century Spanish explorer who searched in vain for the fabled streets paved with gold, the Seven Cities of Cibola. His expedition of 339 soldiers, 4 Franciscan priests, 1,100 Indians, and 1,500 head of livestock set out from Compostela, 750 miles to the south. Indians all along the route confirmed Cibola's existence. It's farther north, the expedition was told again and again. There is some conjecture that the Indians were lying, hoping to push the white men and their horses into a no-man's-land from which they would never return.

Vásquez died without finding Cibola, but he did explore this brutal land of intolerable heat and deadly cold, tracing a crucial overland trade route to the northern territories of the Spanish Crown.

Today, Mexican migrants follow in the footsteps of a conquering Spanish explorer, seeking their own version of the Seven Cities. This is breathtaking and treacherous country, a landscape of eerie, lunarlike beauty, the perfect backdrop for a new Western noir. Here border bandits lie in wait for the vulnerable migrants, and of course there are the Border Patrol, corrupt Mexican police, narcotics smugglers, and DEA agents.

The most recent additions to the tableau are the vigilantes. Dozens of ranchers in the area whose lands are regularly trespassed by border crossers have taken up arms—literally. Like the *migra*, whom they consider inefficient at best, they have availed themselves of such technology as night-vision goggles, but they have also laid in heavier weaponry— some even have assault rifles. The president of the Concerned Citizens of Cochise County has even built a twenty-foot-high lookout station to better patrol his property.

Everywhere I look, there is evidence of migrant journeys. In the brush I come across dozens of discarded bottles of Mexican purified water. Shreds of newspaper lined with shit. A tattered Mexican comic book. A crumpled tube of Mexican Colgate. Along the barbed-wire fence, tiny flags of torn clothing flutter in the breeze. The Coronado National Monument has become a shrine to the migrant. The park rangers might as well as put up exhibit placards.

There are no tourists here. As far as I can tell, I am the only moving thing, the Blazer kicking up a cloud of yellow dust along a road that goes ever higher into the Huachuca Mountains. I look down on the border: a million scrub brushes dot the valley for dozens and dozens of miles southward. The fence is down there somewhere, but it's too small to see from five thousand feet.

I come around a bend and hit the brakes: there is a van stopped by the side of the road, a seventies Dodge Sportsman. I stare at the vehicle as if it were road kill that might come back to life. There is only the sound of my car's motor idling; the Blazer's cloud of dust now flows forward over me.

The van sits off-kilter, its left rear wheel missing, the brake disc half buried in sand. I spot the tire about ten yards ahead. There is a deep rut through the dirt for over fifty yards up to where the van sits; either it took the driver that long to stop or he actually tried to keep moving forward. Probably the latter—all the van's windows have been blasted in with football-sized rocks.

I turn paranoid, wondering if the perpetrators of this violence are still close by. The incident appears to have occurred just a few hours or even a few minutes ago—no dust has settled on the van yet.

Inside the van a thousand glass shards are sprinkled amid the rocks that crashed through the windows. A pair of navy blue men's bikini briefs. An embroidered Indian sash. A flyer announcing a gig by Banda la Judicial, a third-string outfit pictured in red suits with white tassels, snakeskin boots, and white Stetsons. Santa María water bottle, empty. Unopened package of Alka-Seltzer. A cheap vinyl backpack, the classic migrant's luggage, the logo a poorly stenciled map of the world. A Purépecha rebozo, spread on the floor with a canteloupe-sized rock sitting on it.

Arizona license plates. The gas cap is missing; the driver stuck in a red rag. On the exterior right-side panel, there is a splatter that has dried a dark brown. It looks like blood.

The interior side panels have been ripped open, as has much of the floor carpet. The bandits were looking for something, probably drugs. It is impossible to tell if they found anything.

I crest the ridge at the top of the Coronado Pass, leaving the crime scene behind. To the south, the massive, craggy San Jose peak; to the east the savannalike beauty of the San Juan River Valley, promising a temperate respite from the Arizona badlands. Somewhere between the mountains and the flats stands the border, invisible and implacable.

INS agent Laura Privette is a small, sinewy woman with coarse Indian hair cut stylishly short. She is dark—*prieta*, as they say in Spanish—the descendant of immigrants. She is an Indian who's assumed the role of cowboy; tonight, she is field supervisor for Border Patrol operations in the Nogales sector. She has left her silver BMW Z3 convertible behind at the station parking lot and boarded a Ford Explorer BP cruiser to show me how the United States holds the line.

The radio crackles. The dispatcher talks in code: "Five-seventy activity." Marijuana. Every couple of minutes we are apprised of "hits" from the motion detectors buried in the desert along the line.

I like Privette. No woman rises through the ranks of a paramilitary agency—the most macho of environments—without proving her mettle. She grew up Mexican in southern Arizona, where there are lots of Mexicans but precious little space for them in the middle class. As a child, she saw the BP at work on the nightly news, as well as on the streets. The job struck her as heroic; just like a kid in the suburbs who dreams of being a fireman or astronaut, she dreamed of working the line, applying the righteous force of the law against unscrupulous smugglers of human and narcotic cargo. Like many other BP agents, especially Hispanics, Privette professes empathy for the migrants. She believes that there are legal ways to get into this country and illegal ones, safe passage and dangerous crossings. It is pointless to argue with her.

"Things are going pretty good right now," Privette says. With a budget that has tripled in the last five years, the INS's interdiction force has seen its ranks swell by thousands. Its logistical equipment is state of the art.

Privette guides the climate-controlled Explorer, still reeking new-car smell, toward the line—represented in Nogales by a replica of the twelve-foot-high steel wall that blocked migrants from crossing in Tijuana. After claiming success with Operation Gatekeeper in California, the INS proceeded with Operation Safeguard along the Arizona border in 1995, doubling the number of Border Patrol agents, upgrading surveillance technology, and building the wall.

It is late afternoon on a searing late-spring day. There's not much to see yet; the real action starts after dusk. We ride down the avenue that leads to the port of entry, pulling over next to a concrete-lined channel. A Church's Chicken stands nearby, along with a McDonald's, a Jack in the Box, and a taco truck advertising itself as "Parikutín," a Michoacán family enterprise named after Mexico's youngest volcano and a source of endless pride for the Michoacanos.

Back in the days before the massive BP buildup, when a handful of agents battled the mighty stream of migrants who easily cut the chain-link fence, Church's was a kind of migrant drive-through. While the BP was kept busy at the fence, smugglers would bring migrants through the drainage tunnels that traverse the line, hop up to street level, grab a snack, and phone contacts to pick up the cargo. Today, only a trickle comes via the tunnels. It is, however, a popular route for migrants returning to Mexico, a way for them to avoid corrupt Mexican customs officials.

The walls of the tunnel feature generations of graffiti, most of it put there by Barrio Libre, a gang of homeless illegal kids who call the border tunnels home. As Privette sweeps a hand over the scene in explanation, we catch sight of a group of eighteen men double-timing through the wash, headed south. When they notice us, most of them pull up their shirts to cover their faces, but there's no need to worry. The BP rarely bothers to apprehend migrants heading back to Mexico.

Despite laws and technology and the dangers of the road, the border can still be breached dozens of ways. Enterprising smugglers have concocted a scheme that allows an illegal to cross right under the nose of the *migra*. At the San Diego–Tijuana port of entry, a considerable number of crossings take the form of foot traffic through a simple turnstyle past a lone customs agent, who often doesn't press for identification from "American-looking" types. "Nationality?" the guard asks. If you say, "American," in good ole Americanese, you're in like a flint.

For up to $2,000, the smuggler serves more like an acting coach than a coyote. First off, the wardrobe. He gets rid of the invariable polyster threads of your provincial home in favor of 100 percent American cotton. Then he works on your accent and your story, which includes the city, neighborhood, streets, high school, sports teams, and so on of your supposed hometown in the States. If the customs official suspects something, you're merely herded back across the line to try again. And again. The odds, in the long run, are in your favor.

There are still other ways. It is increasingly difficult and expensive to forge the so-called green card (which actually hasn't been green in ages) that denotes legal residency in the United States. Currently, the holographic, "forgery-proof" model looks more like a credit card than a proof of residency. Therefore, there is a brisk business in buying and selling other bona fide documents, including passports, birth certificates, and Social Security cards, which can be conveniently "lost," giving smugglers a window of opportunity of weeks or months to use them until the owner reports them missing.

One day there might indeed be a truly forgery-proof method of admitting people into the country, perhaps the sci-fi scenario of a scanner that identifies on the basis of the uniqueness of the human iris. Such proposals are being seriously considered these days. But for the moment, there is a smuggler's response to every measure the INS introduces.

The Explorer winds into the hills east of Nogales. The border evolves—the towering steel wall becomes a chain-link fence and, a short while later, hip-high barbed wire, the strands cut in many places. We get out of the truck and Agent Privette squats down on one knee, examining hoof marks and the tire tracks that crisscross the line. This examination is called "sign cutting."

"Horses, drugs," Privette says in law enforcement minimalese. "Car. Probably a big old Buick or Impala. Illegals, ten, maybe fifteen."

Sunset. The long, thin fingers of ocotillo bushes stretch into the orange-gold, reaching for the wisps of feathery, gilded cirrus in the darkening sky. Down below, we can see the wall cutting straight across the two Nogaleses. Streets on one side of the line continue on the other. It looks like one huge barrio, artificially divided.

Nothing much is happening in the hills, so we head back toward town.

Suddenly, the radio comes to life. "Hits in sector 1–5." We speed through the barrios on the outskirts of Nogales, past humble homes with front doors ajar in the balmy evening, elders swaying in rockers and kids dashing about the street. No one bats an eye at our Border Patrol truck. In this landscape, the Explorers are as omnipresent as the ocotillos.

We pull up next to a drainage tunnel scant yards from the border, where there is another BP truck, commanded by another Indian agent. His bronze face shines with sweat under the amber streetlight. "I lost sight of 'em. I think they came through here. About twenty of 'em."

Privette commands her subaltern: "I'll go above ground, you go under." The green-suited agent, walkie-talkie tacked to his shoulder, runs off, his black flashlight bouncing madly in the dark.

I run after him. I've purchased a flashlight myself—a rubber-coated, impact-resistant field model—for just such an occasion. But, of course, I've forgotten it back in the Explorer. The BP agent is about fifty yards ahead of me in the tunnel, running east. I can see only the distant, wavering beacon of his flashlight. Around me, it is pitch-black. My footsteps echo strangely, expanding concentric circles of sound with a metallic ring. I kick at unseen garbage at my feet. Now puddles of dank water. Deep puddles.

The flashlight up ahead slows its frantic dance. In a few seconds, I am at the agent's side, at an opening in the tunnel. Above us, there is traffic, American traffic. "Lost 'em," he says into his walkie-talkie. "Stay where you are," Privette's voice crackles in response. We hear running steps approaching above us. Privette looks down at us from street level. For several moments there is only the sound of panting all around.

The two agents try more sign cutting.

"It doesn't look like they came this way," says the male agent. "They might have jumped up to the road. Maybe they backtracked."

Privette: "No, they definitely came this way. I've got tennis shoes going through here. Adidas."

The migrants have disappeared into the night. The BP's billion-dollar high-tech arsenal has failed, at least on this occasion.

The border is not in a war zone, to be sure. But the battle at the line has all the trappings of a low-intensity conflict between two sides, one armed with state-of-the-art surveillance equipment and the other with the kind of ingenuity inspired only by poverty and desire.

It is a tribute to the political furor over drugs and immigration that between them the two Nogaleses host one of the most impressive arrays of public safety infrastructure in the Northern Hemisphere. Consider the battery of forces amassed here, for towns whose combined population is under 200,000: the U.S. Border Patrol and Customs Police, the Arizona National Guard (which assists the Border Patrol in "intelligence gathering"), the Santa Cruz County sheriff's department and the local Nogales Police Department, mirrored on the Mexican side by the Sonora State Police (*judiciales*), the Mexican Federal Police (*federales*, akin to the American FBI), the Grupo Beta (a special force under federal control that deals with border crime), the local police, and, finally, the quixotically named Talón de Aquiles (Achilles' Heel), whose basic charge is to keep the streets of Nogales clear of unseemly characters for the important tourist industry (which includes such border mainstays as greyhound races, bookie joints, countless curios shops, and plenty of bars that won't card American teens).

Sometimes the Border Patrol can almost convince you it's winning the war. Late in the evening, Privette takes me downtown, where, she has been apprised, a large crew of illegals has been detained. When we pull up, they are seated on the benches under the shade trees of the plaza. A brazen smuggler brought them straight across the wall, maybe with a ladder, apparently convinced they would make it precisely because the BP wouldn't expect a crossing right under its nose.

Several agents, with their broken Spanish, interview the illegals, jotting information into their notebooks.

Nombre? Edad? Domicilio? Firme aquí, por favor.

"I don't know how to write," says an elder in a cowboy hat.

"Then just put an *X*."

Eighteen men, two women. No kids. From Michoacán, from Guanajuato, from Sinaloa, from Zacatecas and Puebla. There are looks of fear, of quiet resignation, of lackadaisical boredom. A teenager with a baby mustache winks at me. *We'll be back.*

Privette, perhaps aware that she hasn't shown her department at its best tonight, takes me to the station, where narcotics are being registered after a bust. The agent on duty is a young, chipper African American woman named Eealey. In the evidence room, she empties two burlap sacks, each containing several plastic-wrapped bundles of marijuana. They come to 41.25 pounds on the scale, but she wasn't able to arrest the "mules," the drug runners.

Quite a scene out there, Eealey says. She and another agent arrived after receiving word from a video surveillance officer of a probable narcotics crossing. They caught sight of two kids who, with nowhere else to run, hightailed it back toward the line, hastily dumping their loads on American soil. (There'll be hell to pay on the other side.) Eealey got to one of them just as he was diving down to crawl underneath the fence. She grabbed him by the leg, and the kid actually dragged her halfway into Mexico before she realized this was an international incident in the making and let go.

In Nogales, Sonora, that night, I hang out at a dive called Palas— that's Mexican Spanish for Palace. On the stage, women from every corner of Mexico writhe, women who came to the border thinking of the States but somehow got stuck in limbo. A lot of people got stuck at the line, deferring their American dreams, because there's all kinds of underground business for provincial kids to get caught up in. Many people realized you could make more money playing the black market on the Mexican side than picking fruit on the American side. But then came the wall.

"Isis," from Puerto Vallarta, golden-skinned and Asian-eyed— Egyptian-looking, come to think of it—tells me that business was good until that damn *muro* went up a few months back. Coyotes and narcos used to party here at Palas all night, though they were often scary types with big mustaches, big paunches, big guns, and, often as not, big badges, in the true Mexican corrupt fashion.

"But it's dead now with the wall," says Isis. "Don't the Americans realize that it's bad for business?"

At night, as one looks down from the American side into Mexico, the wall is merely an amber-lit smudge in a swath of small-town light stretching across the valley to the south. Because Nogales, Arizona, is not exactly a model of American affluence and Nogales, Sonora—buoyed in recent years by the *maquiladora* industry of giants like Sony and General Electric—is not the poorest of the Mexican border towns, the Mexican side doesn't necessarily seem Third Worldish.

The two Nogaleses are one, at least geographically, but also in terms of key urban infrastructure—such as the drainage canals and tunnels that traverse the cities north and south. Without this shared drainage system, the sudden summer thunderstorms that toss down a couple of inches of rain within an hour would flood both sides. If there are two cities at this border crossing, they are the Nogales aboveground and the Nogales below.

The city beneath the city is thriving, too. The drainage tunnels are home to all the characters you'd expect at a crossing as contested as this: alien smugglers and narcotics traffickers, down-and-out dope fiends and various other outlaw types. Down below, all these, along with the coyotes and illegals, face off against law enforcement from both sides of the line.

The other player in this border drama is Barrio Libre, whose members range in age from five to their late teens. Barrio Libre is family to a pregnant sixteen-year-old girl, a nine-year-old boy who's been on the streets since he was four, and a few dozen others who pass the time scrounging up meals and occasionally assaulting vulnerable illegals as they cross through the tunnel. For the tunnel kids, as they're called, the battle for the border is simply one of survival.

Some are runaways escaping abusive family situations. Others were separated from their parents in the chaos of a Border Patrol bust. Still others are just plain dirt-poor, restless, and rebellious. Unable to make it aboveground—not with the *migra* and the Mexican police after them—they've descended below, just a few feet under the steps of gringo tourists, Mexican border executives, and squeaky-clean kids their age in blue and white school uniforms.

The only other place these kids call home is a drop-in center on the Mexican side called Mi Nueva Casa, and it is here that I first meet a few members of Barrio Libre. Mi Nueva Casa, funded largely by liberal American foundations, is a humble stucco house just a hundred yards from the border wall.

A typical day begins at about nine in the morning. But Ramona Encinas, the benevolent matriarch of the center, starts brewing coffee and boiling pots of beans and rice much earlier. The kids straggle in one by one or in twos and threes, their faces pale and puffy—a telltale sign they've slept in the tunnel. They are received with a gushy "*¡Buenos días!*" from Ramona, a counselor named Loida Molina and her twenty-something son Isaac (who's known, in the center's lingo, as the "older-brother type"), and Cecilia Guzmán, a schoolteacher. There are hugs and kisses for the girls, street handshakes for the boys, although a couple of them are in a foul mood and plop themselves down on one of the well-worn couches in the living room without uttering a word to anyone.

Mi Nueva Casa lives up to its billing as a *casa*: besides the living room with its TV and couches, there is a dining room with fold-up tables and about a dozen chairs, which doubles as the computer room (three terminals featuring race car and ancient Pac-Man–type games); a bathroom where the kids can shower if they want (or are forced to by staffers); the small kitchen where Ramona holds court; an outdoor patio in back where washing machines are constantly sloshing the kids' clothes clean. The remaining space is taken up by a Foosball center, a dressing room (hung with dozens of donated shirts, pants, sweaters, and jackets), and a classroom.

After a light breakfast of juice or milk with cookies, some of the kids join Cecilia for the day's school session. Through a screen door in the classroom, one can look straight across the street at the grounds of a local public elementary school, hear the shrieks of "regular" kids.

On this particular morning, several kids arrive late, after ten. They were detained by the *migra* on the American side of the tunnel—the place they currently call home. In comes Pablo, a thirteen-year-old wearing a T-shirt featuring Chupacabras (the blood-sucking bogeyman of northern rural Mexico), and his friend Jesús, about ten years old, in an oversize Raiders shirt. They both sport cholo buzz cuts with thin braided ponytails trailing down the backs of their necks. Their shoes are caked with mud. Within seconds of their entrance, the room begins to smell like unbathed kid.

"The *chiles verdes* got us," says Jesús, using the kids' nickname for the *migra* officers, who wear green uniforms. He tells how Border Patrol agents confiscated the only belongings he had to his name: his flashlight and his aftershave—he doesn't have facial hair yet, but it comes in handy to cover up body odor. Now Toño, at nine the youngest in the group, walks in and promptly pulls up his shirt to show off pinkish scar tissue on his side and abdomen, the result, he says, of bites from a *migra* patrol dog.

Officials on both sides of the border agree that incidents of crime perpetrated by the tunnel kids have diminished since Mi Nueva Casa opened. What they don't say is that the law enforcement agencies on both sides have hit the kids hard—with lessons not soon to be forgotten. They are regularly run down, as this morning, by armed Border Patrol agents in four-wheel-drive vehicles. They are chased by Grupo Beta police whose shouts and threats echo terrifyingly along the concrete walls of the tunnel; several kids say they receive regular beatings from the Beta. There is also an unconfirmed report of a youngster sodomized by a Mexican agent.

But at Mi Nueva Casa the horrors of the tunnel are a world away, even though one popular entrance to the underground is barely a block and a half down the street. There are also incentives to behave well. If the kids don't swear, smoke, do drugs, or carry beepers while they're here—and if they attend Cecilia's classes regularly—they can earn "benefits," all written on a sign hanging in the dining room above the computers: "love and tenderness," "food," "clothes," "respect," "bath," "computer games," "television," "videos," "guitars," and "much, much more!"

Cecilia has her hands full, even though there are only six kids in school today. She dissipates a bit of her own nervous energy by chewing gum as she tries to get Jesús to concentrate on math tables. The kids are distracted by me, of course, but also plainly nervous after the morning's encounter with the *migra*. They flip pencils over and over on the desk, bounce their knees up and down.

In walks Gilberto, the coolest of the bunch, dressed all in black, his hair perfectly combed. A ceramic medallion of a classical European baby Jesus floating amid cherubs hangs on his chest. Heavy with attitude, he scoffs when Cecilia asks him if he wants milk and cookies. Says he wants coffee.

Responding to a question about drugs in the tunnel he says, "You can get crack whenever you want." And pot and pills, and if there's nothing else, well, there's always the poor kid's high—paint thinner inhaled straight from the can or spray paint sniffed from a soaked bandanna.

"If you're from Barrio Libre, you can get anything, anywhere," says Gilberto. Barrio Libre, the Free Barrio. With cliques in Phoenix, Chicago, Las Vegas, L.A., and Nogales, Gilberto claims.

Jesús talks of the war between the coyotes and the Barrio Libre kids. "They think we're bad for their business," he says. And they are. When the kids assault the migrants, word gets back quickly to the other side, causing prospective border crossers to eschew the tunnels for coyote crews that breach the line elsewhere. Jesús recounts a recent incident in which a coyote shot at him with what he says was a 9-millimeter pistol.

Gilberto justifies the assaults: he's following the adults' example. "We're just asking for our *mordida* [bribe], a little something to buy a soda with," he says. But there is plenty of evidence that when some Barrio Libre kids don't get what they want form the *chúntaros* ("hayseeds," a nickname for the illegals), they are capable of viciously beating their victims.

It's nearly noon. Cecilia has done her best for the morning. As lunchtime approaches, the kids begin to drift in and out of the classroom. Some head off for a Foosball game, others to wash their clothes. Gilberto is at the chalk board, tagging it up with BARRIO LIBRE. Jesús scratches his arms, which are covered with tiny red lumps, a rash he picked up down in the tunnel. Now Gilberto is twirling about the room, blowing up a paper bag he picked up in the trash and pantomiming the inhaling of fumes.

But one student is still intent on doing class work, practicing his handwriting in his notebook. Cecilia tells me that up until a couple of months ago, José, one of the quieter of the group, was practically illiterate, but today his handwriting is precise. Carefully he draws the curving *o*s and *a*s in Spanish, copying down an exercise in alliteration and assonance:

Dolor, dulce dolor. Pain, sweet pain.
Mi mamá me ama. My mother loves me.

He repeats the lines over and over again, filling the entire page.

Homeless youth would seem to be almost an oxymoron in Mexico, where virtually every mother or grandmother is considered a saint and the family unit is by turns loving, claustrophobic, and dictatorial—all-powerful. Unmarried children typically stay at home well past their teens; many stay at home even after they marry. But something's happening to the Mexican family, and it is not just the economic crisis that's chipping away at the institution; migration has a lot to do with it as well. Hundreds of thousands of households, perhaps millions (no one knows how many) are now single-parent or parentless—Mami and Papi are working in the fields of the San Joaquin Valley or cleaning hotel rooms in Dallas; the kids remain in Mexico until there's enough money to bring them across.

Sometimes the kids themselves leave to try their luck in the north as well. Occasionally they run away; often they're encouraged by their parents. (Wense Cortéz made his first trip to the States at age thirteen; his parents did nothing to stop him.) The family separations are always thought of as temporary, but increasingly (and in proportion to the greater difficulty of crossing back and forth at will) they last for years.

Or forever. Papi, gone for two years, suddenly has a new girlfriend in Illinois or even a new family in Illinois. Or maybe Mami isn't coming back because she's sick of her small town's suffocating morality. In all the hustle and bustle and backbreaking effort to provide for the family—and amid the cultural changes that accompany the migrants' journeys—the kids are getting lost. Mexican family values, ironically, are being undone by the very effort to support family in Mexico by working in the United States.

Mi Nueva Casa does not offer a complete, twenty-four-hour shelter. It can't—funding for the program is chronically anemic. While up to twenty-two young people might hang out here during the day, the doors close at five in the afternoon Monday through Saturday and the staffers go home to their families. The kids, meanwhile, go back to their own "family" in the tunnels.

Despite the clear binational nature of homeless children accumulating on the border, binational policies, free-trade agreement or no, have not made fund-raising or even donating materials easy. Mi Nueva Casa was recently awarded a major grant from the Kellogg Foundation, but the money came with the stipulation that it could be spent only for research and staff training on the American side of the border. On more than one occasion, staffers have had to sneak donated clothes into Mexico from the United States in the trunk of a car because if the items were declared before Mexican customs the red tape would be endless. (A Ping-Pong table given to Mi Nueva Casa by an American benefactor remained in a Mexican customs warehouse for over a year.)

"There've always been problems at the border," says a member of Mi Nueva Casa's board. "But the thing is, the number of people coming up, including the kids, keeps on increasing. The Mexican authorities have been overwhelmed."

But according to American law enforcement agencies, the problem has been taken care of, all because of Mi Nueva Casa. The Santa Cruz Juvenile Detention Center says there has been a dramatic decrease in youthful-offender apprehensions on the border. So does the Border Patrol. "As recently as 1994, we had our hands full," says a BP spokesperson. "But Mi Nueva Casa's made a hell of a difference. Plus, we have the tunnels effectively monitored now."

Which is not to say that the tunnels have been closed or that there aren't kids living in them. There is no way to close the tunnels. They are for drainage, after all. "Effectively monitoring" means that the Border Patrol dispatches a team down into the tunnel two or three times a week to weld shut the steel gate that serves as the barrier between the American and Mexican sides. According to Border Patrol officials, the weld can stand four hundred pounds of pressure per square inch, which means that a dozen or so kids can break it easily. And, in fact, the gate is busted open two or three times a week by the kids, or anyone else who wants to get across.

Romel is one of Barrio Libre's *veteranos*. At seventeen, he's already an old man. He's beaten others and been beaten, robbed and been robbed, known the life of the tunnel for almost four years. Now he is caught between that life and a growing desire to find a straight job. For the moment, he's leaning toward the job.

Romel sits in the living room of Mi Nueva Casa, watching the original Batman and Robin dubbed in Spanish. His father was a drug dealer who was nabbed by the FBI; he lived with his stepmother in Washington State for a few years, but eventually the stepfamily sent him back to the border like a piece of unclaimed luggage. There he fell into the tunnel, into Barrio Libre. He freely admits to *tumbando*, assaulting people in the tunnel for money. But something in the back of his head has been nagging at him lately.

"I'm tired of it and . . ."—he searches for the words—"they're my own people, after all."

Romel's friend Iram shows up, a tall, lithe, good-looking teenager who still lives "down below." He teases Romel about his new life. Ultimately, he goads him into going down for a visit.

We zigzag along the tourist streets of downtown Nogales, looking out for Beta agents, who, Romel says, are after him for a tunnel rape that he swears he had nothing to do with. We head south along Avenida Obregón, Nogales's main drag. A strip joint announces "*chicas sexis.*" A blind accordionist sits on the sidewalk playing for change. A middle-aged gringo tourist in shorts, white socks, and huaraches marvels at a wrought-iron design.

About half a mile from the border on Obregón, we veer left and drop down into a weedy abandoned lot. The kids turn left again around the corner of an apartment building, looking over their shoulders. Now we're underneath the building, in a four-foot crawl space. Knees and backs bent uncomfortably, we walk along a trickle of a river running down the middle of the tunnel. It's not so bad, I think to myself.

But the real tunnel begins only about two hundred yards later, and the space there is barely over three feet high. As if someone had snapped off a switch, suddenly all light is gone. Romel flicks on the only flashlight we have—one equipped with rapidly dying batteries. The light barely cuts through the dark. Staggering along sideways, I can barely keep up with the kids.

The stench hits me: this is not supposed to be a sewage line, but there is obviously leakage from homes and businesses above. The river widens. What appear to be puddles are actually two-foot-deep mini-lakes of stagnant shit and piss. We hear the drip of more sewage coming down. The air is at once too thick and too thin. I breathe heavily and sweat profusely, although it's a few degrees cooler down here than out-side.

I manage to stammer a concerned question about battery life. "Don't worry," Romel says. "Even if it goes out, I can tell you exactly where we are and how to get out of here. I can walk in and out of here without a flashlight." I wonder if he's boasting or serious; there are hundreds of yards of pitch-black tunnel left before we reach the line. *Watch out for the electrical wire—might be live or it might not, you don't want to find out. Careful of this beam. Ouch!*

Concrete dividers are encrusted with surreal collections of goo and trash—baseball caps and egg cartons, underwear and hairbrushes—that rush through here when it rains. My left leg gives way into a shit lake and I fall forward, striking my knee on something sharp. Fetid water splashes up in my face. Giggles from Iram and Romel. My jeans are torn and my knee feels like there's a knife stuck in the socket.

It's deathly quiet down here, no breeze, nothing to see, only the feeling that there are a dozen things that you could knock yourself out cold on.

We approach an ever-so-dim source of light. It's a manhole cover. Through two half-dollar-size holes, the light comes down gray-white in perfect tubes, two tiny spotlights hitting the sandy-muddy floor of the tunnel. Beyond, darkness again. I stand below the iron lid. Directly above us, I see and hear pedestrians along Obregón. A Mexican vendor is earnestly trying to get a tourist to put on a sombrero and pose with his wife next to a burro.

After a while, we come to a stop before another tunnel, running perpendicular to the first. The international line. We clamber over a three-foot-thick black sewage pipe. Iram points east with the flashlight. About twenty-five yards away is the mouth of the north-south tunnel that takes you up to Church's Chicken—where Romel once lived and where Iram and many other Barrio Libre kids still live.

Suddenly bright lights flash ahead. Unintelligible whispers ripple along the dead air, reverberating off the concrete. Iram gets nervous. "Romel—there's somebody up there!" he says. The lights disappear. A few seconds later there is a tremendous metallic bang, loud enough to be felt in the pit of your stomach. Silence again.

"That was the sound of the tunnel opening," Romel says.

But by whom? Other members of Barrio Libre? *Polleros* eager to teach the kids a lesson? Or is it the Border Patrol on one of their strolls into the tunnel, eager to swoop up the day's quota of illegals?

Romel and Iram wait in silence. To the west, a hundred yards away, a veil of gray light—an opening to street level that is part of a construction project on the Mexican side, just a block and a half from Mi Nueva Casa.

Into the darkness or toward the light?

The kids make a run for it, scared out of their wits.

A minute later, alone, I'm climbing up through chunks of concrete and iron reinforcement rods.

The light of the sun glinting off car fenders and house windows is blinding. Above, the deep blue Sonoran sky. And then a man wearing a red beret and aviator glasses is asking me where I am going. Romel and Iram are pushed against the wall, legs spread. I have the presence of mind to show my journalist's credential and the Beta agent calls off the dogs.

"If you hadn't been there," says Romel later, "they would've beat the shit out of us."

The next day, another trip down into the tunnel, this time led by Toño, the nine-year-old I'd met in Mi Nueva Casa—the one with the dog bites. We take the same route, and this time there are no strangers flashing lights.

We turn toward the steel gate the Border Patrol welds shut a few times a week. As we approach, we hear whispers on the other side. Toño slows down, shines his flashlight directly at the gate. It creaks open; the BP hasn't welded it yet. Squinting into the light are a pair of glassy eyes set in a twelve-year-old's face.

"Where you from?" the kid asks.

"Barrio Libre!" Toño responds quickly, and then the door opens fully, revealing half a dozen more kids. Handshakes all around.

The boys show me the weld—it looks like nothing more than a Radio Shack soldering job—that they break open whenever they want. I get a tour of the immediate surroundings, the graffiti-scarred walls. BARRIO LIBRE! on one side, BETA! on the other—the Mexican border agents, not be outdone by the kids, do their own tagging.

We are advised by the older Barrio Libre members not to go farther into the tunnel; there is something going down deep inside. They close the door and scamper back to the Mexican side, maneuvering quickly with their dimming flashlights.

The last time I visited the tunnel, all hell broke loose. I was standing with the kids on the American side, at the mouth of the tunnel, just below Church's Chicken. There were several kids present whom I didn't know. And the ones I did know were high—very high. There was a spray can being passed around with a rag. Gold-fleck paint was everywhere, on the kids' noses and mouths, on their hands, on my tape recorder. The kids were stumbling, twirling, kicking at puddles of water, shouting themselves hoarse.

I was surprised to find Romel among the crew, although perhaps I shouldn't have been. Once you've gone underground, it's hard to stay away. I try to imagine Romel as a mature man in his thirties. I cannot.

Something was about to happen—the combination of the paint and the large number of kids, about twenty in all, was volatile. All they needed was the spark.

There was much drugged banter. Romel announced that he was going to steal a TV set from someone's house on the American side.

"Yeah, we could have cable TV, and beds, and a stove . . ." Jesús enthused. Romel thought there should be a library, too, with comic books and Nintendo games.

The reverie was cut short by the sudden appearance of a man in his thirties coming up from the tunnel. He was dressed in a white shirt opened several buttons down his chest, white pants, smart boots. He was definitely not *migra*, but he wasn't a typical *chúntaro*, either. The kids surrounded him instantly. It was a strange sight: a well-built, mature man mobbed by scrawny preteens and malnourished adolescents, not unlike a bear set upon by coyotes. One of the kids had noticed him stuffing something into his mouth just as he'd come within sight.

"Spit it out!" someone shouted. One kid pried the man's jaws open and took out a wadded-up ten-dollar bill.

"He's with Beta, I recognize him!" someone else yelled. The man remained quiet, amazingly calm considering the circumstances. He was fully patted down, but the kids found nothing else on him. Was he a narco? An illegal? A coyote?

"Are you alone?" a kid demanded.

"No, there are others behind me," he said, his voice devoid of emotion.

I was beginning to think he was bullshitting, stalling for time, but then we heard noises from deep inside the tunnel and saw the flashing of lights. The kids ran into the darkness, and the man in white slowly walked away, jumping up to street level without looking back. There were no Border Patrol agents or Nogales policemen anywhere to be seen. The kids could do what they wanted. From the tunnel I heard them shout "Barrio Libre!" and there were the sounds of scuffling. A few moments later, the kids reappeared, laughing, hoisting the spoils high: a gold necklace, a silver crucifix, diamond earrings in the shape of bunny rabbits, all the real thing. Unlucky *chúntaros*. Romel pulled me aside, breathing hard. He said the victims were about a dozen women. He suspected that the man in white was their coyote. He'd probably told them to wait inside while he checked out the scene at the mouth of the tunnel. There was nowhere for the women to run in the darkness. They sat huddled together, vulnerable as lambs, and then the kids were upon them. "There was nothing I could do to stop it," Romel told me.

As I left, the kids were still sniffing, and there was talk of a big party in

the tunnel that night. When I clambered up to street le[vel]
Patrol Explorer pull into Church's parking lot. I look[ed]
kids were running back into the tunnel, deep into th[e]

Naco, Arizona, is a minor port of entry some fifty [miles]
Nogales. My father was stationed at the nearby army base back in the
fifties. "Wasn't much in Naco," he told me. Nevertheless, I imagine
him knocking back several cold ones in a cantina on the other side with
his army buddies, he the Mexican in GI greens, a Mexican with papers,
a Mexican with an American passport. Mexican only, in the end, for
his brown skin and the memory of his parents' struggle to make it in
America.

Second generation on my father's side and first on my mother's, I
have come back to the line, swimming against the tide, drawn by memory, drawn by the present and by the future. I see the Mexicans pour
into Los Angeles, I see them on the banks of the Mississippi in St.
Louis. I see their brownness, I see my own. I suppose my sympathy can
be summed up simply as this: when they are denied their Americanness
by U.S. immigration policy, I feel that my own is denied as well. They
are doing exactly what my father's parents and my mother did. They
are doing exactly what all Americans' forebears did.

Here in Naco, the border is merely a few broken strands of barbed
wire. There is an obelisk marking the boundary established in 1848, in
English on the north-facing side, in Spanish on the south. I become
giddy. No wall! Just open range, and that's exactly what it is, open range
for cross-border cattle. West of here, on the O'odham Reservation,
there is no wall or fence either. The O'odham people have been caught
in the middle of a transnational caper that has nothing to do with them.
They aren't Mexican, they aren't American, they are O'odham. For
most of the last century and a half, the tribe has moved freely back and
forth across the line, along with their livestock. The Border Patrol
never bothers them; the territory is so far removed from major highways that smugglers rarely think of crossing there.

The O'odham have homes on both sides of the line. "There are no
sides here," an elder tells me. Except that in recent years the Mexican
migrant tide has begun coming across O'odham land because of the

wall in Nogales. And so the Border Patrol has arrived on the res
in its Explorers and helicopters. O'odham people have found dessi-
cated migrant bodies in the middle of their desert.

I leap over to one side; I am Mexican!

I leap back to the other side; I am American!

I dance a jig back and forth across the line, laughing at it, damning
it, and recognizing the mighty power of the very idea of a line that
cannot, does not exist in nature but that exists, nevertheless, in political,
that is, human terms.

And just as I am marveling at the absurdity, an Explorer pulls up
and two BP agents, one Asian, one Caucasian, saunter over.

The Asian asks, in fairly good Spanish, *"Qué hace usted aquí?"* What
are you doing here?

I answer, of course, in English.

I am informed that I am in violation of the United States Immigration Code. I flash my credentials, and after a bit of radio repartee
between the agents and their supervisors, all is fine and dandy. I can
keep walking along the line as much as I want, as long as I stay on this
side—right here happens to be public land so I'm free to engage in
whatever lawful activity I please. But I'm also advised that I might have
many such encounters with BP officers because I will be tripping seismic sensors all along the way, which is why I was detained by the BP
outside of Naco in the first place.

"We get a lot of 'em in through here," one agent says. "Most of
'em are from Mitch-oh-ah-cahn."

And so I get in the Blazer, point it east, and drive toward Douglas,
Arizona, another embattled border village on the forlorn frontier. Hundreds of coyotes and tens of thousands of migrants wait on the other
side in Agua Prieta, and a beefed-up Border Patrol waits on this one,
not to mention mad-as-hell gringo ranchers whose land is being tram-
pled by the migrant stampede.

In Douglas and Naco and Sonoita and El Paso and Laredo, all along
the two-thousand-mile line, it's the same thing each and every day.
Helicopters toss down ladders of light, and the *migra* put their night-
vision goggles and laser grids and seismic sensors and video cameras to
work. Mexican teenagers with slingshots target the BP trucks, so much
so that the Explorers now have iron window grilles. The vigilantes

patrol their properties, fingering the triggers of their assault rifles. A handful of activists protest human rights abuses on both sides of the line, and a few compassionate preachers liken the crossing to wading across the Jordan into Canaan.

It's like this all along the border, and it's a matter of politics, of money, of ideas, desire, death, life.

Joseph Rodriguez

10

WARREN, ARKANSAS

As I cross into Texas in the wee hours, a tremendous windstorm erupts, throwing great bowls of sand and tumbleweeds across the lanes. I'm experiencing the legendary "wild Texas wind," and it brings to mind an old melody. I start humming "El Paso," Marty Robbins's classic ballad about transfrontier love.

> *Out in the West Texas town of El Paso*
> *I fell in love with a Mexican girl*
> *Nighttime would find me in Rosa's Cantina*
> *Music would play, and Felina would whirl . . .*

Border balladeer and Arizona native Marty Robbins, like his Texican brethren Willie Nelson, Waylon Jennings, Joe Ely, and Terry Allen, to name just a few, was a cowboy who'd grown up among the Indians. Robbins not only admitted their musical influence (the waltz rhythms of northern Mexico inflected with cascading passing tones on guitar) but dared to sing of cowboy-Indian romance. The song reached number one on both the pop and the country charts in 1960, the year before my parents were married. My father loved the tune. Born in L.A. and raised in Southern California and Mexico, he was a cultural chameleon. In Mexico, he spoke flawless Spanish and assumed the formality of the Old World. In America, he played the cool teenager with all the accoutrements, including a Brylcreemed pompadour and a metallic-green MG convertible—a brown James Dean. His best friend in high school was Jewish, as was his first love. He returned to his "roots" by courting my mother, a Salvadoran expatriate making a go of her own version of Americana—an independent-minded woman freeing herself from the sexist clutches of the Old World. They conducted their relationship almost entirely in Spanish, but it was clear that, at least in the beginning, they sought in each other contrary cultural currents. My father wanted an Old World woman, my mother an American man. My father wanted tradition, my mother a liberal marriage that would allow her a career. My parents went through some tough times, but they stayed together. I suppose each got enough of what he or she needed, brokering a fragile treaty.

My father was weaned on Old Mexico as well as on the folklore of cowboys and Indians, which was still powerful in his youth, especially in Hollywood. He ate popcorn while John Wayne cleared the West of Indians. At home, he listened to *The Lone Ranger* on radio. He did not dwell on the irony of siding with the cavalry against the Indians; he has never called himself an Indian, and in pure genetic terms, he's not. But when I look at the earthen tone of our hands or stare into the mirror of his dark face, I know our blood is more Indian than Iberian. *Mestizaje*, after all, is the story of how the Indians assimilated the Spaniards, not the other way around.

In any case, my father, despite his turncoat tendencies, has on occasion had trouble reconciling his allegiances to one side of the border or the other; he still does, in fact. For example, he never cared for John Wayne in John Ford's classic *The Searchers*, in which Wayne plays a character seething with hatred of the red man. "A detestable sort," my father said of this definitive Hollywood cowboy. He preferred the more humanist characters played by Jimmy Stewart in Anthony Mann's psychological Westerns, men wracked by guilt, conflicted to the core over the American frontier experience.

An immigrant's son, my father imbibed his parents' ambivalence about life in a place that was once a part of Mexico, that receives a flood of goods and migrants from Mexico but hates Mexicans. He himself deplores the poverty of many of the Mexican migrants arriving in America (he calls them *chusma*, rabble, just as his father did back in his day), but there was no conceivable way he would have voted for Pete Wilson. Wayne and Wilson insulted my father's Mexican soul.

I've always imagined "El Paso" the perfect soundtrack to my father's, and even my own, life. We are Mexicans in America, Americans in Mexico: we are neither, we are both. Within us, the spirits meld and battle: a quintessential unhappy love affair and, therefore, painful and exhilarating. We cannot love ourselves without hating ourselves; we cannot inhabit one territory without forsaking the other; we cannot be one, must always be two and more than two: the sum of our parts will always be greater than the whole.

In the end, "El Paso" is a tragedy, as any good ballad must be. Cowboy falls for Mexican maiden, cowboy shoots another cowboy in a jealous rage, cowboy escapes to the badlands of New Mexico, where he howls in pain alone, cowboy resolves to return to El Paso because he must see his Mexican love again (antimiscegenation laws be damned). A huge posse rides out to intercept the lover and shoots him just as he falls into Felina's arms.

> *Cradled by two loving arms that I'll die for,*
> *One little kiss, then Felina, good-bye . . .*

And so it goes in the borderlands. Even as my father and I suffer and enjoy this impossible love affair, the national versions of it ensure that the kiss remains bloody.

I am eager to get to Arkansas, but Texas is always intent on keeping you from getting to any destination beyond its borders. In El Paso, under a slate-gray sky, above the churning mud of the Rio Grande, the border bridge is choked with traffic: sedans, SUVs, pickups, vans, and trucks, lots of trucks, light, double-axle, eighteen-wheel. Heading north, heading south. By all appearances, the border is open, at least under the terms of the North American Free Trade Agreement. Commerce moves freely back and forth—all you have to do is fill out the paperwork. American raw materials go to Mexico, are given shape by Mexican labor in the *maquiladoras*, and come back across the line, packaged and retail-ready. Cut-rate goods bearing the stamp "Made in Mexico" come north. It is hard to imagine that the line exists at all.

After hundreds of miles, I abandon I-10 for I-20, which takes me northeast through the immense, oil-stained flatlands. The only way to tell time and space is by focusing on the great radio towers blinking their lazy red eyes in the dusty distance. Mexican transmitters vie with their American counterparts on my radio. In this competition, the Mexicans are quite agile; 100,000-watt signals beaming across the line are not uncommon. Thus the sounds of home carry deep into American radio space. Often it's difficult to tell which country a signal is coming from. The fire-and-brimstone preacher ranting in English is easily identifiable as a Christian Identity minister sending his message out from some razor-wired compound in Texas or Arkansas. But then there are the stations that fade in and out, playing rock, techno, hip hop, oldies, and the Mexican border forms, *norteño* and *cumbia*. A *norteño* song might be followed by a deejay out of Crystal City greeting you in English with his Texican twang. The pummeling trance of a techno beat might come from Nuevo Laredo on the Mexican side, the *cumbia* from San Antonio. Occasionally, the signals cross. Johnny Cash struggles mightily to wrest airspace from Pedro Infante's Mexican vibrato. Vicki Carr's purr hovers like a ghostly harmony over Elvis Presley's croon. The border radio—whose sounds persist well into the middle of Texas—is full of songs from artists alive and dead, from this side of the line and that, in all the styles of the twentieth century and the next: the soundtrack of a vast space and time.

About eighty miles south-southeast of Little Rock, Arkansas, is the town of Warren, where the Tapia family of Cherán has made its home. A loose collection of houses surrounding a simple town square, Warren straddles the railroad tracks, one side of which is home, almost exclusively, to African Americans.

The Tapias' path to Warren was long and serpentine. Raúl Tapia's first solo journey to the United States was in 1968, but the story goes back much further; the family has been migrating for four generations. Raúl's grandfather worked in the United States for nearly a quarter of a century and his father made the trip north several times as well. One of his mother's cousins served in World War II, and two of his wife's uncles served in Vietnam. Yolanda, Raúl's wife, was born in San Benito, Texas, where her parents and relatives have lived off and on for three generations, but she was raised in Cherán and returned to the States with her husband.

On his first trip, Rául arrived in Fresno at the peak of César Chávez's farmworker campaign, the year the legendary campesino leader staged his first hunger strike. The moment was immortalized by one of the most famous photos of the era, of Bobby Kennedy sitting alongside Chávez in the fields of the San Joaquin Valley, the New England patrician alongside the poor farmworker. There hasn't been a moment like it since.

"We were invited to a meeting and he was there," Raúl told me, clearly savoring his appointment with history. "The bosses paid very low wages back then. And if you were Mexican, all you had to do was just walk out on the street to have problems with the police."

The young Raúl spent months at a time on the road alone. After picking grapes in California, he scrounged up work in various other states. By chance, a rumor led him to a stint on a tomato farm in Arkansas near Warren one summer. He liked it better than California. The *patrón* was a fair man; Raúl's hard work was repaid with decent wages and respect. The pine-ridged hills reminded him of home. He remembers thinking that Arkansas was the perfect place to raise a family, but with time the idea faded. He returned to Cherán, to his wife and firstborn son, Jordán. Andrés (now Andy) was born and then the family crossed back into the United States, working the strawberry fields of Watsonville, California, for nine years; Raúl Jr. (Rudy) and Adán (Adam) were born there.

But Raúl Sr. remained restless—and ambitious. Tensions between the growers and the UFW were running high in California, and he felt that the presence of so many Mexicans there was causing too much competition, perhaps even driving down wages. He wanted to get his family out of the fields, but the thought of moving to a city—to any of the big, turbulent California cities—was anathema to him; he didn't want his sons to go the way of the cholos. When he heard about work on the Union Pacific Railroad in North Platte, Nebraska, the family packed up its belongings and migrated to the Plains. Raúl Sr. worked on a track maintenance crew, making far better money than the minimum wage of the fields. But the Midwestern winters were too much for a man from the relatively temperate southwest of Mexico; he knew Nebraska was just a way station on a longer journey.

One winter Raúl returned to Cherán to build his dream house. He spent four months working on the home—one month too long. When he returned to North Platte, the Union Pacific told him he'd lost his seniority because his leave had been longer than the ninety-day limit. A layoff followed, and although his boss told him he'd surely be rehired, Raúl grew restless again. Next stop was Carbondale, Illinois, a destination popular with the natives of Cherán going back several decades. By this time, the kids were old enough to work alongside their parents when they weren't in school. After the fruit in one field was exhausted, they headed toward the next harvest. They followed the crops like this for a few years, putting tens of thousands of miles on the family's Silverado.

At the end of one picking season, a friend of Raúl's mentioned that he'd heard about work in Arkansas—timber, tomatoes. Raúl remembered Warren, and they loaded up their truck again. At first, Raúl returned to picking tomatoes on a small farm, work that paid no better than any other farm he'd been on. But he sensed that he'd finally found a home. Warren was a place where you could still leave your car and front door unlocked. Just like Cherán.

The Tapias live in a mostly white neighborhood on the outskirts of town, far from most of the other Mexicans in Warren, who generally live among poor African American families or in the clusters of dilapidated trailers near the tomato fields. Their house is suburban-large, with a stucco and brick facade. The front lawn is big and lush, the backyard equally expansive. Three bedrooms will soon become four; father and sons are remodeling the two-car garage. After a quarter century roaming the picking fields, the Tapias own this house—as well as five cars. The family pride and joy is Adam's 1987 Cutlass Supreme with its classy pearl-white paint job, whitewall tires, and sparkling rims.

"Those people who think immigrants are a drain on the economy are confused," says Raúl, lounging on the living room sofa. In Cherán, I remember him in cowboy-Indian regalia. Here, he wears American casual: a T-shirt, jeans, and Velcro-strapped sandals. A fading tattoo of an idealized Indian maiden is visible on the inside of his right forearm, a memento from his days as a rough-and-tumble migrant kid.

"I own a house, pay taxes," Raúl says. "I have a city job and the government gets taxes from that, too. We have the cars and pay insurance on them. We buy appliances, we buy groceries. What more does it take to be an American?"

A permanent resident on his way to citizenship, Raúl has pinned the family's hopes firmly on an American future. He addresses his children in Spanish, as does Yolanda, but he is not overly concerned that they mostly respond to him in English. He is only one generation removed from a monolingual Indian existence in the highlands of Cherán—his parents spoke Purépecha—he does not lament the loss of language. Just as his parents urged him to learn Spanish, so he's urged his kids into the American idiom.

"Purépecha is a beautiful language, but what place does it have in this world?" he says, draping an arm over the sofa and glancing in the direction of the TV, which flashes with the rapid camera cuts of an NBA game.

The living room looks every bit American: wall-to-wall carpet, a twenty-nine-inch Magnavox TV hooked up to cable, a cluster of the kids' sports trophies on a shelf, framed photos of graduations, the sons wearing white shirts and sports jackets, looking like budding young professionals. On the surface at least, there is nary a hint of the homeland, except in the kitchen, where Yolanda still serves up typical Purépecha meals, long on meat, chiles, and corn tortillas. And yet, for all this, the Tapia family, especially the kids, are changing what it means to be American. The same kind of cultural swirl is turning Cherán upside down.

When I shoot the breeze with the Tapia siblings on the front lawn as the sun sets on a warm Arkansas evening, Adam's Cutlass parked before us at the curb, they each recount how they've made peace with the disparate influences they've inherited.

Jordán, twenty-five, speaks fluent Spanish (the rest of the kids have trouble formulating complete sentences), although he's intent on teaching English to his new wife, a pretty girl from Paracho, Michoacán. Andy looks to be the most enamoured of U.S. culture—white American culture, that is. Although he dresses in urban baggies, he listens to country music. But like his father, who sings praises of the American dream even as he reserves the right to point out its shortcomings, Andy speaks bitterly of his experience in the navy. "They tell you they're color-blind in the service," he tells me. "But that's just a bunch of bull."

Next in line are Rudy and Adam, twenty-one and nineteen, the hip hoppers of the Tapia clan. Rudy has plucked his eyebrows in the latest dance-club style. Adam speaks enthusiastically of the lowrider car shows he's attended in Dallas. Both have some drawl in their speech, but mostly they try to sound like urban warriors.

Rudy's eyes light up when I mention the late, great Tupac Shakur. "Oh, you know Tupac? That's bomb!" Chalk it up to the influence of African American culture—the Tapias live, after all, in a black-and-white town. "We lived in this housing project once," Adam says, "and most of my friends there were black. That's who we be associating with more, y'know."

Sixteen-year-old Maribel, the youngest sibling, already displays the enthusiasm, ambition, and brilliance of her elders. She's taken to reading up on Chicano history, her heroes of the moment César Chávez and Emiliano Zapata. When I first met Maribel in Cherán, she quizzed me about my job. She wanted to publish a story in *Lowrider*, the Chicano zine. But hers is an updated, multicultural version of Chicano style. She says that her friends are white, black, and Mexican. In Warren, she really has no choice.

The Tapia family is hurtling into the middle class. The sons have all gone on to higher education: Jordán has a degree in biomedical engineering, Andy one in accounting. Rudy is just about to start college while Adam is taking a break for a couple of semesters, working at a Burlington Carpet factory, where he is one of two Mexicans among a staff of fourteen hundred. Maribel will surely enter college after graduating high school. The Tapias' journey from a poverty in Cherán to American comfort and mobility seems to have taken place in the span of an MTV video jump cut. The children are fresh-faced and energetic—not haggard like the migrants I've seen in harsher stations of the borderlands. Rosa Chávez is four years younger than Jordán and only five years older than Maribel, but tragedy has aged her.

It is a middle-class existence that has been achieved with peasant sweat, though.

"It was a little hard, we lived in some pretty bad places," Rudy recalls, absentmindedly pulling at leaves of grass. "We were working once in Michigan, I think it was, and we had to live out of the van for a couple of weeks. Yep, you could say it was pretty bad. My dad would wake us up really early in the morning and we'd work all day, no breaks, just lunch, and we'd get off about this time."

The time being, right now as we sit on the lawn in Warren, the dimming twilight. The sky is a deep, nearly cobalt blue above the stand of pines rising thin and tall. Lightning flashes on the horizon, but it's too distant for one to hear the thunder. The chorus of crickets grows louder.

The Tapias are not a typical Mexican migrant family, and I think Raúl Sr. knows this. While he is proud of what he has achieved, he does not minimize the discrimination he's met every step of the way, the racist police, the abusive *patrones*. He and his family have made it in spite of all, but he knows it is not a simple matter of "having what it takes" or even of working especially hard.

Luck is an important factor. Raúl and Yolanda made felicitous decisions on the road, about when to move on and when to stay. Nine years in Watsonville, three in North Platte, only weeks at a time in certain towns on the edge of the vast, stifling fields of the Midwest. Raúl happened to be in the right place at the right time some thirty years ago and heard a fellow migrant tell of jobs to be had in Warren, Arkansas.

And circumstances worked in his favor. The last generation of African Americans and poor whites was leaving the picking fields for city jobs by the 1960s, leading to labor shortages that Raúl and millions of other Mexicans have alleviated ever since. Raúl had clear goals as well. Passing through Los Angeles in the 1970s, when gang strife was beginning to tear at the soul of the Mexican American barrios, he saw first-hand the deterioration of life in the inner city and swore to himself that he would do everything in his power to keep his children off the streets.

The list could go on: the Mexican economic crisis, the deforestation of Cherán, the globalization of culture. And as heartening as the delicate combination of chance and faith and individualism and materialism has been for migrants like the Tapias, in the exact same proportion it is horrific what can happen to people's lives when the perfect coincidence of factors does not occur.

Each year, more Mexicans settle permanently in Warren—by the Tapias' count, some sixty families, most from Cherán, are now working in the fields and lumber mills, edging close to 10 percent of the population. In addition there are growing numbers of Chinese and Indians from the subcontinent. Warren is not exactly, however, a racial paradise. The Tapias have many stories of the kind that you'd expect to hear in the South. It was, after all, only some forty years ago that water cannons and dogs were trained on the civil rights marchers in Little Rock. There was the time Adam, his cousin, and the cousin's young son were hanging out at the mall in nearby Pine Bluff. Unlike the older two, the boy isn't typically Mexican-looking; he's very light-skinned.

"So this white lady come around and says, 'Whose son are you carrying? Is he lost or what?' And I said, 'No, that's my little nephew.' " The story does not end there. The white lady phoned the cops, who showed up with guns drawn, ready to save the white boy from the clutches of the greaser kidnappers.

Rudy tells about being pulled over by the cops when he was out driving his dad's truck. He was only seventeen, but he had his driver's permit in good standing. "And they just stopped me for no reason," he says. "They handcuffed me. I said, 'Hey, you guys can't arrest me,' but they just told me to shut up. 'We'll give you a bigger ticket if you don't,' they said." The arrest was witnessed by a family friend, who rang Raúl Sr. at home. He and Yolanda were at the scene within a couple of minutes, and after Raúl's righteous protest, the cops cuffed him, too. When Yolanda joined the chorus for justice, the cops grabbed her so roughly that the bruises lasted for days.

Adam has another story. One night, cruising slowly through Warren in his Cutlass, just passing the time, he saw a car full of teenagers approaching. The driver leaned out and shouted, "Fuckin' Mexican!" The cars stopped in the middle of the road and the kid cussed Adam out some more. Adam got out of his car, and, in a move he surely learned from the likes of Tupac Shakur, he threw up his hands and said, "Whassup!" His adversary sped off. A little while later, the two cars met up again and there was more dissing. This time, both boys got out of their cars. "I pushed him and he pushed me, but I said, 'I don't want to start no fight.' You see, he had a bunch of his white friends around, and I said, 'I don't want to fight none of y'all.'"

Clearly, Adam has learned when to back down. The irony of the situation is that the racist bully was not white. "He's an Indian," Adam says, meaning Native American. There've also been plenty of internecine battles in the region, the Tapia boys say. When they first arrived in Warren in 1985, only four other Mexican families lived in the area. The Tapias are regularly challenged by fellow Purépechas, for the very same reasons they are challenged back in Cherán: they are resented for their economic success, for the way they have acculturated. *Envidia.*

Whatever trouble the Tapias have had, they say it's nothing compared with what the seasonal migrants endure. During the late spring and summer months, a couple of hundred migrant men work the tomato farms. Adam remembers witnessing a white cop pulling over a migrant worker at a traffic signal. The cop claimed the Mexican hadn't stopped. It was a sizzling summer day. "Put your hands on the hood!" ordered the cop. The migrant did as he was told, but within seconds he pulled his hands off the blazing-hot metal. In Spanish, he tried to explain. The cop did not, of course, speak Spanish, and he busted the migrant for "resisting arrest."

For all the expressions of racism, there are signs in Warren of the kind of multiracial future being forged throughout the country. Adam and Rudy seem to be in the vanguard, brown hip hoppers who say they've dated white girls, black girls, Mexican girls, Mexican American girls. Not that the Montagues and Capulets are happy about such behavior.

"I was talking to this black girl once," says Adam. "She had a kid, and her ex-boyfriend gave me a real hard look. I guess he was thinking that I wasn't just associating with her but with his kid, too. Black people be telling us to be associating with our own kind, y'know."

Adam, a Purépecha, declaims these words in equal parts Ebonics and Arkansan dialect, which may or may not be premonitory. Still, a Purépecha American version of *Guess Who's Coming to Dinner* could be in the making. His dad would probably get on him, Adam says, if he were to marry a black girl. "He's not really racist or anything, my dad's pretty cool. But yeah, he'd probably get on me if I did."

Mexicans have always had an uncanny instinct for finding the soft spots of the American labor economy. Where there are jobs to be had in low-skill, low-wage industries, sooner or later the Mexicans will be there. The difference now is that many are settling in places where Mexicans have never settled before, beyond the border states of the Southwest.

But the town of Warren doesn't offer a plethora of job opportunities. Either you work in one of the handful of lumber mills or at Burlington Carpet in neighboring Monticello or you pick tomatoes. And even these mainstays are vulnerable to the winds of the economy. The lumber mills have seen their share of layoffs, owing to technology and downsizing. Many small farms have failed, and, it occurs to me, Burlington Carpet may relocate to Chihuahua.

Raúl Sr. is one of the fortunate few in town to have a job with the city, working on a street maintenance crew that consists of three employees and a supervisor. He's quite proud of the fact that he's the first Mexican to work for the local government. (Recently, a Mexican was appointed to the city planning commission, the first immigrant to hold such a position.)

We gather at the crack of dawn in the maintenance yard, a couple of blocks from the town square and across the street from a laundromat run by migrants. The Spanglish sign out front reads, WASHETERIA. Harvey Hilton, the supervisor, is in his late fifties, silver-haired and big-jowled. He groggily goes over the day's work orders.

"As far back as I've been around the Mexicans was in 1948," says Hilton. "On our farm we had thirty-eight pickin' cotton. Back then you didn't hardly ever see a Mexican other than at harvest time; through the winter you didn't see any at all. But we had them in the spring choppin' cotton, and then in the fall pickin' cotton."

When Raúl first applied for the job, Hilton says, referring to his employee as "Rudy," he drove the newcomer around town to see if he could read the street signs. "Well, he probably read about 70, 75 percent of 'em. We still every once in a while have trouble communicatin',

you see, we, uh, we get . . . well, Rudy's English is a little rusty sometimes, you see. I just tell him, 'Now, Rudy, if you don't understand
something, you just come back to me, and let's get everything
straight.' "

Raúl is standing next to us during this conversation, and I start to
regret the interview. My presence is reinforcing the hierarchy, it seems.
Suddenly, the man who's challenged cops and held his own in cantina
brawls is the obedient help.

"My English, I cannot speak it too good," Raúl says with a heavy
accent. "But I understand it mostly. I don't read very much, you know.
I never been to school, and it's too late for me. It's sad for me, but my
little English help me a lot."

The New South's labor economy, as seen through the microcosm
of Warren's street maintenance department, looks like this: on top is
Hilton, the supe, an elderly white man; below him are Raúl and two
co-workers, James Woodcut and Willy Marks, African Americans in
their late forties. The first job of the day is to clear out a drainage ditch
on a residential street. Raúl works the Caterpillar backhoe, while Willy
and James take shovels to the muck.

"Harvey doesn't really give us no hard time," says James. "He just
does things in a kind of sneaky way. He figured that for some of the
machines only a white boy can run 'em, like I'm too stupid. He bought
a machine just a couple of weeks ago and said nobody was going to run
it but him and this other white boy who doesn't even work in our
department."

The next job, another drainage ditch, is on the south end of town, in
a black neighborhood called Goatneck. An elderly African American man
in overalls saunters over to watch the work. The Mexicans, he prophe-
sies, will come in ever-greater numbers. "Let me tell you one thing," he
says. "The whites, they want everything on a silver spoon, you know.
They need to lose out for once. Somebody new should take over."

The crew gets a full hour for lunch. Because the town is so small,
Raúl heads for a meal at home rather than brown-bag it at the maintenance yard. Although he gets along well enough with his co-workers,
he just doesn't have much to talk about with them. James and Willy
banter all day long; Raúl only speaks when he has to. At home, he

warms up some leftover stew and tortillas. As always, he sits at the head of the table, his back to the windows overlooking the grassy expanse of the backyard. These days, he eats his lunch alone. Yolanda has taken a job at the local dry cleaners and her half-hour break is too short for her to make the trip home. In my presence, Raúl usually assumes the role of proud father and migrant philosopher. But today we make small talk for a bit and then Raúl grows wistfully quiet.

Maybe the mood reflects the day's humiliations. Lately, Raúl is also preoccupied by thoughts of the changes taking place in his family. Now that the children are approaching adulthood, they will likely be taking to the road. Warren is just not the type of place young people can envision growing old in. In this sense, too, it's much like Cherán. Jordán has married and moved out of the house. Although he lives nearby, his biomedical engineering degree will almost certainly take him farther away soon. Andy is thinking about moving to St. Louis. The Tapia children might very well wind up spread out across the country. Then the Tapias will have truly arrived in America, a place where family ties are maintained by long-distance phone lines, where the dinner table is full only for the holidays. A new kind of solitude is beginning to settle on Raúl Tapia.

After Raúl's early solo journeys, the Tapias avoided the migrant's nightmare of family separation. "I always told my husband that where he goes I go, where he stays, I stay," Yolanda told me. "We never separated." Throughout the years, she worked either alongside Raúl in the fields or at a job nearby. But their very economic success will cause the family to drift apart.

I recall speaking to Raúl in Cherán. His aging, frail mother was in the kitchen, just a few paces away. He hadn't seen her in three years, and he knew that he might not see her again after he returned to the States. The intervals between the Tapias' visits to Cherán had grown steadily longer over the years, especially since the family settled in Warren. It was impossible to live fully in both places, and even the occasional visits had become problematic. There was the mortgage on the house, payments on five cars, and the five children's education to save money for.

Raúl is not the ostentatious type; he long ago gave up on turning his house in Cherán into a migrant mansion. He's too far along on the road now to go back. But what will be left for him here when the children move away? Raúl came to America alone to give his children a future. He just never thought about how that very future might swallow them up.

Joseph Rodriguez

PRINCES OF NORWALK

It is springtime and no matter where you are in America, in the city or in the country, on an interstate or a county road, day or night, there are people on the move, their U-Haul trailers crammed with furniture, their backpacks pressing their shoulders as they lean over the Greyhound ticket counter. There are families, lone drifters, packs of students exploring the world. Sipping coffee at a rest stop, they look glumly at the map behind the plastic case. They gather for a midnight dog at the Amoco or at those surreal commercial islands glowing McDonald's yellow in the drizzly night. This is America, and the travelers are white and black and yellow and brown and red and every mixed-race shade imaginable. They are rich and poor and in-between. The middle-class families are headed to Lake Tahoe or up into the Smoky Mountains, the parents sleepless and the kids kinetic. And those we like to call, in neo-Marxist tribute to long hours, monotonous tasks, slim paychecks, and high-interest mortgages, working class—that is, most of the travelers—are going back home to bury Grandma or pulling up stakes because Dad has heard of a textile factory that's hiring right now.

And at the rest stops and Circle Ks and Piggly Wigglys across this land, in every region from the steamy Mississippi River Valley to the rusty cities of the Northeast, you'll find Mexicans. Always two, three, or more. They just jumped out of a boxcar at the train yard in Davenport, Iowa; they just washed their faces at the sink next to you at the Denny's in Dallas; they just arrived at the Greyhound station or they are just about to leave.

Now and again you come across a "solo," a Mexican who's struck out on the road alone. Perhaps he was separated from his family at the border, or there was some falling out with his comrades one night in a cantina. He'll be standing apart from the pack of day laborers waiting for a ride, ordering coffee at a McDonald's early in the morning with his face puffy from having spent the night outdoors. He'll follow a rumor that there might be work in the next town, in the next state, or on the other coast. His loneliness is immense—I've never known a Mexican man to prefer solitude to the company of others, and there is no Mexican equivalent of the American tradition of lone drifters—but so is his resolve. Speaking only a few words of English, often down to the last of his money, he overcomes his fear and sticks to the road.

I am standing on Main Street in Norwalk, Wisconsin (population 564), a town much smaller than Cherán, Michoacán. The interstate becomes a state route out here and finally a county road, which becomes Main Street. It is gentle country, rolling hills green with prairie grass. And it is God's country, too, an Amish and Mennonite stronghold. The Germans and Norwegians who migrated to the region generations ago have been thoroughly absorbed into the landscape—they are Americans. Like the Spaniards who built cathedrals over the pre-Columbian temples, the new Americans layered their plain Christian aesthetic over Indian land. The memory of the first natives has been reduced to placards at rest stops along the interstate that tell of the Indian wars.

Sunday afternoon at two o'clock. No one's out on the street. The one general store and one restaurant are closed. The bars—two of them—are quiet. The only sound on Main Street comes from the faint flapping of faded American flags affixed to the light poles.

But suddenly there's life. I hear music. And I begin to feel a little of the cultural vertigo I experienced back in Cherán when I caught sight of the Enríquez family's trucks blasting hip hop as they cruise the highway. Because what I hear in the Wisconsin outback are the strains of Mexican *banda* pumping full blast from car stereo speakers. A pickup truck rounds the bend. I am expecting to see a crew of migrant kids in the cab and pickup bed. But what I see is a crew of young white women. As they cruise past me, one of them lets out a cry—not the Mexican "ay-ay-ay" but "yee-haw," the unmistakable American cowboy hoot. American girls in a Ford pickup blasting *banda*. Welcome to Norwalk, Wisconsin, a new kind of upper-Midwest town.

Santiago Enríquez heard a rumor that there were meatpacking jobs for the taking in Wisconsin. *Wisconsin*, he thought to himself. *Is that in Canada?* After years of following the fruit harvests, of living like the Joads out of a van packed with bedrolls and pots and pans, the idea of settling down somewhere, of working indoors, of getting regular paychecks instead of cash under the table sounded like heaven.

On the front porch of an abandoned church I find a local Mexican nursing a beer and I inquire as to the Enríquezes' whereabouts. He wordlessly points at a house just a few doors down. Everything is just a few doors down in Norwalk.

I knock on the door of a handsome old two-story wood-frame house, and Santiago himself opens the front door. He's dressed Mexican casual in a sleeveless T-shirt that highlights his bulging upper arms and healthy paunch. He is midbite into a homemade *carnitas* taco. It takes him a while to recognize me. Once he does, he is fairly astounded.

"I know you said you'd visit one day, but I didn't think you would," he says. "You must have come thousands of miles!"

Soon the entire family is out on the veranda, greeting me like a long-lost relative, in sharp contrast to the chilly reception I got from the Enríquez boys in Cherán. I am ushered into a house that, but for the wallpaper and wood-framed windows, looks much like the Enríquez mansion in Michoacán. A calendar emblazoned with an Aztec warrior hangs in the hallway, advertising a Mexican butcher shop in Chicago. The aroma of stewing pork and freshly made tortillas wafts from the kitchen. Dominating the living room is an altar with a huge white baby Jesus doll, a framed Sacred Heart of Jesus, and a Virgin Mary statuette surrounded by fresh flowers and burning votives. Next to the altar is

ently tuned, via satellite, to a soccer match beamed up
City.

is is a big house by American standards, the quarters are
cramped for the Enríquezes. Here live Santiago and María, their
five children, four daughters-in-law, and five grandchildren. Santiago's
nephew Pedro, up from Cherán for the first time, is staying here, too.
The young married couples each have taken one of the four bedrooms
with their children. Santiago and María sleep downstairs in the living
room with Marta, their youngest child. Pedro unrolls a mattress in the
pantry at night.

The men return to the living room and huddle around the TV,
watching the action live. The Chivas of Mexico City are clobbering the
Tigres, a provincial team, 5–0. The Enríquezes root for the underdog
Tigres—as all self-respecting Mexican provincials must—against the
much-hated representatives of Mexico City. But the score doesn't really
matter. It's a Sunday afternoon, the Enríquezes' only day off, and everyone's in T-shirts, shorts, and rubber sandals, lying back in the dusty
curves of a huge old sofa.

They've spent six days boning cows at the meat plant, where the
supes bark orders in English, and now they're enjoying a Cherán home-
coming of sorts, made possible by a subscription to Primestar, which
offers them four Spanish-language channels.

The Enríquezes' Norwalk home is a labor of love, just like their
migrant mansion over the border. A fixer-upper bought from an American family for $16,000 cash (the Enríquezes have no credit cards, not
even a checking account), it was a rundown eyesore.

"It was ugly, practically in ruins," says María, who chats in the
kitchen with her daughters-in-law, as traditional Mexican women are
wont to do while their husbands partake of the Sunday soccer ritual.
"So we invested some money to fix it up a bit." María is being modest.
The Enríquezes poured their meat-plant salaries into a new roof, new
siding, a full exterior and interior paint job, and new cabinets in the
kitchen and bathrooms. "We'd come home from work and keep working. Ten hours we'd be at the plant and then we'd all pick up hammers
here at the house."

I note the pinkish tone they selected for the interior. María smiles.
"Coral," she says. "The same color we painted the house in Cherán."

María offers me a fresh tortilla stuffed with tasty stewed pork—the same meal, eaten without forks or knives, that I will be offered every day of my Norwalk sojourn. "We don't like the tortillas they sell in the store, they taste terrible," María says. "Too salty." In addition to the tortillas she disdains, the general store now offers several varieties of chiles. About half the population of Norwalk today is Mexican.

On my tour of the spacious backyard, I meet the next-door neighbor, Barbara Hansen, a blonde, slim, no-nonsense middle-aged woman who has lived her whole life in the town and happens to be outside tooling about her yard. She professes delight with the Enríquezes as neighbors but also says that she hears plenty of gossip among her colleagues at the store where she works in neighboring Sparta.

"They say things like, 'I wouldn't want to live in Norwalk, that little Mexico,'" she says, her speech singsongy and slightly clipped—the Canadianesque accent of the upper Midwest. "But I love being exposed to different cultures," Barb Hansen says, clearly and enthusiastically placing herself on the liberal side of the local debate over the changes wrought by the Mexican presence. "It's exciting. I think the Enríquezes are starting to feel okay with me because this afternoon they came over to borrow some salt. I figure that was the first gesture of being a neighbor."

Another major icebreaker, Barb says, was the grand fiesta the Enríquezes threw for their granddaughter's christening a couple of months ago. Anglos and Mexicans mixed easily, stuffing themselves on meat from a pig slaughtered in the backyard for the occasion and roasted in a coal-filled pit in the ground. While most of the Anglos commented favorably on the meal, some thought that killing a pig and roasting it that way was a bit, well, primitive.

As night falls, the air chills fast. The family eats some more pork tacos, watches more TV, the Sunday-night Mexican variety shows. The Enríquez boys will not cruise their cars and blast hip hop along Main Street—they reserve that ritual for Cherán. The streets of Norwalk are absolutely still. The only sign of life is the ghostly flicker of TVs through the drawn drapes of the old homes.

By 9:30, the grandchildren are all asleep upstairs; their parents' whispers gradually fade. María offers me a couple of wool blankets, brought up from Mexico, just like the ones my grandmother wrapped me in as a kid when I slept at her house in L.A. My grandparents turned their house, an architectural oddity that mixed Deco, Mission, and even a bit of Western rustic, into a shrine to Mexican memory. When they talked of Mexico in their later years, they spoke bitterly of the chaos and poverty and corruption, but it was nonetheless in their blood, and so a grand framed Virgin of Guadalupe dominated the living room and votives flickered in the bedrooms.

I settle into the sofa and feel warm as in the womb. María and Santiago crawl into bed, a double mattress on the floor behind a sheet hung on string. Marta is already asleep on a single mattress on the floor next to her parents.

The house is completely dark and silent. Still, I can sense life—the history of lives—in this house, in the old dark wood of the fireplace mantel, in the sagging steps of the staircase and the handrail whose lacquer has worn away from generations of people climbing up and down, in the snaps and pops of the floorboards adjusting to the chill of the night. From the sofa, I can see out the windows covered with lace curtains. Elms and ashes line the street, their branches arching together to form a leafy cathedral. The lights are going out in Norwalk. I stare into a serene and starry sky. For the moment, I am in Mexico—in America.

The alarm clock softly sings Muzak. Santiago stirs, yawns loudly, groans. It is 4:00 A.M. He comes out from behind the sheet, runs his hand through his hair several times, unsuccessful in taming it. María rises about a minute later, quietly walks past me toward the kitchen, and flicks on the light. When Santiago comes out of the bathroom several minutes later, dressed, he puts on the blue helmet that denotes his status at the plant—supervisor of the bone crusher. He must be at work before everyone else who works the line.

The aroma of pork and fresh tortillas fills the house again. After a quick taco, Santiago pads softly to the front door and closes it gingerly behind him. At 4:30, the engine of his prized Silverado growls. It is the first loud sound the neighborhood has heard since early last evening. Santiago Enríquez is always the first up on his street.

I join María in the kitchen. She is wearing the same T-shirt she had on yesterday, Budweiser Clydesdales. Life is so much easier now, she says. This is the first year since she married that she hasn't worked alongside her husband in the endless succession of fields they picked and then at the meat plant. With all the grandchildren to look after and with the daughters-in-law young and able-bodied, María, encouraged by Santiago, decided she would retire and tend to the next generation.

In contrast to the men, who complain that there are just too many laws against having fun in America, María feels she's much freer here than she is back home. She doesn't have to wrap herself up in a rebozo; her daily uniform now is pants and a T-shirt. In the States she worked and received her own salary, and she even has a say in the household's collective finances.

"At first, we women said, 'We'll spend our money the way we want.'" The men, of course, objected. A compromise was struck: everyone contributes to one pot. Essential bills are paid, and what's left is split evenly among all. "Sometimes I'll buy something nice for myself, makeup or clothes."

But she leaves her American wardrobe behind when she goes back to Cherán. "People criticize us back home," she says. "Over there, I do as the others."

There are some Old World rituals that María will not part with, on either side of the border. A couple of years ago she fell ill with a mysterious malady. She became listless and had no appetite, ultimately losing thirty pounds. "I'm going to die," she said. "You're not going to die," Santiago told her. They went to a free clinic in La Crosse, for X rays and tests. Something to do with the thyroid, the American doctor said via the practically unintelligible translation of a young white nurse with high school Spanish. The doctor recommended surgery. But the thought of a white doctor opening her up was too much. "So we went to Mexico," María says. Not to the *brujos*, no, because she doesn't believe in them anymore. But her faith in Jesus Christ remains a rock, and Santiago and María made the pilgrimage to San Juan Nuevo, to the small colonial church where Christ performs miracles for the sick and needy. (After all, the church survived the wall of lava that poured out of Parikutín in 1943, destroying the rest of the town.) There she prayed and left behind *milagros*, little tin replicas of various parts of her body, on the altar. Upon her return to the United States, the symptoms disappeared, and she hasn't had a complaint since.

María speaks openly about the difficult days of her marriage, the early years in Cherán and the first few on the road in the States, when Santiago did his share of drinking—and his wife suffered his behavior. I am surprised at María's openness; such matters are rarely spoken about in Mexican families. Chalk it up to American confessional culture.

"Back home, the man will hit you, and what can you do?" she says, now completely awake and speaking not in a whisper but in the loud, sometimes shrill voice of a Purépecha matron. "But here, they'll go to jail. Maybe that's why they think they're not free up here, ha!"

In Mexico Santiago might have continued drinking, María says. Perhaps she would have left him, though probably not. But here it's different. There are no secrets here.

At five o'clock, Jacinto and Mayela sleepily grab their tacos, followed by a glum Santiago Jr. and Lourdes at 5:15. Enríque and Aurelina come down the stairs at 5:20, Roberto and Maribel at 5:25. One by one, the Silverados purr off down the street for the three-quarter-mile drive to work. The Enríquez boys do not turn their stereos on. In Cherán, they acted like tough rappers, but here they seem to play a quiet, almost humble role. Which probably makes the annual pilgrimage to fiesta all the more necessary. In Cherán, they literally let their hair down (at the meat plant they tuck their ponytails into hairnets) and blast their stereos as loud as they want.

By seven o'clock, Marta and the grandchildren have bathed, dressed, and eaten. Marta rushes out to catch the school bus on the corner. (There is no school in Norwalk; the bus makes the twenty-minute trip to Sparta.) A short while later, María sits in the living room and switches on the TV while the grandkids play quietly before her. She channel surfs until she finds a Mexican station running an early-morning soap.

Sometimes María thinks her life now is a dream. She remembers the decrepit trailers they lived in during the fruit-picking years. She had to knead and pat the maize dough for tortillas by hand. In the cramped quarters, it was impossible for everyone to have time to shower every day. She felt unattractive. Today, she's living it up. She has new sponges and Formula 409 to clean the kitchen and bathroom. She has Pert shampoo in the shower. She has paper towels, a microwave. She has a big rolling pin for the tortillas.

Life is so much easier now, on both sides of the border.

In the lot of the Valley Pride Meat Plant, the five Silverados are parked next to one another, their airbrushed murals glimmering in the early-morning light. It is such an impressive fleet that I almost expect to see the Enríquez name on the curb, reserving these spots for the Purépecha princes of Norwalk.

My first order of business is to get permission for a tour. The personnel director, Rhonda Powell, is sitting at a fairly neat desk inside a trailer at the edge of the parking lot. A tall, striking peroxide blonde, thin but sinewy, tight-lipped and dead serious, she reminds me of a stern Barbara Stanwyck presiding over the Ponderosa. It strikes me that Rhonda's the boss here, despite the fact that Tom Powell, her ex-husband, holds the title of plant manager. He's baby-faced, with a tousle of brown bangs hanging down his forehead, giving him an aw-shucks air of innocence. My guess is that she left him, and not the other way around.

Tom, Rhonda, and I sit at the conference table, more like a card table, for an interview. I mention that I met the Enríquez family back in Cherán and was impressed by their home. Tom nods. He's impressed with the Enríquezes, too.

"Yeah, they did the same thing up here, bought a house that was all run down and they got it all remodeled, cleaned up," he says. "I don't think they're a typical Spanish family. They're pretty clean people."

Rhonda does her best to cover for her ex. "What he means by a 'typical Spanish family' is, we get some trouble in town when the single guys come in and get a house and then fifteen of them move in. That's when the neighbors get mad.

"I don't know," she goes on, "it must be like a custom for that many people to live in one house like that . . ."

This "custom" is, of course, the result of economic conditions, just as the American "custom" of kids leaving home at the age of eighteen is a product of a different economy.

Then Rhonda's off, deploring another social custom, an American one this time: welfare. To hear her tell it, the reason that some 70 percent of her 250 full-time employees are Mexican is, simply, because the locals prefer to live on the dole.

"We can't draw from the town," Rhonda says. "They don't want to work like this."

The Enríquezes showed up, en masse, at Rhonda's trailer three years ago. "They did want to work, and they seemed like a pretty sincere family, but that was quite a crew to start at once, so we basically started a few of them and then other relations came in later on. What is it, twelve of them work here now, Tom?"

Tom nods earnestly. "They're not lazy . . ." he drawls.

Almost all at once, Rhonda, fearing the conclusion of Tom's thought, drums her nails on the table, reaches for her pack of Vantages, and cuts him off. "It's good money," she says. "We figured once that the Enríquezes together made $7,800 a week."

That was during the "fall run," as it's called in the beef industry, when ranchers sell off cattle to avoid barning the animals over the long Midwest winter. The plant record is some nine hundred head slaughtered and boned in one day—that was last December. Plant workers often put in seventy hours a week or more during peak months. They arrive in the early-morning dark and leave in the dead of night, never seeing the sun for weeks at a time.

Rhonda Powell believes that the Spanish presence at the plant will continue well into the future.

"They love the overtime," she says. "The people in this area, they want to work forty hours and go fishing in the afternoons, and that's why we got a lot of Spanish working here instead of locals. The locals whine about having to work, but the Spanish, they love it."

The thing that strikes you immediately is how loud the operation is. The boning room, the kill floor, the bone crusher, guns that blast hot or cold air, the boiling antibacterial vats, the huge refrigeration pumps, the shouts of supervisors, the loudspeakers blaring above it all. The cacophony rings in your ears long after you leave.

Tom leads me to the supply room, where I am given a white plastic hard hat, a white smock, and high rubber boots.

We pass through swinging doors into a large, frigid room, and there before us is the bone crusher, the massive, screeching steel monster that Santiago Sr. supervises, though at present he is nowhere to be seen. Workers toss loads of bone in, and what looks like ground beef comes out one side, bonemeal on the other.

On to the boning room. It is a strange, dramatic sight: about eighty workers are lined up on either side of two conveyor belts, one above the other, about twenty-five yards long, moving at about five miles an hour. I look for familiar faces, but I can't make out individuals, what with the helmets, goggles, surgical masks, and smocks. All I see are dark Indian eyes. Eighty pairs of hands wield knives, rapidly slicing the meat and fat off the bone, then tossing the bones up onto the top belt, which leads to the bone crusher. The meat cuts are left on the bottom belt, sorted, and, at the end of the line, packaged.

As the tour proceeds, the working conditions grow more and more primitive. In the warehouse, where it is always 32 degrees—a temperature drop of nearly twenty degrees from the boning room—hundreds of skinned cows hang from hooks above us. These are fresh from the killing floor; in short order, they will be quartered, then carried over a worker's shoulder—no mechanization for that task—to the boning room. A quarter weighs an average of two hundred pounds. The dozen men of the warehouse detail each carry nearly a hundred quarters a day. I have no idea how the young men (I want to say kids—they're clearly the youngest in the plant) perform the feat. All of them are Mexicans, not a one taller than I am, and I'm well below six feet. Like ants, they seem to carry more than their own weight.

Steam rises from the carcasses. I push my finger into the flesh of one. It is still warm, and now there is blood on my finger. "That cow's probably been dead fifteen minutes," says Tom, smiling. "If you cooked that up right now, you'd have yourself the freshest steak you ever tasted."

The floor is slippery beneath our feet. As we pass from room to room, we step in trays of clean water to wash the blood off our boots, but within seconds we're bloody all over again.

We pass through the wash department, the first step after the animals are killed, where the Mexicans clean the carcasses with blasts of 220-degree steam, hot enough to kill bacteria. The room is easily 80 degrees. We have gone from arctic to tropical in a few seconds.

In the gizzard room, the Mexicans toss the spleens, hearts, livers, and tongues into boiling vats. The stomach and "bag" room is where they sort the intestines and bags of a cow. "You know," says Tom, "the udders, their tits."

The kill pen. Mexican kids prod the unwilling cows—they seem to know where they're going—through a chute and into the tight slaughter corral. The cows are knocked out by a stun gun, which smacks an iron rod through the skull, causing an instant massive brain hemorrhage. The kid wielding the gun is young enough to have trouble growing a decent mustache. He wipes his nose with the back of his hand, waiting for two others to get the cow in position. The air is thick with dust and the pervasive smell of manure. There is no conversation, no music playing to distract one from the job, just the same task, over and over again, save for the fifteen-minute morning and afternoon breaks and the one-hour lunch.

The gun blasts and a cow drops like a sack of potatoes, but it's not dead. Now another kid chains the hind legs, hauls the beast up with the help of hydraulics, slips the electrical bit into its mouth, and watches its limbs go taut with high voltage. Then someone else comes in with a knife to slit its throat and everyone stands back from the quick torrent of blood. The cow moves down the line to the saw room, where the animal is opened up and its stomach rolled out. The carcass is skinned and sent off to the warehouse. Later, other crews quarter the cows and eventually sort the parts, sending the tenders to the boning line, the bones to the bone machine, the gizzards to the gizzard room, the tits to the tit department. Meat for humans, meat for dogs. USDA inspectors roam about with clipboards, determining what is lean, or fatty, or diseased. And everywhere, everywhere, there are Mexicans with bloody hands, bloody knives, blood-spattered smocks, helmets, and masks. The boning line is where you want to be—the pay starts at ten dollars an hour. If you can't keep up with the conveyor, you'll be sent back to packaging or, God forbid, heaving quarters over your shoulder in the warehouse.

At every turn, it seems to me, danger lurks, accidents are waiting to happen. Water and steam can scald. Knives can cut. Nine-hundred-pound carcasses could crush every bone in your body should the chains or hooks or racks fail. Floors are slick with blood. Machines can swallow your arm, your leg, your entire torso.

But Tom says it only looks dangerous, and, of course, the federal Occupational Safety Hazard Administration (OSHA) is overseeing the whole operation, everything's up to regulation, there's no reason for an accident.

But all kinds of accidents happen in Norwalk.

The kid's name is Chance. A beautiful boy, if a bit moody and restless. At the moment he's clawing at his mother's breasts, pulling at her hair. But Kerry Vian, thirty-two years old and a Norwalk native, has the patience of a good mom. We sit on the front lawn of one of Norwalk's migrant mansions, an old white wood-frame with four bedrooms, Midwest-spacious. Kerry, Chance, and Javier, Kerry's boyfriend and Chance's dad, and a crew of migrant solos lounge about on a slow, warm Sunday afternoon.

In late spring the temperatures here are comfortable; in a few weeks, it'll be stifling. A few months later will bring the quickening darkness and the chill of autumn. And then the long, dark winter. This time of year, everyone's out on the porches and backyards and front lawns looking very Norman Rockwell. Kids swing in tires hung from trees and bounce on trampolines; grown-ups snooze in rocking chairs. Front doors are left wide open. Norwalk can see how another long winter has aged the wood of the trees and the houses and the people.

The thick grass of the lawn is littered with the dozen or so Bud Light cans the boys have finished off, a Sunday-afternoon display that elicits a "there goes the neighborhood" response from the town elders. Just a few minutes earlier, a gray-haired local walked by and flashed a scowl. The Mexicans haven't gotten rowdy though. The whoops and shouts, macho challenges and occasional flying fists are usually reserved for Friday or Saturday nights at The Place, one of the two bars in town that the solo boys call home.

Ten years ago a prototypical American family lived in this house. Blond-haired, blue-eyed kids, blond-haired, churchgoing people with roots in these parts going back several generations. Each generation worked the land, like most people around here. There isn't much else to do in middle Wisconsin. Now the house is home to ten Mexican guys from Guanajuato. The landlord is making a killing; each man pays two hundred dollars, when three hundred dollars would probably get a white family an entire house the same size. This is the kind of thing that irks the Mexicans. And they feel unfairly resented by the locals, who are annoyed that the Mexicans work very long hours for whatever pay is available. That's why they're here, after all. To work. To send money home. To return home someday. At least that's what they say. But there are doubts in the minds of the migrants. Go back . . . to what?

There are many houses like this one in Norwalk, peopled by packs of solos; only a few are occupied by families like the Enríquezes. But the big issue here is that women like Kerry—the umpteenth-generation progeny of northern European migrants—are going out with guys like Javier and having babies like Chance. Such relationships are on the rise throughout the United States; the 2000 census even included a category for people of "mixed race." But while mixed couples barely stand out in the big cities, in a town like Norwalk they can't be missed.

Kerry is a big woman with a slightly freckled moonface, blue eyes, and, right now, unkempt brown hair. She rarely wears makeup. She works at the convenience store just outside of town on a county road that cuts through Norwalk. Like most kids growing up in a small town, she'd dreamed of seeing the world beyond Norwalk. In the end, though, the world came to her, in the shape of a man who arrived from Guanajuato.

Javier is short but powerfully built, with a beautiful, deep-brown Indian face, a shock of coarse black hair, and almond-shaped eyes. He has an air of seriousness, unlike his younger solo friends. A couple of years ago he, too, was a solo, a restless, lonely migrant kid on the road. And Kerry was a restless, lonely local in an isolated and ultimately boring village. The couple met at The Place back when Kerry tended bar there and Javier would go cash his check on Friday evenings and knock back a few cold ones. They got drunk together, made love, and then came Chance.

Kerry named the child in the hope that he would have the opportunity to move beyond no-exit villages in places like Guanajuato or Wisconsin. That kind of a chance.

Two years old, Chance is, of course, completely oblivious to the fact that he was born a powerful symbol in Norwalk. He's a beautiful child, but not in the way people are used to around here. Chance has sandy hair, brown eyes, and golden cinnamon skin. His looks are a perfect blend of his mom's and dad's.

Kerry's relationship with Javier was the first of its kind in Norwalk— at least the first resulting in a kid. It just sort of happened, Kerry says. She wasn't thinking of integration, although the lack of young white men in town—this year's graduating class at the local high school consisted of thirty students—probably had something to do with it. Most of the kids who grow up around here wind up taking the highway to Madison, Green Bay, Chicago, or points beyond after they finish school. Norwalk is an aging town, like so many other rural spots around the country these days. There are the families that go back several generations and the middle-aged or retirement-aged folks who come seeking refuge from the cities. Most of the young adults in town are Mexican, drawn to the Valley Pride Meat Plant, Norwalk's only major employer.

The situation makes for tension between generations as well as between ethnicities. Kerry and Javier's relationship only exacerbated the tension. The reaction was predictable.

"Friends of mine I'd known forever said all kinds of things," Kerry says.

But then Kerry's friend Nina got together with José. Jessica hooked up with Pedro. Cora started going out with Pablo. A Mexican kid nicknamed Loco wooed a local girl named Tamacey. Later there were Dawn and Tolingo, and Susanna and Mario, and Monica and Alvaro, and Becky and Ramón, with the attendant pregnancies, sudden marriages, and occasional male flight. And of course these matches—between macho, baroque, Catholic men and independent-minded, plain-styled, and mostly Protestant women—involve considerable negotiation of language and music and food and religious practice.

"There's a lot of women around here who just don't like the *bolillos*," one solo tells me, using the slang term "white bread." He adds that "a lot of them go out only with Mexicans."

"They like us as lovers," says another, dripping with male pride. "And the *patrones* like us as workers. The Mexican is better at working and loving."

The situation does wonders for the Mexican ego. But the Mexican position in Norwalk is tenuous, nonetheless. It was the political wind of nativism in California in the nineties, coupled with labor-thirsty industries in the heartland, that pulled the Mexicans here in the first place. What if a downturn in the economy brings the politics of nativism to places like Wisconsin?

Already, the long arm of Washington has reached the Midwest meatpacking industry. In 1999, the INS, which for years had staged massive work-site raids to deport illegal workers, began implementing a new strategy. Increasingly conscious of a public relations disaster (TV news images of agents collaring brown men, women, and children), the agency went high-tech by randomly selecting businesses in industries known to employ illegals, cross-checking green card and Social Security numbers with the national database, and notifying employers of illegally documented workers. By law, the employers are then forced to fire the workers. The assumption—a big one—is that the workers, now without a livelihood, would deport themselves back to Mexico. The INS has merely passed the dirty work on to the employers. Rhonda Powell says that she dutifully checks all her workers' immigration documents according to the government's instructions; she also admits that she has no real way of knowing whether the documents are real. In any event, the INS pilot program has affected only a handful of businesses, and Valley Pride is but a speck on the industry map. Norwalk probably has little to worry about—for now.

But what if beef prices plummet, what if Valley Pride halves its workforce or closes down? For the Enríquezes and the solos, it'll be on to the next town, next county, next state, maybe even Canada, where not a few Latin American immigrants have trekked over the last two decades, as both political and economic refugees.

Not a few in Norwalk would be glad to see the migrants go. Kerry recalls Donny, a local boy from Sparta, who worked at Valley Pride from 1994 to 1997—the years when the migrants began arriving. He watched as the Mexicans went from about a dozen on the kill floor to the majority of the workforce. A bully always looking to pick a fight and already on probation for illegal possession of a firearm, Donny showed up one weekend night at The Place when it was bustling with Mexicans spending their pay on Pabst draft. He was packing a firearm.

"He pretty much admitted he'd come in there to kill somebody, and that that somebody was going to be Hispanic," Kerry says.

But the guys were ready for Donny. Someone pulled a knife. Somehow, in the struggle, one of the Mexicans got stabbed. Old man Cobb, the bartender, called in the sheriff from Sparta—Norwalk is too small to have its own police force—and Donny and five of the Mexicans were arrested. The victim survived. But according to the Mexicans, and allies like Kerry, the case was a miscarriage of justice. All but one of the Mexicans, who was actually born in Chicago, were deported. And Donny? He got ten more years of probation, a slap on the wrist. The TV reporters came in from La Crosse for the story of drunken Mexican bandits running amok in Amish country.

According to Kerry and several other locals, trouble here has never started between Mexicans and locals from Norwalk. It's always been someone from out of town, like Donny.

If there's trouble, says one of the solos, it's "because they're mad about us going out with their women."

Another chimes in: "And because they think we're taking away their jobs."

Lehrner's Market is on Main Street. Everyone shops at Lehrner's, because it's the only market in Norwalk apart from the convenience store on the highway. I visit in the middle of the day, when there aren't any Mexicans around; practically every Mexican in town is at Valley Pride at that hour. The only people I find are the owner, Theresa Lehrner, and her friend Dennis Hubbard, who's stopped by to chew the fat.

Lehrner and Hubbard are upstanding citizens; they both grew up in the area. The Lehrners have a farm in addition to the store. The Hubbards also have a farm and Dennis sits on the town board. The changes at Valley Pride were so rapid and the social ramifications so immediate and radical that the locals felt compelled to take action. Lehrner and Hubbard were among the leaders who formed what is informally called the Latino Task Force.

254 ▪ CROSSING OVER

"We had to do something," says Hubbard. "There was a complete lack of understanding of the rules of our society. The police had to come down here more than a few times a week."

Indeed, to hear Lehrner and Hubbard tell it, all hell broke loose in the midnineties. There was the loud music, the fights, even a number of incidents that Hubbard classifies as "rapes," although charges were rarely filed and, of those that were, all but one were dropped. It seems that the Latino boys attracted quite a crowd of women—though not locals, Hubbard assures me.

"We had girls coming in from neighboring towns," he says, "and I can't say they were getting paid, but they seemed to be acting like prostitutes, or they were runaways."

Lehrner adds with disgust: "Bunch of tramps."

And there were other things. Like the slaughter of the pig for the Enríquezes' christening, for example.

"Sure did raise some eyebrows," Theresa Lehrner says.

Hubbard leans liberal, coaxing Theresa. "Well, but remember, Theresa, here in this area, twenty, thirty years ago, in the fall you'd have deer hunting and people would bring the dead deer into town and the deer would be hanging on the trees all over."

"Yeah, but they didn't *slaughter* them," Theresa protests, increasingly agitated. "The slaughter is something I personally feel could become a problem here in town. If we let them get away with that, then maybe they'll bring chickens in and slaughter them. I mean, this is a village and there are rules and regulations—you can't just have live animals, livestock, in town. My neighbor used to raise rabbits and kill them and the village board asked him to stop. I just don't think the slaughter is necessary."

There is silence for several beats after this outburst, in the midst of which a young Mexican walks into the store, oblivious to the conversation about him and his animal-sacrificing ilk. He waits patiently at the register for Theresa to turn her attention to him and tries, in tortured English, to communicate what he wants to buy.

He keeps on saying "cahhhr," which Theresa cannot, of course, decipher. She tries out her Spanish. "*Carro . . . comida?*" She picks up the pocket Spanish-English dictionary sitting right next to the register.

She is thumbing through it uselessly when she finally exclaims, "Oh, a phone card!"

Theresa doesn't seem to have been bothered by the game of linguistic charades, quite the contrary. She smiles wide, genuinely glad that the momentary barrier has come down and now she's just a store clerk selling a customer a product. The register rings and opens. The kid walks away, uttering a shy "Goo-bigh." He will soon be talking to loved ones down in Michoacán or Guanajuato.

Dennis Hubbard is above all a practical man. He helped organize the first Latino Task Force meeting, which was attended by local leaders, including practically all the town clergy, the meat-plant managers, and a few of the permanent migrant residents, the Enríquezes among them. Hubbard opened the meeting by asking the natives where their forebears had emigrated from and why.

"Basically," Hubbard says, "most of the people in the village here came from Europe in the mid-1800s, because of political and social rebellion."

Then the question was turned to the Latinos. "And we found out it was social and political for them, too, and in some parts of the world it was war, like El Salvador."

One thing is clear, Hubbard says. The flow of migrants will continue.

"The community's going to have to change," he says. "Even if the meat plant weren't here, there'd be something else. And whether it's the poultry-slaughter operation or furniture factories or these expanding dairy farms—in the past, a family farm would milk thirty, forty cows and now there are two hundred, four hundred, five hundred—they're all going to have to hire labor. In the future, the immigrants are going to be taking on some of those types of jobs too."

And with that, Dennis Hubbard has pretty much explained how a town like Norwalk could, in the course of five years, have gone from being a sleepy Midwest village to a place irrevocably subject to the churning forces of global capitalism, migration, and change.

At first glance, you wouldn't know from looking at The Place that anything has changed in Norwalk. You can get dill pickles, hot Polish sausage, deviled eggs, and turkey gizzards, along with Heileman's Old Style brew and Busch, Pabst, and Schmidt's. There are the requisite cigarettes, candy bars, bags of chips, and tiny packets of peanuts for forty cents. The Place even has red worms for that fishing trip your drunk just inspired you to take. And you can tell the time by the Elvis Presley-with-guitar clock on the wall.

Cobb, the bartender, wears Scotch-taped wide-frame glasses and a polyester shirt with eight ballpoint pens in the pocket. He's a good listener and a good talker, as any bartender worth his salt must be.

"When people think of Mexicans they think of Pancho Villa with a bandolier, not a guy who works at the plant to provide for his family," Cobb says. "I guess that didn't sound too nice," he adds, laughing at himself. Cobb likes making jokes at his own expense.

There's a TV in the corner, just now showing an industry commercial, with the slogan "Beef: it's what's for dinner."

"Meatpacking is a young man's job," Cobb says, absentmindedly wiping an already clean counter with a rag. Cobb did his time at the plant. Practically every man and a good number of the women in town have done theirs. But that was in the old days. Before the youth became restless, before the sons and daughters of Norwalk performed their rite of passage not by getting a job at the plant but by moving to a city, any city. After generations of small-town stability, suddenly the kids wanted no part of it. They left for college. They went to Vietnam and, if they came back, they left again. They went looking for jobs, for wives and husbands, in Madison, Chicago, and St. Louis and on the coasts.

People from Norwalk, Cobb says, have in the last two decades scattered all over the country. The changes in the culture have had something to do with it and so, ironically, has the economy, which has been good to the people in the region. Currently, unemployment here is under 3 percent. So there are many locals who must work elsewhere, at the foundry in Sparta or at points beyond.

The Mexicans weren't the first migrants to arrive for jobs at the plant. Before them there were Poles, Russians, and even African Americans filling positions on the kill floor and the boning line. Mexicans are just the latest.

But something different is happening this time around, Cobb tells me. First of all, the people of Norwalk had never seen a Mexican before. And the previous groups of laborers were itinerants; they pulled up stakes after a few months or, at most, a couple of years. Few spent a lifetime working at the meat plant. Now, Cobb says, families stay here year-round, even buy houses. And Mexican boys go out with the local girls, that is, white girls born and raised in Norwalk.

It all hit home for Cobb when his daughter started dating a Mexican. "And I don't know if this boy's the marrying kind," Cobb says, pushing his glasses up on his nose, then placing both hands on the bar. "But there's been a few marriages between local girls and the Spanish guys in this town, and I tell you, you want to see those marriages work out. You want to see a family stay together.

"I guess what I'm saying is, I don't speak no Mexican, I don't know much about Pancho Villa or anything like that, but I do know how hard they work in that plant. And that's good enough for me."

It's good enough for Frank Ettinger as well. One of Cobb's regulars, Frank is a rugged-looking man with coarse hair blow-dried into a pompadour, an angular face, and steel-rimmed tinted glasses. He wears jeans and a black T-shirt whose pocket bulges with a pack of Merits. He has worked at Valley Pride on a couple of different occasions, performing various tasks in the supply room and on the cleaning detail. During his last stint, Frank was doing a job that usually required more than one man to do, and he couldn't take it anymore. According to Frank, if there's a problem in Norwalk, it's Rhonda Powell.

When he complained, Frank says Rhonda fired him, which was fine with Frank, because he could get on unemployment that way. Frank is convinced Rhonda is really pushing it in terms of regulations and safety. In the boning room, for example, where the conveyor belt brings the meat at a pretty rapid clip. There can't be more than three feet between people on that line and that's exactly where most of the accidents happen. It's not that people cut themselves so much as that they get stuck by their partners.

According to Frank, the killing floor was designed for a plant handling far fewer than the 600 head of cattle Valley Pride averages today. The plant record is 984. And you know what Rhonda gave the workers for that feat? Frank asks. A free lunch. Their bonus was a freakin' free lunch. It's dangerous as hell, Frank says, blowing smoke in the direction of the TV. There are 900-pound carcasses above you swinging on hooks. And a lot of the guys in there have jobs that take them from one section to another, from the ice-cold to the steamy in seconds. The air, of course, is full of bacteria, the floor slick with splattered blood. Everyone's always nursing a cold or the flu.

You can't blame the Mexicans for all this, Frank says, but that's what people in town talk about: Mexicans bring down wages, making it more dangerous, Mexicans this, Mexicans that. Bullshit. It's Rhonda who lowers the wages. It's Rhonda who makes it more dangerous. The Mexicans, after all, don't own anything. Rhonda's the one with a stake in the plant. With her job, Rhonda Powell practically owns this goddamn village.

The reason Valley Pride is the way it is, Frank says, is because lots of the boys working at the plant are illegal. She has to know it, everybody knows it. The police know, Immigration knows, Madison and D.C. know. Immigration only comes through when the boys are reported for getting in trouble. The rest of the time everybody just looks the other way. So if someone stands up to Rhonda and tells her to take her job and shove it, well, there'll be no support from the Mexican boys, no sir. They're just too scared. Hell, if those boys tried to get together and tell Rhonda off they'd all be gone in a minute. All she'd have to do is report them to Immigration.

There won't be a union at the plant anytime soon, Frank says. Hell, in Green Bay, you can make fourteen, fifteen an hour for the same job on the killing floor. It's union over there, but Rhonda won't go for that. And no one in D.C. is paying attention to Norwalk, Wisconsin.

"Who's gonna help us out?" Frank Ettinger asks. "OSHA? The USDA inspectors? The government ain't helpin' no one, I can tell you that."

Frank's been out of work for a month—it's been a month and a day since he told Rhonda his opinion of her and her operation. But he isn't worried. He'll find a job, he always does. There's an Ocean Spray plant in Tomah just up the road a ways, and a carpet factory, too. As long as there's at least one job out there you can do with your hands, that's where you'll find Frank Ettinger.

. . .

Cultural vertigo again. It's always the music that does it to me. This time it's the strains of violins and the strumming of guitars, recalling a place and time far removed from Norwalk, Wisconsin. It is a Purépecha instrumental. As I round the corner, I can see that it comes from a ghetto blaster perched on the Enríquezes' front porch.

The lengthening days of late spring allow for rest and recreation after the day shift ends at Valley Pride. At six in the evening, the entire family is out on the porch, preparing to rehearse a traditional Purépecha dance called *los viejitos* (the elders), a simple, joyous affair in which the young act like the old acting young. It is a pre-Columbian ritual and, as such, older by centuries than the Euro-American presence in Norwalk. Santiago Sr. came up with the idea of presenting *los viejitos* to the community of Norwalk in the spirit of cultural exchange promoted by the Latino Task Force. In fact, Santiago says, the Enríquez kids will demonstrate the dance at the next Task Force meeting. I wonder what Theresa Lehrner will make of it.

Marta, the youngest Enríquez sibling, is sitting on the porch, preparing her mask. She is loosening cotton balls to use as white hair and shaping the ends of Q-tips for the eyebrows. Meanwhile, the older Enríquez boys are whittling long sticks they found in the woods for the canes with which they will furiously, rhythmically stamp the sidewalk. It is a curious sight, the fearsome Enríquez brothers—the hip-hop, low-riding terrors of Cherán—suddenly turning Indian.

Santiago presides over the rehearsal, the proudest of fathers. "They say that traditions like this will never be forgotten," he says. Although perhaps it would be more accurate to say that they'll never be forgotten as long as Mexicans are far from their homeland.

"In Mexico, we just watched other people do it," Jacinto notes. "This is the first time we've done it ourselves."

It is entirely fitting in this cultural hall of mirrors that Marta, the youngest and most Americanized of the clan, is about to dress up for this ancient Indian ceremony. And if there are any contradictions, she doesn't feel them.

"I was born in Cherán, but I'm growing up here," she says simply. Her memories of living in the homeland are dim, idyllic. After all, she's usually only there during fiesta time. She speaks accentless English and Spanish and easily travels between her two worlds. In fact, Marta is already a crucial link between the rest of her family and English-speaking Norwalk. Her parents and older siblings, who speak a basic migrant's English, are not and probably never will be capable of expressing the complexity of their thoughts and feelings in the new language.

Marta knows more of America and Americans than the rest of her family ever will. At the same time, she knows more about the Purépechas than most Americans ever will. Except for the other Enríquez children, of course. The grandchildren in the family will probably wind up speaking English better than Spanish. Thus, in the span of four generations, the Enríquezes will have gone from being Purépecha-speaking Indians (Santiago's and María's parents), to bilingual Indians speaking Purépecha and Spanish, to bilingual and symbolically trilingual Indians speaking Spanish and English with a smattering of Purépecha, to monolingual and symbolically bilingual Indians speaking English, with a smattering of Spanish and maybe a word or two of Purépecha.

But that assumes, of course, that this migrant generation will behave like the ones that came before—which is an open question.

Now, on the Enríquezes' front porch, with the sky tinged peachy pink by the setting sun and the crickets starting to sing, a crew of young Purépecha *viejitos* begin to dance, slapping the asphalt with their feet and festooned canes. The rehearsal turns earnest, and the music is cranked up proportionately loud. The ruckus begins to draw a small audience of friends and neighbors. I get the sense that I am witnessing a second kind of "coming out" for the Enríquezes. They are making more noise and making themselves more visible than ever before. Perhaps along with performing Purpépecha dances, the Enríquez brothers soon will find the confidence to parade their rides through town, hip-hop bass rattling the windows of the old houses.

Jenny Schroeder, a local Methodist pastor and liberal dynamo behind the scenes of the Latino Task Force, stops by. A big, pink-faced, cheerful woman, she chats in pidgen Spanish with María while the kids dance. She compliments María on the food (the famous roasted pig) the Enríquezes provided at their granddaughter's christening. "Yum!" Schroeder says, rubbing her belly.

Schroeder is probably as close as you get to a radical in town. She specifically asked her superiors for an assignment in a Hispanic community, having had the opportunity to learn a little Spanish when she visited Bolivia, where her daughter, a missionary, lives. She probably imagined ministering in a Chicago or even Madison barrio; little did she know she'd be assigned to a place like Norwalk. Having arrived only recently she missed the first couple of years of gringo-Mexican conflict. She's approaching her ministry with both caution and big plans. Mexican immigration and its discontents are a civil rights issue as far as she's concerned, and she's considered a form of nonviolent protest against the U.S. policy that has helped create the illegal class.

"Sometimes I think of harboring an illegal," she says. In Norwalk, harboring illegals would mean giving solos room and board. She approached her bishop about the idea and was told to let conscience be her guide, although she was also told specifically not to hire one. It seems the bishop doesn't realize that knowingly hiring and harboring are both felonies with possible prison sentences, but in remote Norwalk there's little risk of being charged.

Then again, some locals might have a thing or two to say if she made a public issue of defying the law of the land. Schroeder is facing the eternal dilemma of the radical at heart: should her protest be a singular act of compassion and solidarity, bettering the world by helping out one person at a time, or should it aim to spark a debate, challenging the moral underpinning of such laws? During the 1980s, the Solidarity movement loudly challenged U.S. policy toward Central America. Some of my personal heroes put their reputations—and freedom—at stake for that cause. Father Luis Olivares, a charismatic Catholic priest who ministered in downtown Los Angeles during most of the eighties, was among thousands of members of the clergy and laity who helped smuggle, harbor, and hire political refugees from Central America and economic refugees from Mexico. But it was the Central American conflict that made the cause chic. Without the death squads in El Salvador, without the brutality of the military regimes in the region and the U.S. government's support of those regimes in the name of the Cold War, there would have been no movement at all.

David Ray and Joe Bailey, two young missionaries from a church in nearby Hillsboro who have also wandered over to watch the rehearsal, are not of Schroeder's spiritual or political persuasion. They belong to a nondenominational congregation heavily influenced by the Amish and the Mennonites. Ray and Bailey took an interest in "bringing the Gospel" to Mexican immigrants when they noted an influx in their hometowns, Ray in Chicago and Bailey in Davenport. They heard about Norwalk through the grapevine and stopped by one day, which is when they met the Enríquezes. For several months, they've come up from Hillsboro once a week to talk about the Bible, but the proselytizing doesn't seem to be heavy-handed. María maintains that the family is still firmly Catholic, but she nevertheless considers the young gringo men of God good friends.

The kids have one last go at *los viejitos*, Santiago clapping along to the rhythm pounding out from the box. The kids dance in line, oldest to youngest, each holding on to the shirttail or the belt of the person in front. They follow a serpentine pattern, their Mexican leather sandals scraping the asphalt, the canes tapping in unison. Because their costumes aren't quite done yet, they are dressed only half Purépecha. Jacinto wears a Wisconsin Badgers T-shirt. Roberto's long hair is loose, flying this way and that like a heavy metal rocker's. Marta has transformed herself into an old man by donning her just-completed mask.

It is a strange ballet on the streets of Norwalk. David Ray's daughter Joanne, a pretty teenager wearing a blue bonnet and an ankle-length dress in classic Amish fashion, stares quietly from the porch stairs, hands clasped. Her father sits next to her, leafing through his well-worn Bible. María and her daughters-in-law, leaning against one of the Silverados, are cheerleaders, clapping gleefully. A couple of the grandchildren are playing on the front lawn, lost in their hula-hoop world.

At a certain point, the rhythm coming from the old box and the movements of the kids become one, a fluid coordination that would have made Bob Fosse proud. Santiago Sr. suddenly thrusts his right arm into the air, gold bracelet glimmering as it shakes on his wrist. "Now you've got it!" he shouts in Spanish.

Up and down the street, the Enríquezes' neighbors are taking note, peering through screen doors, standing on porches or front lawns, some of them smiling, some of them looking quizzical. A crew of solos hoist their Budweisers in salute to their brethren.

The music stops and so do the dancers, perfectly on cue, frozen but for their huffing breath. Applause.

A little while later, everyone has returned home, the windows growing bright with the coming darkness. The silence of the night takes hold of the town.

I stare out at the highway through the window of 71 Express, Lehrner's only competition for sundries and the only gas station in Norwalk. The road is empty, as it will be for most of the night. The yellow line that divides the asphalt begins to glow faintly in the rising moon's light.

At the register, Nina Edgerton rings up another sale and then heads for the bathroom to touch up. Although our interview is going to be recorded only for audio, she wants to look her best. She's a pretty blonde, thirty-three years old, tall and tomboyish, a gregarious woman with a southern drawl. She made her way to Norwalk from Texas, fleeing a dead-end marriage and endless dreary horizons. Along the way, she worked at meat plants in Kansas and Minnesota, where she heard about Valley Pride. Mexicans aren't the only ones on the migrant trail.

More than half of Nina's customers are Mexican. Funny that she ran into Mexicans in the North Country. She grew up among them back home and she didn't expect to find them here in Wisconsin. But she did, and she found love as well. She married a Mexican in Norwalk, a man she met at the meat plant soon after she arrived. I ask her where he's from.

"I always forget the name," she says. She fishes. "Cheh-something."

"Cherán?" I ask.

"Yeah! That's it!"

But the marriage wasn't the lasting kind. Now she's got two divorces under her belt.

"You'd think the owner of this place would get it and start stocking some stuff for 'em," Nina says, settling into one of the booths by the window. Nina knows all about the "Hispanic market," has plenty of experience in the field. She and her ex started up a small business in neighboring Sparta, where the Mexican presence is strong as well. It was an Old Country store where you could get relatively fresh tortillas, chiles, Mexican films on video or gringo videos dubbed in Spanish—a store like many all along the migrant trail.

Nina is thinking about starting one up in Norwalk. Anyone can see there's money to be made. But for the moment, 71 Express offers beer and cigarettes to the hardworking, hard-partying migrants, who also rent some of the English-language videos, advertised on aging posters on the walls: Michael Jordan hamming it up with Bugs Bunny, Depardieu, Denzel and Meg, Sinbad, *Courage under Fire*. You can also get red worms for fishing here, in case you forgot them back at Cobb's place.

Nina met her new boyfriend, José (who works—where else—at Valley Pride), here in the store one day when he came in to buy a snack. José is from Honduras, a country remote and exotic by local standards. It's easy enough to imagine Mexico—everybody has had a shot of tequila and seen a mariachi, at least on TV—but *Honduras*? José doesn't speak much English, but that's not a problem for Nina.

"I've learned a bit of Spanish, so between his English and my Spanish, we don't have too much trouble. We're teaching each other."

Kerry Vian, who has joined us, mentions that her son, Chance, will grow up speaking both languages. The conversation turns to the growing number of mixed-race children in town.

"I think it's a good thing," says Nina. "These kids will be less prejudiced, if they're half Hispanic and half American. It's only the American guys that have that prejudice, and I think it's mostly a jealousy thing."

Kerry's boyfriend, Javier, stops by the store, and his presence chills the banter somewhat. He's not in a good mood. He's nursing a cold he can't seem to shake. Kerry thinks it's because he's on the cleanup detail at the plant. He starts his shift at 8:00 P.M. and sprays the plant floors with steaming hot water until 3:00 A.M., when he walks out into the predawn chill.

That's exactly why Nina quit the plant. Running in and out of rooms, tropical hot and then freezing. And she never got a raise the whole time she worked at Valley Pride. She toiled in the cooler and in the beef-wash department. She wanted to be out on the kill floor, but there has yet to be a woman on it. There was just no future for her there.

One day, perhaps the Mexicans might feel the same way.

• • •

My last afternoon and evening in Norwalk. The plant horn blows, and a few minutes later the Silverados are parked in a row in front of the Enríquezes' house. No rehearsal today. Santiago Sr. mutters something about taking a day off. Even the older boys and their wives, usually bouncing with energy, seem morose. The men strip down to their shorts, put on their rubber sandals, and plop themselves down on the living room sofa, while the wives retreat for a nap upstairs. The grandchildren play quietly on the porch, seemingly intuiting their parents' need for downtime.

The men watch TV for a long while, a soap about a poor girl falling for a rich guy, the staple of Mexican melodrama.

I notice a scar on Roberto's arm, and this opens the door to some shop talk. He was on the boning line one day, slicing chucks, when the knife slipped slightly in his hand. As he was trying to right it, the point of the blade stuck him just above the plastic arm guard. Six stitches. Before that, a partner on the line lost control of his knife and nearly lopped off Roberto's thumb. Three stitches. Because a nerve was severed, it will probably be stiff for the rest of his life.

Jacinto talks about how he's looking forward to the end of the summer, to the fiesta in Cherán and a few weeks' worth of rest. It's impossible to think of the distant future, both the possibilities and the risks dimmed by the enormous energy required by the present. The grandchildren will receive an American education and maybe have a shot at college. Perhaps Santiago will realize his oft-cited goal of "retiring" in Cherán within a few years, ten at the most, he says. Maybe the sons will go back to Cherán and start a business, once they save up a little money.

For now there's nothing but work and rest. The brothers sink back into the *telenovela*, a rather effeminate indulgence for the macho pride of Cherán. The heroine, a doe-eyed girl, is falling into the arms of her *patrón*, but a pair of prying eyes watch from the doorway. There'll be hell to pay for that kiss.

Joseph Rodriguez

12

ST. LOUIS, MISSOURI

I am riding Highway 61 in honor of Bob Dylan, hugging the Big Muddy, thinking Tom Sawyer thoughts, guessing the width of the river.

I stop for cigarettes in some Iowa town and am walking back out to my car when I see two Mexican kids. I think it's railroad soot on their faces, and I'm right. They just hopped off a train they thought was headed all the way through to St. Louis but has been stopped now for several hours on a lonely side rail. I tell them I'm headed to St. Louis myself and they jump in.

They have several forty-ouncers of Budweiser clinking around in their backpacks. Yes, Budweiser, the King of Beers, fuck that Mexican shit. Think about it: only gringos drink Mexican beer in the States. Why would a migrant risk life and limb on a journey of thousands of miles, braving ruthless coyotes, border bandits, the Border Patrol, and finally the metropolitan police or sheriff's department, just to drink Corona in America? Makes no sense.

Carlos is the younger of the two, from San Luis Potosí, a former windshield cleaner, the best windshield cleaner in San Luis Potosí, he says. Twenty-one years old, thin as a stick, working on a mean Mexican mustache, trying to act hard but coming up innocent. He reminds me of a kid who showed up at the warehouse of the print shop where my father (and, occasionally, I) worked for many years. A dusty-haired migrant from Jalisco, I found him sitting on the curb outside the warehouse, absolutely forlorn, down to his last dollar. He'd come up looking for work and had hit the pavement for two full weeks without any luck. The warehouse foreman, a rock 'n' roller with a heart of gold, gave him a job. That was in 1983. Within a few years he had become my father's apprentice in the litho department. Today he makes union scale, thirty dollars an hour, doing color separations in a room humming with Macs. He's married with children, has a mortgage and a nasty drinking habit. An American through and through.

The other hitcher's name is Miguel, from Monterrey. He's been roaming the northern lands for ten years now. Thirty years old, pudgy-faced and rosy-nosed from drinking. He has a mean streak that doesn't quite obscure the fact that he was as innocent as Carlos just a few years ago. Carlos and Miguel have been on the road together for a while, and on this particular day they started drinking early. They chain-smoke Winstons and speak nonstop, by turns vulnerable, lucid, philosophical, petty, and nasty. They also bicker like lovers. Miguel insists on speaking to me in his heavily accented English and this bothers Carlos, whose English is less than basic.

"EH-SPEEEEK ES-PANEEESH, MODDER-FUCKEH," Carlos snaps, from the backseat.

They've just done a stint in a northern Iowa town (Fort Something—neither can remember the name), where a Mexican widow befriended them, giving them room and board in exchange for work on the house. Before that, they'd both been in *el tambo* (the boardinghouse), as Mexicans refer colloquially to prison, Miguel for assaulting a police officer in Memphis, Carlos for driving under the influence (and, of course, without a license), possession with intent to sell, and resisting arrest. They ought to have been deported after serving their time; there must have been some bureaucratic mistake, they say. Their luck continued when they met the widow. She cooked them three meals a day and the work was easy—painting the garage, raking and burning leaves in the yard.

Miguel becomes more and more wistful and takes longer, wetter hits from his forty-ouncer, wiping his mouth with his sleeve. The woman had just lost her husband of thirty years. He'd been her first and only man, but his illness was a long one and they hadn't been, uh, well, you know, together for the last nine years of his life. You'd be surprised, Miguel tells me. Woman of almost sixty and a wildcat. Had him in the kitchen three times a day, breakfast, lunch, and dinner. She said she'd marry him to straighten out his papers. She said she loved him.

Those were the days. The men painted, they raked, they burned. They drank a lot of Busch beer and watched a lot of TV shows they didn't understand, but why would you need to understand the dialogue on *Baywatch*, anyway?

Miguel shows me the terrible prison-tat rendition of the Virgin of Guadalupe on his back and Carlos grows morose. I'm getting nervous that I'll be pulled over by some heartland cop and sent off to Joliet for transporting illegals. But the stories start coming and I relax.

Miguel dominates the conversation. He wants to get back to Memphis; there's this white girl who loves him there. But he can't, because that's where he took a swing at that cop, *racista modderfuckeh*.

"St. Louis is a good place," Miguel says, even though he's got a warrant out on him there too, for assault. "The *modderfuckeh* Mexican deserved it."

He shoves a beer in my face.

"*¡Qué vivan los mojados!*" Miguel shouts, hoisting his Bud out the window. Long live the wetbacks! "Fuck the *migra*! Let's go see that girl in Memphis, yes? Hey, you hungry? Let's get some pizza . . ."

We pull off 61 at some garishly glowing place where there's a salad bar. Miguel and Carlos act like they've never seen a salad bar before, falling in love with it, all you can eat! They pile their plates with cherry tomatoes and sprouts and iceberg lettuce and keep asking the tall, gaunt white waitress—in loud broken English—for more crackers. The waitress rolls her eyes and everyone in the restaurant looks at us. I see sneers forming on the pale faces as if we're barbarians, and I suppose we fit the part, three brown guys, two with dusty hair, railroad soot on their faces, tattered sneakers, and now a great pile of cracker crumbs and croutons gathering on the table. We head back to the car with a jalapeño pizza. Now the boys' tongues are on fire and they're embarrassed; their chile-eating prowess has been challenged by a gringo pizza.

Farmland stretches over the horizon in every direction; the gray afternoon becomes a gray twilight. Cigarette smoke chokes the car. Carlos is tired of the Winstons raking his throat. He snaps at Miguel to give him a Marlboro Light, and Miguel waves the pack in his face without handing him one. When Carlos asks for a lighter, Miguel pretends he doesn't hear. He's pissed because earlier on Carlos said he should have stayed back in Fort Whatthefuck, where the widow cried when they left.

"You disrespect me!" Miguel yells. "You think I made the wrong decision, just come out and say it, *puto*."

Changing the subject, Carlos tells of the time he got stabbed. One of his best friends attacked him with a kitchen knife in a trailer on the outskirts of Kansas City after a drunken argument. His girlfriend screamed, she rocked him back and forth in her arms, the ambulance came, and the doctor said it was a miracle he survived. It felt good dying, a warm, peaceful thing. Yes, that's what dying felt like—he's not scared of it anymore.

Miguel isn't impressed. He can't take his mind off Memphis, where he got drunk and disorderly on Beale Street. He asks me if I know Memphis and I say I do; he asks me to name the club across the street from B. B. King's place and I can't. Miguel chuckles, satisfied that he's caught me bullshitting. This angers Carlos.

"*Chinga tu madre*, this guy gives us a ride and you're dissing him!"

Miguel ignores the outburst and returns to his musings. He says that he met his first white girl in Madison. He could hardly speak English, but it didn't matter because she was so drunk her English sounded like Spanish. Carlos talks about white girls and black girls and American Indian girls. Miguel says that America's this big place where you can fuck and work and get high.

"No," Carlos says. "That's not it, it's more than that . . ."

"Isn't that right?" Miguel interjects before we get the big picture.

"Isn't that right, *cabrón*?" Carlos calls out to me, asking me to affirm the thought that has yet to be articulated.

A Missouri patrol car comes up alongside us. The boys have their beers in paper bags between their legs. They're suddenly quiet and obviously nervous. The cop looks at us, then finally, mercifully speeds past us. We continue on and on through dozens of small two-bar towns, past grain elevators and graying barns and freshly plowed fields. The sun is setting on the Midwest and I'm 179 miles north of St. Louis on Highway 61. *Don't follow leaders, watch the parking meters . . .*

They ask me if it's a bad idea to go back to Memphis, because of that cop. But there's no way to get to Kentucky, where there's work in the tobacco fields, without going through Memphis.

And then more stories: the evil boss, the beautiful white girl, the train ride at dawn, the fifty-seven-year-old widow. How Miguel remembers her tears! He chokes up thinking of her and Carlos knows not to say anything now. There are angels on the road, Miguel says, angels in the form of Mexican widows, obviously sent by Jesus Christ himself to tend to lost migrant boys.

Yes, they think about family, about doing the right thing. Carlos wants to go straight, he really does. No more drugs! he swears. But he'll never give up the forty-ouncer—ask a Mexican to give up a forty-ouncer and you might as well cut off his balls, he says. And yes, he wants to send money back to his family in Mexico, wants to build a house for his *madrecita*, wants to marry, have kids, stop this journey he's been on for three years now.

And in the end Miguel, who is much more hardened than Carlos, just wants to go home too. But they're a long way from everything and everyone, and there's that cop in Memphis and an immigration detention center in Louisiana with their names on the computer.

At five minutes before midnight, we pull into the Greyhound station in downtown St. Louis. The Gateway Arch glows dimly above the banks of the oldest of the old rivers. They're bleary-tired and I'm past exhaustion, but they'll get on that midnight bus to Memphis, yes, Memphis is where they're headed after all, maybe they'll find a job there to avoid the steaming tobacco fields of Kentucky.

"Fuck the police!" Miguel blurts out. "I gotta see Mary one more time. Did I tell you she have my baby?"

We part at the station. They're cold and I give them a sweatshirt and a sweater and they hug me and say we wetbacks always stick together. We'll meet up again someday on Beale Street, they swear, because Mexicans, they love the blues.

Rosa and Wense live in a sprawling apartment complex in West St. Louis, barely a mile from Lambert International Airport. The family has grown since I saw them six months ago. Wense's father, Rafael Cortéz, and his two youngest sons, Melchor and Gaspar (along with Baltazar, christened in honor of the Magi), have arrived in Missouri after yet another grueling crossing. Gaspar and Baltazar forded the river in Texas on tractor-tire inner tubes; the current was swollen by torrential rains, and Gaspar nearly went under. Baltazar, who was returning to St. Louis after visiting Cherán for a few weeks, held on to him and they made it to the other side. Rafael and Gaspar limped into town after crossing the line in the mountains of eastern San Diego County.

All of them live in a two-bedroom apartment, together with Baltazar's wife, Vicki, and their daughter, Stefani, Wense, Rosa, and Yeni. Within a few months, there will be more arrivals from Cherán— Wense's mother and three other brothers are still there—each representing a leap of faith and considerable sweat in the fields and nurseries of Missouri to pay off the several thousand dollars owed Mr. Charlie.

The neighborhood is mostly African American, but Mexicans now make up perhaps 10 percent of the residents in an apartment complex of some two hundred units—and the enclave is still expanding. Black and brown kids play together on the commons in the late afternoon and early evening, leaping over barriers of language and race as only young children can. Perhaps as older teenagers or young adults they'll be at one another's throats, but for the moment it is multicultural paradise. At two years and a couple of months, Yeni already has a black playmate, a neighbor's three-year-old; together they are inventing their own patois of Spanish and English. Notwithstanding Wense's disdain for the *negritos*, his daughter is growing up among African Americans and will be inescapably influenced by them. "I think she thinks she's the same," Wense says, a bit perturbed. "She only gets upset when she sees a white person."

Thompson Farms, where the Cortézes work, is only about a hundred yards from their apartment. It is a small, diversified parcel, featuring a country store selling fresh fruit and vegetables to retail customers, mostly elderly affluent Anglos who live farther out in the suburbs. A fence separates the complex from the farm, but the brothers have cut a hole in it to make the trek to work even shorter. They walk out their front door and down the stairs (often as not, someone is smoking something, anything but cigarettes, in the stairwell), turn left on the first floor, circle around the building, passing full and pungent garbage bins (occasionally, local teens torch them for kicks—or perhaps to protest the Sanitation Department's neglect of the neighborhood), and slip through the fence's severed links.

Only a few steps away from the gritty apartment complex, the Cortézes find themselves walking through rows of berries, corn, tomatoes, zucchini, and cabbage. From the American inner city to Cherán in less than a minute.

The tomato plants are nearly a foot high now, the dull green leaves giving off a vegetable aroma, and it is the Cortéz men's job to prune them, one by one, along the dozens of rows, which are each a hundred yards long. The plants have budded, and pruning ensures that the tomatoes will ripen faster. It is a timeless, time-consuming task for which no one has invented a machine. In a month or so, the Mexicans will begin picking the field. There's no machine for that yet, either. The tomatoes will be washed and boxed in the warehouse, then driven to the distributor, to wind up in markets, restaurants like Denny's, and family kitchens across the land.

A lonely rail track overgrown with weeds runs along one side of the field; a busy road abuts the other. Every now and again, someone passing by will shout something at the work crew. When I'm there, it's "*¡Andele, ándele!*" from a pickup carrying white teens mimicking Speedy Gonzalez. The Cortézes are used to it. Happens all the time, Baltazar says. They hear all kinds of things—"Go back to Mexico!" and "Fucking wetbacks!" and "Why don't you wipe the shit off my ass!" By and large, it's young men who do this, but one time some white girls rolled past slowly and one of them leaned out the passenger window and pulled up her T-shirt to bare her breasts. She said she wanted some "Mexican cock"; the girls laughed and sped off.

The work's not so bad, Baltazar says, compared with many other fields, where you're paid according to how much you bring in, like the farm in Watsonville where Fernando and Florentino Chávez are picking strawberries. There, you're paid by the box. You've got to move as fast as you can; the aches and pains come on a lot quicker, too. Fields like that are usually on larger farms, and there's not much talk among the rows, because your buddies are often several yards away. You're lost in your own little section of the field, among the plants you've just picked and the ones you still have to do, and your mind races, flashing back to good times and bad, spinning fantasies of lunch or sex. Time is funny that way in the fields, totally fluid. From the middle of a row the end looks impossibly distant, but once you're there you're amazed how quickly you finished and you start the next one. Suddenly the supervisor (*mayordomos*, the migrants often call them, using the language of feudal Spain and the Conquest) will call a break and there'll be small talk and cigarettes and always, in every crew, a jokester telling crass ones. Quitting time feels just like finishing a row of fruit or vegetables: a slow day went by fast and now there's a cold beer waiting back at the trailer or the cantina, and time slows again, the evening mercifully eternal. But when you wake up at five in the morning, it seems like the party went by much too quickly.

On Thompson's field, though, there's no *mayordomo*; if anyone plays supe, it's Baltazar, who speaks the best English and is the senior crew member. While he's a very serious, responsible young man, Baltazar harbors no ambitions to crack the whip. Father and sons squat in parallel rows of tomatoes, all working at the same slow but deliberate pace—snip-snip, snip-snip, snip-snip—leaving only two leaves beneath the white flower at whose center the tomato is still an infant bud. I join in and mangle several plants before I get the hang of it. Within minutes, my knees and back ache. After only a few afternoons in the fields, the soreness will remain with me for several days.

Squatting under the pale Missouri sky, the family is one—father and sons together, working but also talking, swapping stories. Rafael Cortéz, a diminutive, wiry man in his late forties with peppery hair and a deeply creased faced, retells the tale of his crossing. The illegals he joined first tried to cross near Tijuana but were turned back twice after torturous climbs through the mountains east of San Diego. When the *migra* swooped down during a second attempt, he and his son Gaspar were separated as the illegals scattered. Deported back to Mexico, the father did not know of his son's fate for several days, did not know that Gaspar had made it safely across and was anxiously waiting in Los Angeles for word of his father's whereabouts. When the two finally spoke—nearly a week after they were separated—Rafael told his son that he was going to return home, that Gaspar should make the rest of the journey alone.

"I was thinking about the money," says Rafael. "One thousand dollars for each of us. After all the money I spent trying to get across, I didn't have a peso left."

But Gaspar gave his father a pep talk. "You're already on the road," he told him. "Just keep following it and you'll arrive."

Agreeing to give it one more go, Rafael contracted the services of yet another coyote, his third, who wanted $1,000 for the trip to Los Angeles. (Others had offered to take him all the way to St. Louis for the same price.) After a night clambering through the mountains, he arrived in L.A. Back in St. Louis, Wense and Baltazar asked Jim Thompson for an advance on their salaries; then they paid off the coyote through Western Union, and bought two cheap one-way seats on Southwest Airlines. It was the first time either Rafael or his son had been on a plane.

"And now I have the great pleasure of being here with my sons, where I should be," says Rafael. "Back home, I have no idea how they're doing, how they're living. You worry about the things they say, that our children are out drinking and getting into trouble."

Neither Wense nor Baltazar, on opposite sides of the same row, look up from the plants during Rafael's speech. It's pretty clear which son gives cause for worry. There's something of Cain and Abel in these brothers. At twenty-three, Baltazar, the firstborn, is his father's favorite and the de facto leader of the siblings in Rafael's absence. He's bright, light-skinned, and handsome, has an attractive wife from Uruapan (the closest thing to a city in the Purépecha region) and a bouncy daughter. His English is good and his vocabulary improves all the time. He has the nicest car (the 1989 Grand Am in which we drove through the blizzard to pick up Rosa).

And Wense? He's dark, younger, and not very good with words. He has a paunch and a stiff leg. Wense is next in line after Baltazar, but he doesn't wield much power in the apartment or on the fields. In contrast to Baltazar's succession of used but clean and well-running cars, Wense's are always on the verge of a breakdown. Right now he has an '85 magenta-and-silver Monte Carlo, with racing rims and gaudy decals on the rear window.

In his older brother's presence, Wense often turns brooding and testy. But when Baltazar isn't around, Wense will confide his hopes and worries. He's made a tremendous effort at straightening out his life. He now drinks only occasionally, and when he does, it no longer automatically means an all-night drunk. He is a conscientious worker. Although money is tight, he meets his bills, pays back the loans he takes out, and still budgets well enough to send up to three hundred dollars back home to his family each month. He is thinking about the future.

Still, it is Wense who parties the hardest. Wense told me about his most recent escapade when we were alone one morning buying breakfast for the family. Wense, a friend of his named Victor, and a guy from Guerrero they'd just met went out and had some drinks at a local cholo's house, got ripped, in fact. On their way home in Victor's truck, Wense fell asleep in the passenger seat. In a distant, dreamlike way, Wense felt the tumbling blows—the car hitting the retaining wall. He says he woke up in the hospital hearing doctors and nurses wonder, in English, whether they should call the *migra*. But there was also a pretty blonde nurse who treated him nicely and spoke a bit of Spanish and told him that he was too young to be throwing his life away.

It was probably a miracle no one was killed, in Victor's or any other car, but fortunately the freeway had been deserted at 3:00 A.M. Victor and Wense came away with light injuries, but the boy from Guerrero suffered a broken arm and a severe concussion, and, Wense says, he just hasn't been the same since.

Wense wears the evidence of the wreck every day. His prized County J jacket, an oversize piece of blue denim that, true to urban-warrior fashion, mimics what prisoners wear in jail, has a huge hole in the left elbow. Wense thinks it scraped the retaining wall through the open car window; the large scab has yet to heal. For all the terror of that night, the angels of the road didn't abandon Wense completely. Miraculously, no DUIs were brought by the Highway Patrol and no one called the *migra*.

At least one of the reasons Rafael made the perilous trek to St. Louis was to reestablish his authority over a wayward son. "One should think," he says to me, but clearly addressing someone else, "about why it is one comes here in the first place. So that when one returns home, and when one is asked what one did up here, one doesn't say, 'I just drank a lot of beer.'"

The sons remain silent for a couple of minutes, during which there is only the snip-snip of their hands on the plants and the sudden roar of a TWA jet on takeoff.

If it were up to Rafael, all the Cortézes would be back in Cherán within a few years, after some honest work and saving. Melchor, suffering from intense homesickness after only a few weeks in the States, is ready to go back anytime. Gaspar, the youngest, will do whatever his father says. Baltazar is likely to disappoint his father and be swallowed up by an American future.

And Wense . . . who knows? He finally looks up from his row of plants and, like his father, speaks to me when he's really delivering a message to his family.

"There are people who have more than we do, and it's not like we want that much, but now, with my father and my brothers here, we can do *algo*, something," he says. "Together, we can help one another, have enough to at least dress ourselves well . . . to buy some sweaters," he continues, curiously recalling last winter, even as the spring is turning to a humid Missouri summer. "And we're going to send money home, too, so that the rest of the family can share in what we have."

This is Wense at his most earnest and responsible. He goes on, talking about the long road he's traveled. Now that he's got his family's attention—perhaps even their respect—he is going to make himself understood.

He recalls his first trip to the States. Because of his age—he was barely thirteen—he was the butt of the migrants' jokes. "You're too young, you're not going to make it, this kind of life is for a man," they told him, and he set out to prove them wrong. But that very first trip north, he got a harsh lesson in migrant life. At the beginning of the journey, the coyote, a Cherán native fancifully nicknamed *El Chacal* (the jackal), took all his money, a couple of hundred dollars that his family had scraped together. Then, in the chaos of the crossing, Wense somehow lost the crumpled slip of paper with the address and phone number of a relative in Los Angeles. He begged *El Chacal* to take him to St. Louis, where his uncle and his best friend, Alfredo Román, lived. Instead, he was stuck in Long Beach, California, cooped up in a safe house. *El Chacal* used him as a slave, forcing him to do the cleaning and, occasionally, to go out on the streets and collect aluminum cans. A week went by like this, then two, an entire month. *El Chacal* threatened to "sell" Wense to a sheep farmer in Colorado if his family didn't come up with the cash. "You'll be herding sheep the rest of your life to pay off your debt," the coyote told him. Wense, of course, had no way of knowing whether this was true. Finally, *El Chacal* relented and agreed to take Wense to St. Louis, since he had a couple of other *pollos* to drop off in the Midwest anyway. They arrived in Cobden and went in search of Wense's uncle, but to no avail. Then one evening, a car's headlights flashed into the trailer the coyote used as a safe house. Wense looked out and saw his uncle and Alfredo walking up. "I felt like crying," Wense recalls. "I felt so much, I didn't know what I felt." His uncle struck a deal with *El Chacal* to pay him the next day, but on the trip back to St. Louis that night, when Wense talked about the treatment he'd received, it was resolved that the debt would never be honored.

As fate would have it, the Cortézes took a trip back out to Cobden a few weeks later, and there in the town square, where the Mexican flag flies over City Hall alongside the Stars and Stripes and the flag of the Prairie State, the Cortézes ran right into *El Chacal*. Drunk, he walked up to Wense and his uncle, demanding payment. But Wense's uncle, a proud and fair man, declaimed a speech loud enough for all the plaza to hear about how badly the coyote had treated his nephew and how payment would therefore not be forthcoming in this life or any other. *El Chacal* took a wild swing, hitting only air. Wense's uncle stepped up with a flurry of punches and, when *El Chacal* went down, a series of kicks to the gut. *El Chacal*, in desperation, grabbed the uncle's shoe and bit it. "And all around us," Wense says, "people were cheering, because *El Chacal* had treated many people the same way, and to this day his business is bad, very few people travel with him. That's why most of the Cheranes go with Mr. Charlie."

Wense's old man is beaming at the end of the story. Taking his father's cue, Baltazar lets out a chuckle, followed by giggles from Melchor and Gaspar. Everyone is laughing hard now, except Wense, who just smiles, satisfied that he's managed to communicate just a bit of what he's gone through, just a bit of the world's cruelty and its occasional opportunities for justice, even heroism. One day Wense would like to play his uncle's role. He just hasn't had the opportunity yet.

The sun slants across the field, amber through the dust kicked up by Jim Thompson's tractor. It's quitting time. Except for two fifteen-minute breaks and lunch, the Cortézes have been squatting in the field for nine hours. But the hours have gone by fast after all, and the sons are in a playful mood. Baltazar challenges his siblings to a race through the tomato rows. "I'm getting old," he says, "but I can still beat you all by a kilometer." I get them on their marks and send them off. There is much laughter. Baltazar leads by a few paces and thrusts his arms high in victory as he leaps up to the raised earth of the railroad tracks at the end of the field. Melchor comes in second, Gaspar third, and Wense, heavy and gasping, running as hard as he can, never giving up, places fourth. To my mind, Wense's the winner. By a mile.

The Cortéz kitchen is equipped with a microwave oven, an Osterizer food processor, and an electric can opener. A full-sized refrigerator, seventies model, whirs loudly. An MCI phone bill ($142.11) is tacked up with a magnet. In the cupboard there are several large bags of rice and cans of Hunt's Tomato Sauce. On the electric stove, a pot of red chile beef is boiling, and in a pan some strange Michoacán concotion consisting of sour cheese is melting in chicken stock. The table is covered with a white embroidered tablecloth and striped plastic place mats. A Formica bar separates the kitchen from the living room; forming a small altar in the corner are wallet-sized photos of the three dead brothers and votives for each of them, depicting Saint Jude, the Sacred Heart of Jesus, and the Last Supper.

The living room is furnished with a pizza-toned shag rug, medium-sized plaid sofa, two matching stuffed chairs (hand-me-downs from Farmer Thompson), and a particle-board coffee table. The nineteen-inch RCA TV receives, via cable hooked up for a small fee by an African American neighbor, HBO, Showtime, and Cinemax. Opposite the TV, two cinder blocks support a piece of plywood draped with the same embroidered cloth as the kitchen table, on which stand a Magnavox cassette box and a few scattered CDs, *banda* and *norteño*.

A Virgin of Guadalupe beach towel hangs on the wall in loud tones of red, blue, green, and gold, identical to the one tacked up on the roof of Baltazar's Grand Am. The only other image on the wall is a picture of two blond children, a boy and a girl, holding hands and crossing an old wood bridge spanning a raging river, at night, in a terrible storm, with a winged angel watching over them. The picture is a puzzle the family put together and glued to some cardboard. It is the centerpiece of the living room.

In the waning light, Rosa is watering the flowers she's planted in large Costeña-brand jalapeño tins on her second-floor balcony. Baltazar, fresh out of the shower, in shorts and sandals and his perennial baseball cap, sits on the sofa. The Bulls battle the Jazz on the tube. It's a typical night in the Cortéz household in St. Louis. When they're not watching basketball, the family members spend their evenings watching the latest English-language action-adventure flicks, siding with the good guys who speak in a language they can barely understand, against the villains whom they themselves usually resemble.

Wense's in the shower now. The brothers bathe in age order. (Rafael waits until all have had their turn; he sits immobile in the chair next to the couch, eyelids fluttering.) Melchor and Gaspar are napping on the single beds in the bedroom they share across the hall from Baltazar, Vicki, and Stefani's bedroom. Come bedtime, Rosa, Wense, and Yeni sleep on the living room floor, Rafael on the couch.

When Wense gets out of the shower, fully dressed in his gangsta regalia, Rosa comes in from the balcony. They sit next to Baltazar on the sofa, a tight fit, all three mesmerized by the action. Rosa asks Wense whom the Bulls are playing.

"Utah," Wense says, pronouncing it rather well.

"Yew-ka," Rosa tries, and Wense, now a bit testy because he's being distracted, snaps, "Utah!"

Rosa ignores the outburst, although occasionally she snaps back. Rosa has grown more independent with each passing month in St. Louis and gained greater respect from the men of the clan, if not necessarily from her husband. She has endured more than anyone in the family, been dealt life's harshest blows, and the men all know this ("She's very admirable," was Baltazar's understated praise). They increasingly give her space—to speak at the dinner table, to take on heavier tasks at work, including driving a tractor.

"Yew-tah," Rosa tries again, closer, but still aspirating the final syllable the way Purépechas do. She says it mostly to herself, needing no affirmation from Wense or anyone else.

Despite her increased self-confidence, Rosa harbors few illusions about her prospects in America. Now and again, she talks of taking English classes, computer courses, perhaps going to cosmetology school. But she knows that it is Yeni who has the best chance of attaining an American future—linguistically and economically.

Rosa interrupts the commercial, once again talking to no one in particular. Rosa wants Yeni to grow up without having to depend on anyone to make herself understood. "Not like me," she says, "waiting for someone to translate what I'm being told or what I'm saying. It's embarrassing." There are times, Rosa says, when she craves a soda or some chips. The Amoco station right around the corner from the complex has a convenience store, but she hesitates to go there. "I'm afraid I won't know what they're saying and I won't know what to say. I don't want Yeni to go through that."

Rosa wonders how her mother would feel in St. Louis. For some time, Wense has been trying to convince Rosa to bring María Elena north as well. But Rosa's not so sure. If she herself feels so isolated, so utterly lost just a few paces from her apartment door, what would it be like for María Elena?

In Cherán, at least, Rosa's mother has friends and the store to tend to, even if there are few customers. Her life in America would basically consist of baby-sitting Yeni and Stefani in the apartment six days a week. With so much time on her hands, with so little to distract her, María Elena would turn to thinking about the tragedy and she'd begin to suffer mysterious pains again, like in the weeks and months after the brothers' deaths.

"I want to do the right thing," Rosa says, "but I'm not sure this is it." Yet the few times a month Rosa talks to her mother—after calling Salvador Estrada's long-distance booth in Cherán and waiting for a messenger to bring María Elena the good news that her daughter is phoning from the States—the old woman always says she wants to come north. She is willing to face the same risks that her children have faced. She does not want to be left behind.

The second quarter begins. The rhythm of the game picks up as the Bulls begin to work their magic. Fast breaks, layups, steals, dunks. All the Cortéz brothers are now in the living room, watching the action intently. The old man has fallen asleep. Rosa has loosened up, talking about how many trays of houseplant seedlings she moved today in the Thompson nursery, about the Mexican store down the road—has Wense taken me there yet? There's this guy there behind the cash register, a *jotito*, a little fag, and he's so funny . . . She's feeling much better now that the nightmares have subsided—terrible scenes reliving her excruciating crossing, the nights in the mountains, the rocks giving way under her feet, Yeni like a load of bricks in her arms. During the first several weeks in St. Louis she'd wake in terror, crying, bathed in sweat.

"Sometimes I still can't believe I'm here," Rosa says. "But I am. I didn't give up."

It is 96 degrees with 100 percent humidity inside one of the greenhouse nurseries at Thompson Farms. The heat of a suffocating Missouri day is exacerbated by the nursery lights above us. They are always on. At night, the nursery glows like an extraterrestrial apparition hovering above the fields. Rosa Chávez works side by side with Pat Zimmerman, one of the few non-Mexican employees. They sow shoots of Swedish ivy into trays filled with dark soil. Around us are hundreds of plants, from sprouts to fully grown, a riot of color: mint greens, fuchsia reds, soft pinks, canary yellows. Marigolds and sunflowers, petunias and geraniums, a variety of vegetable seedlings. Yeni is running up and down among the flowers under the watchful eye of her mother.

Within minutes, I'm sweating like a Missouri thundershower—and all I'm doing is scribbling notes. Somehow, Rosa and Pat appear cool and fresh-faced. They have little to say to each other; neither speaks the other's language. Pat wears headphones. "Most people don't want to work this hard," she says, rather taciturn. "I don't mind. The heat doesn't bother me." And that's about all the conversation I get out of her.

But Loretta Panhorst, another non-Latino helper, is hungry to be heard. Loretta describes herself as a "Heinz 57 kind of girl," hopping from bedding plants in the nurseries to tending tomatoes out in the field. A heavyset woman with bubbly reddish curls, Loretta grew up on farms in the Midwest; farming is her life. She stands outside one of the nurseries, the huge blades of an intake fan turning above her head.

Loretta has been at Thompson Farms for eleven years and has developed intimate relationships with many of the Mexicans. "I don't

even like to call them Mexicans, they have names, you know." She's
known the Román family, Wense's friends, since she began working
here, and she was even Rosa Román's maid of honor. She practically
saw the Román kids grow up.

But as Mexicans flooded the local farm-labor market, she started
noting problems. There was the language issue, but that's just a minor
frustration, since, Loretta says, "they're not stupid and they pick up
pretty quick on what you're doing." But then she noticed something
beyond language that truly bothered her: the way the Mexican men
treat their women, the way the women allow themselves to be treated.

"I work with the girls a lot, and I tell them that's not how we act
up here," Loretta says. "But the women always seem to get left home
on weekends and the guys go and do their thing."

There's another classic attribute of Mexican machismo that troubles
Loretta. "It's always *joto* this and *joto* that. I guess for them being homo-
sexual is just not the thing to do, you know, whereas up here it's more
accepted."

And so Loretta thinks of herself as an older sister, counseling the
Mexican women, urging them to stick up for themselves. She sees
changes happening before her eyes. Rosa Román was a quiet, submissive young woman, and now "nobody messes with Rosa, she's gotten
tough. She's not Miss Liberation or anything, but she's growing up."

Notwithstanding her clear sympathy for the Mexicans, Loretta professes ambivalence about the continuing tide of immigration.

"I hate the job situation," she says. "I know many Americans won't do
this kind of work, not even for the pay I'm getting. But I'm scared that the
Mexicans are taking the jobs that Americans might want some day.

"I'm just afraid," Loretta continues, "that somebody might need
that job to support their family, but the person from Mexico needs
the job to support their family too, so that's the battle. A lot of the
people from Mexico don't even have a home, they live eight, ten to a
place. It's sad. That's why you don't want to take their job away. It's
hard to be a back stabber and say no, we don't want you, but yet what
are you going to do?"

It's been a long time since I've heard an American so honestly
express the dilemma inherent in the debate over immigration. Loretta is
well aware of the changes in the economy that steered many Americans

away from the jobs that the Mexicans now take. The last generation of African Americans to work on the farms left by the 1960s, and once you leave the farm, there's no going back. The other source of temporary labor for farms in the Midwest—high school kids and even college students—has also dried up. Today these kids gravitate toward the fast-food industry and other service jobs of mall America's retail boom. The pay at McDonald's and at Thompson's is roughly the same, and kids know where the work is easier.

Simply put, there is no supply of manual labor other than the Mexicans, not only for farming but increasingly for other labor-intensive industries such as meatpacking, textiles, and the bottom rungs of the service sector: hotel and restaurant help. The non-Latino workforce seeks such jobs only as a last resort, only in the event of cataclysmic economic change. Before the great economic boom of the late 1990s, nativist forces played on fears of such change. In the early years of the decade, Americans from the middle class down were insecure about jobs, salaries, and benefits, and politicians stoked their anxiety, rallying its force against the Mexicans.

A farmer like Jim Thompson, however, doesn't care where his workers come from. A no-nonsense man in his thirties whose land has been in his family for five generations, Thompson just wants a readily available and cheap workforce. "Everyone should just let the situation alone and allow supply and demand to run its course," he tells me.

Whereas about twenty-five years ago the help on this small farm—at the peak of the season, there are only two dozen employees—was mostly African American, with a smattering of Anglos, today it is almost all Mexican. Moreover, most hail from Cherán. The Román family was the first from Cherán to migrate to the area, then the Izquierdos, and finally the Cortézes. The families live within blocks of one another, just as they do in Cherán. It is a classic migrant enclave.

The working conditions are probably far better than at the turn of the last century, but still may not be up to modern-day standards. The workers say there is no overtime pay (even when the crew works a seventh day, which they often do at peak). Though Thompson doesn't know it, the youngest Cortéz brother, Melchor, is only fourteen. Because he works full-time and does not attend school, there is an unknowing violation of child labor laws. Rosa, Wense, and his brothers get up at six, are at work by seven, and only call it quits at five in the afternoon. A ten-hour day for which they say they are paid nine hours at $5.75 an hour.

But they aren't about to complain. They are all illegal. Most of the time, the Cortézes seem quite grateful to their *patrón*—for the loans, for help in securing housing, for time off pretty much whenever and for however long (a month or two to return home at the end of the year, for example).

"He treats us well," Wense says. "He's good people."

And indeed, Jim Thompson is a personable sort. He looks you in the eye with his sky-blues peering out from under thick sandy-blond hair. He's often in the fields with his crew, his hands usually caked with Mississippi River Valley mud. It would be hard to describe Thompson as an abusive boss. There is a paternalistic benevolence about him.

From a historical perspective, the family's difficult circumstances are perhaps the "sacrifice" made by all first-generation immigrants, just as European newcomers worked in the sweatshops, in the fields, and on the streets with their pushcarts. But earlier waves of immigrants were instrumental in the birth of the American labor movement, which dramatically improved conditions in the workplace, and saw many of their children enter the middle class. The unions, however, have been on the defensive for the last two decades, and there is no guarantee the attempt to revive them—to a large extent by organizing the newest generation of Mexican immigrants—will succeed. Today, by and large, Mexican migrants have no form of redress, no opportunity to challenge the terms of their employment, even when they are in the U.S. legally.

In the tobacco fields of North Carolina, for example, the picking is now done by Mexicans, many of whom possess H2-A work visas permitting them to take short-term seasonal jobs in agriculture. Mexican American labor organizers are active in the area, yet working conditions are often poor and housing not far removed, geographically and qualitatively, from the plantation days. The farms are frequently located in remote areas where the workers are put up in "labor camps." At one place I saw, the men slept in long, one-story, tar-papered buildings with no insulation and prison-issue cots. The outhouses were splattered with feces and swarming with flies. Forty workers were being served by four latrines, two showers, two sinks, and one water fountain. This setup was pretty typical.

Near Benson, North Carolina, a small town surrounded by tobacco fields, I visited a farm where an older worker pulled me aside, leading me behind one of the housing shacks. A native of Tlaxcala, he would not give me his name.

"In August, when picking season begins, the sun can kill a man," he said, speaking in a barely audible whisper. "But it's not just the heat. They spray these chemicals all around us, the pesticides."

One day in the fields, he fell suddenly and severely ill with dizziness and vomiting. He approached the *patrón*, fully expecting to be taken to a clinic. Instead, the boss said he could return to Mexico if he wasn't up to the work. He tried to forget the incident, but it happened again, several times. Some nights, after twelve hours in the steaming fields amid the pale green leaves with their huge yellow veins, he'd awake in his cot, feverish, drenched with sweat, trembling, his head splitting with pain. He wasn't alone. One time, he and three other workers got sick at the same time, vomiting together in a row of tobacco.

"If you speak up, the boss puts out the word that you're a bad worker," he said. There's more. On isolated farms the *patrón* often sells the workers their food and drink, company-store style. A can of soda can go for one dollar, a sandwich for two. He'd heard of fields where the bosses sell beer and even drugs for a profit.

So why did he work there? Why not pick oranges in Florida or lettuce in California, where conditions have improved as a result of the UFW's campaigns?

The man smiled. What could he do? His job was a legal gig. He did not want to risk crossing the border illegally, he said. Hadn't I heard of all the migrants who'd died over the last few years? He just wanted to finish out the harvest here and then move on to another farm, one with zucchini or lettuce or watermelon, anything but tobacco.

Thus the Cortéz family willingly accepts the conditions at Thompson's farm (although Baltazar sometimes wonders whether he might be better off in another job, such as construction). In turn, Thompson's farm manages to hold its own in an economy hostile to small farmers, mostly because of the cheap labor. Thompson also has a source of distribution—the retail store just a few yards away from the fields where the Cortéz family works. A steady stream of custom-ers stop by, shopping for fresh berries and homemade jams. Occasionally, the Mexicans and the whites meet—the workers have to walk through the store to get a drink of water from the faucet in the back room. In St. Louis, this is as close as these two worlds ever get.

On a break from the sauna of the nursery, Rosa tells me that she and Wense are thinking lately of returning to Cherán. For fiesta? I ask. No, she says. Permanently.

Even as Rosa is wrestling with the decision whether to bring her mother across the border illegally, she and Wense have begun to consider buying a parcel of land back home and growing beans or corn, Purépecha staples. Wense is growing weary of the work at Thompson's. There is little hope of a better job or a better place to live. And Rosa is beginning to doubt the value of an American future altogether. At least back home there would be extended family for Yeni to grow up with, she says. And the traditions, the way Mother's Day is celebrated with an outpouring of love and affection, and Children's Day, and the fiesta for the patron saint, and the wonderful social communion during harvest. Surely, this offers something to a child as well. Something less than the hope of a better material existence, but is that the only thing that matters?

Rosa is not sure anymore on which side of the border her future lies. I am stunned by this new turn. I'd always assumed that the family's narrative, born of tragedy, would find resurrection on this side of the border. But Rosa's ambivalence can't be easily reconciled: she is right when she dreams both her Mexican and her American dreams.

As I'm walking between the fields and the nursery, I catch sight of a bedraggled Mexican lifting a battery-powered weeder off a work truck. He wears grass-stained khakis and a red shirt speckled with white paint. His face, a sweaty Indian moon with bloodshot Asian eyes, is somehow familiar. We are walking right toward each other, but he doesn't make any visible sign that he recognizes me, and so I pass him without greeting.

But then it hits me. I turn around. "José?" I call out to his back. "José Izquierdo?" He turns around.

The last time I saw José Izquierdo was in Cherán, stumbling along the highway, howling out the name of his unrequited love. José Izquierdo, the cholo who boasted of running pounds of coke, who'd supposedly been busted in Chicago and sprung by syndicate lawyers. José Izquierdo, the man who changed three crisp counterfeit hundred-dollar bills at the *casa de cambio*, who wore mirrored shades, a denim shirt buttoned all the way up, and a fat gold crucifix dangling on his chest. The first and only time I met him, he'd been fretting about whether to do another "job" for his boss. To the extent that I believed him, I'd always imagined that he went ahead and did it. I imagined him living the high narco lifestyle in Chicago, molls at his side in a Jacuzzi, lighting a fat cigar with a burning C note. José Izquierdo, Wense's cholo hero, is here on a Missouri farm, his weapon not a laser-sighted Glock 9-millimeter but a weed eater.

"Yes, it's me," he says. We exchange small talk. He never mentions Chicago or jobs or anything of the sort, and I don't bring it up. I wonder again if he fabricated the entire story. When I ask Wense about it later, he shrugs his shoulders. "That's what he said. Who knows?"

I offer my hand to José Izquierdo, and he puts me through a convoluted street handshake. We continue toward our destinations. After a few paces, I turn my head and watch him walk slowly in the direction of the retail store, where he'll get a drink of water in the back room. He wipes his brow in the stifling heat, then sticks both hands in his pockets. And then ever so slightly, he leans back against his gait, a humble reminder of the oh-so-cool Pachuco swagger he's known for in Cherán.

It is Saturday night, the one night of the week that Wense allows himself to cut loose, since there's no need to wake before dawn the next day. Baltazar is at the wheel of his Grand Am, but tonight Wense's really the one in charge. He rides shotgun. In the backseat is his buddy Alfredo Román, who, in addition to having a nine-to-five job, two kids, and a mortgage, claims the title of cholo *veterano*, one of the founders of a small set of Mexican gangsters in St. Louis, the O.G.s (Original Gangstas), as it were, of the heartland. We cruise toward downtown. We are headed to an appointment to hang with Wense's heroes and Alfredo's protégés, the cholos of the local Sur XIII clique, who, I am told, are the mortal enemies not of the black Bloods and Crips of St.

Louis but of the Zacatecas-155 boys, a Mexican gang that, if we are to believe Sur XIII, owns all of East St. Louis.

We pull up in an old neighborhood of red brick buildings with big white window frames, a mostly black area with an incipient Mexican presence. Rafael, the Sur XIII crew leader, has a spacious apartment here, with hardwood floors and and elegant carpentry. The place is lovingly decorated, especially considering that Rafael and his roommate are a couple of Purépecha cholo bachelors. On the fireplace mantel, a space every Mexican in America transforms into a pagan-Catholic altar, there are three small framed portraits of Jesus, the Virgin of Guadalupe, and the Madonna and child. Above these hangs the largest image, a poster of an aqua '57 Chevy.

The entire Sur XIII clique sits on a old blue sofa in the living room—five boys ranging in age from sixteen to twenty. Beepers and cell phones chirp. The boys are dressed to the nines. It is Saturday night, after all. Rafael, the oldest, wears a sleeveless T-shirt and khakis ironed to razor-sharp creases, and his red bandanna is snug over his head and low over his eyes, the old-school look. The younger cholitos follow his lead, although they lean toward the hip-hop look.

Apprised that Los Angeles, gangsta mecca, is my hometown, the crew peppers me with questions about the Mexican Mafia, the fearsome Salvadoran gang Mara Salvatrucha, and, of course, the death of Tupac Shakur. It is virtually the same conversation I had in Cherán with Alfredo Román last year, cruising the highway in the dark.

When I turn the tables and ask them about the mean streets of St. Louis, Rafael becomes rather sheepish. "We're the only Mexican set west of the river," he says. "There's no territory to fight over, it's all ours."

By the looks of the graffiti in the neighborhood, black gangs seem to dominate the space Sur XIII calls home. But relations are peaceful.

"There's no beef with them," Rafael says. "As a matter of fact, we respect them. They were here first, after all."

The younger boys are mostly quiet; it is clear they're awed by Rafael. But they start to loosen up when we talk about cultural identity. They are Purépecha, they say. One hundred percent. To prove it, Rafael goes over to the stereo. He shuffles through a stack of CDs and selects one, handling the disc by pulling up one of the long tails of his denim shirt. He brings the disc up to his mouth and delicately blows off the dust. He pops it into the box. A haunting a cappella *pirekua* duet emanates from the speakers, the very voice of the Michoacán highlands.

"This," Rafael pronounces over the Indian melody, "is what it means to be Purépecha."

After a couple of minutes of silent, reverential listening, he punches the "skip" function on the player. We jump to a golden oldie, "Angel Baby."

"This is also what it means to be Purépecha," Rafael says.

Skip again. The romantic god of twentieth-century Mexico, Pedro Infante, an Elvis-like figure who died a young and tragic death, sings the bolero standard "Tú, sólo tú."

The curiously eclectic CD is the soundtrack to *My Family*, Gregory Nava's depiction of barrio life. Rafael has made his point. To be Purépecha is to be part of a "people who travel," whose journey is never-ending, whose identity is as fluid as their journey.

For these kids, their cholo presentation appears to be mostly an emulation of urban hard core, the style more than the violent substance. Nonetheless, their rebellion is daring in a place like St. Louis, where dressing up like a Mexican gangsta is sure to bring on police harassment.

For the most part, first-generation immigrants like the Cortézes and their friends will steer the straight and narrow. How could they live with themselves if they failed their families, their sacred mothers, back home? It would be too great a sin to return home without having made something, anything, of yourself in America. Yet these boys acting like men are still boys, and they will have their time. Even Baltazar, who is so intent on playing the part of responsible husband, father, older brother, and firstborn son—he remains quiet all evening at Rafael's—has a tattoo of his surname on his shoulder, cholo style. Underneath the mask of responsibility, he is, of course, as insecure as any other migrant on this road. He wants to belong to the mythical brotherhood of Sur XIII, too.

It is the members of the second generation who are at risk of losing themselves in the American inner city's endless possibilities for self-destruction. For now, the cholo style is mostly a benign form of protest. For example, tonight Wense has on a Vato Loco T-shirt, a riotous color design of a tough dude with fedora and shades handling a fat pistol. He is wearing his frustration on his sleeve, since he has no other means to express it, no speech with which to utter it. By dressing the cholo, he rebels against his disciplinarian father and against his Abel-like brother. On Monday, though, he'll be back at work in the fields.

The vast majority of residents at the apartment complex where the Cortézes live are African American; the Mexican presence, albeit growing, is still tiny. No matter how much the migrants play their *norteño* music, it cannot compete with the hip hop and R&B of eminently black St. Louis.

It's a troubled place: there is gang and drug activity. But for the most part the residents are hardworking secretaries, mechanics, casino clerks, Federal Express drivers, and the like. Small black children play jump rope and hopscotch on the commons and splash around in the pool, which the Mexicans seem to think is off-limits to them.

Notwithstanding the physical closeness of Mexicans and blacks, there is little social contact between them. On the commons one afternoon, I chat with some of the locals. The Mexican presence is a new development—there hadn't been a nonblack resident as far back as anyone can remember. Leticia Miles cradles her daughter Kinett, a three-year-old I'd noticed Yeni playing with. "She asked if she could go over and play with the little Mexican girl," Leticia says. "When she came back, she told me, 'That little girl don't talk right.' "

Most African Americans in the complex speak of Mexicans in the same way—low key, bemused. It is all too new, too small-scale to really perturb anyone. And while there's surely some prejudice among some blacks toward Mexicans, the attitude of the Mexicans is no less problematic. Except for the kids, every member of the Cortéz family speaks to me about the *morenos* in deprecating tones. Sometimes, they even call them *mayates*, an ugly Spanish epithet that refers to a jet-black beetle of the northern desert lands. The great irony is that the Mexican immigrants—particularly the young—are acculturating black, not just in St. Louis but across the country in the increasingly black-brown inner cities. Wense, who openly expresses dislike of African Americans, often listens to a local black hip-hop station on his car stereo, when he's not blasting *banda*, that is. And in terms of dress, all the kids, black and brown, wear the same warrior uniform.

At least there's been no outright hostility. Perhaps tensions remain low because, at least for the moment, there is little direct competition in the job market.

This is no L.A., where there is open enmity between youth gangs on the streets of South Central and areas like Venice Beach and Hawaiian Gardens, an enmity that is all about outlaw economics: the fight has less to do with race than with the right to run drugs and control the rest of the underground markets. On the other hand, St. Louis is by no means Mt. Pleasant, a Washington, D.C., neighborhood where Salvadorans, Dominicans, and African Americans have at least begun to collaborate on the streets—and in bed. St. Louis is an old Midwest city that's seen its share of mob battles and racism among the old immigrants and the African Americans who arrived with the great northward migration. The current transformation has only just started. It's too early to tell how it will all turn out.

The Cortéz family insists on taking me out for a farewell dinner—to a Mexican restaurant, of course. Las Palmas, it's called, and it is a clean, well-lit place that serves migrants and Mexican-food-loving gringos alike. We are serenaded by a duet that plays songs from the Old Country, like "Qué lindo es Michoacán" (How Pretty Michoacán Is), which Wense asks for. When it comes my turn, I request "Volver, volver" (Return, return), which is a kind of anthem for migrants, whether they left Mexico six months or three generations ago:

Y volver, volver, volver
a tus brazos otra vez
llegaré hasta donde estés
yo se perder, yo se perder
quiero volver, volver, volver

(To return, return, return / to your arms once again / I'll catch up to you / I can swallow my pride / I want to return, return, return)

To migrants this song is about their mother back home, their extended family, their friends, the stroll around the plaza in the early evening, the cornstalks rustling in the wind, the rebozo-wrapped grandmothers, the sublime chaos of fiesta; the object of desire is home itself. The song is also an anthem for Mexican Americans a generation or more removed from the Old Country. They may never have visited the homes of their distant relatives, but the longing remains, reaches mythic, metaphysical proportions.

On the way back to the apartment, Wense, knowing he won't see me again for a long time, maybe ever, turns suddenly earnest.

"You know, I'm really doing something," he says, recalling his speech in the tomato field. He's stopped drinking, his wild years are over. He swears he's not going to wind up like so many drunk fathers back in Cherán or so many of the solos wandering the States, futureless. He's working for $5.75 an hour, nine hours a day, including a lot of Sundays lately. He says he wants to move into a new apartment, where it'll be just him, Rosa, and Yeni. (The plan to return to Cherán has apparently been shelved.) He wants to buy a new car; Alfredo Román has offered him his old Buick, smoke gray with a white vinyl top that is turning a slightly rusty beige, well over a hundred thousand miles on it, but a dignified ride. And he wants to send Yeni to a parochial school—Alfredo has advised him that public schools just won't do. Yeni looks to be a bright kid. She's picking up English rapidly. She says "money" instead of "*dinero.*" The other day I taught her to say "plane" so she could point up at the sky and cry out the word every time a TWA jet roars over the complex. Yes, Wense swears he's going to make something of himself.

Joseph Rodriguez

STRAWBERRY FIELDS FOREVER

I'm heading west on I-70, exactly twenty-nine miles east of Kansas City. Lazy cumuli hang over the highway and the air is bronzed as the sun slants toward evening. My Blazer darts in and out of sun and shadow, over the prairie stretching to the horizon. The skyscrapers of downtown Kansas City rise from the prairie like the Emerald City.

Beyond the city, the land smells like the biggest lawn in the world has just been cut. Fields in all directions and grazing cattle. I flash past a billboard that reads, "The border is closer than you think," a heartland ad for Taco Bell, but prophetic in this part of the country. The border is indeed everywhere now, has moved northward from the Rio Grande clear across the country.

I spend the night in Hayes, Kansas. When I walk out to my car in the morning, there is a gaping hole where my left rear side window had been and beads of glass scattered over the asphalt. Nothing stolen; probably bored teenagers. A couple of Mexican kids at an auto-glass shop are kind enough to tape it up for me, no charge. But if I don't crack the front windows to allow the air pressure an escape, the plastic will blow out. I drive the next fifteen hundred miles with the wind buffeting my face. A red bandanna keeps the hair out of my eyes.

For the first time, the solitude of the road gets to me, bringing paranoia. Maybe the perps back in Hayes were neo-Nazis. Maybe a tire will blow tonight. Maybe the driver in the cab of the semi rig next to me will nod off and swerve into the Blazer. Maybe I'll fall asleep at the wheel.

I reach the Front Range of the Continental Divide and drive into a series of lead-gray storm cells. The plastic sheet that serves as my rear window blows in and out with the rising wind, like some great puffing jellyfish. I don't stop in Denver. I have to keep moving; suddenly, I feel an urgent need to get home. I climb into the foothills. The pioneers looked for passes through the Great Divide and did not always find them. I-70 follows paths blazed by frontiersmen long ago, paths that today's migrants follow: Mr. Charlie steered the van carrying Rosa and Yeni along I-70. Somewhere close by, they hit the storm and the "tornado" of snow that knocked out one of the windows of their van.

Suddenly, the rain comes down heavy as a waterfall. The car in front of me is only a few yards ahead, but I can barely see it through the downpour. I hear thunder rolling all around me. All the semi rigs slow to a crawl and turn on their emergency blinkers, but there are assholes in SUVs still rushing along.

CAUTION: FALLING ROCK. The rain comes down so hard that it seems to bounce up a full foot. At forty miles an hour, I hydroplane whenever I tap the brakes. More chunks of rock, small boulders tumble onto the road.

TUNNEL AHEAD.

It runs through the very heart of the mountain, lit a dim, soothing amber. The asphalt dries up by midtunnel. When I come out the other end, the clouds part quickly and patches of blue appear. My plastic window held through the storm.

Elevation 11,000 feet. Snowy peaks. I light a cigarette, take a couple of drags, and immediately feel dizzy. I ride through the Breckenridge ski resort. A huge mass of rock rises up, dabbed with snow at the peak, pine trees somehow growing out of what appears to be solid granite. There are Mexicans in these parts too, running ski lifts, cleaning hotel rooms. Among those enjoying a vacation are aristocrats from Mexico

City who've traveled two thousand miles to be attended by the same brown brothers and sisters who serve them back home.

In the late afternoon, the highway is an endless silver ribbon winding down the backside of the Great Divide. The craggy gray granite gives way to stratified layers of earth, rusty reds and soft pinks and dull yellows. The Eagle River rushes along to my left. The Eagle eventually merges with the Colorado, which courses along the California-Arizona border. It is this river that will take me back home. The land is gradually becoming the desert that I know and love. I smell the Southwest now: piñon trees, sweet and dry, not tangy like cedars.

JUNCTION I-15 330 MILES.

I-15 descends into the Nevada highlands and then into the Mojave Desert. The road is a luminous thread across the land. Perhaps forty, fifty miles ahead—it's impossible to tell distances in the desert—the thread dips into a basin before rising up before me, and then gradually breaks up into a string of pearls, individual headlights. In the rearview mirror, I see the opposite. The brake lights of each car congeal into an unbroken river of red that, in the distance, disintegrates again into distinct points of light, glowing under the darkening sky like rubies or fire opals.

The story is coming to an end. California is on the horizon.

I navigate the familiar path to my house in Los Angeles. But I am not home to stay—L.A. is, for the moment, just a stopover on my way north to Watsonville, to the strawberry fields that the dead Chávez brothers once worked.

When you want to dash up to San Jose or San Francisco by car, you usually hop on I-5 up through the flat expanse of the San Joaquin Valley and past one of the largest cattle-killing fields in the country. But you take 101 when you're headed for Santa Barbara, Monterey, or Santa Cruz. You take 101 if you're vacationing, and you take 101 if you're working the industries that, in one way or another, make life comfortable for those of us who vacation, or live, in this bucolic region where the pines meet the sea, where rockers retire and meditate on their own private beaches.

The trip from L.A. to Watsonville is 360 miles, about seven hours. As is often the case, there is bumper-to-bumper traffic across the entire San Fernando Valley, the great flat stretch that was worthless until

William Mulholland brought water across the desert and turned it into a citrus paradise and an American bedroom community. Though the region has long been considered the domain of Valley Girls, white pubescent mall rats are now harder to find. These days, wide swaths of the valley are home to immigrants from Mexico, Central America, and Southeast Asia.

During the 1994 Northridge earthquake, one of the costliest natural disasters in U.S. history, the migrants were finally rendered visible. Suburban homeowners, the Anglo old guard, complained bitterly about the authorities' slow response to the emergency. The migrants, meanwhile, well accustomed to quakes and all other manner of natural and man-made disasters, went about setting up provisional shelters in the city parks. They brought out sleeping bags and mattresses, strung sheets between trees, held community cookouts. They lived outdoors for a couple of weeks, until everyone was reassured that another big one was not imminent. One local TV news reporter, marveling at the Old World ingenuity, called the encampments "tepees." While the hardy American stock—erstwhile Reaganite enemies of "big government"—whined for their handouts, the migrants, as always, made do with what they had.

Another recent battle showcasing the disparate worlds of migrants and natives, enclaves of which lie within blocks of each other, involved Mexican street vendors, part of the same informal economy that arrived in New York with the European migrants of the early twentieth century. These days, vendors proffer everything from fruit salad to tacos to pirated music cassettes. When the most recent spate of vending appeared in the valley, as well as across much of the Los Angeles Basin, the white homeowners' associations—one of the most powerful lobbies in Angeleno politics—shouted a chorus of disapproval. Health codes! Unfair business competition! New antivending ordinances were drafted, debated, approved. The police began raiding the sidewalk stands, tossing papayas into the street, levying hefty fines.

The migrants were not to be quashed, however. Los Angeles's Latino population, as measured in the 2000 census, has edged close to a majority. The street vendors fought back. Some of them were Salvadoran women who'd experienced far worse than attacks by the local city council and L.A.'s finest, and they quickly organized their own lobby. They stormed City Hall with activism that amounted to performance art, strolling their carts into council chambers and offering snacks to the legislators. Although the LAPD did its best to portray the vendors as fronts for gangbanger drug dealers, the media image of poor women working an honest living finally swayed the council. The street vendors won a redrafted ordinance that largely legalized their livelihoods.

Then there was the battle over the leaf blowers. Mexicans took over the gardening and landscaping industry from Japanese and Anglos a generation ago. In the 1980s, the main weapon in the Mexican gardener's arsenal became the leaf blower, a rather crude contraption that saved time by freeing workers from the age-old rote of the rake. But as the leaf blowers proliferated, the noise started grating on homeowners' ears, and the associations protested to the politicians downtown. They clamored for a ban, using environmental rhetoric, speaking of "noise pollution" and decrying the fumes from the gasoline-powered blower engines. The gardeners, following the example of the vendors, organized and started making their own trips to City Hall, where they were supplied with translation headsets, as if they were at the United Nations—which is what L.A.'s City Hall looks like these days. They didn't argue the point that the blowers were annoying; they merely asked for a moratorium on the issue, during which, surely, someone would come up with a more environmentally friendly blower. To ban the machines outright would cut too deeply into the gardeners' already meager earnings. The council leaned toward the homeowners—whose taxes and campaign contributions outnumbered the gardeners' by millions if not billions of dollars—and approved the ban. But that's not the end of the story. A committee of gardeners pitched a tent on the steps of City Hall and called a press conference to announce a hunger strike, the duration of which would be determined by the mayor: the gardeners would break bread only if he lifted the ban. Richard Riordan, L.A.'s Republican mayor for much of the nineties, was in a bind on several fronts. A free-marketeer to the core, he chafed at ordinances that placed burdens on businesses big or small; he was also Irish Catholic and known for his sympathy toward L.A.'s burgeoning Mexican population. But the aggressive homeowners' lobby was also his electoral bulwark. The mayor met with the immigrants in hopes of dissuading them from their suicidal mission. The meeting was a disaster. It happened to be lunch hour, and Dick Riordan was hungry. He was munching on a hamburger as the elevator descended to the ground floor. He had finished only half of it when he extended a hand dripping with mayonnaise and catsup to one of the starving workers. The hunger strikers redoubled their resolve. Tragedy seemed inevitable.

A week into the strike, the miracle came. A fellow immigrant, a Salvadoran auto mechanic, had been watching the gardeners' plight every night on the local Spanish-language news. According to migrant legend, one night in his dreams a vision of an environmentally friendly blower came to him. Instead of a gasoline-powered engine, the propeller blades would turn by dint of a car battery. So beautifully simple! He woke in the middle of the night and rousted his teenage son out of bed. They tooled around in the garage for a few hours. By morning, nearly mad with excitement, political passion, and sleep deprivation, he arrived at the gardeners' tent with the new blower. Riordan was quickly apprised and came down—sans food—to give his benediction. Forthwith, the council issued a moratorium on the ban so the prototype blower could be developed and placed in the hands of L.A.'s gardeners.

As sweet as the vendors' and gardeners' victories were, both underscore a much larger issue: the immigrant class serves the white middle class and that is not likely to change anytime soon. It is important that this generation of migrants win dignity and respect, but the real question is what opportunities migrant children like Yeni, Rosa Chávez's daughter, will have when she's ready to enter the workforce, where she'll live, what she'll be able to give her own children. Mexicans from earlier waves of migration have seen their children mostly remain in the barrio, educated in inferior schools, vulnerable to gangs and drugs, the fate of people who have no future, of families who have no mobility.

The traffic opens up, and I leave the last of the suburban bedroom communities behind. Now the view along the highway is old California pastoral: oak trees shading the hills above Ventura under the blue-white sky of early summer. The strawberry fields on the fertile coastal plain of Oxnard will soon yield their fruit. And there they are, figures like ants on the horizon: migrant workers bending into the earth. In an instant they are gone. The car swallows more landscape: grazing hills, only a few short weeks ago bright green and ablaze with wildflowers, now faded to a tannish brown. Near Paso Robles ("Oak Pass"), I see a lone Mexican wading knee-high through a sea of wheat. Vineyards, lettuce fields, garlic fields—row upon row unto the horizon. Oil wells, pipelines. Irrigation ditches, arcing plumes of water from the sprinklers, high-tension towers standing tall next to the highway and diminishing in the distance. To the east, the great valley has no end. To the west, the yellow hills rise toward the cooler, even more fertile coastlands. The razor-wired compound of the state prison at Soledad. The ghost barracks of Camp Roberts. Billboards in English, in Spanish, announcing beer and motels and HIV testing and a Danish theme town called Solvaang.

As I descend into the Pajaro Valley on Highway 129, fog curls over the hills. Gone is the yellow land of the south. There are stands of oak and eucalyptus, now and again a drooping willow next to a ranch house. I remember the highway curving into Cherán, the buses groaning up the incline, the blue-black rebozos of mothers and grandmothers trudging toward market. I have inherited the memories of others, too: I see Benjamín, Jaime, and Salvador Chávez at the Zamora bus station, waiting for their departure for Tijuana. I see them chatting and sleeping and snacking through the day and a half it takes the bus to cross the immense Mexican landscape. I see them boarding the GMC in the darkness; I see the truck flipping over into the ditch. I am arriving in the town where they never arrived.

Watsonville is what a friend of mine, a priest, now dead, would have called a prophetic place. The earliest migrant magnet was the Gold Rush; but most of the new arrivals didn't make their money finding the mother lode. What they did find was a rich soil that would turn California into the nation's cornucopia. These first-generation migrants took their place at the bottom of the ladder, working the fields of the Pajaro Valley or, as in the case of the Portuguese and other ethnic Europeans, in the fishing and canning industries. Since those days, Watsonville has evolved into a center of migrant activism, a constant portent of economic, political, and cultural struggle whose repercussions are felt far beyond the Pajaro Valley.

In the mid-1980s, this town of thirty thousand (the same size as Cherán) hosted one of the most significant labor battles in California history, a strike by the largely Mexican migrant workforce of the Watsonville Canning and Frozen Food Company. The workers—almost all women—won the eighteen-month strike, only to see the company close a few years later, itself a victim of the global economy. At the end of the decade, Watsonville became the site of a landmark political battle that resulted in a federally mandated realignment of voting districts in the city. Mexicans, long the majority in the region, had had little representation, owing to the political tradition of gerrymandering. As a result of a successful Voting Rights Act lawsuit, Oscar Ríos, a second-generation Salvadoran immigrant, became the first Latino to be elected mayor in Watsonville in over a century.

Cementing the town's legendary status was the alleged appearance, precisely during the years of political and labor tumult, of the Virgin of Guadalupe in a beautiful lakeside hollow. Not coincidentally, the Virgin is said to have been seen by one of the leaders of the Watsonville Canning Company strike. In the years since, hundreds of thousands of the faithful have come to see her image, seemingly branded by divine hand into the bark of a tall maple in the hollow.

More recently, the United Farm Workers (UFW) staked its future on a David and Goliath battle in the strawberry fields of the Watsonville region, which include farmlands owned by transnational companies like Monsanto. Years of organizing efforts on behalf of and against the UFW finally led to a representation election at one of the biggest farms in the area; the UFW lost, narrowly, and continues to organize to this day.

Watsonville currently has one of the lowest per capita incomes in the country; unemployment is usually double the national average. Most of the frozen-food plants—once the mainstay of the local economy—withdrew after the cannery workers' strike. In the cruelest of ironies, they relocated to Mexico, to the states of Jalisco, Michoacán, and Guanajuato, where the majority of Mexican migrant workers in the United States hail from.

Depending on your location, Watsonville can look either very Mexican or very American. The brick buildings clustered around the central plaza recall old Anglo California; there wasn't much in the Pajaro Valley until the Americans rolled in and started working the fertile earth. It is still a town with a Dairy Queen and a Winchell's donut shop and a Salvation Army store, a John Cougar Mellencamp kind of town. On the north side, there is a collection of cookie-cutter tract homes, owned mostly by white commuters who work in Santa Cruz, San Jose, and even San Francisco. But south of the plaza, across the Pajaro River, which flooded catastrophically a few years ago, is Old Mexico. There are trailers and shacks, general stores proffering the same products they sold back in Michoacán circa 1925, roosters strutting around front yards. The whites and well-to-do Mexicans (of which there are a smattering) hang out at the mall on the north side; the migrants pack La Frontera bar, whose name, appropriately, means "the border," just south of City Hall. La Frontera is packed with men whose fingernails are grimy with dirt, a place where only Spanish is spoken, a place of migrant solidarity and scandalous, perhaps even occasionally dangerous partying.

On my first night in town, I look for the trailer where Fernando and Florentino Chávez live—and where all five brothers lived together before the crash. The trailer park, an alley of homes that dead-ends on one side, is practically on the banks of the Pajaro River; a storm could easily wash it away. At nine in the evening, there's nary a soul stirring among the darkened trailers. I finally find Fernando and Florentino's place, dark like the others, and roust a surly matron only to be told that the boys aren't home, that they're probably out drinking with friends.

The next day I try again, around lunchtime, thinking that the brothers might be taking a break from the fields, but no one answers when I knock on the door.

Life is stirring among the trailers, though. I'm greeted by the Chávezes' neighbors, Guadalupe, Isidro, and Joel, a trio of veteran migrants who've more or less settled into life on this side. Legal residents, they've done their time on the *files*, as the migrants call the fields, Spanishizing the word, to retirement or, as in Lupe's case, disability payments (he visibly limps) and an intense ham radio hobby. Their collective handle is "Los Guardianes Internacionales." A tall antenna scratches the sky from the roof of Guadalupe's trailer. He is clearly the don of the trailer alley. He has a big belly, a scruffy pepper-leaning-toward-salt beard, and a moth-eaten sweater. He is a native of Michoacán, as are most of the migrants here.

On good days, Lupe says, he can make radio contact with colleagues all the way down in Pátzcuaro, Michoacán. He says he has radio buddies from New York City to the Argentine pampas.

Isidro, from Mexico City, has a CB radio in his car for more prosaic contacts nearby. The car itself is a museum piece—a '65 Mustang, deep metallic blue, in mint condition. Joel is from Jalisco, a quiet man content to sip at his Bud and let the others ramble on. We sit in easy chairs in front of Lupe's trailer, the sun darting in and out of stray patches of fog blowing in from the coast, which is just over the hills to the west.

The ham and the CB transmitters came in handy during the flood of '95, Lupe says. He helped coordinate rescues, directing emergency crews to victims. He notes with pride that even the usually surly white cops congratulated him on a job well done.

Disasters always seem to follow the Mexicans, Isidro says, setting the tone for a long conversation about apocalypse. The reason Isidro left Mexico City was the cataclysmic quake of 1985, in which tens of thousands perished. It struck early in the morning, just after seven, when Isidro was lying in bed, groggily awake, in his cheap fifth-floor apartment near downtown. What he remembers most is the roar of the quake: like a lion let loose from hell. He ran down the stairs as if someone were chasing him with a butcher knife. By the time he got to the ground floor and peeked outside, it was over. Across the street, a plume of dust rose from a pile of rubble that seconds earlier had been an apartment building just like his. He joined the citizen rescue crews and pulled bodies from the destroyed buildings for two full weeks. The trauma convinced him to come north for a fresh start. He'd heard of the strawberry fields of Watsonville—he thought of the Beatles song— and had led a calm life here until October of 1989, when the Lorna Prieta quake rattled the trailer and sent him screaming into the alley.

Now Joel chimes in, recalling Jalisco's great disaster, the Pemex explosions of April 22, 1990, which resulted from a refinery leaking fuel into the city's sewage system. The explosion obliterated dozens of city blocks; hundreds were killed, hundreds more injured. Many bodies were never found.

The Guardians keep on: the peso devaluation of 1994, the drug wars of northern Mexico. The cholo street violence in Michoacán and right here in Watsonville. There was a drive-by shooting just a couple of blocks away recently, they tell me. Lupe's own son was injured, although when I ask him more about it, he mutters unintelligibly and looks away. The Guardians know, everyone in California knows, that one day the Big One will come, the temblor that will plunge the strawberry fields of Watsonville, San Francisco's Market Street, and the barrios of Los Angeles into the Pacific, to become a new Atlantis.

"So you see," Lupe says, "Mexico is fucked up, and so is California, and there's really nowhere to go. Might as well just drink another beer." He fishes one out of his Igloo cooler and tosses it to me.

There have been other signs of impending doom, Lupe says. There was a UFO sighting in Watsonville a couple of months ago, a strange flashing object hovering over the strawberry fields; dozens of farmworkers saw it. "Maybe it's just like the signs the Aztecs saw before the Spaniards arrived," offers Isidro.

When I bring up the Chávez accident, the trio grows quiet. Lupe looks down at the ground, plays with the pop-top of his can of beer. The news sent a shock wave through the trailer alley, through the entire town, much as it did in Cherán. More than half the migrants in the Watsonville area hail from Michoacán. A smattering are natives of Cherán, and everyone comes from a town that's just like Cherán.

The men of the alley gathered around Florentino in his grief, everyone drank and toasted the dead. Lupe took Florentino aside and told him: "Stay. Don't you see that this constant moving around is too dangerous? Stay, save up money, bring your wife up, then your kids." Florentino heeded the advice. He returned to Cherán for the funeral but was soon back in the fields during the day—and drinking in the trailer alley every night.

The Guardians look out for the surviving Chávez brothers; everyone in the trailer park does. They've all suffered backbreaking labor in the fields, abusive *patrones, migra* agents. Many have experienced the terrible pain of a loved one's passing away back home and they carry the guilt of not having been at his or her side. And almost all have felt the terror of crossing the line—through the mountains in winter, through the desert in summer, across the river in a storm. But the Chávez accident was a tragedy almost incomprehensibly large: it was every migrant's dread, a loss that will not be forgotten.

As we are talking, I see Fernando and Florentino Chávez walking toward their trailer.

Fernando is looking thin, almost gaunt, his T-shirt and dark jeans hanging loose. Florentino resembles a pudgy teenager even though he's in his late twenties. They are both grimy from a day in the fields. Fernando passes on the beer offered by Lupe, Florentino accepts. They invite me into their trailer, an old lime-green model whose siding is coated with rust. The interior is gray—two bedrooms and a fairly large kitchen decorated with a single Budweiser poster. The front bedroom belongs to the landlady from Michoacán, who rarely comes out of her quarters; the rear bedroom belongs to the brothers. There is a bunk bed, kiddy-size. A small black-and-white TV with a broken aerial sits atop an old dresser. Out back, there is a tool shed and a couple of badly rusted easy chairs placed on a piece of fraying carpet. A previous occupant made a strange installation out of the fig tree looming over the tool shed; he attached a platform to the tree and piled on it an impressive collection of scrap wood and metal, everything from bicycle wheels and trailer siding to iron reinforcing rods.

Here, in the shade of the fig tree, the five Chávez brothers would drink their beers after work on the long, warm California nights, watching the twilight slowly fade, the melody of *norteño* tunes wafting over from a box in one of the nearby trailers, along with the crackling voices from Isidro's CB or Lupe's ham. Then at around nine or ten the boys would take their work boots off outside, leaving them on the carpet by the chairs. Benjamín, Fernando, and Florentino would make their beds on the floor, with blankets for mattresses, while the youngest took the bunks. They'd turn on the TV for a bit, tuning in Univisión, which beams variety shows from Mexico City. One of the brothers would reach up from the floor and turn it off; by that time, the boys in the bunks would be snoring. They got a good night's sleep in the trailer alley. Except for the times when the drinking parties lasted into the wee hours—almost always Fridays and Saturdays—it was as quiet as the nights in Cherán. Besides, the sheer fatigue from ten-hour shifts in the fields guaranteed dreamless sleep.

Except the night before the accident, when Florentino had just arrived in Watsonville, having left his brothers in Tijuana. He tossed and turned that night, dreamed of being caught in a terrible storm in the highlands; there were torrents of muddy water and great swarms of bees. "I couldn't walk for all the bees," he says of the vision.

Florentino had departed Cherán with Benjamín, Salvador, and Jaime (Fernando, feeling ill, had stayed behind) on Monday night and arrived in Tijuana Wednesday morning. Florentino, legal papers in hand, crossed ahead of his brothers and by Thursday afternoon was in Watsonville, in good spirits because he'd secured a house for the brothers—they could finally move out of the old trailer. Everything was in place for a season of working and saving, of playing soccer and drinking a beer or two together, all of it together. Fernando would join them when he felt up to it. And after a few months, after the interminable days in the fields, after the summer, the last of the strawberries would be picked. The brothers would go shopping at the discount stores on Front Street in Watsonville, loading up on clothes and kitchen appliances for their mother and their wives and toys for their kids. They would buy vinyl bags to take their purchases back home. And just before their departure, the *patrón*, Miguel Ramos, a fair man who'd once picked the fields himself, would throw a party for his workers right there next to the strawberry rows. A great barbecue would be going, and there'd be plenty of Budweiser, and everyone would talk about how they'd spend the rest of their money, how they'd finally get to make love, how they'd see their children, how they'd be home again.

It was going to be a good year, another step forward for a family that had certainly seen its share of hard times. It was going to be a year of rising expectations, of learning a few more words of English, of growing more accustomed to the United States of America. It was going to be a long journey but well worth it.

Florentino was dozing off early Saturday evening when Fernando's call came through from the *caseta* back in Cherán. Florentino had been taking it easy. He'd decided to wait for his brothers before going back to work in the fields; they might as well all start together. They did everything together. That was how they'd managed so far.

Neither Florentino nor Fernando can recall exactly what was said during that phone conversation. All that Florentino remembers is the long ride back to Cherán by bus, sitting in the rear, looking out at the sallow landscape and remembering every terrible and ordinary moment he'd ever shared with his brothers.

Florentino thinks that his dream of rain and bees was a premonition.

He just wishes his brothers would visit him in his dreams. It's been a year since they died and they have yet to do so.

"I'd like them to say something to me," he says.

Fernando says that the dead have spoken to him. Back in Cherán during mourning, the black ribbon hanging above the entryway to the house on Galeana Street, the family, out of respect for the dead, did not play any music. "But Jaime came to me in my dreams," Fernando says, "and said, 'I don't like how you're living without music, so sad.' " The next day he turned the radio on, tuning it to XEPUR, "The Voice of the Purépechas," and the *pirekuas* began to play again.

Fernando says that he regularly communes with his family in his sleep. This past week, four nights in a row, he dreamed that his mother, his wife, and his children were all sick, coughing, running fevers. When he rang them yesterday, he learned that his mother had the flu early in the week and that his children were now sick with the bug.

After returning to Cherán to bury his brothers, Florentino made the toughest decision of his life, to return to work in the States. His mother begged him to stay, just as she did Rosa. She was especially concerned that, returning alone to the trailer and to the strawberry fields, he would be haunted by the memory of his brothers. But Florentino could not imagine remaining in Cherán: his brothers, surely, would have wanted him to continue to carve out the future for which they had died. And so he boarded the bus yet again, after saying good-bye to his wife and his two children. His family had never been the kissing kind, but when he said good-bye, Florentino found himself giving his wife a quick hug and he was surprised to feel tears in his eyes, which he quickly wiped away.

He arrived at the Watsonville Greyhound station and walked five minutes across town to the trailer alley. The memories assailed him, just as his mother had predicted. Soon he was drinking himself to sleep. But the memories came to him, drink or no drink. "You can only forget for a while," Florentino says. But in the end, Florentino does not regret having coming north again. He's fulfilled what he thinks are his brothers' wishes, and he's supporting the family back home with three hundred dollars a month, more than a third of his earnings. He's cut back on his drinking, indulging only on weekends. When Fernando joined him, his sorrow lightened a bit. They work side by side in the fields.

They're practically always together. That is how they will survive their season of loss, how they will reclaim the future.

Before going to sleep tonight, Fernando and Florentino take off their shoes out by the tool shed, leaving them side by side on the strip of old carpet.

La Lupe de Guerrero is dancing with El Luis de Jalisco at La Frontera. At five foot five, she towers over him; he's barely five feet tall. El Luis's hair is matted with sweat, his face glistens; his shirt is grimy from the fields, his jeans fraying at the cuffs, his boots starting to come apart.

As for La Lupe, a *cantinera* (part bartender, part taxi dancer) at La Frontera, she's immaculate, of course, an olive-skinned goddess of long-nosed, thick-lipped beauty, not unlike the Virgin of Guadalupe, her namesake. Come to think of it, El Luis looks not unlike the Indian Juan Diego, to whom the Virgin is said to have revealed herself nearly five hundred years ago, and just in the nick of time. Tenochtitlan, the Aztec capital, had fallen to the conquistadors and disease. It was then, in Mexico's darkest hour, that she appeared, and she continues to appear today, not just in the worldly guise of women like La Lupe but in her celestial form, on both sides of the border, in the provinces and in the cities, always to the poor, who need her the most. She was recently seen at a subway stop in downtown Mexico City at the height of the crisis. And of course she follows the migrants on their journeys: she is said to appear on the border itself, tricking Border Patrol agents down the wrong arroyo while the illegals make safe passage. From her lake-side hollow, she looks out for the migrants in Watsonville.

It is 7:00 o'clock on a Friday night, and La Frontera is rapidly filling up. The men come straight from the strawberry fields without stopping to shower first. La Lupe dances with El Luis through a *banda* number played by a crack three-piece band (synthesizer, bass, drums), the glow from the Budweiser, Miller, and Coors neons her corona.

La Frontera, a mammoth establishment practically a city block long, has five entrances. The first, which I've just walked through, leads into a long hall with a few tables and a bar that stretches some thirty feet; in between the bar and tables is the dance floor. The second entrance is for the pool hall next door, where serious money is exchanged. The third is for the diner, serving tacos and *menudo*, beef tripe stew, in anticipation of the customers' hangovers. The fourth is for another bar area, this one with booths, peopled by older men, many of whom have retired from the fields. The fifth is the back exit, the door the men can run through if and when the cops come. Judging by the building's red brick and mortar skeleton, glimpsed through its crumbling plaster facade, it is an antique from the turn of the century. Everyone says the building has always been La Frontera. The sign out front, painted in brown directly onto the beige plaster, is barely legible after decades of the sea air that arrives with the fog.

La Lupe is the life of the party. The other *cantineras* are mostly overweight, their bare midriffs showing stretchmarks from childbirth. La Lupe, the most sought-after woman, demands politeness and, above all, respect. A drunk sitting next to me has been eyeing her and presently grabs her hand, which she's placed about a foot away from his on the counter. He pulls her close. She stiffens, jerks back, slides her hand out of his. She shoots him a quick disdainful look and that's it—he will bother her no more. He lights a cigarette and stares at her image in the mirror behind the bar. Treat La Lupe right or you'll never get to talk to her, much less share a three-minute *banda* number.

La Lupe has plans. She's been in Watsonville a couple of years; she left her no-name town in the provinces of southwestern Mexico to follow a sister who pioneered the Watsonville area for the family with her husband. She has another sister in the Carolinas—she can't remember if it's North or South; they had a falling out. That sister married some bastard macho who ruined her life and she wouldn't heed La Lupe's advice to leave him wallowing in his own vomit. La Lupe would never get herself in such a situation, never. She has never married. She has no children. She commands respect from men before whom other men grovel. She works at La Frontera because it's easy money and better than she'd ever make in the fields. She's never had to do anything on the job that would compromise her dignity. "I control them, not the other way around," she says.

She swears that she'll return to Mexico with a bankroll and start up a hotel in her town, not a general store like all those migrant losers open, thinking they'll make it big selling Chiclets and deviled eggs, but a hotel, a clean, pretty place for the tourists who need just such a place.

Later, I talk to Lucía, a chubby *cantinera* a few years older than La

Lupe, whose cheerful demeanor is belied by the deep circles under her eyes. She's from Michoacán, where, she says, some wealthy farmer stole her family's land. If it's the last thing she does in this life, she's going to get her family's parcel back. Buy it from him, kill him for it, whatever it takes. She'll build a hacienda and watch the cornstalks rise and fall with the seasons in her old age, and every woman who was ever wronged by a macho fuck will be welcome there, a hacienda for women.

The band plays, the billiard balls crack, the old-timers watch serenely, the *cantineras* serve beer and flirt a little, and the migrants, the new cowboys of Watsonville, are whooping it up tonight, just tonight, just one night a week, because you can't afford to get drunk at La Frontera every night on a field hand's wages. Besides, despite their flirtations, they are almost all family men; the reason why they're here, after all, is to send money back home. The local Western Union branch, one of the busiest establishments in Watsonville, is just a couple of blocks up Front Street, as bustling a place as the *casa de cambio* is in downtown Cherán. In any case, there is a virtual thread connecting the two; Western Union has established Internet links with such Old Country business mainstays as Telégrafos de México, Banca Vital, Banca Promex, and Elektra.

On La Frontera's dance floor, the cowboys, the Indians, the cowboy Indians dance: boys playing men, men playing boys. La Lupe watches over them, pitying them, cursing them, understanding.

Under the old mantilla that covers her thinning hair, doña Anita Contreras's face, pale, gnarled, and with a fairly prominent mustache, is full of emotion; her eyes glisten. It's been years since the apparition, but she is moved to tears every time she comes to the water's edge at Pinto Lake, just east of Watsonville. Even before the Blessed Mother appeared to her, she used to sit here every day since her granddaughter drowned in the waters off the wooden pier just beyond the hollow.

It was the seventeenth of June 1992, at precisely 11:30 A.M., when she saw the Virgin. These had been dark days for Anita. Twenty-six years on the line at the Watsonville Canning and Frozen Food Company and eighteen months of a heroic wildcat strike in which she'd been one of the leaders had led to the unthinkable: she'd been forced into early retirement with a pitiful monthly pension of $382. In the 1980s, some six thousand people, many of them Mexican migrant women, had been employed at several local canneries. By the early 1990s, at least half those jobs had gone.

Earlier that June day in 1992, Anita had had a terrible argument with her daughter. At eleven in the morning, she had stormed out of her house on the edge of town and walked to this place of breathtaking beauty and peace, where the branches of tall maples arch together a few feet from the waters lapping gently at the lakeshore.

Anita walked up to the tallest maple, knelt down facing the trunk, and prayed to her goddess, the Virgin of Guadalupe. In her head she heard a voice, the voice of a woman. Stunned, she looked down at her feet. A seashell. She picked it up. On its surface, she saw the visage of the Virgin herself, dressed like a poor woman, like a "valiant peasant," Anita says. She thought she was going crazy, that her emotional armor had finally cracked after twenty-six years of labor, eighteen months of strike, the death of a granddaughter, and the trouble with her rebellious daughter, who caused her no end of grief. And yet the image on the seashell continued to speak to her. She looked toward heaven, at the sunlight shimmering through the maple leaves, and her eyes came to rest on the Virgin again, this time on the bark of the tree itself, high up on the trunk just before the first fork. A skeptic might say that the image was the natural coloration of the tree's bark, but for Anita there was never any doubt.

Her celestial conversation with the Virgin lasted three and a half hours. "Take my message to the people," the Virgin told her, "so they may hear my wishes: that they pray the *full* rosary in my honor, that they confess their sins and take Holy Communion to become one with God."

The Virgin said many other things that day—"private things," according to Anita. She returned home ecstatic, trembling, and told her daughter and sister what she'd seen. They both thought she'd gone mad. Anita went to her church, where she sought out the priest from Guadalajara, who she thought would surely hear her out, but he didn't believe her either. She told another priest in the confessional, also to no avail.

"For God's sake," a cousin told her, "you'd better keep quiet. They could send you to the asylum, you know."

Her sister pitied her. "So much you've suffered in this life, it's finally gotten to you," she said.

But Anita knew she was not mad, but rather the world was mad for not believing, and she persisted. She brought friends and total strangers to the hollow. She asked them to search for the Virgin's image—without telling them where to look—but for weeks no one saw the mestiza Blessed Mother, she who always offers hope to the Mexican, no matter how far from home, no matter how trying the season.

But word soon spread and people began showing up at the hollow out of curiosity. Anita would hide nearby and hear them laugh about an old woman's insanity. Vipers! People of little faith!

And then one day, all of a sudden, they believed. She doesn't know who told whom, but it spread like wildfire. Dozens, hundreds, thousands came and beheld the Madonna of Watsonville. The poor, the lame, the mad, the faithful, the TV crews. Anita appointed herself minister. The crowds came and she related the tale of the apparition and pointed to the image on the bark. The people knelt and prayed.

Soon, it was a spiritual stampede. People she didn't know sought her out for consultations. A family whose son had gone missing brought her to their home; Anita led them in prayer in the child's bedroom. At the end of the rosary, the boy called from San Francisco to say he was safe and sound.

Then the vendors came, smelling money to be made. Like Jesus at the temple, Anita sent them away, shrieking: "*She* does not want a shopping mall!"

Now a loose chain-link fence is wrapped around the maple—at one point, the faithful had taken to clambering up the tree to touch the holy image and it was a miracle no one was hurt. Hundreds of prayers written on scraps of paper hang from the fence, as do driver's licenses, passports, Social Security cards, legal resident alien cards, newspaper death notices, cannery IDs, school IDs, Polaroid photos, anything identifying the person seeking a miracle. Countless votives and vases of flowers stand at the base of the fence.

O Blessed Mother, I beg you this favor that a mother asks of you, that you ask God our Father to assist my son at his court hearing, may his bail be lifted and may he be set free.

Dearest Virgin, I only ask that you watch over my children in the fields, protect them, dearest Mother, from the hands of the migra.

Little Virgin, I pray that you might take mercy upon my husband, who has suffered a heart attack; if he should leave me, what would I do all alone in the world?

Day after day, year after year, doña Anita comes to the hallowed hollow. She still hears from the Virgin now and again; she says that the Blessed Mother's pleas to her children are ever more desperate. They are not listening, she tells Anita. They have not become one with God. There's not much time left.

"She wants us to stop the alcoholism, to stop the drugs, to stop the violence," Anita tells me, rocking back and forth, oblivious to the steady stream of the faithful, some of them taking out pocket mirrors to cast the reflection of the sun on the Virgin's image.

When Anita isn't speaking about the Virgin, she rails against the *patrones* of the cannery where she worked ten hours a day and where you couldn't even yawn without having supervisors breathing down your neck. "All the *patrones* in the world can't win against all the workers when they're united," Anita says, with her old activist fire. The women on strike had had a Catholic sense of their mission, infusing their actions with religious symbolism. One night, they trekked from the cannery to the church, almost a mile, on their knees, a physical representation of their suffering.

Anita raises a finger and continues.

"This world is not dignified enough to stand before her without guilt!" she says. "We should bury our heads in shame!" And then she shouts a torrent of almost incomprehensible pain, the words so rapid they slur together, almost like speaking in tongues, but the gist of it is this: There is still so much injustice, still so much work left to do, so many sins to confess, so many battles to wage, so much change to bring, so many tears that must be shed for the sheer tragedy of this wretched earth, of these poor people of the fields. Of which she, Anita Contreras, is only one.

The note was tacked to the garage door of Reyna Guzmán's new house: "Since you Mexican wetbacks arrived, our property values have gone to hell." Then came the garbage cans overturned in her driveway, the rotten eggs and vegetables thrown at the house.

It is a five-bedroom house, one story high, twice as long as it is wide, with a wood-shingle roof. The walls are painted a rather drab green, but that doesn't take away from the house's undeniable beauty— American beauty on a hill, a gentle rise overlooking the Pajaro Valley.

The house was Reyna Guzmán's grandest dream: large enough for each of her children to have a bedroom. For Ignacio, an agronomist turned truck driver because his Mexican degree is worthless in the States; for Aaron, the son who married a Mexican American woman (rather than a girl from Cherán), much to Reyna's disappointment; for Iván, who at age fourteen was flirting with gangs and drugs but has since calmed down and is now obsessed with Native American spirituality; for Blanca, who ran off with a boy Reyna doesn't care for; and for Beatriz, the youngest, who's following in Iván's footsteps, mesmerized by the teachings of a local Indian elder.

A native of Cherán, Reyna is a former Watsonville Canning Company rabble-rouser, all-around activist, and single mother. She saved diligently even as she raised five children alone. She wanted the family under one roof and arrived at the realtor's with some $30,000 in the bank. She remembers the look of shock on the agent's face; she ignored it. Show me some houses, she demanded. When she saw the house on the hill, Reyna swore to make it hers.

The realtor announced an asking price of $300,000—the going rate in neighborhoods like this one, full of big houses occupied, strangely, by small families, mostly Anglos. The owners rejected Reyna's initial offer. She looked elsewhere, but nowhere did she find the five-bedroom home of her dreams. The economy was on Reyna's side in the recessionary early 1990s; the realtor called back. Would she care to reinstate the offer, since the owners hadn't been successful in selling to another party? She offered $200,000. They accepted. She put $30,000 down, took on a large mortgage, and the house was hers.

At first, the chilly reception from Reyna's neighbors depressed her to the point that she begged the realtor to tear up the contract. But then she reminded herself that she had worked all her life to buy the house, and she swore to herself that the ones to move would be the neighbors. Five years later, her wish came true: the neighbor she believed was behind most of the harassment, a white police officer, has placed a For Sale sign on his property. Soon he'll be gone.

Reyna Guzmán is a lot like other Purépecha women I've met. She is dark-skinned, raven-haired, and short but strong. Contrary to type, though, this Indian mother is anything but submissive. Reyna is a tireless fighter, outspoken and even foul-mouthed when she needs to be. She speaks Spanish, some Purépecha, and working English. One morning she said "Fuck you" to the wife of her police officer neighbor. The woman had walked past Reyna, who was tending the lovely garden in her front yard, and had called out a cheerful "Good morning." They never spoke again.

The garden is Reyna's other pride and joy. It is rare for poor Mexicans to cultivate gardens back home—horticulture is the domain of the upper classes. At most, people in Cherán fill a few old tin jalapeño cans with earth and plants picked from the wild. But Reyna's years of hard work have given her the middle-class right to her own garden. There's a long, carefully cut lawn and rows of peach trees budding with new fruit. Beds of geraniums bloom a bright red. There are also begonias, lilies, and gladiolas. Bright green ferns crawl up the side of the house. Among these plantings, which are not uncommon in American gardens, Reyna has placed a bit of Mexico: nopal cacti and maguey plants, a guava tree, and an avocado as yet too young to bear fruit. She's particularly proud of the avocado. She planted the seed in a soda can two years ago and transplanted it just recently.

And then there are the herbs she uses for cooking and home remedies, also part of her memory of home: sage, mint, rosemary, cumin. Every day she spends at least an hour gardening in the early morning and then another hour or longer in the evening, "until I can't see what I'm doing anymore."

"The garden gives me so much happiness," Reyna says. "To see the buds appear and then break open and flower is so beautiful."

Reyna Guzmán has been married three times and insists that she kicked all of her husbands out. She first came north in 1973, practically dragged along by her first husband. Like everyone else, she started out picking in the strawberry fields, but within a year she'd gotten rid of her husband, leased four acres of land, taken on thirty-five workers, and generated a $20,000 profit for herself with the first harvest.

Despite her success, Reyna remained ambivalent about her new life in the United States. "I've spent twenty-five years thinking about going back to Cherán," she says. She thought of her savings as her ticket to return. She did go back once, in the late seventies, when her children were still quite young (Blanca and Beatriz weren't born yet), and opened a restaurant. Though business was good at first, she had to close down after three years because of a series of unforeseen events—including some hefty *envidia* and obstacles raised by the Mexican bureaucracy. She came back to Watsonville, to a job on the line at the cannery, packing broccoli, cauliflower, spinach, and chiles from six in the evening to three in the morning. She'd sleep for three hours and rise at dawn to get the kids ready for school. For five years she worked without a vacation. The strike began on September 9, 1985, at 5:00 A.M. The next eighteen months would be the hardest, most fulfilling time of Reyna's life.

A clipping from the Watsonville *Pajaronian* shows Reyna, up against a line of policemen; she has a fearsome scowl on her face and is giving the cops the finger. She marched on City Hall, she marched against the Teamsters (whose old-guard leadership was cozy with the cannery's management), she marched against the cannery bosses. And though few of the strikers' original demands were met by the company, they did keep their jobs, until the layoffs of the early nineties. Many would say that they won the battle only to lose the war, but according to Reyna, the workers "won respect."

Reyna's been involved in politics ever since, helping to elect Oscar Ríos to the city council after the Voting Rights Act lawsuit remapped the district boundaries and made it possible to bring a Latino to power. She led a boycott against a McDonald's outlet because the owner, a Mexican woman, supported Proposition 187. Today, her front lawn is her political platform, sown with signs supporting candidates and measures during election season.

It doesn't look like Reyna will be returning to Cherán anytime soon; maybe she never will. And so she's done what she can to bring Cherán to Watsonville. There is an altar in her living room with candles and ribbons and the favorite saints of the Purépechas, Santo Niño de Atocha and the Virgin of Guadalupe. Posters announcing fiestas and competitions back home hang on walls throughout the house, as do masks worn by the Indians for the traditional dances. In the kitchen, bowls brim with the ingredients of Purépecha cuisine: cilantro, onion, pasilla chile, cabbage.

Today, with her daughter Blanca at her side, Reyna is cooking a blazingly spiced *churipo* stew for her guests. Tradition, Reyna says— clearly addressing Blanca—acts like a vaccine against the contamination of influences on this side of the border. She cites Iván, her son, who appeared headed down a path of self-destruction in the gangs. She encouraged him to visit Cherán. "He found himself there," Reyna says. Upon his return to the States he left gang life behind.

On the other hand, there are influences on this side of the border that have helped the Guzmáns. It would have been impossible for Reyna to divorce her first husband back home, much less to have married and divorced twice more. She wouldn't have had the chance to lease a strawberry field and act as a *patrona* of her own work crew and become a labor leader. And she certainly would never have been able to buy a five-bedroom house.

The thing is, only two of Reyna's children live at home with her now, Iván and Beatriz, leaving two of the bedrooms empty. And because Blanca and Aaron have troubled relationships with Reyna, family reunions are rare. The fragmentation of American family life has affected her own home, but it would have done so if she'd stayed in Cherán, too; a husband or son or daughter would eventually have gone north.

This is Reyna's life: she is physically present in Watsonville but conjuring up Cherán at her altars and in her meals and in the lessons of tradition she teaches her kids, even as the influences of their new home inexorably pull at them. It's a classic immigrant story: she has lost some precious things and gained some others. It would be hard right now for Reyna Guzmán to easily answer the question of whether the bargain was worth it. But then again, who can?

Early summer in the Pajaro Valley is bright with the green of wild grasses and crops nearing their peak. The Santa Cruz Mountains are a dozen shades, with stands of eucalyptus and pine and fir and the fog curling over the ridges in the early mornings and late afternoons. The contrast between all the greens, which battle one another across the valleys and hills, gives the area a tense beauty.

I am standing on a large hill curved gently like the sky, the strawberry field where Florentino and Fernando Chávez work, where all five brothers once worked together. Miguel Ramos, *el patrón*, tells me how the harsh winter destroyed some farms with flooding, but not his; he'd taken all the precautions.

"The rains actually helped wash away the salt that had built up in the soil because of the pesticides and fertilizers," he says. "I'm doing great."

Ramos is, however, experiencing a shortage of pickers this season, which he attributes to fallout from Operation Gatekeeper. Before, women and young men were common in the fields. Now, it's mostly men in their late twenties and even their thirties. Ramos thinks that only the most hardy and experienced migrants are getting across the border.

"The Border Patrol knows that it is putting people in the position of risking their lives," he says. "It knows that they will risk their lives as long as there are jobs and a shot at the future here. I don't know how a country that calls itself civilized can promote such a policy."

Miguel Ramos, like Reyna Guzmán, has realized his American dream, although were the two of them to meet, a brawl surely would ensue. Reyna is a heroine of the Watsonville left; the UFW has painted Miguel as the archetypal evil *patrón*. A lawsuit brought by the union claimed that Ramos helped organize and fund the Agricultural Workers Committee, which the UFW alleged was a union-busting outfit. Ramos denied the charges, and the lawsuit against him was eventually dropped.

The accusations come as a shock. Conditions on Miguel's fields are among the best I'd ever seen: clean toilets; morning, lunch, and afternoon breaks dutifully observed; wages fairly distributed; no complaints from the workers. Morale among the work crew also seemed quite high. Florentino and Fernando spoke of their *patrón*'s generosity: he'd frequently throw barbeques for the workers on holidays.

At forty-two years old, Miguel is a tall, striking man with a shock of peppery hair parted in the middle over a handsome bronze face, an Indian face of almond-shaped eyes, blunt nose, and full lips. A native of San Luis de la Paz, Guanajuato, Miguel came to Watsonville in the late sixties and began at the bottom, picking strawberries. Today, he is the *patrón* of a few dozen acres of strawberry plants, worked by about fifty field hands, mostly from Michoacán.

In his office, Miguel has hung a poster of Emiliano Zapata, a few pictures of bullfighters, and a map of Michoacán. I look for Cherán. The map is detailed enough to prove its existence.

Miguel identifies himself politically as neither a Democrat nor a Republican. "But if I could vote," he says, "I wouldn't be a Democrat." (He is a legal resident and on the waiting list for naturalized citizenship.) More than anything, Miguel considers himself an American. And, of course, he is, living out the classic "up by his bootstraps" story. He tells of the terrible conditions he encountered in the fields of Watsonville when he first arrived—the lack of bathrooms and drinking water, the white *patrones* (he calls them "*yanquis*") cracking the proverbial whip over their brown underlings.

But then he looks at today's migrants and shakes his head. "They need a change in mentality," he says. "I'm in this country, my kids were born here, I contribute to this community. These guys save their money to build homes back in Mexico. They should stop resisting feeling American."

For Miguel, becoming American comes down to letting go of Mexico, sinking new roots in the United States, speaking English, applying for citizenship, and participating in the political process. "To be an American is to be in this community and give to it. It's going to city council meetings and getting involved, not just playing soccer.

"We start living on our memories," says Miguel. "The migrants go back home and tell spectacular stories. They say, 'I made $120 in one day!' And when we're here, we don't want to be American, we say, '*la raza*,' we say, 'Chicano.' " He pronounces the radical monikers with pronounced distaste.

Miguel's assimilationist position places him on the right of the political spectrum, as do his antiunion views. "The UFW paints us all as poor little workers, but they're just out for power for themselves," he says. But in other ways, Miguel sounds quite, well, Chicano—at least in the cultural sense. He frequently returns to his bitter memories of the *yanquis*, of the bosses who were always white. And he's taken the decidedly nationalistic step of giving his first son a Mayan name, Quitze Balam, which translates as "smiling tiger." Thus his son's American friends will always refer to him in the ancestral language.

So there is clearly a split in Miguel's soul. He now finds himself in the thick of union politics, on the side of the very *yanquis* that he loathes. He does not admit it, but this must be a painful irony. Miguel has staked out very lonely territory: at odds with the prevailing politics of "his people," he is still also the odd man out among the growers of the Pajaro Valley, who are practically all white.

From the doorway of Miguel's office I look out to the fields and see the workers bending over the endless rows on a cold, gray, drizzly afternoon. The workers are wrapped in garbage bags to keep from getting soaked to the skin. "Those are our disposable raincoats," Miguel says. With both hands, each worker rapidly snips a few berries from the plant with quick flips of the wrist, carefully stacks them in the cardboard bin, then pushes a small iron cart another few feet down the row through the increasingly slimy, muddy earth.

Late one afternoon, while the workers are still in the fields, Miguel and his brothers set up a barbecue in a small gorge that serves as a parking lot. Soon, the aroma of *carne asada* is wafting over the fields. Miguel has also bought a few cases of beer; he is hosting a modest fiesta for his work crew, as he does several times each picking season. He allows the workers to quit early.

At the barbecue, the normal hierarchy is inverted: the Ramos brothers serve the migrants strips of meat, tortillas, chiles, and beers. The day is hot, and everyone seeks shade underneath several small oak trees, kneeling or sitting on a bed of dead leaves. The scene is thoroughly pastoral. It could be Cherán. But it's not. This is no harvest-time meal among friends and family. The *patrón*'s presence puts a slight damper on things, of course, but the party also never quite takes off because the workers are mostly strangers to one another. They are friends or family only in twos and threes, and there are a great many solos among the crew.

There is a fair share of drinking, though, and a few tongues are loosened. Miguel Ramos waxes optimistic, claiming he'll bequeath his children hundreds if not tens of thousands of acres—strawberry fields forever. Miguel is among a select few in a migrant narrative that, a hundred years into its history, is still more about poverty than about success. No doubt, Miguel's hard work and imagination helped him get where he is. But it took more than that. It took being in the right place at the right time, finding a tiny portal in the vast wall that stands between the migrant and social mobility.

The sun dips toward the horizon and everything takes on its golden afternoon glow. The migrants drink the last of their beers and head toward their battered cars. Fernando Chávez comes up to me. He's never been the gregarious type, but today he's in a talking mood. He peppers me with questions about my travels. "I wish I could go with you," he says. "I wish I could just keep moving and never stop."

Florentino rushes up behind Fernando and collars him playfully. "You're not going anywhere without me," he says, and then looks at me. "So what do you think of Watsonville? Isn't it a beautiful place?" I say that yes, it is. "As beautiful as Cherán?" he pushes, and I hesitate. The brothers giggle.

Fernando lets me off the hook. "It's a trick question," he says. "They're both beautiful, no?"

The brothers hitch a ride back to town. By the time I get in my car, Miguel's field is empty. I look out at the dimming rows. The mint-green leaves of plants rustle softly in the evening breeze.

It is Sunday afternoon in Watsonville. On my way out of town, I wind through the Mexican barrio. The neighborhood is bustling. The migrants hang out on front porches and front lawns, the children play. Music is blaring. Everyone is dressed in bright, clean clothes, the one day of the week they can be because there'll be no dirt or mud from the fields, no grease splattering, no dirty dishwater from the restaurant. One day of rest. Most everybody here works six days a week, and at the peak of the picking season, many work seven. Tomorrow morning the town will empty out again and the picking fields will be full.

I head south, to the desert, where I will sit down to write. They say the desert is God's country, and I find a place where the migrants have found him, the Apostolic Church of Indio. In the pews are grandmothers with mantillas and faces wrinkled like prunes, teenage Chicano boys with heads shaved and oversized shirts transforming their lithe Indian bodies into manly hulks, virginal girls with long auburn-highlighted black curls and floor-length dresses blooming a hundred flowers, an endless stream of young parents carrying newborns in portable seats and leading toddlers by the hand.

A banner on the wall to the left of the altar shows an amateurishly drawn clock bursting through chains. JESUS SAVES HEALS AND DELIVERS, it reads, followed by a quotation from Scripture: "For a just man shall fall seven times and shall rise again: but the wicked shall sink down into evil."

The preacher, a short, round man with a round face, thrusts his hands heavenward to punctuate his unmistakably black Baptist cadences:

I was DOWN in the VALLEY
of the SHADOW of DEATH
and then I was LIFTED UP
SOMEBODY give me an AMEN!

He cruises between Spanish and English effortlessly, with a slight gringo accent in Spanish and a slight Mexican accent in English.

"You are not down for the count—*no estás vencido*. The devil ain't got you yet—*todavia no te ha derrotado el enemigo*. The theme of Christianity is of rising up, rising up, rising up, again and again—*el tema principal del cristianismo es de levantarse, levantarse, levantarse una y otra vez*. Winter is over, the sun is shining—*cómo brilla el sol!*"

The spirit is with the musicians today, too. First a trio of teenage Chicanas in white mantillas and long, flowery dresses sings a spiritual more black than white or brown. Wonderful vibratos from deep down, moving the congregation to ecstatic applause and hand waving.

And now I hear the tongues, leaping out of a choirgirl's mouth. The spirit has moved her to jump up and down like a fan at a ska concert. Her lips and teeth and tongue move like an auctioneer's, so fast that even the fantastic rapid sounds she's making don't seem to keep up. She begins jumping in place, arms swinging. Her voice pierces through the band's beat, rising above the entire congregation.

Slowly, the faithful sit back in the pews, wiping tears and sweat with handkerchiefs. The band grows quiet, the elders take their seats at the front.

It is time for the rite of baptism, to make good on the promise of salvation. At the alcove above the altar, red velvet curtains with gold drawstrings sweep open to reveal the baptism font, a large round tank of water. An elder and a teenage girl, both in white robes, stand waist-deep in the water.

"Claudia Ramos," the elder intones, the name booming through the cathedral, big and holy, her name belonging not to her body but to her eternal soul. "Claudia Ramos, I baptize you in the name of the Holy Spirit."

The elder places one hand under the girl's back and the other on her own hand, which covers her nose and mouth, and he gently and quickly pushes down into the waters. She comes back up after a couple of seconds, her hair now a wet blanket and her face reflecting the light.

The band and chorus break into a boogie-woogie vamp, and one thousand hands clap. Another soul saved.

And so it is for the others who are baptized today, for Jonathon González and for Jorge Villarreal, young pilgrims who've come to California, who've crossed the river and arrived in what they believe is Canaan. The currents beneath the river's placid surface might suck the pilgrims under, and many do die, whether by drowning in the Rio Grande or by being crushed in a truck in Temecula. But to cross over, to be a wetback, is itself a baptism into a new life. The river anoints the pilgrim, and the pilgrim enters the Promised Land.

It is here, in the middle of the desert, among the migrants looking for *la vida mejor*, that my journey ends. With life, not with death.

My father recently told me again of those journeys back to Old Mexico with his parents in the early fifties, a time when my grandfather, longing for home, was perhaps having thoughts of ending his stay in the United States. Grandfather was a slight, wiry man with a booming baritone in song as well as in drunken rages. When I was a child he was bedridden with a bad heart, so the image I have is of him frozen in a plump, gray chair next to the large picture window in the living room of my grandparents' house in Los Angeles, a thick Mexican wool blanket covering his legs. The window looked out onto a lush garden, but it also gave a view of another place and time: the center panes were painted with a simple desert landscape that glowed beautifully in the late afternoons.

He did not smile a lot, this hardworking, hard-loving, hard-drinking man—a migrant to the core—and tension deep inside him was forever locking his jaw into something of an angry pout. I've always believed that the bitterness was the result of his body having betrayed his wanderlust. He was stuck in that chair by the window, and it drove him to despair. Before his illness, he probably imagined himself in his later years, as so many migrants do, finally able to enjoy the fruits of his labor both in America and in Mexico, homes here and there, friends and family here and there, life here and there. But his American home was where he sat, motionless, the window landscape, a place that looked a lot like the northern Mexican town he'd left behind, just out of reach.

I have inherited my grandfather's wanderlust. In the last few years I've flown the L.A.–Mexico City route perhaps two dozen times—I know each and every valley, snowcapped volcano, alluvial fan, duned desert, and sandbar beneath blue-green sea, have memorized each detail of the landscape from 33,000 feet. And I always know when the plane crosses the border, because when it nears the edge of the Sea of Cortés, I put on my headphones to listen for the controllers ordering the pilots to lock their guidance equipment on the radar beacon at Julian, a small town east of San Diego, just above the border. That's the only way to tell, because there's no sign on the ground below. No line in the sand, no wall at that point, nothing but semiarid land, sparsely populated, and the beginning of a great desert that stretches for more than a thousand miles until it reaches the Gulf Coast. From that height, there is no border; the line is an idea.

EPILOGUE

Not long ago I got a call from Wense in St. Louis. He talked about the heat and humidity in the picking fields in the summertime. The desert was also very hot, I replied, but the heat was dry and more bearable. He asked me if there were any jobs in the area.

Then he said he had a favor to ask: he needed to borrow some money.

What for? I said.

To pay Mr. Charlie. Rosa and Wense had decided to bring María Elena up from Cherán. He had already raised most of the money, he just needed a little more.

I wired Wense the money. A few weeks later, he called back. Everything had worked out fine, he said. I could hear the TV roaring in the background. He said he'd pay me back soon. Then he put María Elena on the line.

I told her I never thought she'd come north.

Well, she said, in the end she decided that if she didn't cross the line her sons' deaths would have been in vain. She had to complete the journey for them. Only this way did their deaths have meaning.

Not long before she left Cherán, María Elena received word from the family's American lawyer that the Border Patrol had offered, without admitting liability, a settlement in the lawsuit stemming from the accident in Temecula: $7,000 for each of her dead sons. Because legal precedent in wrongful death claims involving pursuits conducted by law enforcement agencies made a jury trial a risky venture, the lawyer recommended that the family accept the offer, and they did. But the Chávezes have not, as yet, received any of these monies. Another lawsuit was filed on behalf of the family against the Santa Rosa Community Services District (SRCSD), which maintains the private road on which the Chávez brothers died. The road, the suit claimed, was not built to the State of California's safety standards and thus played a key role in the accident. In late spring of 2001, a jury in Riverside County Superior Court found in favor of the plaintiffs and established liability for damages as follows: the smuggler driving the truck the migrants rode in, 95 percent; the migrants themselves, 3 percent; and the SRCSD, 2 percent. Under California tort law, this judgment opens the door to recompense from the SRCSD to the plaintiffs equal to 2 percent of the overall damages. As of publication, this amount has yet to be determined.

The Chávezes took the news with a grain of salt. "I don't believe anyone anymore," María Elena said. She learned long ago that there was no kindness in the hearts of strangers. If the family was going to have a future, she said, they would have to go it alone.

We talked a while longer. Before we said good-bye, she told me to come out and visit the family again, at their home, which, as the Mexicans say, is mine, in St. Louis, Missouri.

ACKNOWLEDGMENTS

I am greatly indebted to the many residents of Cherán, Michoacán, who, in their hometown and in their second homes scattered across America, opened their doors and their lives to this outsider.

Ofelia Cuevas accompanied me on this journey—sometimes at my side, always in my heart.

My dear friends David Reid and Jayne Walker in Berkeley always received me graciously with history, vision, and Chardonnay; without them, the trek would have been much lonelier.

My editors at Metropolitan, Sara Bershtel and Riva Hocherman, worked splendid magic on the text. Whether at the other end of a phone line or sitting across the table, Sara helped me believe that I could write this book in spite of all.

My agent, Susan Bergholz, stuck by me despite my stumbling.

Sandy Close at Pacific News Service helped me shape the initial vision, and without her support this book would never have been written.

Pedro Meyer, Trisha Ziff, and the Zonezero crew got me to sit down and write.

Brujas Mona Yehya and Margarita Velasco gently pointed out the signs on my path, even if I didn't always see them.

Elia Arce, Ted Quinn, John Pirozzi, and the Desert Dwellers took me in when I got lost on the road.

Roberto Lovato in the north and José Luis Paredes-Pacho in the south were, and are, the epitome of friendship.

For their generosity (and patience) during my stay in Mexico City, my most heartfelt thanks to: Rogelio Villarreal, Elisa Bernard, José Wolffer, Cristina Miranda, Marco Barrera, Cuahutémoc García, Willy Fadanelli, Pablo Hernández, Victor del Real, Guillermo Gómez-Peña, Roger Batra, Naief Yehya, César Martínez, Tania Barberán, Vicki Fox, Beatríz Nava, Joel Simon, Rolando Ortega, and Sam Quiñones.

Jesús Velo, Willie Herrón III, Joe García, and Johnette Napolitano helped compose the soundtrack that played in my head while I wrote.

Jack McGarvey, border scribe, appeared to me one day in cyberspace, and his passion reminded me of what was at stake.

Yael Flusberg, Quique Avilés, Hillary Binder-Avilés & the D.C. Kids offered me art, politics, friendship, and fun.

I would also like to thank, for their friendship, hospitality, inspiration, and support on the migrant trail: Marcus Kuiland-Nazario, Mandalit del Barco, Betto Arcos, Marco Vinicio González, Benjamin Adair, Todd Melnick, Ernie Chávez, Isaac Mizrahi, Randy Williams, Chuck Moshantz, Colin Campbell, José Delgado, Diane Rodríguez, Joe Loya (Sr. and Jr.), Elaine Katzenberger, Gustavo López-Castro, Gilbert Rosas, Mary Ana Carsillo, Luis J. Rodríguez, James Diego Vigil, Raúl Hinojosa, Juan Felipe Herrera, Rubén Guevara, Richard Blair, Joy Russell, Andy Wood, Kit Rachlis, Marcelo Rodríguez, Sue Horton, Ellen Weiss, John Brenkman, Gary Spiecker, Kim Ridley, Joie Davidow, Julie Reynolds, Kathy Dobie, Rebecca Taichman, Alisa Solomon, Joel and Betsy Bard, María Beatríz Alvarez, Michael Bettencourt, Steve Williams, Jonathon Friedlander, Fred Dewey, Raúl Villa, Mario García, George Lipsitz, Michael Riley, Bonnie Snortum, Martha Barajas, Carlos Martín, Richard Rodríguez, Lydia Chávez, Edward Soja, Mike Davis, Miguel Algarín, Mark Torres, Josie Aguilar, Abelardo de la Peña, and, last but hardly least, Bear, who sat at my feet while I wrote.